# CLASSICS IN PSYCHOLOGY

# CLASSICS IN PSYCHOLOGY

# MIND
# IN EVOLUTION

L[eonard] T. Hobhouse

**ARNO PRESS**
A New York Times Company
New York ★ 1973

Reprint Edition 1973 by Arno Press Inc.

Reprinted by permission of John Cushman Associates, Inc.,
executors of the estate of Leonard T. Hobhouse

Reprinted from a copy in The University of Illinois Library

Classics in Psychology
ISBN for complete set: 0-405-05130-1
See last pages of this volume for titles.

Manufactured in the United States of America

----◆----

**Library of Congress Cataloging in Publication Data**

Hobhouse, Leonard Trelawny, 1864-1929.
    Mind in evolution.

    (Classics in psychology)
    Reprint of the 1915 ed. published by Macmillan,
London.
    1. Ethnological jurisprudence. 2. Intellect.
3. Evolution. 4. Psychology, Comparative.
I. Title. II. Series. [DNLM: BF701 H683m 1915F]
BF701.H7 1973    156'.3    73-2968
ISBN 0-405-05140-9

## A NOTE ABOUT THE AUTHOR

LEONARD TRELAWNY HOBHOUSE, British sociologist and philosopher, was born in 1864. He was educated at Oxford and, during the first years of his professional life, was active in social and political movements. He contributed to and edited newspapers, was secretary to a trade union, and developed a doctrine of social liberalism based on the relation between individual freedom and state control. After his appointment as the first Professor of Sociology at the University of London in 1907, Hobhouse devoted himself increasingly to scientific and philosophical pursuits, writing a number of seminal works. He died in 1929.

Hobhouse's key concept was development, but he viewed this process differently from the Spencerian evolutionists and from the metaphysical rationalists. Striving to synthesize empirical and rational approaches, he focused on the facts of the animal world and the transition to human mental processes. He also sought links to the development of laws, morals, religion, scientific and philosophical thought. For Hobhouse, development was the liberation and structured association of elements which had previously been indifferent to one another; and mind was the principle of orderly growth within reality. His major scholarly contribution was a full working out of these ideas in a number of treatises, including the one reprinted here.

# MIND IN EVOLUTION

# MIND
# IN EVOLUTION

BY

## L. T. HOBHOUSE, D.Litt.

MARTIN WHITE PROFESSOR OF SOCIOLOGY IN THE UNIVERSITY OF LONDON
LATE FELLOW AND ASSISTANT-TUTOR OF C.C.C., OXFORD
FORMERLY FELLOW OF MERTON COLLEGE

MACMILLAN AND CO., LIMITED
ST. MARTIN'S STREET, LONDON
1915

*First Edition,* 1901
*Second Edition,* 1915

# PREFACE

The form of the present work needs a preliminary word of explanation. Its subject is "Mind in Evolution," but no one will expect that such a subject should be treated with any pretence of adequacy within a single volume or by a single writer. The contribution offered in the following pages is of a double character. There is, first, an attempt to sketch in outline what seem to the writer to be the main phases of mental development. There is, secondly, an attempt to fill in this outline so far as the lower phases are concerned. To put the same distinction in different words, a hypothesis is propounded as to the general trend of mental evolution, and an attempt is made to test this hypothesis so far as animal intelligence and the generic distinction between animal and human intelligence are concerned. For the rest, that is to say in all that relates to the higher development of the human mind in society, the outline is left to be filled in upon a future occasion. The whole subject naturally falls into the two main divisions of animal and human evolution, and the mass of matter to be dealt with is so great that it is convenient to keep the two parts separate. At the same time evolution is a single continuous process the different phases of which are only seen in their true significance when treated as parts of the whole to which they belong. This is my excuse for combining a general design with a partial execution.

Even as to that portion of the hypothesis which I have described as being tested in the present work I cannot pretend that the test is in any sense final. The hypothesis, though it appears to me to stand the test thus far, remains a hypothesis. The nature and limits of animal intelligence in its higher forms are matters of keen controversy, and will long remain so. In a science so little advanced as Comparative Psychology the justification for publishing any opinions or arguments must lie not in any pretence to finality, but in the hope of suggesting further investigation.

The general conception of mental evolution presented in this volume was formed some fourteen or fifteen years ago when I had come into close contact with the criticisms then current on Comte, Mill, and Spencer. The conception has been in my mind ever since, subject to constant modification as it was confronted with fresh facts or the better psychological analysis of other thinkers. The general view of evolution which most closely corresponds to it, is to be found, I think, in Dr. Lester Ward's *Outlines of Sociology*, published in 1898. I mention these points as indicating the general character of my obligations to other writers.

My more special obligations in the present work are, first, to Principal Lloyd Morgan and Professor Alexander, who have read the manuscript, and made numerous valuable suggestions. I hasten to add that they must not be held responsible for anything that appears in the text. In the preparation of my material I was helped by Mr. A. E. Taylor, some of whose work done originally in this connection will, I hope, see the light in another

form.    Many references to be found scattered through the
volume are due to his suggestion, and for some he is
wholly responsible.    I have to thank Mr. W. E. Hoyle,
of The Owens College, for help in a number of technical
points, Miss M. V. Vernon for help in the preparation
of the MS., and several friends for aid in experiments.
Last, but not least, I am under a special obligation to
Messrs. Jennison, proprietors of the Belle Vue Gardens,
Manchester, for their courtesy in placing their great
collection of animals at my disposal for the purpose of
my investigations.

# PREFACE TO SECOND EDITION

In the years that have elapsed since the first edition
was published, the subject of Comparative Psychology
has undergone a great change.   It is hardly too much to
say that, owing to the activity of a group of workers
in the American Universities, the investigation of the
animal mind has, roughly within this period, established
for itself a place among the recognised sciences.   Hence
much that was within the hands of pioneers when this
book was first written, has now been thoroughly
examined.   Much, of course, still remains undetermined.
In some material respects I have found it necessary to
modify opinions formed on the data available in 1900.
In particular, the observations of Mr. H. S. Jennings
have shown me that something of the nature of mind
is to be carried further down in the organic world than
I supposed.   His results, together with other work in
general psychology, have led me, however, to extend
rather than to narrow the view taken in the first edition
of the function of mind in evolution, and even to raise
the question whether mind (in the infinitely varied forms
of its activity from the groping of unconscious effort to
the full clearness of conscious purpose) may not be the
essential driving force in all evolutionary change.   In

any case, the revolution which has overtaken biological theory during the same period is profound. Its significance is as yet imperfectly grasped, but it will, I believe, be found, as time goes on, to have invested the constitution of the living being as against the environing conditions with a new importance, and in this constitution the fundamental fact everywhere is that the living being is not passive but active, not mechanical in its reaction to things, but assertive, plastic, and, in a measure proportioned to its development, self-determining. If this is so, psychology will in the future have a larger part to play than has hitherto been supposed in the study of the rise and decay of forms of life.

My obligations to many contemporary writers will, I think, appear clearly enough in the text, but I should like, in particular, to thank Professor Yerkes for information kindly supplied in correspondence ; Mr. Bullough for a valuable note on the Elberfeld Horses, and the Society for Psychical Research for putting much literature on this subject at my disposal at a time when it was otherwise difficult to come by. In general psychology I, like everyone else, have gained many new suggestions from the work of Professor Stout, Professor Graham Wallas and Dr. McDougall.

L. T. H.

HIGHGATE,
*September*, 1915.

# ANALYSIS

## CHAPTER I

### MIND AS A FACTOR IN EVOLUTION

1. The normal tendency of evolution is not towards a higher, but (2) a divergent type. 3. In the resulting diversity old types survive, and there is deterioration as well as improvement. 4. Within these divergencies there is one line of true development. This is the evolution of Mind. 5. The generic function of Mind is to organise Life by correlating its parts. 6. Its growth consists in the widening scope and increasing articulateness of correlation, (7) with which it replaces that organisation of life which rests on heredity. To trace this growth in outline is the object of this work.

## CHAPTER II

### MIND AND MECHANISM

1. Two generic types of correlation, (2) of which one is logically attributed to Mind. 3. Reserve necessary in attributing specific mental functions, especially in interpreting animal behaviour. 4. Conation and Purpose . . . . . . . . . . . . . . . . . .

## CHAPTER III

### ORGANIC ADAPTABILITY AND THE VITAL PROCESSES

Without deciding the question whether organic processes are to be explained by mechanical laws we may characterise organic activity in general terms, (2) as that which tends to keep the

## CHAPTER IV

### REFLEX ACTION

## CHAPTER V

### CONATION

## CHAPTER VI

### INSTINCT

## CHAPTER VII

### ASSIMILATION AND READJUSTMENT

1. Generically, Intelligence is distinguished from Instinct as a correlation of experiences and actions effected by the individual within his own life-history. 2. The experience on which intelligence rests is generically an experience of relations. (3) The operation of experience begins with Primary Retentiveness. 4. The simplest form of the inferential use of experience is Assimilation, (5) which involves a modified revival. 6. The main function of experience at this stage is to define general instinctive tendencies. 7. Cases in which a response is not modified, but created, by close association with a feeling may also be referred to assimilation. 8. For such operations of experience ideas are not necessary. 9. Their results in human consciousness are acquired perceptions and perceptual impulses. 10. Intelligence at this level is Inarticulate. 11. Evidence for the diffusion of this form of intelligence in the animal kingdom

## CHAPTER VIII

### CONCRETE EXPERIENCE AND THE PRACTICAL JUDGMENT

1. Judgment as a synthesis of distinct elements is to be distinguished from Assimilation and from the Association of Ideas. As a synthesis of perceptual elements, it may be called the Practical Judgment. 2. The Practical Judgment rests on the revival of Concrete Experience. 3. It involves ideas. 4. The conditions of revival differ from those of Association. 5. Such a synthesis is the condition of the knowledge of individual objects, of memory and anticipation, of purpose and desire. 6. The knowledge of objects also makes possible (*a*) a rudimentary analogical inference, and (*b*) the selective application of the data of experience. 7. The effect of the Practical Judgment as seen in behaviour is that instead of a mere modification of response the results of experience are applied to the guidance of action. 8. There is thus in this stage of intelligence a correlation of articulate complexes, which may be compared to the logical inference from minor premiss to conclusion on the basis of a perceived parallel . . . . . . . . . . . . . . .

## CHAPTER IX

### LEARNING AMONG THE HIGHER ANIMALS. THE METHOD OF TRIAL AND ERROR

1. Acts of apparent purpose can hardly be explained by Association of Ideas, but may grow up through Trial and Error. 2. Mr. Thorndike's experiments show that many novel acts can be learnt in this way. 3. But his results do not prove that all cats and dogs learn by habituation. 4. Nor is it universally true that animals learn nothing by being put through an action. 5. Experimental results are in the main unfavourable to reflective imitation, but the preliminary question should be settled whether an animal can learn by perception of results affecting itself. . . . . . . . . . . . . . .

## CHAPTER X

### SOME EXPERIMENTAL RESULTS

## CHAPTER XI

### THE KNOWLEDGE OF CONCRETE OBJECTS

## CHAPTER XII

### ARTICULATE IDEAS

## CHAPTER XIX

### SELF-CONSCIOUS DEVELOPMENT

## APPENDIX

# LIST OF ABBREVIATIONS

| *Abbreviation.* | *Full Title of Work.* |
|---|---|
| Bethe, Ameisen . . . . | Dürfen wir den Ameisen und Bienen psychische Qualitäten zuschreiben? von Albrecht Bethe, 1898. |
| Dahl . . . . . . . . | Versuch einer Darstellung der psychischen Vorgänge in den Spinnen—F. Dahl, Vierteljahrschrift für wissenschaftliche Philosophie, Vol. IX. |
| J. A. B. . . . . . . . | *Journal of Animal Behaviour.* |
| J. C. N. P. . . . . . . | *Journal of Comparative Neurology and Pathology.* |
| Müller and Schumann . | Experimentelle Beiträge zur Untersuchung des Gedächtnisses.—Zeitschrift für Psychologie und Physiologie der Sinnes Organe, 1894. |
| Preyer I. . . . . . . . | *The Senses and the Will,* by W. Preyer (Eng. trans. by H. W. Brown, 1896). |
| Preyer II. . . . . . . | *The Development of the Intellect,* by W. Preyer (Eng. trans. by H. W. Brown, 1896). |
| M. E. A. . . . . . . . | *Mental Evolution in Animals,* by G. J. Romanes, 1885. |
| Romanes . . . . . . | *Animal Intelligence,* by G. J. Romanes, sixth edition, 1895. |
| Wasmann, S. d. A. . . | Vergleichende Studien über das Seelenleben der Ameisen und der höhern Thiere, von Erich Wasmann, S. J., second edition. |
| Wesley Mills . . . . . | *The Nature and Development of Animal Intelligence,* by Professor Wesley Mills 1898. |

# MIND IN EVOLUTION

## CHAPTER I

### MIND AS A FACTOR IN EVOLUTION

1. EVOLUTION is a natural process, moving without regard to human judgments of what is good or bad, right or wrong. So its exponents, who are often also its apostles, assure us. None the less, it is held up to our admiration as a process which makes for good. The term itself, indeed, suggests a growing fulness of existence, the unrolling of latent powers, a tendency towards perfection, the process by which a thing comes to be that for which it was destined. Evolution is used as synonymous with progress, and progress, at least before its association with commercial statistics, meant a movement towards better things. The doctrine that whatever is is right reappears in the modernised form that whatever comes to be is justified. Nature thus conceived is not perfect, but is always on the way to become perfect. If only the fittest survive, each generation since the world began must be able to boast with Sthenelos that its members are much better than their fathers.

Unfortunately for the biological enthusiast, the perfection which Nature seeks is not always a perfection which man as a rational being can welcome or love. If the struggle for existence has produced the wisdom of man, it has also sharpened the tiger's claw and poisoned the cobra's fang. Nothing lives "unless helped by another's death," and the

B

progress of each species includes advance in the means of destroying others as well as preserving itself. Nor can it readily be conceded that the various species which thus learn to destroy each other more efficiently are necessarily higher or nobler in type than the ancestral forms from which they are derived. If, indeed, the "higher" type simply means that which is best capable of dealing with the circumstances in which it is placed, then it is undeniably true that the highest survive in the struggle for existence. But the truth is at this point a truism not worth mentioning but for the mischief which it has wrought. In the current theories of organic evolution, more particularly in the doctrine of Natural Selection, there is nothing whatever to prove that the individuals who prevail over others in the struggle for existence must necessarily be in any way "higher" in the sense which we human beings attach to that word. There is nothing in the nature of the struggle itself to show that the type which prevails must always be one which we should recognise as morally better, intellectually more developed, physically more beautiful, or in any way more desirable. It all depends on circumstances. In some parts of Africa the horse is driven out by the Tsetse fly; in others the white man succumbs before the malaria germ, just as in this country the honest investor goes down before the swindling company promoter. If it be said that in the end the better type will prevail, that man is upon the whole dominant among animals, and honesty upon the whole among men, I do not wish to deny, nor yet at this stage to affirm it. I am only concerned to protest against its being affirmed upon a thoroughly false ground, and in a thoroughly false form. The worst type very often survives, and evolution is not always upwards.

2. It is not even normally upwards. If we take man as the highest type of animal, and regard the line of evolution which ends in man as the upward line, then, as we know, at every point from the lowest upwards there are countless diverging lines. Evolution is not serial. Its plan is not that of a straight line or even a spiral, but rather that of a tree. For the species that has moved some distance along

a branch there is little or no chance of returning to the main stem, and for such a species further development means movement further away from the line of ascent. Look at any general scheme of organic evolution (Haeckel's, for example), and consider the lines of divergence.[1]   We find, for example, Echinodermata, Arthropods, or Mollusca, ranked as co-ordinate with the Tunicata from which Vertebrates are derived.   They are not stages in the evolution of Vertebrates, nor can their further evolution bring them nearer to the Vertebrate type.   The crab does not become more perfect by approximating insensibly to the Vertebrates, but rather, if the expression be allowed, by becoming more decisively and perfectly a crab—that is, by developing those features, strength of grip, hardness of outer shell, or whatever they may be, which distinguish it from other Crustacea.   The evolution of the dog, under the guidance of man, has not made him more human, but has brought out all sorts of canine qualities—scent, strength, swiftness, and the rest—and carried each to perfection after its own kind.   Normally, evolution accentuates the existing tendency, whatever it be.   By whatever organ or faculty a species is struggling to maintain itself, that organ or faculty will be brought by the survival of the fittest to the finest point of perfection.

3. This perfection may, from any point of view but that of success in the struggle for existence, be nothing but degradation.   Eyes become atrophied as a useless encumbrance to animals that dwell in caves.   A general degradation of type is suitable to the parasite, and the thick-skinned man gets on best in the world.   There are many instances of sheer deterioration in organic as in social evolution, and in each case the lower type is that which most successfully adapts itself to circumstances and manages to survive.   Nor, though the higher type may become in some degree dominant, is the lower eliminated.   The primitive organic forms appear to have subsisted with comparatively little alteration to the present day.   At any rate, no organism could be very much simpler than the

---

[1] Some good diagrams illustrating this point are given by Mr. Herbert Spencer, *Principles of Biology*, Vol. I. Ch. XI. p. 388.

lowest Rhizopods, which must either have remained nearly
unchanged through many geological periods, or represent
a process of degradation equal in extent and scope to that
of their previous evolution. But indeed there is nothing
in the physical conditions of Evolution to imply the
necessity of perpetual change. The fundamental fact of
Evolution is that through differentiation multiplication becomes easy. Ten beings requiring precisely the same food
would have much less chance of supporting themselves in
a given space than the same number feeding on different
things. Thus, if one of the ten develops a liking for food
of a different kind, the pressure on the others is lightened,
and their chance improved. If we apply this to variation
in a species, we see that, while its first effect will be very
adverse to the old stock, the future consequences may be
quite different. It may be that by striking out a fresh
line the variation relieves the old type from the pressure of
competition. Its reduced numbers find means of subsist-
ence again, and increase finally to their old point. Especially in social evolution, however rapid the rate of change,
we constantly find, if we look for them, survivals of the
primitive type. The small general shop is not utterly ex-
tinguished by the mammoth store. The village cobbler
remains, even if it be only to botch the boots that are
made at a Leicester factory. So also do the Protista survive, and there is not the slightest reason to suppose that
they are passing away. Many of them indeed in the
form of disease-germs wage an equal struggle with the
lords of creation. The tendency of biological evolution in
general is not to produce the highest type, but rather to
produce as many types as possible, filling in all the lacunæ
of organic possibility, not necessarily destroying any but
those which have not the character of their own kind in
sufficient strength. Evolution tends to space out the types
that it suffers, to cut them deep and true. It multiplies
and it defines, but it does not necessarily elevate.

4. We have spoken already of at least one upward line
in the evolutionary tree. Can we trace this line? Is there a
development in the true sense? Is there progress, or the evolution of a higher type? To answer these questions, we must

first know what is higher and what lower. To say that the highest thing that man knows is Mind, or Soul, or Spirit, may be to state an axiom, or to make an assumption. If the latter, I must, at any rate, for the sake of clearness make the assumption here. Evolution "upwards"—Orthogenic or, as it has been called, Aristogenic Evolution[1]—is the growth of Mind, or of the conditions which make Mind possible.[2] Evolution in any other direction is the growth of any other qualities whatever that assist survival. The main purpose of this work is to inquire into the character, tendency, and scope of Orthogenic Evolution: in other words, into the growth of mind. It will be best to say at once that we shall not be concerned with what is called (as I think, confusedly and inappropriately called) the ultimate nature of Mind. We shall not endeavour to trace the origin of Mind out of something else that is not mind. We shall take it as a factor in organic evolution which we shall endeavour to trace backwards to its germ and forwards to its mature development, ascertaining at the same time its relation to other factors. In this inquiry we shall have to do not so much with the inner nature of Mind as with its functions, not so much with what Mind is felt to be by its possessor, as with its operations as apparent to an onlooker. What bearing these investigations may have on the nature of Mind, its origin in the organic world, or its function in the whole of things, are questions upon which our results must speak for themselves. We shall be occupied with its evolution, not in the sense of its origin, but in the sense of that unrolling of its full nature which is what evolution most strictly means. If Mind is the highest thing, Orthogenic Evolution must consist in the unfolding of all that there is of latent possibility in Mind, the awakening of its powers, the development of its scope. It will be well to take a preliminary view of this development.

5. Mind, as we are to deal with it, is known by its functions. The function which modern philosophy seized

[1] By Mr. Sutherland, *Origin and Growth of the Moral Instinct* Vol. I. p. 29.
[2] Taking these conditions into account we shall be able to substitute a more comprehensive definition at a later stage.

upon as expressing the vital essence of Mind was that of bringing things together so that they have a bearing upon one another.  Where there is mind there are order and system, correlation and proportion, a harmonising of forces, and an interconnection of parts.  The organism which is gifted with intelligence shows it by arranging its actions on a certain plan.  It adapts means to ends, which is one sort of correlation, and in so doing it perhaps brings a past experience to bear, interpreting a perception, for example, by memory; and this is another sort of correlation.  Its scheme of action may include the good of its young, or its mate, or its friends, along with its own, and this is again another sort of correlation.  In proportion as its acts tend to promote the same end, its conduct may be termed organised, and its several actions correlated.  And the organisation, as we have just seen, may include several individuals, a pair of mates, a community, or conceivably a whole species.

Not all organised action, as we shall presently see, is intelligent.  But all unorganised action is, just as far as organisation is lacking, unintelligent.  Where action is random, blind, unconnected, conflicting, there is no mind at work, or there is a failure in its control.  Where action proceeds on the impulse of the moment without relation to permanent values, where past experience is not used in interpreting perception, there is lack of mental faculty, while, as between different people if their purposes, however cleverly planned for the good of each, tend to thwart one another, it is clear that, as the ordinary phrase rightly expresses it, they are not of one mind. In the latter case, which is important for our purposes, there is mind—a mind in each individual—but there is no mind which comprehends the ends of all in a single plan, and makes of that plan its purpose.

6. Where minds differ is in organising power—that is, in comprehensiveness or in scope.  The dog who begs for his dinner acts, to all appearance, intelligently.  He adjusts means to ends, and correlates a simple action with its immediate result.  So also does a statesman who drafts a clause in a Bill, or an engineer who decides on strengthen-

ing a girder.    In each case there is a certain correlation.
Actions are fitted together so that they form a connected
whole, or an intelligible plan.    The difference is partly in
the scope of the plan, partly in the method of its construction.    The dog performs a single action with a view
to an immediate gratification.    The man, whether statesman or engineer, has to deal with a problem which it
would perhaps fill many pages even to formulate, and, in
adjusting each detail, has to think out a series of complicated interactions, lest in filling a void at one place he may
disturb equilibrium somewhere else.    If we turn to the
data by which dog and man are guided, we find a similar
result, of analogy and of contrast.    The dog was trained
to beg ; that is, he learnt that by begging he obtained
food.    When he applies the lesson, and begs of his own
accord, he connects this experience with his present
needs, brings it to bear on his present action.    The
man also correlates experiences, but he has a thousand
and one data to take into account.    A great proportion of them may rest, not on his own observation,
but on the testimony of others, and he has to work
them up in all manner of ways, to reconstruct and
to calculate, before they can serve his purpose.    There
is the same process of interconnecting distinct facts at
work, but as the interconnection is immeasurably broader
in its scope, so it is infinitely more subtle and intricate
in its methods.

The growth of mind in life is, then, manifested in the
wider and more subtle interconnection of what is otherwise
separate and even inconsistent.    The rise of reason is a
swelling harmony which gradually subdues discord, and
uses it to its own ends.    To the true rationalism the
supreme reason is no dry pedant living apart and blighting
the free spontaneous life of impulse, but the animating
spirit that interpenetrates experience and gives to its otherwise scattered fragments new and harmonious meaning.
Aristotle,[1] with much quaint nobility of phrase, has described the inner harmony of the man in whom the real
or thinking self [2] is supreme, how he " agrees with him-

---

[1] *Eth. Nic.*, IX. 4.    [2] Τὸ διανοητικόν—ὅπερ ἕκαστος εἶναι δοκεῖ.

self," and "feels with his own joys and sorrows, because
the same thing is at all times pleasant or painful to him,
and not one thing at one time and another at another,"
since with him is no variableness neither shadow of turning.   Modern thinkers [1] have worked out in some detail
this correspondence between the "inner harmony" of the
moral or practical reason, and the "outer harmony" of
man's relations in society.   Both within the soul and in
the relations between men, reason, as her sway extends,
harmonises, correlates, and connects.   The clash of wills
is subdued, without loss of vigour or of personality, in
a common will.   The experience, not merely of the individual but of the race, is brought to bear on the
problems which the race must solve.

7. At this point it will naturally be urged that, after
all, things are not, in the absence of reason, as anarchic as
might appear from our argument.   If the lower animals
do not act from purpose, they still behave in a perfectly
determinate manner, and in the way best suited to their
needs.   The singing of the birds or the play of the butter-
fly is no mere frivolity, but is serious courtship.   Even
the kitten that seems to be amusing itself with a ball of
string is really preparing, after the fashion that Nature has
provided, for the serious business of hunting mice.   In
short, in the brute creation Instinct replaces intelligence
as the correlating or unifying principle in life.   On the
basis of instinct, means are adapted to ends, food is obtained, danger avoided, the young cared for, and long connected trains of action, like the nest-building of birds or insects, carried out with undeviating persistence. And not only
does instinct adapt means to ends, but, it may be further
urged, in so doing it uses the very same means which we
have dwelt upon as the peculiar property of intelligence.
For on any theory of Evolution it is the past experience
of the species which directly or indirectly conditions the instinctive reactions of the individual.   Just as in human
life the arts develop from stage to stage as new experiments are made and found successful, so in the animal

[1] See particularly Prof. Alexander, *Moral Order and Progress*
p. 117, &c.

world slight variations which turn out well are preserved.
The physical structure which made them possible is handed
on, and becomes the basis from which a fresh start can be
made.  The structure of eye, wing, beak, and claw that
makes perfect the swoop and pounce of the falcon is the
result of countless ancestral variations in the course of which
the structure which made some slight approach to this
point of perfection prevailed over others, and prevailed
more surely the more nearly it reached its goal.[1]

Now Instinct, a term which has here been used in a
popular sense, is not when fully defined to be taken as
exclusive of Intelligence.  On the contrary, as we shall
see later, the relations are subtle and closely interwoven.
But we may put the criticism in more radical fashion by
substituting for Instinct the conception of hereditary
physical structure acting in accordance with mechanical
laws.  Every living being, it may be said, possesses such a
structure.  It has grown up bit by bit under the conditions of heredity and of the struggle for existence, every
variation that helped to keep the organism alive and
to perpetuate the stock being preserved, while every
adverse change is weeded out by the destruction of the
stock which it entails.  This structure effects the correlations which we find in the world of life.  The spring of
the cat involves a cunning adjustment of numerous processes, from the rise of the retinal excitement which we
call the sight of the mouse to the combination of muscular
contractions which lands the cat with her prey in her
claws.  This adjustment subserves what, from the out-
sider's point of view, we call a purpose, the purpose of

---

[1] Later researches on heredity have thrown grave doubts on the
permanent value of small individual variations.  Biology seems to be
reversing the old adage and proclaiming that in evolution *natura nil
facit nisi per saltum*.  If this view is finally substantiated it must
profoundly affect the entire philosophy of development.  Clearly it
postulates some originating factor of organic change the nature of which
is at present wholly unknown.  Nevertheless the argument of the para-
graph stands, if it is clearly understood that "experience," *i.e.*, realised
success in meeting the conditions of life, is not spoken of as the cause of
new experiments in behaviour but the condition governing the survival
of the individual making the experiment and of his line.  We may still
regard a complex instinct like a complex structure as growing by stages,
though we may have to take each stage as a definite step, not as the
infinitesimal prolongation of a continuous curve.

securing a meal. But purpose as a conscious process in the cat has no causal efficacy. What works is the physical system, and we ought to attribute to this system not the fulfilment of a purpose but the performance of a function in the life of the cat. Indeed, according to one theory all actions of living beings from the pounce of the cat to the inventions of the engineer or the creations of the poet are in the last resort to be explained in this fashion. All are the reactions, highly specialised it may be, but still the reactions of a complicated machine. If we keep to the facts, however, we recognise great differences of type in the behaviour not only of men but of animals. Some forms of behaviour conform to the mechanical type. They serve a function, but in doing so they proceed with a machine-like uniformity. Others bear no resemblance to machine-processes, and the more closely we analyse them the more definite does the difference become, and these are the modes of behaviour usually attributed to Mind. Now whether this distinction is fundamental or superficial, whether the apparent independence of Mind is an illusion or a reality, how the relations between the mental and the physical are to be understood are philosophical questions which we can only approach with any advantage when we have all the apparent differences before us. But that there are differences between forms of behaviour, and in particular differences in the kind and degree of correlation that they exhibit is, as we shall argue in the next chapter, simple matter of fact. Our main object in this volume is to exhibit these differences, to distinguish the principal types of correlation that are found in the behaviour of living beings. These will be found to range themselves under the two great classes of the mechanical and the mental. Even if ultimate analysis should resolve one of these into the other or both into a more ultimate unity, within that unity the distinction would still hold. There would still be specific differences in correlation of the highest significance for the evolution of life. In particular we shall see that the kind of correlation which we attribute to Mind is wider in scope and more complete in the detail of its adjustment than that which we call mechanical, and the more so in proportion as Mind develops. Thus if our study of orthogenic evolution is an inquiry into the growth of Mind, it will also follow the successive stages by which the life of animals and men become more completely organised, and if a completer organisation may fairly be called a higher organisation, that is some justification for our provisional application of the term to the work of Mind. Our subject then is the development of Mind as seen in its functions, and this will involve a review of the principal types of correlation, whether attributable to Mind or to any other factor, that are discoverable in the world of life.

# CHAPTER II

## MIND AND MECHANISM

1. Our object being the study of correlation in general, and of correlation as effected by Mind in particular, our first task must be to justify the distinction drawn in the last chapter between the mechanical and the mental. We must establish, first, that there exist two generically different modes of correlation, and, secondly, that one of these may justly be attributed to Mind. The data on which the first of these conclusions rests must obviously consist of external facts of behaviour. There must be positive differences in the relation of act to act or act to circumstances to justify a deep distinction between the correlating functions. The data of the second conclusion cannot consist in external behaviour alone, for we know Mind each of us directly within himself. The relation between these two arguments is the chief source of difficulty in our subject, and we must at this early stage do our best to make it clear. Let us begin by re-stating the mechanical theory of correlation and examining it from the point of view of an observer of external behaviour alone. By general admission many of the processes of the living body can be explained upon mechanical principles. Given the contraction of the muscle the movements of the limbs illustrate simple principles of the lever. Given the pulsations of the heart, the broad fact of the circulation could be inferred from the action of the common pump. Given the respiratory centre and its control over the muscles that move the ribs

and the diaphragm, respiration follows as a matter of pneumatics. In all these cases there are indeed qualifications induced by more searching inquiry. Not all the facts of circulation are explicable on the principles of the common pump. When the dilatation and contraction of the arteries, for example, are taken into account, we can no longer think of the blood as circulating through a simple system of elastic tubes. When all the facts are known the phenomena of digestion are not found to correspond accurately to the chemical laws of osmosis. Moreover, in stating each of these processes in mechanical terms, we have to assume certain forces which are not like those of an ordinary inanimate mechanism. Nevertheless the advocates of the mechanical theory of life point with triumph to a series of successes. Time and again they have reduced some mysterious process, which seemed distinctive of living beings and explicable only by the assumption of some vital force, to mechanical terms. Their belief is that the residue which is at present unreduced only requires further investigation to be set upon the same basis. If we knew enough about the structure of the heart and the nature of nerves and muscular action, we should be able to state the law of its pulsations in mechanical formulæ. A similar extension of our knowledge would explain the adaptation of the arteries to the fluctuating requirements of the body, the control of the respiratory mechanism by the medullary centre, the absorption of foodstuff by the cells lining the alimentary canal, and so forth. Finally, a still more perfect knowledge would enable us to reduce purposive action, artistic creation, philosophic thought to a complex of mechanical changes in nervous tissue. All would be recognised as mechanism if we could only know the whole of the intimate structure of the body.

In order to examine this theory and to decide what part, if any, is played by Mind in modifying mechanical processes, we must ask in general terms what is meant by the mechanical and what sort of function we suppose mind to introduce in the business of correlating vital activities. Now if we take a confessedly inanimate machine, the work of human hands, it exhibits, like the human body itself, a complex dovetailing of various parts, such that when the whole is put in motion some definite result is produced, and in the production of this result every part of the machine, like every organ of the human body, performs some specific function, thus contributing to the whole. But in the machine, though each part performs this function, its motions do not directly depend upon the result that does, as a fact, come about from them, and though the machine when perfect acts as a whole, yet the movement of each part is dependent on its own structure and on the behaviour of those which are immediately in contact with it, not on the unity and entirety of the machine. This particular wheel is turned by cogs fitting in, let us say, to a ratchet. If the ratchet moves the wheel turns. It does not matter whether the machine as a whole is in order or out of order, whether it is doing the work for which it was made or doing nothing at all ; given that the wheel is in place and that the ratchet is moving, the wheel will turn. It has no regard to the performances of any other part. It has no concern with the effects that it produces by turning. It turns in response to the force immediately impressed upon it. These conditions hold generally of mechanical aggregates. Every element in such an aggregate acts uniformly in response to the force immediately operating upon it and without relation to the contemporaneous behaviour of any other part or to the result which will in fact accrue from its action.

Now, whenever Mind is at work, these conditions are in appearance reversed. It may be only appearance, but even so it will have its importance as bearing upon the methods of correlation. Let us then examine the difference. Mind, as studied from outside, in its functions, is most clearly recognisable in the purposive act. Now the purposive act, again studied not from within but from without, is an act apparently directed by relation to its result. It chooses means to ends, rejects those that are unsuitable, varies its behaviour in accordance with circumstances, surmounts, destroys, or circumvents obstacles, adapts itself to an indefinite number of varying circumstances in accordance with their relation to the matter in hand. If a philosopher from another planet, ignorant of all forms of life as they exist upon this world, were to watch a stone rolling down hill and a man running to catch his train, he would come to the conclusion that the stone and the man were actuated by very different principles. He would, for example, see the man go round the obstacle which caught up the stone, and if he proceeded to compare their behaviour under many circumstances and in different relations, he would arrive at the result that the broad difference could be most easily formulated by conceiving the stone's action as determined always by the reaction of its inherent qualities upon the forces directly impressed upon it without regard to the ultimate issue, while the man's action would be, in the majority of cases, determined by its relation from moment to moment to some result more or less remote. If, further, our observer was to extend his investigations to the operation of man-made machines, he would discover in their working a co-operation of parts, a correlation of processes, in subservience to certain results. But if he carefully analysed and compared different cases, he would arrive at the conclusion that the working of every part of the machine rested on causes fundamentally identical with those which urge the rolling stone. He would see that the bearing of its act upon the outcome never affects the behaviour of any cog in the machinery. If, however, he looked into the workshops where the machines are made, and especially into the offices where they are designed, he would discover that the behaviour of the beings that made them is continually adjusted and readjusted in accordance with the relation of the act to the result. That is to say, proceeding purely by inferences based on comparison of behaviour, he would discover two fundamentally distinct types of correlation, one in which each element of behaviour is conditioned by its relation to its result, the other in which no such relation is operative although the result is in fact produced. Now he might ultimately decide that these two types are reducible to one. He might, for example, find that all mechanical correlations are to be referred to a plan in which the result is pre-arranged. Or he might find that the apparent determination of behaviour by result is due to an infinitely more subtle combination of purely mechanical arrangements which at first escaped him. But even in the latter alternative he would still acknowledge two clearly distinct types of correlated behaviour, in one of which the bearing of act on result is operative, while in the other it is not. He would now hold that this relation is made operative by a mechanical arrangement. But operative it still would be, and this would generically distinguish the type of correlation from the type in which there is no such element operating.

2. So far, then, our first point. There exist two types of correlation, the first conforming to that of known machines, the second radically differing. Whatever more ultimate unity may be suggested between them, this difference in the nature of correlation will remain, and this difference is established purely by observation of behaviour. But now comes our further question. We provisionally attributed the second type of correlation to Mind. In so doing we are deserting the test of behaviour pure and simple. Mind is something of which I have direct knowledge within me, and you within you, but neither of us sees, hears, or feels it at work in another. By what logic then is behaviour of any kind attributed to Mind ? The broad answer is as follows. → In my behaviour I am conscious of certain states, acts, processes. For example, when I effect that kind of correlation which I call acting with a purpose, I am aware of the acts and have an idea of the end, and such awareness is within my experience essential to activity of that kind. The sum of all such conscious activity together with the processes involved in it and the permanent conditions underlying it constitute that body of my experience which I call my own mind.) Now in referring any act of my own to my mind as a cause I may be mistaken. It may be that physical processes of brain and nerve of which I am unconscious form the true vehicle of the act. But in

speaking of my mind as implicated in my purposive behaviour, I am only recording facts of my experience just as certainly as if I were noting the movements of the barometer. On the other hand, it is only my own individual mind that is thus given to a direct experience, and if all reference to mind other than that based on direct experience were ruled out, each of us would have to be a Solipsist.[1] I find, however, that many other objects, constituted externally much like myself, also behave in ways broadly corresponding to my own and I attribute to them also minds and states or acts of Mind accordingly. The inference is quite logical, and within limits is being repeatedly corroborated by the whole of my intercourse with my species. Within limits, because I may err by too great simplification, taking others as more like me than they really are, or again by failing to recognise a common element which is really at work. These are the ordinary fallacies to which all generalisation is liable and from which it is saved only by a rigorous inductive logic. The application of such logic to the details of our subject will be examined presently. Meanwhile on the main point we must maintain that the attribution of Mind to others on the basis of behaviour is a perfectly consequent logical inference. Here is a situation A upon which I react consciously in a definite manner, B, the result being certain overt behaviour C. Here is another being in a corresponding situation A', which displays corresponding behaviour C'. To infer a corresponding link B' is a valid logical procedure, and its validity is corroborated by the ever-repeated test of daily intercourse with our fellows.

3. This being the logical basis of our attribution of one class of correlations to Mind, it is open to two criticisms, which have been hinted at but must be more fully stated before we can proceed. First, Mind may not be the operative cause of correlation. Internal consciousness does not prove that it is so in me. Therefore no observa-

---

[1] It may be said that other beings communicate their minds to me by language, but in the last resort the use of words is an element of behaviour of which only the external result is an immediate object of my experience.

tion of behaviour can prove that it is so in another. This criticism we must provisionally accept. What our reasoning can prove is that the operation of Mind is implicated in certain forms of correlation, and it is on this ground that for the time being we call them mental. The proof that Mind is the operative cause must rest on the analysis of the nature of mechanism on the one hand and of mental causation on the other. For our present purposes the names mechanical and mental must be held to import, the one correlation corresponding to that of known machines and not involving mental activity, the other correlation involving mental activity and radically different from that of known machines. Secondly, in imputing a specific mode of consciousness to another we argue from the situation and the behaviour. If these were in all respects similar from case to case, there would be no difficulty. But no two situations are absolutely alike. If we argue from our own behaviour in one case to that of another person in his case, we are justified only if the cases are alike in all relevant points. What is relevant we decide, as in all induction, by comparison of instances wherein those things which go uniformly together are distinguished from those which vary independently. But now when we come to beings which differ permanently from ourselves, a graver difficulty is introduced. This difficulty appears even in human psychology in our judgments of the other sex or of another race, even of another class or another age than our own. It is still more serious when we are dealing with animals whose whole organisation presents points of difference from ours, who are relatively poor in means of expression, and whose behaviour does not therefore afford so many opportunities for testing a doubtful point. The attribution of consciousness to animals rests ultimately on the same logic as its attribution by you or me to our fellow men. But the differences which already give us trouble in judging our fellows are deeper, and the tests by which we may measure their effect more difficult to apply. But this at least we can say: if the behaviour of another being corresponds precisely in all its outer relations to that which I know of in myself as carried out in consciousness and never without consciousness, it is clear that in that other being *some* process occurs which performs the same functions as consciousness performs in me. The antecedent situation corresponds, let us suppose, in every detail which experience has shown to be relevant to its causation. The resulting act corresponds. It is an inevitable inference that the linking process corresponds in function. The organisation of the animal being different, it is possible that the state of consciousness may differ in any respect not essential to its function. This is a possibility which our method cannot exclude. But it can establish the existence of corresponding functions. We shall confine ourselves to the analysis of such functions without attempting to ascertain the nature of the animal mind in other respects. That is to say, we shall not try to form a picture of the animal consciousness. But we shall in the course of this work use the term consciousness and terms importing consciousness or specific modes of consciousness to describe any function corresponding precisely in its outer relations to one which among ourselves necessarily involves consciousness or the particular mode of consciousness which is in question. Given the criteria as we have stated them, this attribution is logically justified. The similarities between the functions which the terms are used to describe would subsist whatever the differences may be, and no other way of describing them lies to hand that does not involve repeated and intolerable periphrasis.

We conclude then (1) that there exist two generic forms of correlation distinguishable by the observation of external behaviour alone ; (2) that one of these is held on sufficient logical grounds to involve the operation of Mind. Further, we propose to distinguish and compare types of mental correlation on the basis of the behaviour involved. We shall find that the method of correlation involved will give us a common measure applicable to every stage of mental development from the lowest to the highest, enabling us, therefore, to determine at any point how much is achieved. Lastly, to each form of observable correlation we shall impute a corresponding mental function, and shall hold ourselves justified in so doing even in the animal world so far as we restrict ourselves to terms importing function and do not attempt a picture of a state of consciousness as known only to its possessor. We remark finally that any doubt attaching to the use of such terms will not apply to the description of the types of correlation effected, which depend entirely on accuracy in the analysis of observed facts of behaviour.

4. In order to apply our conception of mental correlation and distinguish it from the mechanical, we must include within it every class of action in which the relation to results enters in as a factor. For purposes of illustration we have employed purposive behaviour. But fully developed Purpose is not the only practical operation of Mind. This we may ascertain by regarding operations either from within or from without. If we look at purpose from the inside the relation to the result is a matter of consciousness. We have an idea of the end in view, and this idea is a factor in promoting and guiding our behaviour until the end is reached. But the employment of ideas is a relatively advanced stage in the life of mind. We shall find types of action that resemble purpose in that they are determined by relation to the result, although no idea of the result is consciously formulated. We shall find that, viewed externally as modes of correlation, they differ in a manner corresponding to the difference ascertained by conscious analysis. We need, therefore, a generic name for all action which is in one way or another determined by relation to the result which will accrue from it, whether there is a full antecedent awareness of that result or not. For this purpose psychology employs the term Conation. Conation is a mental state which as such tends to pass into some other. The " other " may be clearly or ill defined. The method of operation may be precise or wavering and uncertain. We shall have to take up these points at a later stage and seek a closer understanding of the relation of Conation to purpose. Meanwhile it results from our

definition that relation to some other state that is to come out of it is essential to conation, and the name may therefore serve to characterise the activity of mind in general as a factor in the organisation of conduct. What is involved in conation as such and what is peculiar to its distinctive forms, will be questions occupying us at a later stage.

# CHAPTER III

## ORGANIC ADAPTABILITY AND THE VITAL PROCESSES

1. To determine the part played by Mind in behaviour we must begin, as the preceding discussion will have suggested, with its opposite. We must seek to determine the scope and measure the achievement of the mechanical factor in the life of organised beings. For this purpose we naturally turn to those processes which in ourselves go on without the aid of conscious mind. We may begin with the ordinary vital functions of nutrition, respiration, secretion, and the like which are common to all organisms. These functions exhibit a measure of adaptability which is the common character of all living organic matter. We find it in plants no less than in animals, in Protozoa no less than in Mammals. This adaptability, however, is commonly referred by physiologists to mechanical causes. The prevailing view is that the white blood-corpuscle which makes its way through the blood to the bacteria which it is about to devour is as certainly moved by mechanical forces, if we could only detect them, as the red corpuscle which is carried along passively in the blood-stream. The waving of the cilia, or delicate threads which proceed from the lining of the windpipe, and by a constant upward swish sweep away any chance foreign body from the approaches to the lungs, is held no more spontaneous than the alternate bending and recovery of the long grass in the wind. We can tell what it is that bends the grass. We do not at present know what moves the cilia. It is no massive outer force ; it is

a series of molecular, presumably chemical, changes. But physiologists for the most part agree in the hypothesis—which it is well to remember is no more than a hypothesis—that if we knew all about these changes, we should find them to be only very complicated results of the same set of physical laws in accordance with which the grass bows before the wind.

Before discussing this question let us look at the broad facts of organic adaptability as we find them, and form from them a conception of what the organism can do. If we assume that the prevailing physiological conception is correct, and that the organism is in fact a cunningly contrived machine, we may remember that every machine has a function and character of its own. It is composed of parts which, taken by themselves, are common to many machines, and work in accordance with highly general laws, yet in their combination make up a machine which may be quite individual, and work in a way peculiar to itself. The machine as a whole may draw a train, or spin cotton, and any one, an onlooker or a purchaser, may be allowed to ask what it does without asking how it is built. If the organism is a machine, if it is made up of parts each of which can be found also in the inorganic world, and acts in accordance with the very same laws which prevail in that sphere, still the combination of these parts may be distinctive, and the work it does may be peculiar. It may be to evolve carbonic acid, or it may be to produce poetry. We can learn something of the character of its work, and of the way in which it does it, even if we can form no satisfactory theory as to the structure of the machine.

2. The normal life of any organism from highest to lowest is a process of unceasing change. It involves a constant interchange of substance with the outer world, an equally constant metabolism or transformation within itself of the substances which it takes up from without, and a no less constant transformation of energy. Such processes are common to all organisms. If we spoke only of the higher forms, many other activities could of course be added. Throughout this unceasing process of change,

which differentiates it from inanimate matter, the organism preserves its own identity as clearly as the unchanging rock. This feat of preserving itself in the midst of change could not be accomplished as it is in the midst of ever varying circumstances unless there were a certain equilibrium point, as we may call it, which the organism is always striving to maintain. It is true that the equilibrium is a moving equilibrium. The process of rapid growth in youth, of slow change during maturity, and of gradual decay ending in death (or internal transformation ending in fission), is of course the normal orbit of every organism. The equilibrium point moves along this orbit, and the momentary changes of which we speak are so many oscillations about the equilibrium point as it moves. What immediately concerns us is that every organism is so built, whether on mechanical principles or not, that every deviation from the equilibrium point sets up a tendency to return to it. This is true both of the normal and of the abnormal circumstances that affect the organism. A few illustrations may make this general statement a little clearer.

The normal breathing of the healthy man serves among other things to maintain a certain balance between the demand and supply of oxygen within the body. In the alternate expansion and contraction of the lungs we have a simple instance of oscillation about a mean point, in which by whatever mechanism the deviation in one direction itself tends to bring about the contrary motion. Under certain circumstances, normal breathing does not supply oxygen in sufficient quantities. If the atmosphere is deficient in oxygen, or if by violent exercise the muscles consume more than their due share, we begin to pant, to take deeper breaths, and take them more quickly. The same action has the effect of eliminating the extra quantity of carbonic acid[1] evolved by the muscles during violent exercise. The organism makes an effort to maintain as nearly as possible its normal state.

Still more instructive for our purposes is the mainten-

---

[1] It seems doubtful, however, whether the carbonic acid has a direct effect. See Foster, *Text Book of Physiology*, II. pp. 632 and 634, sixth edition, 1895.

ance of an almost even temperature by all warm-blooded animals. In man, the temperature of the blood is maintained, no matter what the temperature of the surrounding air, at 98·4° F. The fluctuations around this point during health are so narrow that any marked deviation is at once taken as a symptom of illness. Without going into detail, it is sufficient to say that this balance is maintained principally by two mechanisms, the vasomotor system and the perspiration. The vasomotor nerves govern the calibre of the small arteries which supply the surface of the body with blood, dilating or constricting them as the case may be. The application of something cold to the skin acting through these nerves causes constriction of the blood-vessels. The result is that less blood comes to the surface, and as it is the blood that brings the heat the skin is cooled, but the body as a whole gives off less heat than usual. Exactly the opposite result follows from the application of heat. Now the small arteries are dilated, the surface is flushed with blood, and heat is rapidly lost. Similarly, the increase of heat again acting through a nervous mechanism throws the sweat glands into activity, and the consequent evaporation keeps the body cool.

" The working of this heat-regulating mechanism is well seen in the case of exercise. Since every muscular contraction gives rise to heat, exercise must increase for the time being the production of heat ; yet the bodily temperature rarely rises so much as a degree centigrade, if at all. By exercise the respiration is quickened, and the loss of heat by the lungs increased. The circulation of blood is also quickened, and the cutaneous vascular areas becoming dilated, a larger amount of blood passes through the skin. Added to this, the skin perspires freely. Thus a large amount of heat is lost to the body, sufficient to neutralise the addition caused by the muscular contraction, the increase which the more rapid flow of blood through the abdominal organs might tend to bring about being more than sufficiently counteracted by their smaller supply for the time. The sense of warmth, which is felt during exercise in consequence of the flushing of the skin, is in itself a token that a regulative cooling is being carried on. In a similar way the application of external cold or heat defeats its own ends, either partially or completely." [1]

---

[1] Foster, *op. cit.* Part II. p. 849.

It is merely a familiar instance of the same well adapted rhythm, that work makes us hungry, that being hungry we find something to eat, that eating it makes us able to work again, and thereby earn our next meal. It is a more special application of the same fact that the muscle which we especially exercise gets an extra supply of blood and grows in proportion.

3. Thus both in general and in special ways the normal healthy life is a process of unceasing oscillation about an imaginary equilibrium point, departure from which tends of itself to set up processes which take the organism back again. The same feature of organic action appears in a more curious shape in more or less abnormal life. A machine can be made to regulate its own action within certain limits. Thus, in the steam engine, the forward thrust of the piston opens and shuts valves by which the backward thrust is at once brought about. Here there is perhaps a parallel to the automatic rhythm of breathing, or of the heart's beat. More than that, by the device of the " governor " a steam engine can regulate its own available energy in accordance with the work required of it. There is a close analogy here to the laboured breathing of hard exercise where more oxygen is required. But I do not think that any machine can repair itself when its own structure is in some way injured. This, within limits, every organism can do. Even the human body can repair its skin and its broken bones. This repairing means that in the healthy organism a lesion sets up processes which tend to restore the normal condition. Let us first observe the degree and kind of adaptation involved in the healing of a broken bone. The spongy substance of the long bones in the higher vertebrates is—

" . . . . arranged on a similar mechanical principle to that of arched structures in general; it is composed of numerous fine bony plates, so arranged as to withstand the greatest amount of tension and pressure, and to give the utmost firmness with a minimum expenditure of material. But the direction, position, and strength of these bony plates are by no means congenital or determined in advance : they depend on circumstances. If the bone is broken and heals out of the straight, the plates of the spongy tissue become rearranged, so as to lie in the new direction of greatest tension and pressure ; thus they can adapt themselves to changed circumstances." [1]

But it is among the lowest organisms that "Regeneration" performs the most remarkable feats. As long as one condition is maintained, a Protozoon may be not merely injured, but divided into several pieces, and yet each piece will, in a few hours, grow into the entire animal again, dwarfed perhaps, but otherwise, to all appearance, healthy and content. The condition is that each fragment should contain a portion of the " nucleus " of the cell in addition to some of the surrounding protoplasm. If this condition is not observed, if, for example, a portion of the protoplasm is cut off by itself, it retains for some while activities as similar as may be to those of the entire animal, but it shows no power of reconstruction or recuperation, and in the end it perishes. But a *Stentor*, for example, may be divided into twenty-seven parts, and the twenty-seventh fraction may, if containing a fragment of nucleus in its protoplasm, live to become a complete *Stentor* again.[2] The remarkable nature of this process is best illustrated by the diagram on the following page, which I take from Prof. E. B. Wilson's work, *The Cell in Development and Inheritance*, p. 250.

It will be seen that, however much the fragments differ, they end by reproducing the entire organism, the reproductive process having in each case the same equilibrium point at which waste and repair balance one another and growth ceases.

Equally remarkable is the tendency of a mutilated embryo to develop into a perfect animal. When the fertilised ovum divides into two distinct cells, it would be natural to suppose that each one of these was destined to develop into one half of the body, and it might be inferred that if one were destroyed, the other must either perish or develop into one half of the embryo only. But it is found, in point of fact, that there are further possibilities. In

---

[1] Prof. Weismann, Romanes' *Lecture*, p. 15, quoted by Mr. Lloyd Morgan ; *Habit and Instinct*, p. 313.

[2] Wilson, *The Cell in Development and Inheritance*, p. 249.

some cases the half embryo is formed first, and the missing half is regenerated from it later on. In other cases the half-embryo formation is found only in the earliest stages, while in others again it is entirely suppressed. Thus, to illustrate the first case, Roux destroyed one of the two "cleavage cells" into which the ovum of a frog divides, and found that the other grew into an embryo which

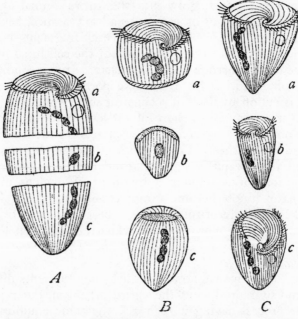

REGENERATION IN THE UNICELLULAR ANIMAL *Stentor* [Gruber].
A. Animal divided into three pieces, each containing a fragment of the nucleus. B. The three fragments shortly afterwards. C. The three fragments after twenty-four hours, each regenerated to a perfect animal.

wholly lacked one half of the body. The missing half could, however, grow out of the existing half at a later stage.[1] For the second case we may quote experiments on the ova of sea-urchins, which divide first into two and then into four cells. If at either stage these cells are isolated, they continue to segment—

"as if still forming part of an entire larva, and give rise to a half (or quarter) blastula. The opening soon closes, however, to

[1] Verworn, *General Physiology*, trans. F. S. Lee, 1899, p. 534.

form a small complete blastula, and the resulting gastrula and
Pluteus larva is a perfectly formed dwarf of only half (or quarter)
the normal size."[1]

In Amphioxus the isolated blastomere cells produced
by division of the ovum segment from the beginning
like a smaller ovum.[2] Lastly if the gastrula of sea-urchin
or starfish be bisected either along the axis or at right
angles to it complete little organisms are obtained.[3]

One might say, looking at these cases alone, that the
embryo was determined to do its duty, and grow up true
to type, whatever happened. Or, dropping metaphor, one
might infer the existence of internal forces in the germ
cells absolutely determining the lines of growth, irre-
spectively of the material supplied to them. This inference, however, would not be altogether sound. Both regeneration and development are largely conditioned by
external circumstances. Thus a *Tubularia* has the very
useful faculty of growing a new head, in case it should
have the misfortune to be decapitated. But this regeneration can only go forward in water, and if the decapitated
end is buried in the sand, it is the other end which
develops the head.[4] Either end of the worm is able to
grow a head with the help of water, neither end without
it.[5] So again if growth were fixed by internal causes
alone, a tadpole must necessarily develop into a frog when
the time comes. But if at that point in its career a tadpole is prevented from leaving the water, it retains its tail
and gills while increasing in size.[6] Similarly the crus-
tacean Artemia salina assumes two specifically different
forms according as it is brought up in sea water or in
fresh water.[7] Thus while on the one side we find the
organism clinging, as it were, to its type, in spite of

---

[1] Wilson, *op. cit.* p. 308.     [2] *Ib.* p. 309.
[3] Driesch, *Science and Philosophy of the Organism*, vol. I. p. 8.   See
the whole of Part I. (especially A and B) for numerous illustrations and
a full discussion of the problem.     [4] Wilson, *op. cit.* p. 325.
[5] Another remarkable point is that the "head" does not bud out from
the wound (and is therefore not technically regenerated) but can be
shown to be restored by the combined work of many parts of the stem.
Its position and size depend on the length of the section, and the growth
will occur at whatever point the stem is cut (Driesch, vol. I. p. 127).
[6] Verworn, p. 182.     [7] *Ib.* p. 183.

adverse circumstances, we find it, on the other, departing from its type to suit special circumstances. The growth and maintenance of the organism are due, not merely to a complex balance of internal forces, but also to complicated reactions between these forces in their successive phases and the forces of the environment.

4. What appears to be the distinguishing mark of an organism is that, through all these complications, it maintains its hold on the balance of forces necessary to its existence. It is not merely that its functions run smoothly in the particular groove marked out for them by its structure, but that, within tolerably wide limits, it can survive accidents, which cause a considerable departure from its normal course, and either struggle back to the typical life of the species again, or effect some compromise with circumstances by which life is maintained in some more or less modified form. Adaptability of this kind does not seem to be found in the inorganic world. A stone maintains its existence for centuries, it may be, but maintains it unchanged. If the stone could be said to have a life, it would be one of dull mechanical persistence in the established fact. If it is scratched, dinted, or broken, it remains scratched, dinted, or broken, and there is no more to be said. There is nothing comparable to the recuperation of the living being.

It may very well be true that, if we take the common characteristics of organised beings one by one, and look about us for comparisons, we can find something to match each one severally in the inanimate world. Thus the tendency to regain the equilibrium point is common to mechanical arrangements, like the pendulum, and to all bodies so far as they are elastic. The analogy is real so far as it goes. In one particular way the elastic body can be made to deviate from, and then will tend to return to, an equilibrium point. But the tendency is limited to a single kind of reaction ; it is called into being only by the application of an external force, to which the reaction is strictly proportioned, and the existence of the object as an elastic body does not consist in, nor depend upon, a state of constant activity in oscillating about the point of equilibrium.

It is possible, again, to take up those points of difference, and urge that each can be matched in the inorganic world. The pendulum, for example, is in fact constantly oscillating about the equilibrium point, and its existence as a pendulum may not unfairly be said to depend upon its so doing. But the continued motion of the pendulum depends upon an outside force. It has no power of accumulating afresh the energy which it loses at each swing. It is not like the organism, self-maintaining. That is to say, it does not of itself find the means of maintaining the process which constitutes its existence.

This last point of contrast is, indeed, challenged by Dr. Verworn,[1] who compares an organism with a steam engine in its need for being supplied with energy from without. The steam engine is supplied with fuel, and this, he urges, is analogous to the supply of energy to the organism, through its food. But here, again, the analogy seems only to carry us a part of the way. The steam engine does not go to look for coal when it runs short, nor would it dream, as the engineer has dreamt, of substituting oil in case coal were not available.[2] The case of machinery

---

[1] *Op. cit.* p. 123.

[2] A similar criticism applies to an ingenious example adduced by Dr. Verworn to show that continuous metabolism, by which a body is continually being built up from certain materials which are as constantly broken down and excreted, is not peculiar to living organisms.

"A simple example of this is found in the behaviour of nitric acid in the production of concentrated sulphuric acid. If nitric acid be mixed with sulphurous anhydride, which is obtained in the manufacture of sulphuric acid by roasting sulphur ore, the sulphurous acid withdraws oxygen from the nitric acid and passes over into sulphuric acid, while the nitric acid becomes nitrous acid. If the constant entrance of fresh air and water be provided, the nitric acid is constantly reformed from the nitrous acid and gives a part of its oxygen again to new quantities of sulphurous acid, so that the molecule of nitric acid is continually being alternately broken down with loss of oxygen and built up with absorption of oxygen. In this manner, with the same quantity of nitric acid, an unlimited quantity of sulphurous acid can be changed into sulphuric acid." *Op. cit.* p. 125.

This continuous process can be maintained under certain uniform conditions. An organism will maintain a number of such processes at once, digesting, respiring, secreting, and at the same time adapting its actions to the acquisition of new material, and all under more or less varying conditions of the outer world. Could the nitric acid adapt itself to a change of diet? Of course, the adaptability of the organism is also limited. But the point seems to be this :—If we change the conditions which affect the nitric acid, we shall inevitably increase or decrease its

is, indeed, not a little instructive. Human ingenuity has succeeded in mimicking one form of organic activity after another. Up to a certain point the steam engine can be made self-acting. We have already drawn attention to the opening and closing of the valves by the piston as comparable to the rhythm of respiration. In speaking of the pendulum, we might have referred to the " compensating" arrangement whereby it is made to adjust itself so nicely to differences of temperature that its length remains approximately constant, though every portion of it expands. Here is an adaptation as remarkable in its way as the vasomotor adjustments which maintain the even temperature of the warm-blooded animal. If finally we were to take refuge in the uniformity of machinery, and contrast it with the infinite capacity of the organism for adjusting itself to the changing details of its surroundings, which are never twice the same, if we urged that machinery must always turn out the same pattern, and cannot achieve individuality, our last card of this suit is trumped by the linotype. No two consecutive lines of a book or a newspaper contain the same number of words of the same size. Hence the " spaces" required to bring the line to the right length differ from line to line in a manner which it is absolutely impossible to predict. There is no rule and no uniformity in the matter. The human compositor puts in the spaces as he sees that they are needed, and one would say that this was a point at which the service of the human eye could not be dispensed with. But, by a very simple arrangement, the same end is achieved by the linotype, and with equal accuracy.[1]

bulk and the rapidity of its formation, and this in direct proportion to the change in the conditions. If we change the conditions affecting an organism, it will, up to a certain limit, adapt itself to the change, and after, perhaps, an interval of disturbance, appear very much as it was before. Its bulk, for example, will not uniformly increase or decrease in direct proportion to its food supply.

[1] It is of some importance to notice the limitation of the achievement. The number of spaces in the line is determined by the human compositor. What the machine does is to thrust a wedge in between the words so as to space them to the required length of the line. The method of response given by the machine is unvarying. The variations are effected in accordance with a plan by which the objects acted on, viz., the length of the several words, determine the extent of the mechanical movement.

In these and no doubt in many other ways that might be specified the machine is made to perform functions which in this or that feature recall the behaviour of a living organism. Such examples are instructive both in their success and in their failure. For the condition of success is a combination of mechanical forces expressly designed to meet the end in view, and this suggests that whatever the creative force that brings the organism into being, the organic structure is a combination of parts determined in a general way by the functions which they will have to perform in the structure as a whole. They are so arranged as to maintain a certain balance, to regain it from within tolerably wide limits of variation, and even to readjust the principle of the balance itself (*i.e.*, to modify the organic structure), if this is demanded by the environment. Any single characteristic in this self-maintaining process can probably be paralleled from the inorganic world ; but whether the process as a whole can be paralleled is quite another question. It seems rather from the illustrations I have given that the thing that resembles an organism in one respect differs in another, and that where this difference is overcome a new one breaks out.

5. In the most fundamental feature of self-maintenance, it may be doubted whether any inanimate substance can be fairly matched against the living organism. It is by suitable response to stimulus in the main that organisms preserve themselves. Now the excitability of living tissue differs from the response of an elastic spring to pressure in that the energy evolved in the response bears no definite relation to the energy of the stimulus. It is interesting to see how Dr. Verworn deals with this point.

" It can be said in general that irritability is the capacity of a body to react to an external influence by some kind of change in its condition, in which the extent of the reaction stands in no definite proportion to the extent of the influence. As a matter of fact, irritability, or excitability, is a property of all living substance, whether the organism responds to the external influence by the production of definite substances, as with secreting gland-cells, or definite forms of energy, as with muscle-cells, phosphorescent cells, and electric cells, or whether it responds by depression or even standstill of its vital activities. But irritability is not the exclusive property of organisms, for lifeless substances are likewise irritable and respond to external influences by definite changes, *e.g.*, by the production of definite substances or of energy, in which process the extent of the production by no means corresponds always to the extent of the external impulse. The clearest examples of such cases are afforded by explosive substances. By a slight shock nitro-glycerine is decomposed into water, carbonic acid, oxygen and nitrogen, the process being accompanied by a powerful evolution of energy ; in other words, nitro-glycerine responds to an external influence by an enormous production of energy and a change of material. Hence irritability is not an absolute sign of difference between organisms and inorganic bodies, and it is seen that a fundamental contrast between the two is afforded no more by their dynamical than by their structural and genetic relations." [1]

Here again then an analogy can be found, but here again the analogy does not carry us the whole way. After the explosion the nitro-glycerine is gone once for all. Its identity is lost. It is dissipated into component parts. But the muscle which has violently contracted in response to a slight tickling of the skin remains as good a muscle as before. Doubtless it has lost a certain amount of potential energy, and its cells have undergone a chemical change parallel to that experienced by the nitro-glycerine. But there is the muscle sound as ever, and already actively engaged in assimilating new substances from the blood which will restore the proteids oxidised in the contraction. The organism in short in letting energy loose still maintains itself, and the letting loose of the energy is ordinarily a means of maintaining it. The organism is apparently the only thing that maintains itself by the liberation in response to a stimulus of its own energy.[2] In other words, the liberation of energy is controlled by a principle of organisation or correlation of changes whereby fresh substance or fresh energy is stored up which will bring the organism back to the very same condition in which it was found before the liberation of energy took place. The example of the muscle will recur to the reader as illustrating what I mean.

[1] *Op. cit.* p. 124.
[2] I owe this point to some remarks made to me some years ago by Sir J. Burdon Sanderson.

6. An organism then, as we are led to conceive it, may be roughly described as a whole consisting of parts each of which is conditioned in its behaviour, and even often in its existence, by its relation to the remainder. These relations are such that as the parts interact with one another and with the outside world they tend to undergo a regular series of changes which constitute the development of the organism from birth to death. The general course of the development is to this extent fixed by the original constitution of the organism. But as the surroundings with which it is brought into contact are infinitely various, what may be called the typical course of development is a purely imaginary line from which the life-history of any organism diverges at every moment in greater or less degree. But the forces that keep its various parts together are such that within tolerably wide limits it can accommodate itself to changes in the forces acting on it, maintaining its existence, and even its general character, unchanged in their despite. This is achieved by an appropriate modification of its action, a change at one point for example compensating a change at another, whereby under novel circumstances, or perhaps with grave modification of some part of the organism itself, the plan of the whole is as nearly constant as may be. If we sum all this up by saying that the living organism is distinguished by its *tendency to maintain itself through process and against change* we are merely formulating the known facts. Underlying this formula is the question whether this tendency is a true conation or the result of an intricate combination of mechanical parts so dovetailed that any disturbance of the organic equilibrium at any point automatically sets up compensating processes which tend to restore the balance. The strongest argument against this view is provided by experimental mutilations. We can with difficulty conceive a machine so intricately planned as always, in all the varying assaults to which the living being is exposed, to yield that reaction which tends to restore its normal method of working, as long as all its parts remain intact. But the very delicacy of such a machine would lead us to suppose that a breakage at any point must at least be fatal to the opera-

tions of the part affected. Now this is what mutilations, particularly those of the embryo, disprove. If the embryo is a machine for the assimilation, storage, and modification of material or of energy whereby the mature organism is to be produced, then there is no doubt that in its normal life-history one portion of this machine resides in one blastomere and another in another. But experiment shows that one blastomere artifically separated can generate the entire organism, and the advocates of the mechanical view are thrown back on the suggestion that nature has provided a secondary set of these highly perfect machines in case of accidents—accidents, moreover, which are by no means likely to occur except in the laboratory, an environment which nature can hardly have foreseen. Machines, as Driesch has elaborately argued, can do wonderful things, but what do we ordinarily expect of a broken machine ?

On the other hand, the teleological view is full of difficulty. We do not by taking thought heal our wounds. Our purposive activity supplies unguents and bandages, but "the rest nature transacts within." Our tissue is not, as far as we know, consciously aware of the purpose of restoring itself. Nor can we suppose the stem of Tubularia to plan the production of a new head. What we do know is that an organism subject to injury or distress not sufficient to overwhelm it, is stimulated to intense effort. If it does not know how to act it nevertheless acts, and continually varies its action, abandoning that which is fruitless and persisting in that which yields relief. We shall see in the following chapters how by this method living beings frequently obtain satisfactory results which apparently they could not plan or foresee. To conceive restorative vital processes to depend on conation in this rudimentary form, we must suppose successive stages in the process, each of which is satisfactory by comparison with the preceding, but gives rise to renewed efforts. We must also suppose the effort to be made by each part of the organism affected, and must assume a possibility of co-operation. This is to postulate an arrangement certainly, but not an arrangement that is

mechanically perfect.    It is rather an arrangement which
sets effort at work and provides a basis of co-operation
between parts.    In the most general terms the organism
is a structure which maintains, reproduces, and develops
itself by co-ordinated conations, the basis of the conations
and their co-ordination being laid by the inherited arrangement of the structure.    We shall see that this formula is
applicable to higher and confessedly intelligent as well as
to lower activities, and serves to indicate the connection
between them.    Whether it supplies a basis for the
explanation of vital processes, whether these can after all
be referred to some peculiar complication of mechanism,
or whether some wholly distinct agent, neither mechanical
nor teleological, is to be prayed in aid, the future of
physiology must decide.[1]

[1] Driesch's *Entelechy* which is neither conation nor mechanism,
comes at the end altogether to transcend the individual (see especially
vol. II. p. 318).   If the directive forces are within the individual I know
of no alternative between the mechanical and the conational.   Both of
these are at least *verae causae*.   The study of conation is still in its
infancy, and to say the least, further light may be expected from the
exploration of its possibilities.

# CHAPTER IV

## REFLEX ACTION

1. THE organism maintains itself by continual adaptations. There is adaptation in every process of life, inward as well as outward, in absorption, secretion, respiration, no less than in those movements of the limbs which for the observer constitute pre-eminently the actions of an organism. These actions, however, whereby it modifies its relations to other organisms and the outer world generally, form one case, and for us the most important case, of the exercise of its powers of adaptation.

Actions whether inward or outwardly apparent may be due to purely internal changes. Just as the kettle goes on quietly simmering till presently the lid lifts and the water boils over, so in a nerve centre, or for that matter in any mass of protoplasm, internal changes may go on, while for the outward observer all is peace, till suddenly a culminating point is reached, and a limb or the whole body is thrown into decided, perhaps sudden and violent, movement. Internally initiated movements are found in the fœtal life of the higher animals. Movements of the chick in the egg from the fifth day are reported by Preyer,[1] and according to the same observer the "outstretching and bending of the arms and legs" of new-born children is "nothing else than a continuation of the intra-uterine movements.[2] The aimless waving about of arms and legs noticeable up to the third quarter of the first year are referred by him to the same class.[3] Actions of this

[1] Preyer, I. p. 201.   [2] *Ib.* p. 205.
[3] *Ib.* p. 207. It may be, of course, that these motions have a casual good effect as exercise, but this would not exclude them from the scope of our definition.

class, according to Dr. Verworn, make up a considerable part of the life of Protista.

" A Stentor draws itself suddenly together, stretches itself out, draws in again after a short time, may remain stretched out a long time without the slightest contraction, till presently it gives vent to a whole series of contractions at irregular intervals."

There is no appearance of purpose in these irregular movements, and Dr. Verworn [1] points out that by imperceptible degrees they pass over into periodical, that is to say, automatic movements. Automatic movement indeed, as we see it in the pulsating vacuole among Protista, and among higher animals in the beating of the heart or the action of the respiratory centre, is a development and adaptation of the persistent structural activity to special requirements of the organism. It is due to the interaction of internal forces (though it may be modified by outer influences) but it is repeated at regular intervals, or rather, like the beating of the heart, it forms a connected cycle of events each of which introduces the next, till at length the cycle is completed and starts afresh.

To understand movements of this class we must bear in mind that in any living cell chemical changes are constantly going on. The protoplasm of the cell is building itself up out of materials supplied by the surrounding medium. This is the assimilative process. At the same time an opposite process of dissimilation is going on, in which the constituents of the protoplasm form new combinations, and ultimately become waste products of which the cell gets rid. These changes involving a constant molecular movement, the cell is never in a condition of stable equilibrium. But the outer results may be very different, according as the internal changes do or do not tend to balance one another. If they merely oscillate slightly about the point of equilibrium, there will be no outward sign of change. If there is a slow but decided gain of one set of forces in one part of the cell, an amœboid movement will result. The cell will slowly put out a projection or

---

[1] *Protisten Studien*, p. 142.

" pseudopodium " in one direction, or draw in another from an opposite quarter. If the nature of the molecular change is to produce a large mass of unstable chemical compounds in a certain part, then the effect of the final touch will be to " explode " this mass, and a sudden and violent contraction follows. In the higher organisms, besides the interaction of molecules in each cell, there is the interaction of many distinct cells, and indeed distinct organs, to be taken into account. The restless movements of the infant may be due to changes in the nerve centres, but they may also arise from a thousand and one different stimuli from the muscles, joints, digestive organs, or any part of the body, and indeed of other things with which the body comes into contact. It thus becomes impossible to draw a clear and certain line between actions of this class and the lowest kind of reflexes, with which we shall have presently to deal. It remains only to add that in the case of automatic actions the internal changes of which we speak appear to have become regulated, presumably under the influence of natural selection, so as to follow one another in a fixed order and at a determinate speed. There are the same processes of building up and breaking down, and they give rise in the same way to contraction and expansion, but they have become more accurately adjusted to one another in their proportions, so that each contraction is of measured length, force, and speed, and is succeeded at a fixed interval by an equally determinate movement of expansion.

2. *Reflex Action.*

Hitherto we have dealt with actions resulting from inward changes. We have now to consider actions brought about by the influences of the environment. All organisms may be affected by the direct contact of outer things with their surface, and most organisms, except the lowest, can be affected in other ways as well as through their organs of sense. Such an affection is called a stimulus, and the resulting change in the organism a response. It is of course principally by its responses to stimuli that the organism succeeds in adjusting its behaviour towards changes in the outer world in a way favourable to its own existence. If the mouse were not stimulated to run away by the sight of the cat, it would not be long for this world, and if the cat were not so excited by the sight of the mouse and of other food as to make the movements necessary for catching, seizing, and eating, she in her turn would starve. The most primitive form in which response is adapted to requirements is that in which a simple sensory stimulus calls forth a uniform reaction on the part of the organism. Such a response is known as a Reflex action. This is an extended usage, and etymologically is, it must be admitted, not altogether appropriate. The term applies strictly to animals with a developed nervous system. In such animals the reflex act consists of two distinct movements or processes, a sensory or afferent process, and a motor or efferent process. Thus if one inadvertently touches a hot iron the burning of the hand sends a wave of excitement along the sensory nerves to some part of the central nervous system. This is the sensory or afferent process. From the brain descends a back wave of excitement causing the contraction of several muscles whereby the hand is withdrawn. This is the efferent or motor process. The two together with whatever central process is required to connect them[1] make up a reflex action.

But the above definition, which corresponds to the extended usage of the term now common, applies very clearly to the responses of many animals which have no nervous system at all. If the long hair-like " flagellum " of a Poteriodendron be lightly touched as it waves about in the water, the effect is instantaneous. The waving thread suddenly rolls itself up in a coil, while the body, which consists of a mass of protoplasm standing on a sort of stalk, fixed to the bottom of a miniature cup, is withdrawn hastily to the bottom of the cup, where it

[1] The more modern definitions of reflex action make a different partition, distinguishing a receptor organ, where the excitement starts (*e.g.*, the retina), an effector, which carries out the response (*e.g.*, the muscles of the arm), and a conductor, which includes the entire nervous portion between the two. The centre is in this description only of importance as a name for any point or points where different conductors may meet and different impulses impinge on one another (see Sherrington, *Integrative Action of the Nervous System*, p. 7, &c.).

lies for a few seconds, after which it begins to rise again.[1]
If the pseudopodium—or temporary arm of protoplasm
stretching out from the cell body—of a Rhizopod, like
Difflugia urceolata, be touched with a needle it becomes
wrinkled, and if touched somewhat harder withdraws into
the cell mass.[2] It is needless to multiply instances.
Reflex action in the sense of uniform response to simple
stimulus is found all along the scale of organic evolution
from the Protista to man.

3. If we regard only the function that it subserves in
the life of the organism, reflex action impresses us as
purposive. If we look only at the method by which it is
carried out, it impresses us as mechanical. If something
comes straight at my face, I blink. The action is well
adapted to the purpose of protecting my eyes from the
blow. But it is unintelligent. I may know perfectly well
that the object is not going to hit me, but notwithstanding
every effort I blink. Whether itself to be regarded as
intelligent or not, reflex action proceeds independently of
the conscious intelligence of human beings. It is in many
cases both among men and animals independent of the
higher cerebral centres which are essential to intelligent
action in the ordinary sense. There are some reflexes of
which we are not conscious at all ; for example, the contraction of the iris under the influence of light. There
are others of which we may or may not be conscious, but
which we cannot hinder. Such are, for many people,
blinking, and probably for all people vasomotor reflexes
like blushing and growing pale. There are others which
we can interfere with in some slight degree, like breathing,
coughing, sneezing, and laughing. Others again can be
inhibited by a strong effort of will, such as weeping,
screaming, and groaning. But in all alike the conscious
intelligence seems to have nothing to do with initiating or
directing the action. The action proceeds of itself. It
does not need consciousness nor the other activities of the
organism. I remember being thrown by a sudden accident
over the handles of an old-fashioned high bicycle. The
thing happened so quickly that I realised nothing about

---

[1] Verworn, *Prot. St.* p. 86.          [2] *Ib.* p. 83.

it till I found myself on the ground. Yet I fell on my
hands, and my face and head were not touched. And the
throwing out of the hands is a complex action involving
the well adapted duly proportioned contraction of quite a
number of muscles.

4. There are certain fallacious arguments against the
mechanical conception of reflex action which it will be well
to consider. Take first the fact of adaptation. Many
reflexes among the higher animals involve very complex
co-ordination of muscular movements, a definite order and
simultaneity of contractions, a careful adjustment of the
length and vigour of each contraction, and so forth. In
this respect the higher reflexes contrast very markedly
with the simple contractions of, for example, a muscle-
nerve preparation, or the slow withdrawal of a pseudopodium by a Rhizopod.

"When the peripheral stump of a divided sciatic nerve is
stimulated with the interrupted current, the muscles of the leg
are at once thrown into tetanus, continue in the same rigid
condition during the passage of the current, and relax immediately
on the current being shut off. When the same current is applied
for a second only to the skin of the flank of a brainless frog, the
leg is drawn up and the foot rapidly swept over the spot irritated,
as if to wipe away the irritation ; but this movement is a complex
one, requiring the contraction of particular muscles in a definite
sequence, with a carefully adjusted proportion between the
amounts of contraction of the individual muscles. And this complex movement, this balanced and arranged series of contractions,
may be repeated more than once as a result of a single stimulation of the skin. When a deep breath is caused by a dash of
cold water, the same co-ordinated and carefully arranged series of
contractions is also seen to result, as part of a reflex action, from a
simple stimulus." [1]

All this, of course, only proves that the machinery, if it
is machinery, is complex, and well adjusted to its end.
Put a penny on a balance, and it weighs down the scale
by the simple action of the lever. Put it into the slot of
an automatic machine, and it produces a stick of chocolate
by I know not what complication of levers and cogs.
Complexity of adjustment does not take us out of the
region of machinery.

[1] Foster, I. p. 184.

A second fallacious argument may be founded on the disproportion in a reflex action between stimulus and result.

"When we stimulate the nerve of a muscle-nerve preparation the result, though modified in part by the condition of the muscle and nerve, whether fresh and irritable or exhausted, for instance, is directly dependent on the nature and strength of the stimulus."

. . . "In a reflex action, on the other hand, the movements called forth by the same stimulus may be in one case insignificant, and in another violent and excessive, the result depending on the arrangements and condition of the central portion of the reflex mechanism. Thus the mere contact of a hair with the mucous membrane lining the larynx, a contact which can originate only the very slightest afferent impulses, may call forth a convulsive fit of coughing, in which a very large number of muscles are thrown into violent contractions; whereas the same contact or the hair with other surfaces of the body may produce no obvious effect at all. Similarly, while in the brainless but otherwise normal frog a slight touch on the skin of the flank will produce nothing but a faint flicker of the underlying muscles, the same touch on the same part of a frog poisoned with strychnia will produce violent lasting tetanic contractions of nearly all the muscles of the body." [1]

It might be inferred from this that the reflex is, in a sense, originated by the organism, instead of being, as in a machine, a transformation of energy from one shape to another. But the truth is that the stimulus is not to be compared to the fuel which supplies the engine with its energy, but to the touch which turns the handle and sets accumulated energy free to work.

"The nerve centre may be regarded as a collection of explosive charges ready to be discharged, and so to start efferent impulses along certain efferent nerves, and these charges are so arranged and so related to certain afferent nerves, that afferent impulses reaching the centre along those nerves may in one case discharge a few only of the charges and so give rise to feeble movements, and in another case discharge a very large number and so give rise to large and violent movements." [2]

This fundamental feature of the reflex mechanism must, however, be kept carefully in mind in judging the true character of certain modifications of the reflex act to which we shall shortly come.

[1] Foster, I. pp. 182, 183.　　　[2] *Ib.* I. p. 183.

5. So far we have found nothing to differentiate the reflex mechanism from any other piece of machinery. There is a certain arrangement—a sense-organ, an afferent nerve, a nerve centre consisting essentially of a more or less complicated ramification of nerve fibres, one or more efferent or motor nerves, and one or more muscles. Apply a stimulus, and the machinery works. Nerves, nerve centres, and muscles are thrown into activity. As in a machine the parts not merely act, but act together in a prearranged harmony, the general tendency of which is to deal with the stimulus in the way best suited to the needs of the organism.

These last words recall us once more to the conception of purpose, and we may now put the question thus. Is it the needs of the organism that determine the action, or is it the preformed structure? Is the act the result of a structure that is already there, or is it adopted as a means to an end, which is still to be realised? Broadly speaking the facts leave us in no doubt as to the answer. In the typical reflex the structure is "already there." The organism or part of it is attuned to a certain kind of stimulus so as to react to it in a special manner. It is so attuned that the manner of reaction adopted for each stimulus is under ordinary circumstances beneficial to the organism. Of the structure we may perhaps say with certain reservations that it has grown up because it is useful to the organism. But of the particular act we must say that it is performed not because it is useful at the present moment, but because it is the necessary result of the action of a given stimulus upon a given structure. Circumstances may be such that this response does not serve the normal "purpose," but unless these "circumstances" are counter stimuli acting on the nerve centres, they have no effect. Taking this last qualification into account, we may say that a reflex action is a response to the present operative stimuli as such. This differentiates it from an act of purpose. Purposive action may also from one point of view be regarded as the response of a structure to its surroundings in accordance with laws which are uniform after their kind. But here the fundamental law is precisely that action is determined not by the immediate, perceptible surroundings as such, but by whatever consideration affects the attainment of the end.   Hence, far from being tied to a uniform response to a given stimulus, purposive action deals with the whole present situation at any moment by correlating it with any relevant facts, however remote, finally shaping its action in the way which, all things taken into account, will be most likely to lead to its desired end.   Hence the purposive act is determined by its end, and it is thus to be contrasted generically with the predetermined response of structure to stimulus, the adjective "predetermined" meaning that the structure must respond to the stimuli acting upon it as such, and cannot bring them into relation with remote but relevant facts so as to modify its behaviour appropriately.

To illustrate.   The blinking reflex is carried out by the muscles of the eyelids quite independently of real danger to the eye, and most people are unable to hinder it even if they try.   Darwin[1] has told us how he tried to prevent himself from starting back when a snake struck at the plate glass which was a perfectly safe screen.   Darwin's intelligence grasped the truth of the situation, but his lower motor-centres were rigidly bound to act in accordance with ancestral custom.   In a mammal the whole machinery of breathing may be destroyed, but the suitable movements of the nostrils and glottis still continue if their connection with the medulla remains intact.[2]   The nostrils dilate and contract not to let in air, but because their muscles are governed by a rhythmic alternation of stimuli emanating from the respiratory centre in the medulla.   As long as the centre and the connections remain intact, they go on with their work whether it assists in breathing or not.[3]   In the same way might the screw of a sinking steamer rotate wildly in the air as the bows plunge down.   The screw rotates not to propel the ship, but because its motion is governed by connections with the engine, and as long as

[1] *Expression of the Emotions*, p. 40 (2nd ed.).
[2] Foster, II. p. 616.
[3] A friendly critic points out that respiratory movements are automatic rather than reflex (though constantly subject to reflex influences), but I let the illustration stand as exemplifying a highly mechanical process in the life of the organism.

these remain uninterrupted, rotate it will. Similarly the sucking reflex is well adapted to the needs of babies and other young animals for food, but it is a response not to the nipple nor to the food, but to anything that comes into the lips.[1] Hence the infant in its leisure moments sucks its thumb or anything else that comes handy.

What has been said is perhaps sufficient to show that, speaking generally, the reflex is determined by the structure, or a portion of the structure, of the organism which is specially arranged to meet a specific sensory stimulus with a specific reaction. It is easy to see, first, that such a type of action can readily be conceived of as arising under the influence of natural selection, where, under ordinary circumstances, one sort of reaction, A, to a stimulus α, is decidedly more often beneficial than any other. It will also be seen that a mode of action so arising will, in a preponderant number of cases, but not necessarily in all, be suited to the actual needs of the individual in a given case. While, lastly, such an action would not imply on the part of the individual any sort of intelligent purpose in the sense of a power to remodel its behaviour at need in such a way as to bring about a result to which it looks forward.

6. Uniform reaction to present stimulus is the characteristic of unintelligent response in general. But given such response, there are still two possibilities. It may depend on the condition of the organism as a whole, and if so, the normal reaction to one stimulus may be modified by the effect of other simultaneous stimuli, internal and external. Or it may be a response of a definite part of the bodily structure assigned to one particular element in

---

[1] Preyer, I. p. 127. "Experiments on little guinea-pigs, only eight to sixteen hours old, and separated from the mother after two hours, proved to me absolutely that concentrated water-solutions of tartaric acid, soda, glycerine, introduced into the mouth through glass tubes, are swallowed just as greedily or eagerly as cow's milk and water, with vigorous sucking. But then the empty tube, placed with the end upon the tongue, occasioned just such sucking. The experiments conducted in this manner cannot, therefore, yield much that can be depended upon. Touch, as a reflex stimulus to sucking in hungry new-born creatures, overpowers any taste-stimuli acting at the same time. Newly-born animals that have eaten enough do not, however, suck regularly in general." For human infants, see p. 110.

the sensory surroundings. The latter kind is the typical reflex, and is illustrated in the examples drawn above from the respiratory mechanism. It is in such cases that the reflex act especially impresses us as mechanical. But we are not to regard all reflex actions as of this type. In all higher organisms the reflex is the act of a part rather than the whole of the bodily structure, but it is an act dependent in very varying degrees upon the condition of the whole. If there are some reflexes that proceed with the fixity and sureness of fate, there are others that may be inhibited by a counter stimulus or by a reaction of the whole organism, which we call an effort of will. Such an interaction clearly brings the reflex into closer relation with the condition of the organism as a whole. And this process is carried a step farther where we find reflexes that are not set in motion at all unless the general bodily condition is suitable. Thus "the babe that has had enough does not suck." [1] To put it generally, in addition to the stimulus and the permanent structure there must be a general condition of excitability, or susceptibility to the specific excitement, and this condition will depend very much on the requirements of the organism. We here get adjustment to needs again at a higher remove. If the condition of the organism is such that a reaction would be beneficial, then normally the state of excitability is present, and the animal is ready to react as soon as the stimulus appears. The dog's stomach being empty it is good for him to eat, and he is accordingly hungry (ready to be excited by food), and therefore pounces on the bone when he sees it. Conversely the sated dog either buries the bone or neglects it. All this goes to show that the reflex machinery is a part of the whole organism, and may be very dependent for its working on the condition of the remainder. Reflexes vary from the extreme of independence to a comparatively close connection with the general state of the organism. All alike are mechanical in the sense in which mechanism is opposed to purpose. Only the former are mechanical in the sense in which the rigidity of a machine is contrasted with the adaptability of an organism.

[1] Preyer, I. p. 152.

7. The controlled reflex may look externally very much like a true conation.  In particular cases indeed it may be impossible to determine with certainty the class to which an act belongs.  If an irritant is not removed from the windpipe by a cough, one goes on coughing.  The action is continued till satisfaction is obtained.  In this case our will seems at times to co-operate.  Yet the mechanical element may suffice of itself and the coughing fit may in fact be uncontrollable.  In this case the explanation is simply that the stimulus is capable of calling forth repetitions of the response as long as it persists or until exhaustion sets in.  In other cases additional stimulus may increase the excitement so that it spreads to other parts of the body, which by acting suitably give relief. Thus :

. . . " if a flank of a brainless frog be very lightly touched, the only reflex movement which is visible is a slight twitching of the muscles lying immediately underneath the spot of skin stimulated. If the stimulus be increased, the movements will spread to the hind-leg of the same side, which frequently will execute a movement calculated to push or wipe away the stimulus.  By forcibly pinching the same spot of skin, or otherwise increasing the stimulus, the resulting movements may be led to embrace the fore-leg of the same side, then the opposite side, and finally, almost all the muscles of the body." [1]

It would seem from this account as a whole that the successive modifications of the response, which at one stage have a purposive appearance, are due rather to something of a mechanical nature such as the overflow of nervous excitement.  Even an excised muscle varies its response to stimulus in a manner suited to the ordinary behaviour of muscle when doing its work within the organism. For if under a certain stimulus it lifts a given load a certain height, it might be inferred on mechanical principles that it would only lift double the weight half the height. But this is not necessarily true.

. . . " The height to which the weight is raised may be in the second instance as great, or even greater, than in the first.  That is to say, the resistance offered to the contraction actually augments

Foster, I. p. 183.

the contraction, the tension of the muscular fibre increases the facility with which the explosive changes resulting in a contraction take place. And we have other evidence that anything which tends to stretch the muscular fibres, whether during rest or during contraction, increases the metabolism of the muscle." [1]

Here again physiologists offer a mechanical explanation of something which looks like a special effort. We have not in this place to pass on these explanations in particular instances. It is enough for us that any action may be considered reflex as long as it is (1) a response of uniform type to present sensory stimulus, or (2) a resultant of tendencies to such uniform response acting together. Action that can be so explained is mechanical. That which cannot be so analysed is conational.

8. To put together our results up to this point. We have found two classes of actions which proceed uniformly from pre-existent structure and are not determined by relation to the results accruing from them in the particular instance. The first class are initiated by processes within the organism, the second by stimulus from without. The latter we call Reflex action, which we define as the action of a structure which is specially framed so as to respond to present sensory stimulus in a uniform manner. Such structures may be formed under the influence of natural selection,[2] where it is in general beneficial to the organism to respond in one way rather than another to stimuli of any given kind. The reflex action is not called forth or determined by the purpose that it serves in the economy of the organism, for it persists even where useless or injurious. It is, however, subject in varying degrees to the condition of the organism as a whole, and thereby arises a further adaptation of its action to what is required. In the typical reflex this subjection is at a minimum, and there is uniform response of a special structure to appropriate stimulus. The more absolute this uniformity, the more close does the reflex approach the dead-mechanical type. But the response of the special structure may, in

---

[1] Foster, I. p. 143.
[2] They may also be formed at least in higher organisms by habit, and when so formed have the same general character.

higher cases, depend in some measure on the state of the organism as a whole, and this not merely in the negative sense that it is liable to inhibition, but in the sense that a certain state of the organism is a positive condition of its exercise. Such an adaptation though more complex is still a response of preformed structure to present stimuli, and is as such unintelligent. But in proportion as it thus becomes adaptable to the whole state of the organism, the reflex has in reality become a constituent element in action of a higher type. In this capacity we shall meet it again in subsequent chapters as the servant of Instinct and Intelligence.

9. *Reflex action in development.*

Reflex actions are not always perfect from birth. There is in this respect a remarkable difference between one action and another, and also between one animal and another. Even the young chick, whose pecking was taken by earlier observers to be almost perfect from the first, has been shown by later very careful records to require practice, and to take some days to reach perfection.[1] The human infant has but few established reflexes in the first week of its existence. Darwin[2] found sneezing, hiccoughing, yawning, stretching, sucking, and screaming to be "well performed" during the first seven days. On the other hand, the blinking reflex, which is so markedly mechanical later on, does not appear on the first day, and the ability to direct the eyes to an object—to "fixate"—is utterly lacking.[3] Even breathing—in which reflex as well as automatic movements are concerned—is less regular with babies than in later life, and of the more complicated reflexes involved in walking and grasping, it is needless to speak.[4] The rapidity and uniformity with which many reflexes are learnt suggests that the mechanism is almost but not quite perfected by heredity. At the best it is

[1] Shepherd and Braid, *The Development of an Instinct*, J. A. B., 1913, pp. 278 ff.
[2] *Mind*, Vol. II. p. 285.           [3] Preyer, *op. cit.* pp. 25 and 41.
[4] The grasping of an object placed within the fingers appears from the first; but grasping at a thing, or even looking at it in the hand, is delayed for some weeks. See Darwin, *op. cit.* p. 286, and Preyer, I. p. 47, &c.

probably at birth like a new machine which needs to be worked two or three times before it is thoroughly in order. In the machine the thousand strains and stresses upon different parts have to adjust themselves to one another in actual working before the running is really smooth and easy. We may readily suppose an even greater degree of self-adjustment in the living organism, the result of which is merely to smooth and facilitate the working of a structure which is already there in all its essential parts.

Such a structure, we have seen, is conceived by evolutionists as growing up under the influence of natural selection.[1] Among the higher animals, and not least in man, the reflex structure also grows more rapidly under another influence. We have all experienced the growth through practice of true reflexes. If we have forgotten our experience in learning to walk, we remember learning to shave, skate, swim, or ride a bicycle. We remember learning, though we might have a good deal of difficulty in explaining how we learnt. In general what we know is that we attempt to follow certain instructions and in so doing flounder about, making random shots which go on all sides of the mark, and every now and then hit it. The cyclist as he learns is always falling, and his attempt to save himself from a tumble on one side merely lands him in danger of a fall on the other. As our training advances, there are some things which we are definitely conscious of finding out. We see how the thing is done by doing it, though the most careful explanation on the part of our teacher could not show us the way. But having done it once, we know how to do it again. There are other things, and perhaps they are more numerous, in which consciousness does not seem to play by any means so important a part. We learn to do them unconsciously. Each time that we succeed we find it becomes easier to repeat them. Success in these cases plays the part which conscious intelligence plays in the former class.

[1] Whatever difficulties there are in such a conception are those that beset the whole problem of variation. There is at least no reason to doubt that the conditions of existence determine which of several variations survive.

Each action that achieves its end leaves behind it a tendency to repeat that action, while the unsuccessful actions are inhibited. Thus in the individual life, below the level of intelligence, success—the attainment of the equilibrium to which the organism is tending—plays the part which in the life of the species falls to Natural Selection. It confirms the tendency which makes for organic equilibrium, and checks the opposing tendencies.

This selective force acts equally upon reflexes with a hereditary basis. In the co-ordinating movements of the eyes or the legs many irregular and unsuitable movements occur at first, but are gradually discarded in favour of the movements required by the organic equilibrium.[1] Children make random movements about the breast and often suck at the wrong place.[2] Even the localisation of a part of the body by the hand is arrived at after this fashion, as is shown by the following very instructive instance given by Prof. Preyer.[3]

. . . " In the case of two children, who in the first half-year suffered from local itching eruptions of the skin (milk-crust), the reflexive movements of the limbs were quite irregular, and at the beginning absolutely unsuited, afterwards not in all cases suited, to relieve the pain or the feeling of tickling ; at all events, apart from the turnings of the head, which was the most tormented, and which was moved hither and thither like a pendulum when the arms were confined (fourth month). Many times when the arms had escaped from the tethers in the night, the face was scratched to bleeding in several places that were evidently not troublesome (fourth to sixth month). At every unguarded moment the hands went to the head, and the skin, even the sound part of it, was rubbed and scratched. These scratching movements cannot be inborn, they must be acquired. The result of an accidental contact of the head and hand appearing in the diminution of the tickling sensation must have induced a preference of the movement of the hand to the head among all sorts of movements." . . .

[1] Preyer, I. p. 39.
[2] *Ib.* p. 134. Puppies also miss the teat, and will try moreover to suck one another or the master's finger. (Wesley Mills, pp. 118, 119.)
[3] *Ib.* p. 223. Mr. Lloyd Morgan suggests, by way of contrast, the apparent accuracy with which young birds, only a day or so old, scratch a spot artificially irritated.

Understanding that this comparatively rapid process of acquisition in individual experience, which we find in the higher and more adaptable animals, is replaced in the lower orders by natural selection acting in the course of generations upon the race, we have in this instance the whole scheme of the development of the reflex in a concrete illustration. There is a stimulus which disturbs the equilibrium of the organism. A certain reaction would restore that equilibrium. The first result of the disturbance is a series of random actions. These fail to remove the source of disturbance. At length one succeeds. This one has an advantage subsequently over others if the individual is capable of training, and in course of time the tendencies to perform this act preponderate over all others. If the individuals of the species are not capable of training, those which in their random movements come nearest to the one required will have a certain advantage in the struggle for existence, and thus in a more roundabout way the reflex mechanism is built up by inheritance.

10. The random, undifferentiated actions out of which we suppose the reflex to be hewn are no mere fiction of the scientific imagination. The random movements of internally initiated activities are matched by numerous instances of quite random reflexes. The latter occur in all conditions of over excitability. Great joy and pain throw the whole body into motions not adapted to serve it in any way unless the draining off of the excitement be itself regarded as a service. If any stimulus be greatly increased in intensity, it not merely calls forth the movements suited to dealing with it, but brings more and more muscles into action till the whole body may be convulsed.[1] There is a tendency,

---

[1] Instances of undifferentiated or purposeless nervous discharge are well seen in pathological states. In cases of injury to one hemisphere, Göltz speaks of a regular "Entfesselung der reflektorischen vorgänge" (*op. cit.* p. 59). In another dog a curious special reflex—putting out the tongue and licking the nose—appeared regularly in response to tickling of the back. Evidently the response has nothing to do with the stimulus, and we can only suppose that the excitation of that particular part happened for some reason to find the line of least resistance in discharging along the nerve paths, ending finally in the muscles of the tongue. On the permanent inhibitory function of that part of the cerebrum which he calls the association centres, see Flechsig, *Gehirn und Seele*, p. 32. The

well seen in the naked protoplasm of many unicellular organisms, for an excitement to spread like a wave in proportion to its initial strength. A slight shake will make Amoeba princeps hesitate in putting forth its "legs." A prolonged concussion will gradually affect the entire organism and make it roll up almost into a ball. In strychnine poisoning, where the excitability of the nerves is abnormally heightened, a slight touch produces general convulsions.

The primitive fact to which these considerations bring us back is the excitability of protoplasm. Protoplasm, in whatever form, is a substance in very unstable chemical equilibrium. Since it is never at rest internally, the equilibrium is often upset by changes within the mass of the protoplasm itself, and we get internally initiated movements. But various external events—the impingement of a ray of light or heat, a chemical affinity, or a purely mechanical contact—may also, in ways which at present can only be surmised, gravely disturb the equilibrium of the substance at every point. The disturbance has a tendency to propagate itself, a tendency which goes on until its energy is dissipated, or until a countervailing force of some kind restores the balance. The result of such a disturbance is or may be a movement of the mass, or an alteration of its form. Unless there is something in the previous history of the individual organism or its species to direct the movement, there is no reason why it should be in any way suited to the needs of the organism in relation to that stimulus. It will be a random movement which may be useful, harmful or neutral to the organism. It is clear that variations in the direction of useful action will be helpful to a race in the struggle for existence, and that a race in which they occur would be likely to survive. But action at this stage depends on the

---

reflexes, if not held in constant quiet restraint, would run riot. The due response of a lower centre is an application in an appropriate manner of a portion only of the nervous discharge which the stimulus sets going. This general discharge may be regarded as the matrix out of which suitable or adaptive action is hewn. Or, to vary the metaphor, it is the flow of water for which experience and natural selection find a useful channel, while they also devise means of absorbing or damming up the overflow. The primitive thing is the flow. The channel is formed later.

molecular relations of protoplasm, whether in its undifferentiated form or as later in the highly conductile form of nerve fibres.  The preponderance of a certain type of action therefore means the prevalence of a certain structure. In this way structures are built up under the influence of natural selection so planned that a stimulus of a given kind inevitably produces a certain reaction.  Such a reaction is a reflex.  It is mechanical in so far that it is the result of a pre-existing structure which acts uniformly in response to stimuli of a particular kind.  Though it produces a certain result, it is not the fact that it will produce the particular result which brings it into being, but the fact that similar actions have in the past produced similar results.  It is thus a consequence, not a means.  It is also in some degree mechanical in another sense, viz., that it is in part independent of the rest of the organism and its condition. But that is a matter of degree, and we get many variations from the extreme type in which a reflex appears to go on quite independently of the organic life, up to cases in which it is dependent on the general state of the organism, and may be subordinated to some higher type of activity. This interdependence gives occasion for ambiguity in the interpretation of special classes of action, but in no way obscures the principle on which the classification depends.

# CHAPTER V

## CONATION

### 1 *The influence of present conditions. Conative selection*

WE have seen that a reflex response may be repeated as long as the stimulus persists. We have now to deal with a class of cases in which what persists is a certain condition of the organism or of its relation to the environment while the reactions vary until the condition is changed. Suppose we find ourselves in an uncomfortable position. We turn this way or that. It may be we get no relief. In that case we are apt to continue our uneasy motion without any definite method, until in fine we happen into a more comfortable posture. Of course we human beings always have intelligence at our side, which can foresee the process, give a reason for it, and perhaps in some particular direct it. But at the basis of behaviour of this type, even in man, there seems to be an effort directed rather by the general need of some escape from the disagreeable present than by a clear idea of the condition to be substituted. If so, the effort is less than a purpose yet it is more than a reflex, because it is the outcome of a persistent uneasiness. It is a state actively seeking to change itself, to pass into something different, even though that something different be not clearly defined. Further, the result acts upon the effort, for if it does not bring relief one effort is abandoned and another is tried, and the process continues until the relief is in fact obtained. That is to say, the series of efforts as a whole is governed by the results that come out of it. We may formulate these facts by saying that the determining element in

57

effort is its own tendency to produce a result other than itself, and this conforms to our general definition of conation and distinguishes it from reflex action, in which, as in everything mechanical, the result is indifferent.

The simplest form of conation then seems to be action directed vaguely to a change of conditions, persisted in or varied until new and more suitable conditions are obtained. Such action is not purpose because it does not clearly foresee these conditions, but it is conation because it is determined by the contrast between the existing state of the organism and the relief which in fact it tends to bring about. Conation at this stage is found to all appearance among unicellular organisms. Thus Paramecium, in normal conditions, swims gently forward, absorbing food by whirling its cilia. If it encounters a solid body it backs a little, then swings round through an angle of varying magnitude and advances again. If again it strikes the object, the process is repeated and various directions are tried, so that in the end, if there is any egress, it is found. The animal seems in a fashion to explore the object, but the exploration is indirect and persists through the inhibition of repeated errors. Paramecia will behave in the same way to a drop of many chemical solutions. It swims up to the edge of the drop if not too strong, and then reacts in the way described, so that, seen through the microscope, the drop remains empty, while the weaker solution around is crowded with Paramecia. This occurs when the reaction to the drop is what is called negative. The converse case has a special interest. When a drop of weaker solution is contained in one of a stronger the Paramecia appear to be positively attracted to it, and superficially it looks as though they swam deliberately to the spot preferred, which is soon crowded with Paramecia, while the rest of the liquid is empty. But in reality the result is only reached by an indirect method and the continued repetition of the negative reaction. The organism swims at random, but any individual which enters the drop proceeds across it until it reaches the edge of the stronger solution. There it gives the avoiding reaction and starts off swimming in a new direction till it reaches another edge. Here the same process is repeated. The result is that individuals which have once entered the drop do not leave it, and as in the course of random movements many are constantly entering, the majority and in the end all the individuals will finally be congregated there, just as though they had sought the drop deliberately.[1] Both these illustrations are instructive. The second one shows that what appears as an act definitely directed towards a particular end is in fact achieved by an indirect process of successive movements, some of which are inhibited while others are persisted in—the process known generally as Trial and Error.

Paramecium's action then does not seem as though directed to a definite result apart from the conditions in which it finds itself. On the other hand, when it is unpleasantly situated or confronted with an obstacle, its actions do appear to be in a manner directed to the avoidance of the obstacle and the resumption of its normal course. Now it is just conceivable that in this case the reactions are a series of reflexes, but as a minimum we must suppose a persistent state of the organism, which, under certain disturbing influences, maintains a series of reactions and repeatedly varies them until a new situation is achieved. This differentiates the case from that of the cough, which continues till the crumb is expelled, for that is a single reflex indefinitely repeated. Here we have as a minimum varying reflexes with rejection and selection. The internal state which governs them may or may not correspond to the kind of consciousness which we have when we make an effort, but it arises under corresponding circumstances and has an exactly corresponding effect. In accordance with our criteria, therefore, we are justified in speaking of it in the same terms.[2]

---

[1] Jennings, 48–58.

[2] Cf. Jennings on the *Amoeba*, p. 22. The entire reaction method may be summed up as follows : The stimulus induces movements in various directions as defined by internal causes. One of these directions is then selected through the fact that by subjecting the animal to new conditions it relieves it from stimulation.

## 2 *Sensori-motor action*

So far we have dealt with cases in which the internal
need selects one among a number of type actions. We
pass to cases in which type actions are variously combined, measured and adjusted to suit the position or
motions of an outer object and so achieve some effect
in relation to it. A simple reflex is indeed related to
an outer object. If a pencil is put into a baby's fingers,
they close over it and we classify the grasp as a mere
reflex. The baby's eyes will also follow the light reflexly
and its lips will suck anything put into them. But the
new-born infant does not grasp at a thing, and it is not
for some weeks that a change occurs in this respect. The
child will then direct its hand towards anything that
catches the eyes, fixating vision upon it at the same time,
and if it succeeds in catching hold will convey the object
to its mouth. Much of this is still automatic, but we
observe, first, a combination of processes which were
previously distinct, and secondly, what is more important
for our purpose, an adaptation, at first exceedingly
imperfect but rapidly improving, of the grasping movement to the position and movements of the attractive
object. Now the position and movements of outer
objects are highly individual, and we can attain no success
in dealing with them until we can similarly individualise
our response. The cricketer who catches the ball no
doubt discharges type-motions which have become habits,
but all depends on his judgment, that is to say, on a
rapidly formed combination of a number of relevant
data—his own position, the speed and direction of the
ball, and possible allowance for wind, and so on. This
combination is unique and varies from case to case, and
it is so adjusted as to secure a satisfactory result. Is it
then purposive? Is the cricketer inspired by the idea
of the catch and of its glorious results? The answer
appears to be in the negative. Such an idea may of course
be present, but our experience teaches us that if we think
we shall probably miss. Success is obtained by concentration on the field of perception, and the slightest

emotional disturbance imported by ideas of results gets on our nerves, as we say, and disturbs the coolness which is requisite to the exactness and freedom of our poise. The phenomena of learning point to the same conclusion, for though we certainly set out to learn a game with a purpose, connected ideas play but a very small part in the process. We are roughly told what to do, and then we proceed to do it wrong. We do it wrong many times and we do it a little less wrong. We make a hit, and then, after failures, we make a second hit, and the hits and the failures appear by an automatic process, certainly by a process of which we can give no conscious account, to effect our training. Practice is the divinity which shapes our ends, which conscious purpose merely rough-hews, and the beginner on the bicycle is far more acutely conscious of effort to keep his balance in which he fails, than the expert cyclist who rides merrily along looking at the view or thinking about metaphysics. We conclude that in man the part of consciousness in action of this type is purely perceptual. It is concentrated on the object with mere fringes of survival from past perception, which aid in its interpretation and are strictly subservient to the combination of present elements which is the focus of the whole proceeding. This perceptual consciousness then discharges the required motion, and so we speak of response of this type as sensori-motor action. What, then, is the precise function of consciousness in these actions ?

"We have as the basis of the skilled act a structure fitted to respond to stimuli of a certain order. But a structure, as we have seen, can only be adapted to general requirements, *i.e.*, to meet a certain type of stimulus, A, with a type of response $a$, and a type B with a response $\beta$, the response in each case being that which is generally suitable. Now, what happens in any matter requiring much skill in the treatment is that the situations are often unique, that what is wanted is not $a$ or $\beta$, but a certain combination of $a$ with $\beta$, involving perhaps some grading or modification of each. The function of the close conscious attention to the precise position, distance, movement, size, etc., of the object dealt with at any moment is to combine or correlate these distinct data, to yield us the precise combination, A—B, of sense-elements which corresponds accurately to the situation as a whole. Each element in this combination discharges its appropriate motor impulse $a$, $\beta$, but their union in consciousness effects through a machinery which does not enter into consciousness a corresponding modification of impulse by impulse, of $a$ by $\beta$. The precise function of consciousness then in sensori-motor action is to grasp the unique combination of stimuli, each of which having its special reaction modified by the concomitant reactions, there follows a response appropriate to the unique situation as a whole." [1]

Now, consciousness we know only from within. But the function which consciousness performs in sensori-motor action is definite, and wherever a corresponding combination of data and adjustment of action is formed an exactly corresponding function must exist. We shall therefore in accordance with our criteria treat all sensori-motor activity as conscious. The same reasoning will apply to conative selection, which we know in ourselves as involving conscious uneasiness and conscious effort. This consciousness in us determines our behaviour, sustaining repeated movements, checking, encouraging, and varying them in relation to their results. A corresponding function must exist when corresponding behaviour is found, and again in accordance with our rule we shall describe this function as a conscious act. We arrive then at this result, that conation even in its lowest stages is a conscious function. As we know it internally it is a state seeking to pass into some other. In terms of behaviour it is not a uniform response to stimulus but a state governing action by relation to the results at the moment. The grasp of the unique and changing relations involved is the function which we attribute to consciousness. [2]

---

[1] From the writer's *Development and Purpose*, p. 54.

[2] It may be asked whether variation to suit unique circumstances is a good test of conation in view of the possibility (suggested above, Ch. II. p. 32, by the example of the linotype) that a machine may be constructed

Among ourselves sensori-motor action is acquired. It is a matter of trained skill and disciplined judgment. The type reactions employed are themselves for the most part acquisitions, the perceptive judgment which combines them a still more difficult acquisition. But there is no difficulty in conceiving that hereditary type reactions should be uniquely combined, provided there exists in the animal some power strictly corresponding in origin and function to our perceptual consciousness which can combine present data. It would seem that we must in fact carry such power down to the lowest grades of animal life. The amoeba, which is pursuing a prey, employs not one reaction but a number of type reactions selectively, in combination or in succession, in accordance with the behaviour of the prey, which again varies as the play of circumstances may direct. Here is the description of amoeba's hunting from Mr. Jennings's work :

" I had attempted to cut an Amoeba in two with the tip of a fine glass rod. The posterior third of the animal, in the form of a wrinkled ball, remained attached to the rest of the body by only a slender cord—the remains of the ectosarc. The Amoeba began to creep away, dragging with it this ball. This Amoeba may be called a, while the ball will be designated b. A larger Amoeba (c) approached, moving at right angles to the path of the first specimen. Its path accidentally brought it in contact with the ball b, which was dragging past its front. Amoeba c thereupon turned, followed Amoeba a, and began to engulf the ball b. A

to adapt itself in specified cases to the variations of individual circumstances. The reply is that in conation the act is so adjusted to indefinitely varying changes in an outer object as to meet not the present situation but one that is just about to occur. Now if there is a uniform correlation between the acts, states or position of the object such that a series of variations in its present state $A_1, A_2, A_3 \ldots$ are always succeeded in definite time and space relation by a series $a_1, a_2, a_3 \ldots$ such adjustment might be mechanical. That is, the stimulus administered by $A_1$ might by a uniform process discharge the movement suited to deal with the object at $a_1$ and so on. This would be an admissible explanation in, say, the chase of a prey in open country. We might suppose all the responses of the hunter to be adapted by heredity to those of the prey, which, though endlessly varying, may vary on a fixed pattern. But when we consider the synthesis of several independent objects which we find in sensori-motor action, we are dealing with things that vary independently and pass from one unique relation irregularly to another. In this case the given situation varies in no uniform relation to the situation which will emerge from it. The only thing that is common to the several responses is their suitability to the result accruing from them.

cavity was formed in the anterior part of Amoeba c, reaching back nearly or quite to its middle, and much more than sufficient to contain the ball b.  Amoeba a now turned into a new path ; Amoeba c followed.  After the pursuit had lasted for some time the ball b had become completely enveloped by Amoeba c.  The cord connecting the ball with Amoeba a broke, and the latter went on its way, disappearing from our account.  Now the anterior opening of the cavity in Amoeba c became partly closed, leaving only a slender canal.  The ball b was thus completely enclosed, together with a quantity of water.  There was no adhesion between the protoplasm of b and c ; on the contrary, as the sequel will show clearly, both remained independent, c merely enclosing b.

" Now the large Amoeba c stopped, then began to move in another direction, carrying with it its meal.  But the meal—the ball b—now began to show signs of life, sent out pseudopodia, and became very active ; we shall therefore speak of it henceforth as Amoeba b.  It began to creep out through the still open canal, sending forth its pseudopodia to the outside.  Thereupon Amoeba c sent forth its pseudopodia in the same direction, and after creeping in that direction several times its own length, again enclosed b.  The latter again partly escaped, and was again engulfed completely.  Amoeba c now started again in the opposite direction, whereupon Amoeba b, by a few rapid movements, escaped from the posterior end of Amoeba c and was free—being completely separated from c.  Thereupon c reversed its course, overtook b, engulfed it completely again, and started away.  Amoeba b now contracted into a ball and remained quiet for a time.  Apparently the drama was over.  Amoeba c went on its way for about five minutes without any sign of life in b.  In the movements of c the ball became gradually transferred to its posterior end until there was only a thin layer of protoplasm between b and the outer water.  Now b began to move again, sent pseudopodia through the thin wall to the outside, and then passed bodily out into the water.  This time Amoeba c did not return and recapture b.  The two Amoebae moved in opposite directions and became completely separated."  (Pp. 17, 18.)

This behaviour, as Mr. Jennings justly remarks, is evidently complex, and " analysis into simple reactions and simple stimuli is difficult if possible at all."  Undoubtedly the impression made both by this and other observations is that the amoeba's action is of sensori-motor type.  It certainly uses only two or three type methods, which belong to its structure and may be regarded as hereditary, but it appears to vary and adjust them from moment to moment in relation to the behaviour of an external object. If this is the case the action is sensori-motor.[1] With regard to higher animals that follow the turnings and twistings of a prey, or, if themselves dogged, the rapidly changing movements of an enemy, the case admits of no doubt. Mechanism may be wholly hereditary or may be improved by experience as the case may be, but the combination and adjustment from moment to moment require the combination of many co-present elements, and the only question which we shall have to raise later on will be whether we must not carry some of these actions a grade higher and frankly regard them as purposive.

[1] To go a little higher in the animal scale we may usefully compare the behaviour of a starfish that has been placed on its back. First of all it moves its tube feet about and twists the tubes so that some are directed downwards. In this way one or more find the bottom. "They begin to pull on the arm to which they belong, turning it further over, and bring other tube feet into contact with the bottom. These now assist in the process. If two or three adjacent rays become thus attached, the other rays cease their searching, twisting movements and allow themselves to be turned over" . . . If two or more opposite rays become attached, "one releases its hold." The righting reaction is by no means performed always in the same manner but is various and flexible (Jennings, p. 239). I do not know whether the righting reaction should be classed as sensori-motor directed to the ground as an object, or as a selective adaptation. It is certainly an interesting instance of the determination of a series of acts by reference to the immediate requirements of the animal.

# CHAPTER VI

## INSTINCT [1]

1. WE were taught in our childhood that man had reason, while animals had instinct. What instinct precisely was, was not, so far as my own memory goes, made particularly clear. But it was generally understood to be a somewhat mysterious power, the limits of which were exceedingly ill-defined, while its workings were undoubtedly a conspicuous instance of that Providential ordering of things whereby the fly is endowed with wings to escape the spider, and the spider with jaws to devour the fly. I cannot find a better statement of the traditional, popular, and, one may say, pious conception of instinct than that given by Captain Marryat's *Masterman Ready*—a work written for edification.

" ' Instinct in animals, William,' continued Mr. Seagrave, ' is a feeling which compels them to perform certain acts without previous thought or reflection ; this instinct is in full force at the moment of their birth ; it is the guidance of the Almighty's hand unseen ; it was therefore perfect in the beginning, and has never varied. The swallow built her nest, the spider its web, the bee formed its comb, precisely in the same way four thousand years ago as they do now.' "

It may be said to be the breakdown of this conception which made animal psychology possible as a science. As

---

[1] The following chapter was written before seeing Mr. Lloyd Morgan's final expression of his views in *Animal Behaviour*, with which I am glad to find myself in close agreement. My debt to him, however, is none the less, since the chapter is largely based upon his earlier work.

soon as it was seen that instinct, like other animal functions, rested upon conditions many of which can be assigned, that it does not spring into existence all at once in full perfection, but is subject, like other features of organic life, to growth and change and possibly to decay, that it is not always perfect or unerring, that no impassable gulf severs it from intelligence, but rather that intelligence first arises within the sphere of instinct—when instinct was thus brought into relation with more commonplace facts, the awe and mystery surrounding it were dissolved, and the central feature of animal psychology became susceptible of scientific treatment. No one supposes that all instincts are explained, or are easy to understand in the present state of our knowledge. The central conception of instinct itself is not as clearly defined as might be desired. But instinct is no longer a mysterious faculty which may at once be set down as a sufficient explanation of anything in the behaviour of animals that we do not understand. Instinct cannot do anything and everything. It has limits even if we have difficulties in drawing them with precision. And secondly, its territory is not apart, but strictly continuous with other powers of organised beings. Instinct in short is a product of evolution. It presides at a certain phase, and has, all in due order, its beginning, its rise, its culmination, and its decline.

To give the full proof of what I have said would be merely to repeat or summarise the works of authors far more competent to deal with the matter than myself. I may merely advert briefly to the abundant evidence showing that instinct is not always perfect in its working ; that it does not proceed on an unchangeable model ; that it is on occasion applied mistakenly, uselessly and injuriously ; that it is often incomplete at birth, and requires development ; and that, at any rate among the higher animals, it is so interwoven with intelligence that the two factors become exceedingly difficult to disentangle.

Nothing seems more instinctive than the impulse of the young mammal to suck its mother's breast. Undoubtedly there is an innate tendency to suck, and an impulse to suck the breast. But there is no unerring inward guide leading it to obtain its needed nourishment. On the contrary, good observers state that many young pigs, puppies, and kittens would fail to find the teat altogether unless helped by the mother, while of the lamb Mr. Hudson says :—

" It does not know what to suck.. It will take into its mouth whatever comes near, in most cases a tuft of wool on its dam's neck, and at this it will continue sucking for an indefinite time."

It is, he thinks, the strong smelling secretion of the udder that at length attracts the lamb.[1]

Heredity is the main guide in the matter and manner of eating and drinking, but the young bird, however much in need of drink, gives no response to the presence or even to the touch of water till it has once got it inside its bill by a more or less accidental peck.[2]

There is no more wonderful operation of "instinct" than the nest of the bird, or the web of the spider. But neither of these is in all cases immutable in type nor perfect from birth. Dahl[3] found with one species of spider, which makes a web with one section omitted and the space occupied by a single thread, that the first web spun is of a more primitive type. It is made complete, like an ordinary web. The more developed form is found sometimes in the second web, sometimes after several repetitions. One individual combined the single thread with the perfect web. The nest-building of birds is unquestionably instinctive, but as unquestionably it is an art which different individuals of the same species possess in different degrees of perfection,[4] and which is modifiable in many different ways, as circumstances suggest or require.[5]

Few instincts seem more mysterious than those which lead insects to choose for depositing their eggs precisely those places which are best adapted for hatching out the larva. Yet the flesh fly has been known to deposit its

---

[1] Lloyd Morgan, *Habit and Instinct*, pp. 114-116. Cf. Preyer, I. pp. 138-140, and Wesley Mills, pp. 118, 119.
[2] See Craig, *Observations on Doves Learning to Drink, J.A.B.* 1912, pp. 273-279, and Lloyd Morgan, *Habit and Instinct*, pp. 44-46, there cited.     [3] Dahl, p. 168.
[4] See Lloyd Morgan, *Habit and Instinct*, p. 234 *et seq.*
[5] For abundant evidence, see Romanes, *M.E.A.* p. 209 ff. and Wallace, *Natural Selection*, p. 110 *et seq.*

eggs in the flowers of the carrion plant, the smell of which resembles that of putrid meat.[1] No case of this kind is more wonderful than that of the Sitaris beetle,[2] the larva of which begins life by attaching itself to a bee which has afterwards to provide for it. Does one ask how the larva knows the bee ? The reply is, it does not.

"Although they are close to the abodes of the bees they do not enter them, but seek to attach themselves to any hairy object that may come near them, and thus a certain number of them get on to the bodies of the *Anthophora* and are carried to its nest. They attach themselves with equal readiness to any other hairy insect, and it is probable that very large numbers perish in consequence of attaching themselves to the wrong insects."[3]

These and similar instances go to show that what guides the larva or the fly is no unerring internal or external guide, but the contact of the hairs, the smell of the meat. The mechanism of the instinct consists in this : that at the time when the fly is ready to lay the eggs, the smell (or the diffused chemical stimulus which, for us, is a smell) attracts the fly, and contact with the smelling substance gives the final touch which sets the process of laying to work. Similarly the cuttlefish at the due season has the impulse to embrace its mate. Here the stimulus appears to be the shape of the mate, for a piece of wood appropriately shaped will be so violently and persistently embraced that it can be used as a bait with success.[4] A tame dove will give the instinctive sex reactions to the most inappropriate object, bowing and cooing ludicrously to a shoe or to the hand of the owner, behaving in perfectly characteristic fashion, but with complete ineptitude.[5] Similarly a young hawk strikes a harmless piece of meat with ruffled feathers, spread wings, and savage thrust of beak and claw, in fine with all the instinctive adaptations and expressions appropriate to the pounce on living prey, in response to some stimulus of odour or touch, but quite fruitlessly for the purpose in hand.[6]

[1] Romanes, *M.E.A.* p. 167. Cf. Schneider, *Der thierische Wille*, p. 268. [2] Lloyd Morgan, *Habit and Instinct*, pp. 15, 304.
[3] *The Cambridge Natural History*, VI. p. 272.
[4] Schneider, *Der thierische Wille*, p. 173.
[5] Craig, *Male Doves reared in Isolation*, *J.A.B.* 1914, pp. 123, 132, &c.
[6] Haggerty, *A Case of Instinct*, *J.A.B.* 1912, p. 79.

These few instances will serve to show that instinct is not the mysteriously unerring guide that tradition has made of it. It is not invariably perfect from birth ; it often needs and undergoes development in the lifetime of the individual ; it often misleads its possessor, and, as we shall show later, it is, at any rate in its higher forms, capable of well-directed modifications.

2. Indeed, instinctive action of the more plastic kind bears at first sight all the signs and tokens of deliberate purpose—and deliberate purpose implies intelligence. Can we then regard instinct as a form of intelligence? The question would hardly be entertained by any psychologist, but it may be well to assign briefly some of the reasons for dismissing it. If we impute intelligence to an animal, we do so on the same ground ultimately as that which justifies us in imputing intelligence to another man. We reason outwards to other men from ourselves, and similarly we reason outwards to animals from men. And the test of our reasonings is in the end the same—corroboration of our results by inferences proceeding from different data and along different lines. Bearing these principles in mind, we observe :—

*a.* Instinctive and intelligent actions are opposed in their genesis.

To grasp fully the nature of what he is doing, a man must have some experience of it. Instinct, on the other hand, is often almost perfect, and sometimes quite perfect, without any experience at all. At that stage its action is, even in an otherwise intelligent being, carried on without consciousness of its end or its nature. Thus when an otherwise intelligent youth falls in love for the first time, he has little or no conception of what has befallen him, until little by little he begins to compare his experiences with what he has seen and heard and read. Then he knows. To assume that a canary bred in captivity has a conception of the nest which she builds is to suppose something utterly opposed to that human experience which is the real basis of the original assumption. Men do not evolve conceptions out of nothing, in the way which the canary would, according to the assumption, have to do.

On the other hand, men do perform actions without knowing the reason why, and come at the reason afterwards by reflection. In short, instinct is a "vera causa." We know it among ourselves. Innate conception is not a "vera causa." To impute it to an animal is to infer, on the ground of actions similar to those of man, an intellectual method opposed to those of man.

β. Instinct and Intelligence are opposed in the nature of their contents.

If we were to regard as the work of thought actions which we usually attribute to instinct, we should have to impute to the animals which perform them a marvellous capacity for intricate scheming and planning. A single instance will be a sufficient illustration.

"The caterpillar of the emperor moth spins at the upper extremity of its cocoon a double arch of stiff bristles, held together above only by a few fine threads. The cocoon, *i.e.*, opens at the very least pressure from within, but is able to resist quite strong pressure from without. Autenrieth writes of this in his *Ansichten über Natur- und Seelenleben :* 'If the caterpillar acted from reflection and with understanding, it must, on human analogy, have pursued the following train of thought : that it had reached its chrysalis stage, and would therefore be at the mercy of any unlucky accident, without possibility of escape, unless it took certain precautionary measures in advance ; that it would have to issue from its cocoon as imago without having organs or strength for breaking through the cover it had spun as caterpillar, and without possessing any secretion, like other insects, which would, if emitted, eat through the threads of silk ; and that consequently, unless it took care to provide as caterpillar a convenient exit from its cocoon, it must certainly come to a premature end in imprisonment. On the other hand, it must have clearly recognised during its work upon the cocoon that, in order to have free egress as imago, it would only be necessary to construct an arch which could resist attacks from without while opening easily from within ; and that these conditions would be fulfilled if the arch were made of stiff threads, inclined together in the median line, and with their ends left free. At the same time it must have realised that the plan could be carried out if the silk employed for the construction of the other parts of the cocoon were employed with special care and skill at the upper end. Yet it could have learnt nothing of all this from its parents.'" [1] . . .

[1] Wundt, *Lectures on Human and Animal Psychology*, pp. 391–392.

It is out of keeping with anything that we know of Thought to suppose that it could reach such a pitch of perfection in relation to a single series of acts, and not show itself in any other way.   But it is quite in keeping with the nature of heredity to suppose that in a species to which a certain method of protection has become important, that method should go on under the influence of natural selection, becoming more and more perfect in its mechanical precision.   And that instincts no less complex are of this mechanical character is proved by instances which we have already quoted, and to which we might add indefinitely. The truth is, that it is precisely the highly complex development of apparent purpose in certain relations, combined with entire absence of any corresponding manifestation of intelligence in other respects, that forces us to recognise the purposiveness as only apparent.   One has seen incautious writers attributing high unselfishness to an insect because it sacrifices itself for young whom it will never see.   It is precisely this apparent refinement which removes the action out of the moral category altogether, by making it impossible for the insect to know what it is about.

3. *Instinct and heredity.*

The explanation of instinct by intelligence does not accord with the facts.   If the intelligence is regarded as a sort of providential guidance of the animal, the explanation founders on the mistakes of instinct and its variability.   If it is the animal's own intelligence that is called in, we have seen that it must be an intelligence opposed in the method of its growth and its structure when grown to any sort of intelligence of which we have clear knowledge. These explanations have accordingly given way to the biological theory which explains Instinct by heredity.   If a structure can arise through heredity under the influence of natural selection, so also can the function which such a structure performs, and instinct, upon this view, is nothing but the specific function of a definite inherited structure. The evolution of wings is not a separate process from the evolution of flying.   The growth of claws and teeth implies the development of a particular habit of fighting and obtaining food.   These broad correlations of structure and functions are everyday matters too familiar to strike us. The observant naturalist can carry this correspondence further into detail, as when Dr. A. R. Wallace shows that the absence of nests among the Megapodidae is correlated with the large size of their eggs. This involves an interval of ten or twelve days between the maturation of each egg, and makes it impossible that all should be hatched together.[1] But to complete the account of the relation between structure and function, we should require a knowledge of the molecular structure of the nervous system of which we are as yet only at the beginning. The reason why the bird uses its wings, or the tiger its claws, is not merely that they possess wings and claws, but that the muscles of wings and claws are connected through a ramification of nerve fibres with their sense organs. If we could trace out these ramifications in detail, we should be able to specify the actual hereditary structures on which the flying of the bird or the crouch and spring of the tiger depend. We are only on the threshold of the investigations necessary for such a purpose.[2] But we have no reason to doubt that as in general so in detail we should find a close correspondence between inherited structure and inherited mode of action, which would justify us in regarding the latter as the response made by the former to accustomed stimulus.

4. Treating instinct, then, as the response of inherited structure to stimulus, comparative psychology at one time inclined to regard it as closely related to reflex action. The smell of putrid meat attracts the gravid carrion fly. That is, it sets up motions of the wings which bring the fly to it, and the fly having arrived, the smell and the contact combined stimulate the functions of oviposition.

[1] *Malay Arcihpelago*, Vol. I. p. 418.

[2] Here and there by good fortune we come upon a progressive series showing the stages by which evolution *may* have gone forward. "The Synagris are a genus of Eumenidae ... *S. calida* ... stocks the cells with caterpillars, lays an egg in each, seals the cells and takes no more notice of them. *S. sicheliana* ... places in each (cell) enough caterpillars to last the larva a little more than one day, and replenishes the store daily." *S. cornuta* completes one cell, lays an egg in it, does not store it but feeds the hatched larva till it is full-grown, when the wasp seals the cell and constructs another." E. Roubaud as summarised *J.A.B.* 1912, p. 391.

The sight of appropriate food stimulates the chick to peck, just as the contact of the food with the interior of the bill stimulates the swallowing reflexes. And just as the sight of food stimulates the chick to peck, so the sight of the chick stimulates the hen to cluck, or to scratch for food, or to protect it against danger, and so forth.

But the last instance shows us that if we actually identify instinctive with reflex action, we shall be running into paradox. In the maternal care exercised by the hen many reflexes are involved as constituent elements. No doubt a certain optical stimulus may by a purely reflex process make the hen utter the "danger cluck"; the sound of which in the same way induces the chicks to hide. As they run to her she spreads out her wings to receive them and so forth. Each particular act may be described without obvious violence as reflex, but the whole is an adaptive combination of reflexes in which the combination is as important as each separate act. That is to say it is of sensori-motor type. Nor is this all. The sensori-motor act is only one incident in what may be a long and complex series all of which tend to one result, the production and safe rearing of the chicks. Throughout this series there appears to be in the hen at least some permanent state corresponding to what we call maternal feeling, or the parental instinct, which dominates her actions throughout, and without which the various reflexes would not be discharged by their appropriate stimuli nor the perceived situations have their effect in combining reflexes suitably. If she had no chickens to think of, the hen would pick up the food which she finds, and would seek her own safety when frightened.

To this it may be replied that the adaptive combination of the reflexes is itself a part of the mechanism provided by heredity for the maintenance of the species. Those who hold with Mr. Herbert Spencer that instinct is merely compound reflex action, will point out that each action that we have mentioned naturally calls for the next until the chain is complete. This concatenation is no doubt adaptive, but it is also mechanical, and to impute to the hen maternal feeling unless we can show that this feeling has some outward effect in modifying her actions, is a piece of pure anthropomorphic imagery. Upon its own conditions, this argument is sound. In comparative psychology the legal maxim must hold, that the thing which does not at some point or other appear in action must be treated as non-existent. And it may freely be admitted that in many actions we ordinarily class as instincts, instances of rigid adherence to type-action may be found. But alongside of these, often intertwined with them in the very same series of acts, will be found adaptive modifications, combinations, inhibitions. Some of these are sensori-motor, some of higher type, but they agree in this that they are adapted to the changing and even the unique and therefore they fall outside our definition of the mechanical. Instincts present such modifications in very various character and degree. In proportion as an instinct is poor in them and therefore rigid in its execution it approaches the compound reflex type, but at the limit where plasticity disappears we should as a matter of terminology say that the sphere of instinct is left behind and reflex mechanism reigns in its stead.

The true compound reflex is of two kinds. In the first, a single stimulus sets in motion a co-ordinated series of muscular contractions. Thus the contact of a foreign substance with the interior of the windpipe produces the series of contractions which we call a fit of coughing. Here the whole machinery must be prearranged. There are in the arrangements of muscles, nerves, and nerve centres certain lines of communication as complex but also as definitely and rigidly fixed as those of a telephone when the connection is made. The impulse having once set the wave of excitement in motion, the wave travels along the ordained channel till the end is reached, and organic equilibrium is again restored. In the second and more complex case, there is a series of stimuli as well as a series of actions, the actions being so adjusted as to bring the new stimuli into play. This arrangement may be wholly internal, the stimuli themselves being changes within the organism, as in the case of respiration. But this is not essential. Under ordinary circumstances walking—the act of walking as distinct from the purpose with which we set out—is for every one but an infant a true compound reflex. The contact of the foot with the ground sets in motion a number of waves of excitement directed in part to maintaining the balance, in part to the onward movement. The resulting contractions bring the other foot forward, and the result is a fresh contact, setting similar contractions to work, and so forth.[1]

This familiar instance may serve to illustrate the general plan of a compound reflex, and to show that there is nothing to prevent a train of action of considerable complexity being carried on through a succession of responses each following with rigid and predetermined uniformity upon its proper stimulus. Where an "instinct" is of this character, it may be made to betray itself by some slight variation in the circumstances which render the action useless or injurious. When we apply this test we get some very strange results, and what at one moment we take for instinctive behaviour of a high order seems at another to sink to mechanical action of a rigid type. A well-known observation by M. Fabre will illustrate my point.[2]

. . . "A solitary wasp, *Sphex flavipennis*, which provisions its nest with small grasshoppers, when it returns to the cell, leaves the victim outside, and goes down for a moment to see that all is right. During her absence M. Fabre moved the grasshopper a little. Out came the Sphex, soon found her victim, dragged it to the mouth of the cell, and left it as before. Again and again M. Fabre moved the grasshopper, but every time the Sphex did exactly the same thing, until M. Fabre was tired out."[3]

[1] Walking is subject to the permanent disposition to go forward. In purposive acts such a disposition exerts a controlling influence from the background which is roughly parallel to that exerted by the permanent condition in the instinctive series. But subject to this condition the acts involved in walking as long as everything is straightforward are, I think, reflex. The slightest obstacle, of course, brings consciousness into play.

In low organisms movements of the whole body may be analysed into chain reflexes in which the activity of one part stimulated from without is itself the stimulus to the appropriate act of the next part, and so on. (S. J. Holmes, *Phototaxis in the Sea-urchin, J.A.B.* p. 135.)

[2] Lubbock, *Senses of Animals*, p. 245.

[3] It does not follow that the wasp was destitute of intelligence, or that it is not under any circumstances able to bring intelligence to bear on the action. Indeed, a subsequent experiment of Fabre's on another individual

Equally well known is the same observer's experiment on the larva of Chalicodoma.

"This genus is enclosed in an earthen cell, through which at maturity the young insect eats its way. M. Fabre found that if he pasted a piece of paper round the cell the insect had no difficulty in eating through it, but if he enclosed the cell in a paper case, so that there was a space even of only a few lines between the cell and the paper, in that case the paper formed an effectual prison. The instinct of the insect taught it to bite through one enclosure, but it had not wit enough to do so a second time."[1]

What seems like unremitting maternal love is suddenly shown in quite a different light by a slight alteration of the conditions. The Bembex carefully feeds her grub, and never makes a mistake in finding her way to her cell, although it is covered with sand and is then undistinguishable to us from the surroundings, but when M. Fabre removed the earth and exposed the cell, the Bembex did not appear to recognise the young that she had so carefully tended.[2] One is driven to infer a very different mental process from that of the bird, which will follow her young if taken from her, or even from that of the perch, that will remove a nest that has once been disturbed.[3]

Traces of this mechanical method of response are found side by side or blended with intelligence in the higher animals. Mr. Lloyd Morgan quotes an amusing story of a tame squirrel which would " bury " a nut in the floor of a room.

"He would press the nut down on the carpet, and then go through all the motions of patting the earth over it, after which he went about his business as if that nut were safely buried."[4]

The dog's habit of turning round before going to sleep is of a similar character, and so are numberless little irrational habits of which we are aware in our friends.[5] A

proves the contrary. See also Peckham, *Solitary Wasps*, p. 39. Many human actions are performed mechanically day by day, but a sufficiently strong stimulus directs attention to them, and brings intelligence to bear.

[1] *M.E.A.* p. 166.      [2] Lubbock, *loc. cit.* p. 254.
[3] Romanes, p. 251. Cf. Schneider.      [4] *Habit and Instinct*, p. 123.
[5] Habit and Instinct, though of different origin, have so many points of resemblance that we may be allowed sometimes to illustrate the one by an example from the other.

man likes to adhere to his particular way of doing a thing, even though a better way be shown him. In proportion as they exhibit this fixed and unadaptable uniformity of response, instincts approach the compound reflex limit and deserve to be called relatively mechanical.

5. Instincts recede from this type in proportion as the persistent internal disposition[1] influences the response. We may illustrate the influence of such a condition from human actions, where not heredity but an acquired habit is the basis of co-ordination. As I walk down the street, I avoid obstacles without thinking about them. The sight of each passer by, of the lamp post or an approaching cab discharges suitable movements of my legs without—unless the danger is sudden or unusual—distracting my thoughts from the conversation which I am carrying on. The process is reflex. If, instead of walking, I am bicycling, I avoid the perils of 'bus or cab no less "instinctively," that is, automatically. But here quite a different set of muscles are called into play. I steer not by my feet but by my hands and the swinging of my body. If a cart suddenly stops in front of me, I grasp the brake. If I were briskly walking, I should pull up quite differently, with one foot out, and knee bent but tense. In a word, the reflexes excited by the same objects or circumstances differ according to the pursuit in which I am for the time engaged. While that pursuit continues the reflexes are set to play a particular tune as each is touched. In this instance, the setting is fixed by habit, but the effect is the same where it is inherited. But it is not only reflexes that are so determined but sensori-motor actions as well. The clutching of the bicycle brake in the presence of an obstacle may be mechanical, but if a child runs out into the road, the cyclist executes a swift but graceful curve and avoids it. The act may be unreflective but it needs that element of judgment, of grasping several distinct sensory data in relation which distinguishes the sensori-motor from the reflex act. Now the sensori-motor act

---

[1] The German *Stimmung* used by Preyer (I. p. 197) in this connection expresses my meaning better. Mr Lloyd Morgan calls the internal factor a craving (*Animal Behaviour*, p. 102).

involves, we saw, attentive concentrated perception. In us this is a consciousness. In the animal under the same circumstances we see all the corresponding outward signs, the pricked ear, the sniffing nose, the fixed eyeball, the tense musculature ; we have also corresponding antecedents and corresponding consequences. There must, therefore, be some state of the animal's organism corresponding in causes, expression, and functions to our attentive perception, and though that state cannot be more directly known to us, we describe it in accordance with our avowed method by the same name. Now we have to ask what determines attentive perception, and what causes it to discharge actions of a particular kind. The answer in our case is that (apart from the intensity or other peculiarity of some external stimulus) there is some interest which directs perception, is served by the response which the perception discharges, and is in fact the motive force behind the perception. This interest does not necessarily form an independent state of consciousness, but it qualifies our consciousness as long as it lasts, giving our conscious perception an emotional tinge and impregnating it with the sense of effort and excitement. Now such an interest may be connected with a conscious purpose and may arise out of experience. But there is no difficulty in conceiving a similar interest as an innate or hereditary disposition brought into action by an appropriate situation as stimulus or possibly even in the course of the purely internal changes of the organism. Precisely such a state so arising, so enduring till its function is performed, and so directing the series of constituent actions is what we find in Instinct.

To this direction Instinct mainly owes it plasticity of adjustment. As we ascend the scale this feature develops and the divergence from the reflex type becomes more pronounced. Alternative methods of action are used and used appropriately. Different kinds of reaction are combined in ways that must vary, more or less, from case to case. Lastly within certain limits special obstacles or deviations from the normal course of events seem to call up special reactions fitted to deal with them. This

plasticity is partly a matter of degree, partly of the processes at the disposal of the instinct.   At one end of the
scale we have mechanical sequences approximating to the
reflex type.   Moving upwards from these we have
adaptations, at first slight and afterwards important.
The simplest of these may be explained as sensori-
motor acts, where the instinctive interest determines the
manner in which sense data are combined so as to yield
an appropriate response, but, still within the sphere of
instinct, we reach a point where the new combinations
effected in surmounting obstacles or in dealing with
difficult situations  must be referred to intelligence.   The
criteria of intelligence will be dealt with separately.   We
cannot in all cases decide with certainty whether it is a
factor, but it is impossible to deal with the higher instincts
at all without admitting its possibility.

Whether intelligence is present in the following case must
be left to the judgment of the reader, but it will suffice to
illustrate the manner in which actions are combined and
adjusted under the instinctive interest.   A sandhopper is
feeding amongst seaweed and a crab[1] approaches behind a
clump of weed, which he uses as " cover."   There was a
distance of about eight inches between the two animals,
which the crab had to cross without alarming his victim.
Presently he left his cover, and, crouching down, crept
towards the sandhopper.   When he had got about half
way, the sandhopper stopped eating, and turned towards
the crab, which immediately disappeared in the sand.
Presently the sand rose nearer the sandhopper, the
crab reappeared, took a stealthy step or two towards
the victim, and then sprang upon him.   There are
here a succession of acts of diverse character—
watching, stealthy creeping, hiding, and pouncing, all
brought into operation as the case requires.   The whole
series turns upon a fixed point—the seizure of the prey ;
and each of the varied set of acts is adopted in accordance
with the varying actions of the prey, or the varying relations between it and the hunter.   If we try to regard

[1] Dr. Oscar Schmidt in Brehm's *Thierleben*, as quoted by Schneider,
p. 324.

each several movement as a reflex, we should find at once that it was a reflex in which the response instead of varying uniformly with the stimulus, varied in accordance with circumstances. The sight of the prey at a certain distance, and with its back turned, induces stealthy approach ; at close quarters a sudden leap. The turning of the sandhopper's head sets in motion the responses. This is a complex series involved in burrowing under the sand. Everything varies according to the position and movements of the animal pursued, that is to say, the action is sensori-motor, and indeed there is a series of sensori-motor acts adjusted from moment to moment, not to a series of simple sense stimuli, but to the changing phases of a complex situation.

By the " situation " here is meant those objects and changes in the immediate surroundings that have a bearing on the attainment of a particular end, and operate on the sense organs of an animal. The influence which we have to ascribe to the situation implies the existence of an abiding internal state of the organism which deals with it, adjusting action to its changing phases in the way described. Just as the reflex excitability is the correlative of the sense-stimulus, so this relatively permanent state, which dominates many reflexes, is the correlative of a combination of circumstances, or a " situation." To mate and breed the female dove requires not only the male but facilities for nesting, courting, and generally a suitable environ-ment—" no one factor determines it." The transform-ation of the dove's attitude is " determined by the entire social situation." [1] It is this relatively permanent state,

---

[1] *The Stimulation and the Inhibition of Ovulation in Birds and Mammals*, Wallace Craig, *J.A.B.* 1913, pp. 214–221. Conversely, when the brooding instinct is once aroused the appropriate stimuli act almost as reflexes. " Contact with the nest under appropriate conditions excites a powerful suggestion or an almost hypnotic influence upon the bird, which somehow involves the ovaries. This attitude leads her to work further upon the nest. Such work causes the stimulus from the nest to be repeated. Thus the circular activity goes on and on." Of the influence of the male on laying, the writer said earlier that it was a psychological influence. In this passage he withdraws the term in favour of the reflex, but he adds : " It is not a simple reflex. It is a reflex which is set working, not by any one sense stimulus, but by the total situation, including both the totality of present sense stimuli and also memory factors " (p. 217).

directing a series of actions towards a definite result, that forms the basis of Instinct. The construction of a cocoon by a caterpillar, or a tube by a worm, may be quite mechanical, but there is evidence of something not quite mechanical in the power of repairing the things constructed, or of dealing with any special obstacle to construction in a suitable way. The Ant Lion, according to writers quoted by Romanes,[1] has some capacity of this kind, and even among worms we find traces of adaptation. Thus, the Terebella builds its tube by selecting grains of sand— in captivity it is less dainty, but generally rejects glass— seizing them with its feelers, drawing them in, and, after secreting a certain cement upon them, protruding its head and depositing them where required. It not only repairs holes, but if a piece does not stick at first, it repeats the process of cementing, while if the object is too big to be drawn in, it protrudes its forepart to the entrance of the tube, and cements it on the spot.[2] Caterpillars show a certain power of adaptation in repairing injuries to their cocoons, and the methods used by different individuals are not necessarily the same. Thus, according to Kirby and Spence, Bonnet

. . . . " having opened several cocoons of a moth (*Noctua verbasci*), which are composed of a mixture of grains of earth and silk, just after being finished, the larvæ did not repair the injury *in the same manner*. Some employed both earth and silk ; others contented themselves with spinning a silken veil before the opening." [3]

Mr. Romanes also quotes an instructive observation of Réaumur on the larva of the Tinea moth, which eats out the parenchyma of the elm leaf, preserving the outer membrane as a coat, and being careful not to separate them at the outer edge where they unite. This edge becomes one of the seams of its coat. The other seam the larva makes for itself. " Réaumur cut off the edge of a newly-finished coat, so as to expose the body of the larva at that point."

---

[1] Romanes, p. 235.
[2] Brehm, *Thieleben*, Vol. X. pp. 127, 128.
[3] Quoted by Romanes, p. 236.          [4] *Ib.* p. 237.

It thereupon

" sewed up the rent ; and not only so, but ' the scissors having cut off one of the projections intended to enter into the construction of the triangular end of the case, it entirely changed the original plan, and made that end the head which had been first designed for the tail.' " [1]

Lastly, according to Dahl,[2] a spider will not only repair an injury to its web if sufficiently serious, but if it finds that a thread which it has spun does not fit the rest of the network, it will reject that thread and substitute another.

The converse case to the repair of damage is the utilisation of a special opportunity so as to dispense with unnecessary labour. Thus we find, again, according to Kirby and Spence, that the

" common cabbage caterpillar, which, when building web under stone or wooden surfaces, previously covers a space with a web to form a base for supporting its dependent pupa ; when building a web beneath a muslin surface dispenses with this base altogether. It perceives that the woven texture of the muslin forms facilities for attaching the threads of the cocoon securely enough to support the weight of the cocoon without the necessity of making the usual square inch or so of basal support." [3]

This instance [4] is thrown into relief by the conduct of Huber's caterpillar, which has been already referred to.

. . . " P. Huber has described a caterpillar which makes, by a succession of processes, a very complicated hammock for its

[1] An entomological friend remarks on this story that the caterpillar would probably (as in the previous example) merely set about to spin a piece of web where it was exposed, and this would have the effect, not planned by the insect, of "sewing" the edges together. If so, both this and the previous example show how an adaptive modification would result from the persistence with which the instinct operates until it is satisfied.

[2] Dahl, p. 166 ff.          [3] Romanes, p. 237.

[4] A parallel is the action of the dung beetle, which normally makes pellets for its eggs, but utilises any that it finds ready made. (Quoted from Kirby and Spence by Romanes, *M.E.A.* p. 244). Mr. Romanes goes much too far in calling this an "intelligent adaptation." On the face of it, it is merely an instance where an appropriate object calls out the instinctive reactions, that part of the normal instinctive operation which is rendered unnecessary remaining suppressed.

metamorphosis ; and he found that if he took a caterpillar which had completed its hammock up to, say, the sixth stage of construction, and put it into a hammock completed up only to the third stage, the caterpillar did not seem puzzled, but repeated the fourth, fifth, and sixth stages of construction. If, however, a caterpillar was taken out of a hammock made up, for instance, to the third stage, and put into one finished to the ninth stage, so that much of its work was done for it, far from feeling the benefit of this, it was much embarrassed, and even forced to go over the already finished work, starting from the third stage which it had left off before it could complete its hammock. So, again, the hive-bee in the construction of its comb seems compelled to follow an invariable order of work." [1]

We have here a case of the mechanical type approaching if it does not touch the boundary of the compound reflex, while in the other illustrations from caterpillar life we had instances of the adaptive, plastic type.

The power of overcoming obstacles, and also the limitation of that power as long as we move in the region of pure instinct, is well illustrated by another " caterpillar story " communicated to Mr. Romanes by Mr. G. B. Buckton :

"Many caterpillars of *Pieris rapæ* have, during this autumn, fed below my windows. On searching for suitable positions for passing into chrysalides, some eight or ten individuals, in their direct march upwards, encountered the plate-glass panes of my windows ; on these they appeared to be unable to stand. Accordingly in every case they made silken ladders, some of them five feet long, each ladder being formed of a single continuous thread woven in elegant loops from side to side. . . . The reasoning, however, seems to be but narrow, for one ladder was constructed parallel to the window-frame for nearly three feet, on which secure footing could be had by simply diverting the track two inches." [2]

The larva has, it would seem, a definite method of dealing with the particular difficulty of a smooth surface. It does not matter that a much simpler method is at hand. The caterpillar acts *more majorum*, and would doubtless be shocked at the suggestion that it should depart from tradition. This suggestion, however, its perceptions are incapable of making to it. Lastly, we may take a case

[1] *M E.A.* p. 179.          [2] Romanes, p. 236.

where simple patience is the method prescribed for over-coming an obstacle :

"Very young hermit-crabs, not long after leaving the egg, rush with extraordinary animation for suitable shells that are given to them in the water. They examine the opening at the mouth, and take up their quarters inside with remarkable alacrity. But, if it chances that the shells are still occupied by molluscs, then they stay close by the opening, and wait till the snail dies, which generally occurs soon after the beginning of the imprisonment and the strict watch. Upon this the small crab pulls out the carcass, devours it, and moves into the lodging himself."[1]

On this Preyer remarks :

"What foresight ! On account of the preference of the empty shells, the whole proceeding cannot be hereditary. But the young animals are not instructed. They were from the begin-ning separated from their parents, and had no time or opportunity for experiences of their own. They must, therefore, have in-herited their practice of waiting from their ancestors, as a rule of conduct for the case where the shell is occupied, and they can at once distinguish such a one from an empty one."[2]

The element that is not hereditary seems to be supplied by perception. The empty shell invites immediate entry. The full one sets in motion a different train of actions, equally hereditary, and also adapted in the end to give possession of the shell.

In the last illustration given, and in some of the others, it will be seen that instinct overcomes its obstacle by bringing up as it were a reserve method not ordinarily employed. It has alternative methods. We may say if we please that the reserve method is merely a response to a special stimulus, but we must keep in mind that the speciality of the stimulus lies precisely in this, that the success of the instinct cannot be compassed by ordinary means. The cat-like patience of the hermit-crab is only called forth by the necessity of getting into a shell, and by its finding the shell occupied. The same general explanation would apply to the action of the vine weevil, which makes a nest for its eggs by rolling up a young vine leaf. If

---

[1] Preyer, p. 240.          [2] *Ib.* p. 241.

the tender young leaf fails it, it shaves off one membrane of an old leaf, and uses that.[1] More remarkable, if correctly reported, is the account given by Romanes of a spider which, being so injured that it could not spin effectually, took to stalking its prey.[2] Not only will a hungry wolf attack a man from whom he would otherwise fly, but according to Dahl,[3] a fasting spider, which was normally shy of dangerous insects, fought fiercely with a wasp. The contrast between the ordinary gentleness of the female of many mammalia and her fierceness and bravery in defence of her young is in reality another case in point. An example both of persistence in overcoming obstacles and of variation in method is supplied by the larva of *Cecidipta excoecaria.*

"The female moth lays an egg on a gall, and the resulting larva bores into the gall and nourishes itself on the interior till all is eaten except a thin external coat ; the caterpillar then pupates in this chamber. The galls vary in size and shape, and the larva displays much constructive ability in adapting its home to its needs by the addition of tubes of silk or by other modes. Sometimes the amount of food furnished by the interior of the gall is not sufficient ; the larva, in such cases, resorts to the leaves of the plant for a supplement, but does not eat them in the usual manner of a caterpillar ; it cuts off and carries a leaf to the entrance of its abode, fastens the leaf there with silk, and then itself entering, feeds, from the interior, on the food it has thus acquired."[4]

Lastly, the behaviour of crabs in finding means of concealment gives examples both of the "mechanical" and of the more adaptive type. Many crabs have the habit of covering themselves with seaweed or other readily adherent objects, the utility of the action lying in the disguise. In one case, that of Dorippe, the habit appears to have degenerated into a merely mechanical reflex, the crab, as described by Schneider, constantly taking up bits of stone, sponge, or anything else of suitable size and shape, and fixing them on to itself. As it tears away one

[1] Schneider, p. 271. He notes it as a rare instance of an insect altering a custom on encountering an obstacle, and thinks it implies a certain degree of reflection.

[2] *M.E.A.* p. 209.     [3] *Op. cit.* p. 178.

[4] *Cambridge Natural History*, VI. p. 424.

bit to make room for another, it will often use the same object a second or third time over, while it will throw away objects much better suited for its "purpose," in favour of bits of glass which do not conceal it at all.[1] On the other hand, a crab described by Mr. Bateson[2] shows more capacity for adjustment. It takes the weed in its chelae, tears it across, puts one end in its mouth and chews it, and finally rubs it on its head and legs until it is caught by the hairs. If however the hairs do not catch the piece, the crab puts it back into its mouth and chews it up again. Here the non-fulfilment of the function has a direct influence. The crab persists or repeats the necessary steps. Whether this implies intelligence or not is a question on which opinions may differ. We may content ourselves with noting the fact that, whatever the means employed, special actions are brought to bear by which the ends of the instinct are achieved. Still more instructive is Schneider's[3] experiment on some "sea-spiders" to which he gave pieces of paper and linen as well as bits of algae, which they generally use. The paper and linen were at first utterly neglected, but when Schneider removed the algae, a divergence appeared. Of the five crabs, three grubbed in the sand, and so covered their backs with bits of shell and pebble, while the other two betook themselves to the paper and the linen. In the former case, a second kind of habitual reaction is evoked. In the latter, one object is substituted for another. The paper does not, as long as algae are present, excite the crab to seize it ; but the algae being gone, the paper steps into their place so that the instinct may still be fulfilled. The instinct is thus in part independent of stimulus. It needs objects in order to work itself out, but it is not entirely set in motion by the influence of those objects.

7. At this point it may be asked how far we are justified in referring well-devised adaptations of hereditary methods to mere instinct. An alternative explanation suggests itself. It is possible that within the sphere of instinct, intelligence plays a certain subordinate part. Though the

---

[1] *Op. cit.* p. 210.  [2] *Journal of Marine Biology*, 1889-90, p. 213.
[3] *Op. cit.* p. 318.

impulse to a particular course of action is hereditary, there may be sufficient intelligence, not indeed to devise the whole plan upon which the animal proceeds, but to carry out those minor modifications which peculiar circumstances demand. This would be an intelligence operating within the sphere of instinct. But there are many modifications which do not seem to require this explanation, and may be ascribed to what we will call pure instinct ; *i.e.*, instinct operating without intelligence. Thus, to begin with, some of the examples of variation adduced above are, as has been already suggested, to be put down to the existence of more than one hereditary reflex mechanism subserving the same end. A normal stimulus A excites the reflex *a* ; a less frequent stimulus B excites $\beta$ ; the reaction of *a* to A and $\beta$ to B giving essentially the same result. Thus one sort of danger may cause a creature to run away ; another may prompt it to hide, or perhaps to stay quite still (to " sham dead "). Here we clearly have to deal with hereditary methods of reaction, though they are different methods. But there is a more complex case. Though the whole mechanism employed may be hereditary, and so in a sense reflex, each reflex element may be suitably modified and adjusted by the pressure of the totality of conditions. We have seen already that in some degree this applies to reflexes from an early stage. The replete child does not suck. That is, the reflex excitability depends on certain relevant organic conditions.[1] In a more general way we can now understand how an adjustment, and seemingly a very intelligent adjustment, may be effected to different circumstances through the influence that different stimuli have in counterworking one another. Mr. Romanes tells on the authority of Mr. E. L. Layard a " snake story " which may perhaps be explained in this fashion.

---

[1] Another excellent illustration of the variation of response according to the general state and requirements of the organism is seen in Prof. Whitman's observations on the leech Clepsine, quoted in Mr. Lloyd Morgan's *Animal Behaviour*, pp. 159, 160. This leech has two distinct methods of behaviour in danger. One is to hug the surface on which it is resting, flattening the body and stiffening the flesh. The other is to roll itself up into a ball, free to roll away in any direction. " If by chance the animal has eggs, it will not desert them to escape in this way "— otherwise it may adopt either mode of defence.

" I once watched one (*i.e.*, a cobra) which had thrust its head through a narrow aperture and swallowed one (*i.e.*, a toad). With this encumbrance he could not withdraw himself. Finding this, he reluctantly disgorged the precious morsel, which began to move off. This was too much for snake philosophy to bear, and the toad was again seized ; and again, after violent efforts to escape, was the snake compelled to part with it. This time, however, a lesson had been learnt, and the toad was seized by one leg, withdrawn, and then swallowed in triumph." [1]

Here there appears a sort of conflict between the impulse to seize, and the necessity of withdrawing the head. The result is a kind of compromise which happens to suit the case well. The toad is seized, but the swallowing reflex is kept in abeyance till the withdrawal is performed. Without dogmatising about this particular instance, one sees how the conflict of impulses *may* work out to a harmony : how different stimuli, each severally exciting an unsuitable reflex, may act upon and so modify one another as to produce the required adjustment. Where each stimulus acts alone, we get the pure reflex. Where they act together we may get merely an adjustment produced by mutual modification, but where their action is not once nor twice but frequently so combined as to adjust itself to the peculiarities of an outer object, we have sensori-motor action. Where sensori-motors and reflexes are combined in series so as to lead to a definite result, though this result is not foreseen, we have instinct. Where, finally, it is impossible to explain the act except as determined by relation to an end beyond the compass of sensori-motor response, we must impute intelligence. Now the basis of instinct is heredity, but in sensori-motor action we have a factor which is not purely hereditary, namely, the combination of data by present consciousness. We shall use the term " pure instinct " for all behaviour that depends upon these elements alone, and shall contrast them with instincts that involve intelligence, meaning by intelligence processes which the individual devises for himself upon the basis of his own experience. Of intelligence operating within the sphere of instinct there is ample evidence. There are modifications of instinctive action directly traceable

[1] Romanes, p. 262.

to experience. There are adaptations which cannot be explained by any interaction of purely hereditary tendencies, and there are cases in which the whole structure of the instinct is profoundly modified by the experience of the individual.

The habits of solitary wasps have lately been the subject of a charming monograph by two very careful observers, who have corrected the somewhat startling conclusions of earlier naturalists, and have made a notable contribution to the whole question of Instinct.[1] I may quote some of their observations :

"When the provisioning is completed the time arrives for the final closing of the nest, and in this, as in all the processes of Ammophila, the character of the work differs with the individual. For example, of two wasps that we saw close their nests on the same day, one wedged two or three pellets into the top of the hole, kicked in a little dust and then smoothed the surface over, finishing it all within five minutes. This one seemed possessed by a spirit of hurry and bustle, and did not believe in spending time on non-essentials. The other, on the contrary, was an artist, an idealist. She worked for an hour, first filling the neck of the burrow with fine earth which was jammed down with much energy, this part of the work being accompanied by a loud and cheerful humming, and next arranging the surface of the ground with scrupulous care, and sweeping every particle of dust to a distance. Even then she was not satisfied, but went scampering around hunting for some fitting object to crown the whole. First she tried to drag a withered leaf to the spot, but the long stem stuck in the ground and embarrassed her. Relinquishing this, she ran along a branch of the plant under which she was working, and leaning over, picked up from the ground below a good sized stone, but the effort was too much for her, and she turned a somersault on to the ground. She then started to bring a large lump of earth, but this evidently did not come up to her ideal, for she dropped it after a moment, and seizing another dry leaf carried it successfully to the spot and placed it directly over the nest."[2]

We find here, first, variation as between individuals, so marked that we can hardly suppose heredity alone to account for the details of each method. Secondly, what

[1] *Instincts and Habits of Solitary Wasps*, by Mr. and Mrs. Peckham ; *Wisconsin Geological and Natural History Survey*, Bulletin No. 2.
[2] P. 21.

is more important, we find in the later case a series of trials by which, after one or two failures, a satisfactory result is obtained. We cannot describe this second wasp as responding in a reflex manner to a particular kind of object. We can only say of her that she has *an impulse to bring something suitable to cover her hole*. A leaf, a stone, a lump of earth, and again a leaf, are tried in succession until one suits. The objects used differ greatly, the muscular reactions differ materially. What is constant is merely the end to be achieved, and in some sense or other we must regard the wasp as determined by this end, that is to say, as acting with purpose.

The writers give several instances of the dexterity with which wasps get spiders into their holes. In one case the wasp

"was holding it by the under side of the body, the venter being toward the hole, and the legs spread out and stopped its entrance. A moment's tugging convinced her that this would not do, and she then turned the spider over, holding it by the back, whereupon the legs at once folded themselves across the underside of the thorax and the spider was drawn out of sight." [1]

Writing of the same species (*Pompilus fuscipennis*), they say:—

"The spider never went in easily, always requiring to be shifted and turned and tugged at. There was an especial tendency to bite at the legs at this point of time, when the wasp, standing within the tunnel, was trying to drag the spider down. In one instance she managed to get it past the entrance, but it stuck in the gallery, and after working at it in that position for a time she brought it out, subjected the legs to a severe squeezing, and tried again. It was still a very bad fit, but by turning it about and pulling at it she succeeded in getting it in." [2]

Another individual, of *P. marginatus*, stored her prey in a hole from which she had to remove it.

"The task, however, was not an easy one. She exerted all her strength, so that we expected to see the poor victim dismembered before our eyes, and still it did not come. At last she seemed to realise that there was more than one way to accomplish her end, and turned her attention to cutting away the earth to make the opening larger. After a few moments' work she

[1] P. 141.    [2] P. 143.

tried again, and although the passage was still much too small for convenience, the spider was at length dragged forth, looking much the worse for wear." [1]

Lastly, they think that a *P. scelestus* actually compared spider and hole before attempting to get the prey in.

" Presently she went to look at her nest and seemed to be struck with a thought that had already occurred to us—that it was decidedly too small to hold the spider.  Back she went for another survey of her bulky victim, measured it with her eye, without touching it, drew her conclusions, and at once returned to the nest and began to make it larger.  We have several times seen wasps enlarge their holes when a trial had demonstrated that the spider would not go in, but this seemed a remarkably intelligent use of the comparative faculty." [2]

Whatever the correct interpretation of this last observation, enough has been said to show that these wasps adapt means to ends in a way suited to the individual occasion.  They are by no means confined to a series of reactions evoked with mechanical uniformity by a uniform stimulus.  On the contrary, they are able to deal within limits with each emergency presented by the individual differences of the prey they have captured.  Once again, we cannot say that, given a spider and the hole, the " dragging reflex " is excited.  What is excited is the *impulse to get it in*, and this is accomplished, by dragging, biting, turning over, or enlarging the hole, as the case may be.  We are dealing not with reflex action but with the impulse to achieve a particular object to which many muscular actions are subordinated in ways that vary according to the needs of each case.

Without multiplying instances unnecessarily, we may quote one further statement showing that like birds [3] and

---

[1] P. 150.        [2] P. 158.

[3] A detailed account of nest building, describing in particular the methods of overcoming obstacles is given by Mr. F. H. Herrick, *J.A.B.* 1911, pp. 336-373.  He describes a robin bringing strings to his nest, which " brought him up to a short turn by catching on a stub.  He at first tried to release them by facing the nest and putting his whole force into a lateral strain.  Failing in this he faced around and pulled ; failing again, he advanced and taking up a little of the slack pulled again.  I suppose no one would deny that intelligence was displayed in this act, but it should also be noted that his intelligence did not carry him to the

ants, wasps and bees are capable of modifying their whole method of nest-building in well directed adjustment to novel circumstances.

" Pelopœus, instead of building in hollow trees or under shelving rocks, as was the ancient custom of the race, now nests in chimneys, or under the eaves of buildings. We have found *T. rubrocinctum* taking advantage of the face of a straw stack that had been cut off smoothly as the cattle were fed through the winter. The same power of adaptation is shown by Fabre's experiment with Osmia, in which he took two dozen nests in shells from a quarry, where the bees had been nesting for centuries, and placed them in his study along with some empty shells and some hollow stems. When the bees came out, in the spring, nearly all of them selected the stalks to build in as being better suited to their use than the shells." [1]

8. By extending the field it would be easy to multiply indefinitely instances of what we may call provisionally the play of intelligence within instinct. I have taken the solitary wasps because their case is typical. There is no doubt of the instinctive character of their plan of action. They can have no " education " from parents, and practically none from one another. Moreover, in many instances their action, otherwise so intelligent, becomes strangely blind. Indeed, some of the strongest instances of " mechanical " instinct may be drawn from this very field. It is among the Hymenoptera, and especially among bees and wasps, that we find instincts most wonderfully plastic in their adaptability on one side, and most strangely stupid in mechanical persistence on another. Some such examples have already been quoted.[2] Many may be added from Mr. and Mrs. Peckham's work. Both among the wood-boxing and mud-dauber wasps they find frequent cases of

point of going to the obstruction and actually freeing the thread. In this instance the yarn was released, but in others it held fast and there remained when the nest was completed " (*J.A.B.* . p. 348). With this he compares the behaviour of birds endeavouring to carry into their nest-boxes straws or twigs which were too long—behaviour like that of a dog trying to carry a stick through a fence, the object being shoved backwards and forwards in the mouth until held in a certain position when it can be pushed through. In the case of a pair of house wrens the male was an adept in slipping the bill to one end of the twigs and the mate soon acquired the habit from him (p. 371).        [1] P. 235.
     [2] Those of the Chalicodoma grub, pp. 55, 56, and the Bembex, p. 56.

the nest being carefully made and sealed up—empty![1]  A single fact of this kind is enough to wreck the suggestion that the nest-building of the wasp is a fully intelligent process as we understand intelligence. If, again, a wasp understood that her business was to store a nest with food, she would hardly reject a suitable insect when she finds one ready to hand. But there are many such instances. Having, for example, dropped a beetle in her disturbance at being watched, a wasp let it lie for three days close by her web without picking it up again.[2]  The behaviour of others was still more irrational.

"While Cerceris was away hunting, some dry sand was thrown into the nest and the entrance was then stopped with damp sand. She returned laden with prey, and seeing herself forced to resume the profession of a miner, abandoned her victim, cleared the entrance, penetrated within, came out again, and flew off in search of new prey. After two successive trips she penetrated a third time into her dwelling and began to reject the dry sand which had been thrown in. In the midst of this sand was a bee. It was evident that in one of the trips that we had seen her make she could not reach directly to the cell which she was provisioning and dropped the victim at the place where she had to stop. Presently the wasp flew away. The hours passed on, and she returned without a bee, entered, and threw out the other one which she now considered an encumbering object. Thus of two victims which were procured with great trouble, one was abandoned on the threshold, and the other was dropped half way in—neither served as food for larvae. What of that? Cerceris had given the sting—that was enough.

"At another time a nest, one of the cells of which was not entirely provisioned, was destroyed at evening. On the next morning Cerceris brought a newly stung bee and placed it in the hole. On the following day she came again, charged with prey, and dropped her bee, which rolled to the bottom of the excavation. She had not brought the full number for provisioning the nest. Instinct commanded her to bring them, and she obeyed, but not knowing where to put them, let them fall."[3]

Such cases bring us back by a sharp turn to the conception of instinct as a mechanism that must run down in its own way. So does the following. A specimen of *P. marginatus* is seen dragging a small spider along.

[1] P. 84.        [2] *Ib.* p. 114.        [3] P. 209.

"The spider was so small that she held it in her mandibles well above the ground, and we only speak of her as dragging it because she walked backward and acted as though she were obliged to exert herself. Quite often the spiders taken by this species are too large to be carried, and then it is necessary to drag them, and this habit is so ingrained that, when it would be much more convenient to go straight ahead, they stick to the ancient custom, and seem unable to move in any other way." [1]

We may perhaps best understand this behaviour if we compare it with our own little foibles. We all have our own way of doing things, and though our reason may tell us that somebody else's way is better, still we like our own. The basis of this liking is a kind of structure—which we may indifferently call mental or cerebral—built up by past actions. The structure once formed, we find satisfaction in its exercise, and a certain dissatisfaction in anything which excites the structure without bringing it into full exercise, e.g., when we do the same thing, but are made to do it in a different way. So it is with the wasp. It wants to act in its own way, but we cannot infer that it is wholly unaware of what it is doing, or in all respects incapable of guiding its actions.

9. Still, this contrast of dull and often wholly irrational uniformity with highly adaptive contrivances remains the most remarkable feature of insect psychology. Is the dung-beetle wonderfully intelligent, or crassly mechanical? Reading of its powers of co-operation—how one beetle will push another's ball for him and so on—one is ready to exclaim in wonder at this high development alike of intelligence and social feeling. Reading again of their habit at breeding time of rolling any small balls, even if made of wood or stone,[2] one is ready to swing to the opposite extreme, and to explain what before appeared as co-operation as due to the lack of discrimination enough to distinguish between one pellet and another. But then, again, what is one to think when a good observer describes such a beetle getting out of a difficulty in a manner one can hardly conceive of as provided for by heredity? Mr. Lloyd Morgan tells us of a beetle getting his ball into a

[1] P. 146.          [2] Schneider, p. 187.

hollow, and finding the sides too steep to roll it up, whereupon

"leaving the ball he butted down the sand at one side of the hollow so as to produce an inclined plane of much less angle." [1]

Once again, the beetle's nervous system seems to be lifted out of the class of hereditary mechanisms.

Of the many contrasts that might be quoted from the bee world I will give only one, where the power of adaptation and the tendency to mechanical persistence are illustrated in a single case.

"Fritz Müller has recorded a singular case bearing on the instinct of these social Insects. He says that a nest of a small Trigona was built in a hollow tree, and that as a consequence of the irregularity of the hole the bees were obliged to give a very irregular shape to their combs of honey. These bees were captured and put in a spacious box (presumably together with the irregular comb, but this he unfortunately does not mention): after a year, 'when perhaps not a single bee survived of those which had come from the canella tree,' they still continued to build irregular combs, though quite regular combs were built by several communities of the same species that he had kept." [2]

Though the bees are not so dominated by mechanism but that they can, at need, adapt their building to the required space, the strength of inertia is still such that the very modification once acquired tends to go on of itself.

Had we been concerned to disprove that wasps have an intelligent conception of their whole plan of operations for feeding their young, we might have quoted the numerous cases in which they tolerate, or even feed, parasites, which live upon the food which they store up for their own grubs. But we may quote one even stronger case from among ants, whose power of adaptive modification far exceeds that of any other insect. Every one knows the tender care which ants bestow upon their larvae. Yet they freely tolerate in their nest the Lomechusa beetle, the larva of which eats their cherished young. It is as though we bred and tended cattle which habitually devoured our children. Does any one say that this proves the nursing of larvae to

---

[1] *Animal Life and Intelligence*, p. 368.
[2] *Cambridge Natural History*, VI. p. 64.

be wholly blind? If so, let him mark what follows. The ants not merely tolerate the Lomechusa, but actively tend its larvæ, on the same methods by which they nurse their own. Now, it happens the nursing suited to an ant larva is fatal to a Lomechusa larva, and in course of time the ants appear to find this out, and modify their whole system of nursing.[1]

Difficult as it is to conceive the psychological conditions under which such contrasts are possible, we may still get some help from the analogy of human action. When comparative psychologists take occasional inconsistency as proving the utter absence of intelligence they are using an argument which would equally disprove the existence of intelligence in man. After all, is an ant nourishing parasites that destroy its young guilty of a greater absurdity than, say, a mother promoting her daughter's happiness by selling her to a rich husband, or an inquisitor burning a heretic in the name of Christian charity, or an Emperor forbidding his troops to give quarter in the name of civilisation? The mother really desires her daughter's happiness, but her conception of the means thereto is confused, and rendered self-contradictory by worldly ambitions. The

---

[1] Wasmann, *S. d. A.*, pp. 125-8. He says that the modified system is applied to the ant larvæ as well, producing as a result many pseudo-females instead of mere neuters.

Wasmann thinks the whole proceeding an insoluble problem for the theory of animal intelligence and morality, and sees in it an illustration of the Divine wisdom that maintains the equilibrium in nature. Whether it is a conceivable attribute of a Divine wisdom so to make its creatures that they can only be preserved by destroying each other is a problem which Dr. Wasmann does not raise. One may ask whether such a wisdom, though supposed to be infinite, is not more self-contradictory than the limited intelligence that may be attributed to ants. That a limited intelligence should exhibit contradictions in its different processes is not surprising, and it is the chief defect of Dr. Wasmann's book that he overlooks this point. In the present case, for example, he attributes the modification of nursing methods by the ants to "sense knowledge," but refuses the name of intelligence, because Intelligence, he says, would teach the ants that the better they nurse the Lomechusæ, the more certainly their nest will perish. That depends on the degree of intelligence. There may be intelligence enough to grasp simple and immediate results that does not extend to wider or more remote results. Be that as it may, the intelligence of the ants appears equal, on Wasmann's own showing, to defeating the manœuvres of the "Divine wisdom." The truth is that the whole proceeding illustrates, not merely limitation of intelligence, but, still more, perversion of instinct, disregard for the young, otherwise so carefully tended.

inquisitor's conception of Christian charity is similarly corrupted by the subtle corporate egoism of a Church and the
cruel pedantry of bad theology. Even the Emperor has
some conception of civilisation, but it is the civilisation of
militarism. In all cases there impinge on the avowed plan
of action conflicting impulses of a kind not to stop the
course of action, but to merge in it and distort it. Speaking generally, man is only in part conscious of his own
purposes in their real meaning and value. It is his own
nature—of which, after all, he only knows the surface—
which sets him his purpose, and impels him to carry it out.
Hence, between the course in which his own character is
driving him and the end which he recognises and formulates to himself, there is room for wide discrepancy. Now,
if we imagine this original structure more elaborately
worked out in its details, so as to dominate action more
completely, and the sphere of intelligence reduced, so as to
grasp ends less adequately, we seem to approach a condition
realised in those instincts which admit some play of intelligence within their sphere. To reach "pure instinct"
we have only to conceive the sphere of intelligence gradually reduced to zero, while the original mechanism is further
elaborated so as to provide for each separate response to
each new phase of a normal situation.

There is a further point. The psychologist is apt to
characterise an instinct by what he knows of its function
in the life of the species, and either to attribute to the
animal the purpose of fulfilling that function or to deny
it all intelligent purpose whatever. Thus, at first blush,
the neglect of parasites by the wasp, or the sealing of an
empty nest, seems to reduce all the other care and trouble
which the insect shows to a piece of meaningless stupidity,
which we can only explain by referring it to an elaborate
but blindly working mechanism. But here, again, the
human parallel should help us. To the evolutionist, the
youth courting the maid is merely obeying an impulse
cunningly contrived by Nature for the preservation of the
species. But suppose the courting fails, and in the end the
youth dies an old bachelor for the sake of his only love,
what become's of Nature's cunning contrivance? The
youth, so far as his conscious interests go, has nothing to

do with Nature's purposes. Her plans are not his. Yet he has plans and purposes of his own, none the less intelligent because they do not wholly fit in with what Nature, with the approval of the evolutionist, has planned for him. The relation is rather that our personified Nature has a plan into which she inveigles the youth. He never sees more than the next step, but the plan is so cunningly contrived that, as he takes that step, the next again comes into view, and he feels himself attracted or, it may be, driven towards it. So it is also with the solitary wasp. We cannot, for reasons given, attribute to her true understanding of her performances as the evolutionist understands them, but we must think of her as led on by her impulses and the stimulus of outer things, to dig a hole, to catch and sting caterpillars and spiders, to drag them to her hole, to store it, lay her egg, seal it up, depart and begin anew. Each stage, we may think, is to her as attractive or inevitable as the course of courtship and marriage to the youth.

10. The difference would seem to be this. A well developed instinct determines a long course of action. The more it becomes suffused with intelligence, the greater the proportion of the whole course which may be grasped as a conscious purpose. In " pure " instinct, each stage by passing brings on the next, and the instinct must run through its course by a prescribed series of stages or not at all.[1] It cannot, outside narrow limits, adopt alternatives. Intelligence, on the other hand, grasping the ultimate aim, is indifferent as to the method by which it is reached. Thus as intelligence rises, the fixed processes of instinct dissolve. But intelligence does not spring into being fully armed from the head of Zeus. It is born within the sphere of instinct, and at first grasps only a little bit of what instinct prompts. It apprehends, say, the next stage, and, ordinary means failing, guides some special effort to reach that stage, the next stage, not the ultimate end, being the purpose understood and realised by the animal. It is easy to see how from this point it may develop, taking remoter stages or ends into account, until

---

[1] This is to be read with the qualifications given above as distinguishing pure instinct from the compound reflex.

it grasps the final purpose and meaning of conduct. Clearly also, as this development proceeds, the need for detailed determination of response by heredity disappears.

We may perhaps make the matter clearer by symbolising the whole process somewhat in this fashion. Let A be the beginning and z the final purpose of a life process. Pure instinct proceeds from A to z through a uniform series of stages B, C, D, &c. If the conditions for any one of these fail, the instinct is wrecked. Fully adequate intelligence makes z its goal from the beginning, and is indifferent whether it reaches it through B, C, D, or through any other intermediaries, b, c, d, $\beta$, $\gamma$, $\delta$. Nascent intelligence acting " within the instinct " grasps a proximate end—e.g., at the stage A it aims at c, and if the conditions leading to B are not present, may substitute $\beta$ ; or, it may be, the stage B, except as a means to c, drops out altogether. As intelligence develops, remoter stages become direct objects of action, the means cease to be prescribed by hereditary tendency, and instead are chosen with increasing freedom from the possibilities present.[1]

At this stage the impulse to do a certain thing is fixed by heredity, but the means of doing it are not so fixed, but are in part or altogether left to the individual to find out for himself. On this basis it appears at once that the conception of instinct becomes very elastic. The thing to be done may be something which only requires one step to effect it. If so, it is but one degree removed from the reflex response. Or it may be very remote, and a number of steps must be devised to work it out. Or, lastly, it may be of a general character, and then the circumstances of the individual may not only determine the means, but may give its whole concrete filling to the end itself. Thus in man the desire to marry is based on an instinct, but the love of one woman is based on

[1] To put the same idea in more popular fashion, we may say that the youth's consciousness when he first goes courting, is to be expressed, not in the form, " I want a wife and family," but in the words, " I must just see her to-day." Similarly, attributing language to the wasp struggling with the spider, we must suppose her to say to herself, not " If I don't give it this spider my grub when it hatches will starve," but, " I must get this spider into this hole"; and if you asked her why, the mere gift of language alone would not enable her to tell you.

circumstances peculiar to the individual. Broadly speaking, it is in the last two forms that instinct remains important in the life of man, as laying down a scheme of life to which experience supplies the concrete filling, and as positing ends to which intelligence supplies the series of intermediate steps.

To sum up. There may be much plasticity of instinct without intelligence, but the fact that instinct is an abiding state of the organism related to an end that may be remote, and that the behaviour which it dictates is from the first determined by complex conditions, and not by a single stimulus, makes possible those more individual and original adjustments of means to ends which we call Intelligent. Intelligence, if this view is correct, arises within the sphere of instinct ; indeed, we can draw no sharp and certain line between them in nature. Yet in idea they are quite distinct. In so far as an act is instinctive, it is not intelligent, and conversely. We will not here try to determine the point at which intelligence first arises in the animal world, but we may say that so far as action is based upon hereditary modes of response, or the composition of such responses, it remains pure instinct. When, on the other hand, means are devised by the individual on the basis of its own experience for compassing the ultimate or proximate ends to which it is impelled, a new principle appears which we identify provisionally with intelligence. At first narrowly limited in scope, intelligence deals with proximate ends. As it expands, it comes to embrace the remoter and at length the ultimate end to which action is directed. Along with this advance the power of choosing the means best suited to the purpose expands, and the determination of successive stages of action by hereditary structure simultaneously disappears. Thus, whether involving intelligence or not, instinct is the abiding state directing action to the attainment of certain results, but if it is pure instinct the actions are all reflex or sensori-motor. They are modified and directed without prevision of results by the interest which forms the abiding state. Modification of hereditary action not thus explicable must be referred to the assistance given to instinct by a nascent intelligence. Where there is no prevision of the end we must suppose the interest to shift as the instinct proceeds through its stages. While the wasp is boring her hole she is wound up to bore. She will get over obstacles in the boring process, but nothing else will interest her. When she has finished, the egg-laying impulse supervenes, and when that has done its work, there follows, we may suppose, the impulse to fly out and explore. Exploring she sees a caterpillar and there follows the interest in stinging, seizing, bearing it back, and finally getting it into the hole. This concatenation of inward states, not wholly self-determined but related also to the outward and in particular to what has already been done, is a special characteristic of the more elaborate instincts and distinguishes them from the simple sensori-motor act, for in the sensori-motor act there is an adjustment which relieves the tension of the moment, but in the instinct there is this further adjustment that the only thing which will relieve the tension at any given moment is the act which, under the circumstances, is required to serve the ultimate result. The study of instincts reveals that a complex adjustment of this sort is possible without foresight of the ultimate end. Where there is such foresight, the tension involved in purposive effort itself secures the corresponding adjustment of interest and conation at every stage.

11. *Human Instinct and the hereditary element.*

Instinct, as involving sensori-motor action as a unit, lies within the limits in which we use the term consciousness. This alone differentiates it fundamentally from the reflex which does not involve consciousness. It is true that reflexes may supply a sensation to consciousness, as in the case of coughing, but the sensation is in no way essential to their performance. Of many reflexes or internally determined acts such as breathing we are not normally aware. If consciousness interferes with them at all it is more likely to be for the inhibition of the reflex than for any other purpose. But though reflex behaviour thus stands outside consciousness, there are elements of consciousness which themselves almost appear as reflex states. The sudden anger which one feels on being thwarted arises without reflection or any complexity of adjustment. It is a response which though conscious seems to come about mechanically. In popular language we use the term instinctive to describe it, but I am not sure that we do not pay it too much honour. I doubt if it reaches the instinctive level. Nor are emotional impulses the only acts of this class. On the contrary, all sensation is the conscious accompaniment of a response to stimulus by the nerve structure. I see, not merely because the image of an object is cast upon my retina, but because optic nerve and brain react to that stimulus in a particular way. Experience, of course, rapidly acquires a share in modelling sensation, but there seems no reason to deny that "crude sensations," representing the reaction of the inherited structure as such to the appropriate excitement, contribute at least one element to our complex consciousness.

We find, then, a certain raw material of our conscious life, which arises in direct and uncomplicated response, determined by the hereditary structure, to outward objects, or from physical changes of the internal structure. Furthermore, heredity lays the foundation of our entire mental life. We inherit not only capacities for sensation and emotion, but also capacities for distinguishing, analysing and combining them. We have opposed intelligence as the work of the individual to instinct as the product of heredity, but intelligence as a capacity is also hereditary. The propensity to inquire, and the methods of analysing and comparing used in inquiry, all have a foundation in the hereditary structure. It is what we do with these materials and these tools that is our own. It is the product that is the work of the individual, not the means by which he makes it. He may, indeed, in the course of the operation, deal with the means themselves, polishing the instruments with which nature furnished him, or even combining them to build up some more subtle organ. But throughout he is working upon and with the hereditary endowment. We cannot, therefore, in classifying the works of the mind place heredity and acquirement in two perfectly separate portions. Our division is analytical. It is a separation of functions which in working are combined, and an attempt in resolving a joint product to assign to each what is its due. This must be borne in mind in any attempt to estimate the part played by instinct in human life. The older psychology expressed the contrast between the human and the animal mind in terms of the opposition between intelligence and instinct. Recent psychology has emphasised the part of instinct in human nature. But to begin with, it must be clear that in human nature there is very little that is pure instinct. Man is always capable of reflection. Even if instinct sets him the aim he can appreciate it, distinguish what is essential from what is indifferent, and vary the means that he uses indefinitely. Nor is this all. As a rational being he is capable of criticising the instinctive interest, if such we are to call it, itself. He brings it in relation to his life as a whole and to the lives of other people. It is modified by the social atmosphere in which he grows up. It takes its particular shape from the traditions of his society, his class, his school, his family. It never governs him as long as he remains mentally and morally sane, but is merged in that moral organism of many inter-acting parts which is called the self. Not only the separate parts but the characteristic unity of each individual—what used to be called the temperament—that by which the several elements are interfused—is part of the hereditary structure, though, like everything else that is inherited, it grows under the plastic hand of experience. Nor is the behaviour determined by the kind of interests popularly called instinctive specifically defined and fixed, prior to experience, apart from a few exceptional elements. The range of behaviour determined by what is loosely called the sexual instinct, for example, is of extreme width. It may be said to cover the frenzy of physical passion, the romantic devotion which would lead a man to risk his neck for a girl, equally with the expansion or possibly the reserve provoked by contact with the other sex, or the deference and attention which social tradition, acting upon some innate tendency, has developed. In relation to

behaviour, not only in externals but even in such fundamental matters as the occasions for jealousy, the rôle of
social tradition is a preponderant influence. A savage
who would kill his wife for unpermitted license will lend
her cheerfully to a guest. We cannot attribute to the
uniform operation of an instinct conduct which may vary
from the extreme of licentiousness to the pattern of faithful
continence, or from the extravagance of devotion to a girl
to the courtesy which leads a man to open the door for
her grandmother. We have here human nature acting as
a whole in all its varied capacities, that run the gamut
from the bestial to the heroic. What is hereditary in
man is capacity, propensity, disposition,[1] but the capacities
are filled in, the propensities encouraged or checked, the
dispositions inhibited or developed by mutual interactions and the pervading influence of the circumambient
atmosphere. Elements of true instinct remain, but in a
state of dilapidation. Heredity does not operate by itself
in human nature, but everywhere in interaction with
capacity to assimilate, to foresee, and to control.[2]

To sum up, instinct is an enduring interest determined
by heredity and directing action to results of importance to

[1] This term has been suggested by Mr. Graham Wallas in "The Great
Society."

[2] In particular I see no reason for identifying instinct as it exists in man
with certain primary emotions. To begin with, I am by no means clear
that emotion is at the root of all conation. On the contrary, emotion
appears to me to be that form of feeling which arises when conation is
obstructed or when there is an overplus of excitement which action does
not satisfy. Further, as Mr. Wallas has cogently argued, the intellectual
processes have quite as much title to be founded on instinct, if the term is
to be used of all inherited propensity, as any other. Thirdly, as indicated in
the text, the emotions belonging, say, to the sex instinct are not simple but
indefinitely various. And, lastly, I see no appropriateness in using the
term instinct, which in the animal world we apply to a definite train of
acts, in relation to a state of consciousness which does not necessarily
arise in response to a particular class of object, nor necessarily promote
any particular train of acts. But the main question is whether the
fundamental elements of human nature are of the nature of separate
units which inter-act like independent powers, or whether what is
inherited is an abstraction and what is acquired another abstraction, the
two together forming the concrete whole of actual behaviour. In the
main I believe the latter account to be true of human nature, the former
to be true of the lowest and partly true of the higher animals, and it is
this increasing unity of the organism as a whole which I take to be one
of the distinguishing marks of the human as compared with the animal
mind.

the organism without clear prevision of those results. Pure instinct is an interest so controlling internally determined activities reflexes, and sensori-motor actions. A single sensori-motor act would fall within the limits of the definition only if the interest prompting it were hereditary and enduring. In point of fact, all instincts of any high degree of development involve a combination of many such acts. Instincts may also be served by intelligence, in which case we do not speak of them as pure, but at the point at which intelligence is able to grasp the entire trend of action, to foresee the end, and determine the means freely without reference to any hereditary propensity to a specific form of approach, we pass out of the region of instinct and enter that of intelligent purpose.

# CHAPTER VII

## ASSIMILATION AND READJUSTMENT[1]

1. UNDER the names of reflex action and instinct we have dealt with one method by which animal organisms adjust their actions to suit their needs. This adjustment, as we have seen, rests in a sense upon the correlation of the experiences of the race. For if instinct is based upon heredity, and heredity conditioned by natural selection, the growth of an instinctive tendency is determined by the aid which it gives in preserving the race. From the germ of an instinct onward, those individuals in which it is more vigorous or more advanced have an advantage in the struggle for existence over others, and thus in accordance with the current theories of the origin of species, an instinct attains its perfect development. The same thing may be said of reflex action, and of all that part of animal behaviour which depends directly upon the response of hereditary structure to stimulus. Thus by the action of purely biological causes a correlation is effected between the past experiences and the subsequent behaviour of a species, whereby action is adapted to circumstances, as the conditions of race-maintenance require.

But, as we saw in Chapter I., this is not the only nor the most efficient form of correlation between experience and action. Throughout the greater part if not the whole

---

[1] In this chapter I am largely indebted to Dr. Ward's articles on Assimilation and Association in *Mind* (*N.S.*, Vols. II. and III.). The corresponding portions of Mr. Stout's *Manual of Psychology*, which unfortunately I had not seen when the chapter was written, contain a clear and cogent statement of views which are, in the main, the same as those expressed below.

of the animal kingdom, the individual organism has a
certain power, greater or less as the case may be, of
effecting a similar correlation within its own lifetime.    It
does not come into existence with all its actions predetermined in every detail by inherited structure, for we find
its behaviour modified as its life advances.    We have seen
that a measure of such modification arises within the
sphere of " pure instinct."    But to complete our account
of instinct we were forced to take notice of certain more
thorough-going modifications which could not be explained
in the same way.    Such modifications we referred provisionally to intelligence, meaning by intelligence the
power of an organism to adapt action to requirement
on the basis of its own experience.    We have now to ask
what proof there is that any given adjustment is thus
discovered, so to say, by the individual, and is not merely
some subtler or less usual device of heredity.    The broad
answer to this question is that modification in accordance
with the results of experience must be our main criterion.
When we find an animal, for example, first acting in one
way, and then, after experience of results, acting in
another, we must ascribe the change to the effect of its
experience.    The modified action is not hereditary ; it
arises in and out of the experience of the animal, and
indicates that in some degree the animal can correlate its
own past experiences with its subsequent action.    In this
correlation we have already found the generic essence of
intelligence, and our task will now be to describe the form
in which it first appears, and then to trace its further
evolution.    In the growth of this power of correlation
lies the evolution of Mind.

2.    *Experience and inference.*

Physiologically considered, the effects of experience
upon behaviour form a special case of organic adaptability.
But it may be remarked here once for all that when we
speak of experience we shall mean a special kind of
experience and a special case of organic adaptability.
Wherever after a certain experience the organism adapts
itself better to a certain sort of stimulus, it has undoubtedly been modified by its experience, but it has not

necessarily learnt anything by experience of results. Thus any organism, from Protozoa to man, is likely to tolerate unusual heat or cold better after a certain amount of exposure to it than at first.[1] But we do not tolerate extreme heat better because we have found its effects to be beneficial. The exposure puts a certain strain on the organism. If the organism responds to the strain, and does not sink under it, it is able to bear a similar strain better a second time. We are not, without further evidence, warranted in attributing such a change to experience of the results of such a response. For it is part of the general law of organic adaptability that a thing done once is more easily done a second time, and a thing suffered once is, if recovery is complete, more easily suffered a second time. So far as this law applies, the organism is modified not by experience of the consequences of what it does, but by the doing itself. Many of the effects of practice and exercise seem to be referable to the direct influence, as we may call it, of experience. Thus, as we have seen, many reflexes are more or less imperfect at birth, and are improved by practice. But it does not follow that the improvement is due to experience of the results of the reflex. In any exercise involving strength in a particular muscle we improve with practice because the muscle itself grows stronger, and it grows stronger, not because we find that it is better so, but through a reflex arrangement by which exercise increases its blood supply, that is to say, secures it more nourishment.[2] In the same way there is every probability that a reflex mechanism improves not only through the confirmation of well adapted actions and the inhibition of others, but also because usage makes the different parts work better together. In learning to ride a bicycle, we are told to turn to the side towards which we are beginning to fall. We do this at first consciously and awkwardly. By degrees we respond at once more rapidly and more gently

[1] For adaptation of this sort among Protozoa see Verworn, *Prot. St.*; for Flagellata, p. 42 ; Stentor, p. 72, &c.

[2] This is, of course, a result of the exercise, but it is not through learning that this result follows that we modify our use of the limb, but the result itself is such as to give us an improved limb.

to the stimulus, and in this way we soon, or late, learn to balance without perceptible oscillation or conscious effort.  The improvement is, doubtless, largely due to the confirmation of more and inhibition of less successful responses.  But it would seem that something must also be set down to the readier appreciation and more perfect conduction of the excitement by the nerves—their more perfect control of the muscles.  At any rate, this explanation has to be taken into account wherever we have to deal with an action which is the same in general character and apparent purpose from the beginning, and merely improves with practice in its execution.  It probably explains the slowly acquired mastery of its reflexes by a young child, and the rapidly growing perfection of pecking by a newly hatched chick.[1]   And I should be inclined to apply it to most of the many human accomplishments in which what one is definitely taught bears but a small proportion to what muscles, nerves, and nerve centres have to learn in the way of execution.

But there are other cases in which action is not merely improved in execution, but profoundly modified in character by experience.  We may say that it is re-directed.  And in these cases we can point to the results of the act as the operative cause.  The burnt child that dreads the fire does not grasp at the flame more efficiently, but refrains from grasping at all.  The direction or aim of the action is reversed, and reversed, as we know, in consequence of its result when tried.  It is because the child has modified its behaviour in consequence of a relation experienced between act and consequent, that its conduct has been taken as the type of experience acting as the basis of rational conduct.  The unit of reasoning is a relation of datum and consequence, whether the act of reasoning be merely to apply the knowledge of the relation in a fresh case, or to use it as a brick in building up some more complex mental structure.  There are vast differences between the ways in which this relation is grasped and used by minds of different order, but the relation

[1] See Lloyd Morgan, *Habit and Instinct*, p. 36.  See also Preyer, I. p. 236, and Thorndike, *Psych. Review*, Vol. VI. pp. 284 *et seq.*

itself seems to be the pivot of all inference. It is through this relation that an object of experience points the mind to something beyond itself. Hence any action resting implicitly or explicitly on an experienced relation between datum and consequence may be said to be of the inferential type. Such a " relation " may be " experienced," as we shall see, in very different forms and in very different degrees of explicitness, but we ought not, as I think, to exclude from the type any action based on an experience into which, however inarticulately, such a relation enters as an essential element. I should say, then, that when we experience a certain result as flowing from a certain line of conduct, and modify our behaviour accordingly, we are drawing a simple inference. Action of this kind is of the *inferential type*, and is in line with the general development of intelligence. When, on the other hand, we bear heat or pain better merely because we have borne a good deal already, it is not our conscious intelligence that is directing our conduct in accordance with experienced results, but the heat or pain which have had a physical effect on us that has left a permanent trace. When I speak of experience, then, I mean experience of the kind on which inference is founded, and that is, to speak generally, experience of data in relation.

3. *Primary Retentiveness.*

When an inference is based on a past experience it is clear that the effects of that experience must in some way or other endure, or, in the ordinary phrase, be retained by the organism. Needless to say, it is not the experience itself which is retained. That is a temporary state, an event which happens once and passes. What is retained is some result manifesting itself in the subsequent life of the organism. Nor is this result necessarily a memory of the past experience. Memory is a form of retentiveness, but not all retentiveness is memory. The result may show itself simply in some modification of future be- haviour, and among such modifications are inferences, or modified responses which look like inferences, based on results that have at some previous time been experienced. But there are forms of retentiveness which neither involve memory nor inference, but are even simpler and more direct in their operation. When we look attentively at an object—a flower, for example—several features emerge successively into our consciousness—the shape, the colour, the petals, and so on—and the result of each earlier stage of perception endures, qualifying and enriching the latter stages, so that at the end the whole character of the object is more fully and clearly appreciated than at first. The utterance of the concluding words of a verse carries with it a penumbra of sound and meaning attaching to the verse as a whole. This atmosphere that surrounds a later perception has been termed its meaning, and, so far as it is due to the result of earlier perceptions, has been ascribed to primary retentiveness.[1] In very simple forms of behaviour this primary retentiveness persists beyond the moment of sense perception, and has an effect in directing and modifying instinctive response. For example, in the case of the crab stalking the sandhopper, quoted above, the hunting impulses of the crab are concentrated for the moment upon this particular sandhopper. They persist while the crab buries itself, and prompt its subsequent approach and leap upon the prey. Schneider[2] describes a turtle hunting for a hermit crab, which had taken refuge between some big stones, and regards this as proving the existence of an idea of the crab in the mind of the turtle, but all that the behaviour of the turtle actually implies is that the perception of the prey maintains its influence after it has passed. It causes the same sort of efforts to get at the victim as would be put forward were the victim still in sight. Similarly, the particular spot chosen as a resting place or home must be admitted to influence the animal which returns to it, although the home is no longer in sight. The snail, after it has eaten and is well filled, returns along its trail to rest in the corner that it has already found secure and comfortable. The instinct to return is of course directed by the particular place which serves as home for the time being. These seem to be the most elementary cases in which an experience has a certain after-

---

[1] Stout, *Manual of Psychology*, Book I. chap. 3, pp. 169–184.
[2] *Tierische Wille*, p. 312.

effect in directing or refining impulse. In some such cases
we may have to do with experience of results, but in the
main they appear to be instances of primary retentiveness.

4. *Assimilation.*

In human beings, the operation of experience in
simple form is seen when impulsive, reflex or random
actions are modified by the pleasure or pain immediately
resulting. But this operation of experience is, to all outward appearance, as familiar among animals as among men.
The burnt puppy, as some one has said, dreads the fire as
much as the burnt child. Is it making an assumption to
say that both dread it for the same reason—namely, that
both feel ? If it is an assumption, we must make it provisionally, for the sake of compendiously describing the
simplest cases of the action of experience. After a preliminary description, we may refer to our assumption again.

Experience does not, it must be remembered, arise in a
vacuum. The senses do not furnish a dark room. On the
contrary, experience begins to operate on organisms that
have already certain tendencies to act, and its first effect is
to modify those tendencies. We find this effect in two
related but still clearly distinguishable forms :

(*a*) *Selective modification.*

Animals of very low organisation possess, as we have
seen, certain type reactions, with which they often
appear to respond mechanically to a given stimulus.
But in certain instances it is found that they have more
than one type reaction to which the same stimulus may
give rise, and if one fails the other is tried until success
is obtained. Thus a stentor stimulated with carmine
will bend aside, and, if it does not succeed in ridding
itself of the annoyance, will reverse the movement of its
cilia. If this too fails it will contract strongly upon its
stalk, and finally uproot itself and swim away.[1] This
is one of those cases of persistent effort to avoid discomfort which have already been discussed. Something more than reflex action is in question here, because
different methods are tried until the result is secured,
but what follows is the point of importance for our

[1] Jennings, p. 176.

1

present purpose. When the stentor anchors itself again, it has apparently learnt something, for if again touched it does not bend aside, but at once contracts and finally moves off. It prefers the remedy previously found successful. The effect very soon wears off, but none the less we see here, clearly marked, the germ of that kind of retentiveness which brings the experience of past results to bear upon present action, in such a way as to secure similar results a second time. We should observe exactly what is learnt. The stentor does not discover that it should avoid some object or seek some object. What it discovers is that one method of avoiding is more fruitful than another. It learns to prefer the most effective of three type reactions. Among ourselves selection of this type is prominent in the acquisition by practice of skill of all sorts, though not so much in the selection of one type of action in preference to another, as rather in the precise adjustment of the magnitude and direction of the method, which at first is made clumsily and needs refining. As we learn to balance on a bicycle or on skates, we begin with rough attempts under the direction of a teacher. These are conscious and purposive, but they land us continually in failures through excess or defect. We swerve not enough, or too much, and experience bumps on this side or on that in consequence. These experiences have a gradual effect upon our movements, checking the excess, and super-exciting what is defective until we arrive at the mean. It is to be noted, as bearing on the psychological factors involved in acquisitions of this kind, that with us, although the end itself is purposive, and the grosser movements are clearly present to consciousness, the method of adjustment escapes our consciousness. We learn in the end without knowing how, and the processes of inhibition and encouragement go on somehow below the conscious level.

(b) *Confirmation and inhibition.*

So far we have had actions confirmed or inhibited according as they succeeded or failed in securing a constant result. We pass to cases in which the direction of the response is itself modified by the result, in which, that is to say, an object to which we begin by reacting in a certain fashion, which we may call positive, yields some further stimulus which checks that reaction, and in which this effect persists so that we no longer react positively to an object of the same kind. With these we may class, conversely, cases in which an object, to which we are at first indifferent, becomes, as the result of experience, a stimulus to reaction, which is confirmed every time it is repeated. This operation of experience, in its simplest and also its completest form, is beautifully illustrated by Mr. Lloyd Morgan's observations on young chickens.

"With regard to the objects at which domestic chicks peck, in the absence of any parental guidance, one may say that they strike at first with perfect impartiality at *anything* of suitable size : grain, small stones, bread-crumbs, chopped-up wax matches, currants, bits of paper, buttons, beads, cigarette-ash and ends, their own toes and those of their companions, maggots, bits of thread, specks on the floor, their neighbours' eyes—anything and everything, not too large, that can or cannot be seized is pecked at, and, if possible, tested in the bill. . . . There does not seem to be any congenital discrimination between nutritious and innutritious objects, or between those which are nice and those which are nasty. This is a matter of individual acquisition. They soon learn, however, what is good for eating, and what is unpleasant, and rapidly associate the appearance with the taste. A young chick two days old, for example, had learnt to pick out pieces of yolk from others of white of egg. I cut little bits of orange-peel of about the same size as the pieces of yolk, and one of these was soon seized, but at once relinquished, the chick shaking his head. Seizing another, he held it for a moment in the bill, but then dropped it and scratched at the base of its beak. That was enough ; he could not again be induced to seize a piece of orange-peel. The obnoxious material was now removed, and pieces of yolk of egg substituted, but they were left untouched, being probably taken for orange-peel. Subsequently, he looked at the yolk with hesitation, but presently pecked doubtfully, not seizing, but merely touching. Then he pecked again, seized, and swallowed.

"To some other chicks I threw cinnabar larvæ, distasteful caterpillars, conspicuous by alternate rings of black and golden-yellow. They were seized at once, but dropped uninjured ; the chicks wiped their bills—a sign of distaste—and seldom touched the caterpillars a second time. The cinnabar larvæ were then removed, and thrown in again towards the close of the day. Some of the chicks tried them once, but they were soon left. The next day the young birds were given brown loopers and green cabbage-moth caterpillars. These were approached with some suspicion, but presently one chick ran off with a looper, and was followed by others, one of which stole and ate it. In a few minutes all the caterpillars were cleared off. Later in the day they were given some more of these edible caterpillars, which were eaten freely ; and then some cinnabar larvæ. One chick ran, but checked himself, and, without touching the caterpillar, wiped his bill—a memory of the nasty taste being apparently suggested by association at sight of the yellow-and-black caterpillar. Another seized one, and dropped it at once. A third subsequently approached a cinnabar as it crawled along, gave the danger note, and ran off. Then I threw in more edible caterpillars, which again were eaten freely. The chicks had thus learnt to descriminate by sight between the nice and the nasty caterpillars." [1]

The inference from these observations seems clear enough. The inherited tendency of the chicks is to peck —to peck at "anything and everything, not too large." But experience very rapidly teaches that it is pleasant to peck at some things—such as yolk of egg or cabbage-moth caterpillars—and very unpleasant to peck at others, such as cinnabar caterpillars or bits of orange-peel. The tendency to peck at the one sort of object is accordingly confirmed. The tendency to peck at others is inhibited. And the result is that pecking, from being an indiscriminate tendency, becomes a definite mode of response to certain objects. The instinctive tendency is regulated, narrowed, and defined, as it becomes a habit in which experience has played its part.

This form of the action of experience is very widely diffused in the animal kingdom, and is too simple to need much further illustration. But I may note one or two cases illustrating an important difference in one point. One instance was sometimes enough to teach Mr. Lloyd Morgan's sharp little chicks. But the effect of the experience tends to wear off with time. The chick that had learnt to reject the cinnabar larva at one hour would perhaps try it

---

[1] Lloyd Morgan, *Habit and Instinct*, pp. 40–42.

again later in the day, or perhaps he would make a movement to try it, and then, as we should say of a human
being, recollect himself. More marked cases of this gradual
growth and equally gradual obliteration of the effects of
experience may be seen in other animals. Thus Dahl[1]
gave a spider a fly dipped in turpentine. The spider
sprang upon it three times, and, disliking the turpentine,
withdrew on each occasion. After the third attempt it
turned aside when the fly came in sight. Three instances
sufficed to inhibit the impulse to spring. Nor would the
spider for some hours attack a fly of the same species that
was innocent of turpentine. The next day the spider
attacked the fly in turpentine again, but once only.

Here three experiences were necessary to establish the
result in the first instance, and on the following day the
effect was partially obliterated, so that one instance was
needed to renew it. Every one is familiar with similar
points in the working of human memory—the "fixing" of
a verse by repetition, its fading with time, and its revival
by perhaps a single reading.

It may be worth while to place in contrast with the instances given above a case of extreme stupidity in this
respect. Speaking of a number of fish in an aquarium,
Mr. Bateson says :—

"None of the fish seem to get any lasting appreciation of the
nature of the plate glass wall of the tank. The same fish will
again and again knock its head against the glass in trying to
seize objects moving on the other side."

A dangling button, or even a curl of smoke, may attract
them. After repeated attempts they will desist, but some
of the oldest inhabitants, which have been living in the
aquarium about a year, will try again next time. This
failure is no doubt partly due to dullness of sense perception, but, considering the length of time allowed for
learning, it implies a surprising incapacity for turning experiences to account—a stupidity surpassing even that of
Möbius's pike, which, after dashing itself for three months
against a glass partition in the attempt to get at some
minnows, became at last so firmly persuaded of the danger

[1] *Op. cit.* p. 173.

of attacking them that, when the partition was removed, it left them quite unmolested.

The cases which have been quoted, and which might be indefinitely multiplied, admit of a simple general description. A certain stimulus, in the case of the chick some small object within striking distance, evokes a reaction—in this case pecking. This reaction has a certain result, connected in this case with the swallowing or tasting of the object, and in future the same stimulus evokes a modified reaction. The modification may be in either of two directions. The "result"—the tasting or swallowing—may be to *confirm* the original mode of reaction, so that in one instance that sort of object is in future preferred for pecking at and swallowing to others. This was the case with the yolk of egg and the green caterpillars. Or it may be to prevent or *inhibit* the reaction, as in the case of the orange-peel or the cinnabar larvæ. In either case, we have a sequence of facts which we may symbolise thus :—

| Stimulus | Reaction | Consequence |
|----------|----------|-------------|
| $s$ | $r$ | $p$ |

followed by

| | | |
|----------|----------|-------------|
| $s$ | $\rho$ | $\pi$ |

In this sequence, all the links mentioned but one are matters of direct observation. That one is the consequence which I have called $p$. Now, in our human experience, we have also direct knowledge of $p$. It is in such simple cases as those described a feeling, and if its action is *confirmatory* of the reaction which caused it, it is a pleasant feeling ; if *inhibitory*, a painful feeling. We need not labour this point. The burnt child dreads the fire because it hurts, and continues to steal the sugar with increasing avidity because it is sweet. In the case of the chick we cannot directly observe the feeling. We can, however, be sure that something happens in the place where we have put $p$, otherwise there would be no cause to account for the subsequent change—and the action of this something is precisely analogous to the action of pleasure and pain in human experience.[1]

[1] We feel sure about the child, first, because we know our own feelings, and it is so like ourselves ; and secondly, because it expresses itself in ways which we understand. The chick is not quite so like ourselves,

The analogy may be carried a little further. Confining ourselves for the moment to the action of pain and the case in which a mode of reaction is inhibited, we have to remark that the act of inhibition is of a twofold character. We have spoken already of the subsequent and more or less permanent effect of the painful experience, but this is only a sort of repetition of its immediate effect. If there is time, pain inhibits or arrests the particular action that is causing it. A nasty morsel is spat out from the mouth; the hot potato is dropped before it is well seized. It is the same with the chicks. The orange-peel, the very first time it is seized, is " at once relinquished, the chick shaking his head." Another is held for a moment, and then dropped, the chick scratching "at the base of his beak "— to rub away the taste, as a child would explain. Significant in this relation is the behaviour of another chick, which had already had experience of cinnabar larvæ. When, later in the day, more were given him, he "ran but checked himself, and without touching the caterpillar, wiped his bill." Mr. Lloyd Morgan explains this as due to " a memory of the nasty taste " being " suggested by association at sight

and we do not understand all its expressions so readily. Still, the inference is at bottom the same, and the attribution of feeling to the chick is in conformity with the general principles of method laid down in Chapter II.

Here and elsewhere I use the term " feeling " as the generic expression for every state in so far as it interests the agent. Of such interest two things seem universally true. It is not a detached, so to say self-subsistent, state, but adheres to or inheres in some object, or if the term be preferred, some content. Thus in sensory feeling it is an object of sense which is felt as pleasant or painful. In some experiences, e.g., in internal pain, it is true that the feeling is itself the predominant factor, but even here there is some more or less definite recognisable quality, e.g., a diffused ache or pressure, or a sharp sting which so to say is the subject carrying the pain as predicate, and we approach rather than reach the limit of pure feeling without sensory content. Secondly, feeling is the basis of conation but not the same thing as conation. In the simplest forms the two tend to identity—simple sensory pain, e.g., involving either flinching or efforts of rejection as part of itself, but the feeling as such is not the act as such. It is its immediate basis. Pain, moreover, as I use the term, is always (in the absence of inhibition) the basis of a negative conation. Apparent exceptions arise from the fact that intensity is an essential element in feeling, whence it comes about that some sensations, e.g., those of a prick or a slap, while normally painful may be indifferent or even in certain states of organic tension pleasurable in low degrees of intensity. In these cases the sensory experience has acquired the name of a " pain," and so we hear of pains in which there may be a certain pleasure.

of the yellow and black caterpillar." We may be content to point out that a movement of rejection, a movement adapted to getting rid of a nasty taste, is evoked by the sight of the caterpillar just as it was in the original experience by its presence in the chick's mouth. In the same way, to swallow very disagreeable food may produce in us retching or actual sickness, and if the impression is very strong, the mere sight or even the bare idea of such food may subsequently produce a certain feeling of nausea, or perhaps evoke gestures expressing violent rejection.

The upshot of these considerations is that the pain felt in such cases,[1] is the expression in consciousness[2] of inhibitory movement—withdrawal, shrinking, flight, rejection, whatever it may be that is best adapted to cutting short the effect of some stimulus, or some reaction which one has incautiously made. Conversely, pleasure is the expression of confirmatory movement tending to prolong the reaction, or carry it out strenuously to its final development—to swallow with gusto, or to expose more and more of the surface to the pleasing contact.

5. From this slight account, we can gather a certain conception, however inadequate, of the nature of the change whereby experience modifies a reaction. The first point which emerges clearly is that the inhibitory movement, which on a superficial view may seem to appear for the first time after the organism has once had a " painful " experience, really first appears in the first experience itself, and is merely repeated under somewhat modified conditions, and accordingly with different results, in the later experiences. Let us analyse this modified repetition. The sight of the cinnabar caterpillar was at first a stimulus to pecking. The result of the peck was the *taste*,[3] and the taste involved the movement of rejection. But the taste also of course involved contact of the food with the

---

[1] I am far from saying that there is no other source of feeling than the motor reaction to sense stimulus.

[2] The term "expression" is meant to convey a concomitance of the intimate nature of which we are ignorant, though we know it must be something other than bare concomitance.

[3] The word is used, of course, with the provisions and on the grounds explained above (Chapter II).

tongue or palate, and if we divide these two stages of the consequence $p$ of the reaction, we get altogether not three stages, but four.

| $s$ — | $r$ — | $c$ — | $\rho$ |
|---|---|---|---|
| (the sight) | (pecking) | (" unpleasant " taste) | (movement of rejection). |

Afterwards we have $s$ followed at once by $\rho$
(the sight)                         (rejection).

Strictly, what is altered is not $\rho$, which came into existence, at any rate, in tendency and effect, in the first experience, but the effect of $s$. $s$, which before called forth $r$, now excites $\rho$, and the intervening stage $c$ seems to have nothing to do with the matter. How then is the action of $s$ modified ?

We can partly answer this by understanding accurately how far it has been modified. In this way : that instead of evoking as before a pecking movement, it either has no outward result at all, or it evokes a contrary movement of rejection or aversion, which movement is of the same character as one that it previously excited through an intermediary. This gives us the broad character of the whole proceeding. The excitement aroused by a certain stimulus has taken to itself or *assimilated* the character of another excitement which it has previously brought about. The excitement originally produced by the sight of the orange-peel prompted pecking. Pecking produced a contact with the inside of the bill, which in its turn produced a violent movement of rejection. Now the first excitement becomes clothed with the character of the second in greater or less degree, so that either the two motor excitements —the original and the acquired—cancel each other and produce absolute indifference, or the acquired effect predominates, and there is a movement of disgust.[1]

[1] Mr. Stout, with whose very clear account of this process the above is, generally speaking, in close agreement, passes one criticism on the alternation theory which seems to go too far. This theory attributes to the chick a " faintly revived sensation of disgust " accompanying the sight of the caterpillar. Mr. Stout objects (*Manual of Psychology*, p. 88) that this would lead to two movements which would interfere with one another only so far as they are " mechanically incompatible." " One would expect a nondescript blend of the two movements, or an alternation between them." Mr. Stout seems to overlook the point that it would be two divergent cerebral processes that would be set up, and that these might fight it out within the brain and without appearing in outward action.

There is a further point.   In the instances taken, the inhibitory movement in the first trial follows close upon the heels of the instinctive response.   Now we know that a wave of excitement once started in the nervous system persists for a certain short time.   Hence the inhibitory wave arises before the original excitement has subsided, and as we have seen, impinges on and perhaps modifies or half cancels it in the very first instance.   And this modification tends to persist, or at least leave a trace.   For we find that as painful experiences are repeated, the original impulse is not merely checked, but sooner or later dies away.   This part of the process of learning is therefore suggestive of the fusion of two immediately consecutive waves of excitement.   If this is what actually occurs in the lowest forms of learning, the element of time would be important, but we may doubt whether it is merely the co-presence of two waves of excitement that is essential.   The element of unity we may conceive is the conation which is excited by the sensory stimulus and is inhibited by the painful, insipid, or fruitless result.   The effect of this inhibition persists.   The special type of conative tendency that has been frustrated, is weakened, possibly cancelled, for a shorter or longer period, while the reverse result happens if the conation should succeed.   It is the conation which furnishes the unity to successive acts and explains how it is that a result, supervening when sense excitement is over, nevertheless appears to modify corresponding sense excitements in the future.   Be this as it may, in the

But, in point of fact, the two processes do at times (as some of the above instances show) give evidence of themselves in action.   We really get occasionally something like a blend or an alternation.   Mr. A. A. Schaeffer has shown that with the frog avoiding habits might be formed in both ways.   In some instances a disagreeable object is first taken into the mouth and then rejected.   In other cases it is eaten without any effort at rejection but subsequently refused (J. A. B., 1911, p. 324).   In an experiment with newts described by Mr. A. M. Rees (J. A. B., 1912, p. 191) we find various intermediate stages.   One newt seized and half swallowed a piece of filter paper but disgorged it.   It then swallowed a piece of filter paper soaked in meat juice, afterwards disgorging the paper.   Two days later it followed and snapped at a roll of yellow cloth, but after once seizing it, refused to follow it again.   It seized and immediately disgorged a piece of black cotton, and then refused to follow a piece of white paraffin.   " Usually after snapping at the tasteless object a few times the animals refuse to follow any longer, but in such cases they would nearly always follow and try to seize a piece of raw meat of the same size."

instances taken the results which go to modify the effects of an excitement are in point of fact based on a second quality of the same object which by its first perceived quality excites the reaction. Modifications of this type are far more easily achieved than others by animals of low intelligence. Thus, Professor Yerkes, testing frogs with maze experiments, found that from 50 to 100 trials were necessary to perfect the habit ; and in placing the frogs in a box with a glass bottom, 20 to 30 experiments did not suffice to teach them that the glass was to be avoided. On the other hand Schaeffer's frogs learnt to avoid disagreeable earthworms after a number of trials varying usually from 2 to 7, and in at least one case on the basis of a single experiment.[1]

These simple cases of Confirmation and Inhibition then should apparently be grouped together as examples of a specific and very primitive type of learning by experience. The characteristic of this type is that the " experience " which operates is an excitement resulting immediately from the reaction of the organism to some prior excitement. Very often it arises from a second property of the object to which the first stimulus is due. This would for example be true of the instances of tasting, burning, bruising, etc., which we have used. But what seems essential is that the result should follow immediately upon the first re-action, and by "immediately" we mean closely enough to impinge upon and so confirm or inhibit the conational impulse by which that reaction is initiated and sustained. With this understanding we may briefly define this type of learning by experience as consisting in the modification of the reaction to some stimulus through the immediate effects of that reaction. The process is a case of that which we have called Assimilation, because by its means the excitement to which a stimulus gives rise is merged in the consequential excitement and (at least for purposes of guiding action) takes on its character. It is assimilation in what is certainly one of its simplest forms. We can see, however, that the process is closely analogous to that of Selective Modification described above, and

[1] Schaeffer, *loc. cit.*, pp. 324–25.

though the field of action is somewhat different we may suppose it to rest on substantially the same psychological and physiological conditions. In both cases it is the satisfaction or dissatisfaction, to use terms derived from our consciousness, the success or frustration of the conation, to use terms which are more objective, which operates to confirm, modify, or inhibit subsequent conation under similar circumstances.[1]

6. The effect of this kind of modifiability is best seen by considering its bearing upon instinct. It acts upon a certain sort of instinctive reaction, and tends, as Mr. Lloyd Morgan has well said, to "define" the instinct. We have seen that an instinct may be congenitally more or less perfect, more or less definite, as the case may be. There is nothing in the general nature of instinct to make it inconceivable that a chick should be born with an inherited tendency, working with certainty and precision from birth, to peck at one sort of caterpillar and avoid another, just as a certain fly passes over other places, and lays its eggs where a horse will lick them, and so get them into its alimentary canal where they are destined to be hatched. But chicks are not born so. They peck at small things indiscriminately at first, and experience cuts them off certain things and concentrates them on others. Just as the fly reacts to one particular very definite object so the chick reacts to the very indefinite object "small thing within reach." Experience circumscribes this object. It excludes from it yellow and black striped caterpillars, bits of orange-peel, and so on, while it promotes green caterpillars or bits of egg to prominence within the class of objects that remain. What is true of the chick is true in

[1] The above description of the elementary workings of experience must not be taken for an attempt at explanation. How a fleeting experience can have a permanent effect is strictly a metaphysical rather than a psychological question, and beyond saying that there must be something permanent, whether we call it mind or brain, on which successive experiences act, metaphysics can, I fear, do little to answer it. It may be well, however, in view of certain misunderstandings which have arisen, to remind the reader that the "excitements," "feelings," &c., of which I speak have no substantial existence, but are states of the permanent subject, and that when we speak of their "interactions," the "effect of one excitement on another," and so forth, we are merely using a familiar form of speech to describe relations between different states, or the effects of an experience on the permanent susceptibilities of its subject.

varying degree of numberless other birds and mammals in instincts of various kinds. It is natural to look on the aversion and terror manifested by a kitten when it first sees a dog as based on an instinctive dread and horror of dogs as dogs. But in fact what is congenital appears to be a reaction to the dog's smell,[1] which can be inhibited, moreover, by familiarity with friendly dogs. It is natural to speak of a chick as instinctively dreading the cry of a hawk, or as " knowing " its mother's warning cry or her inviting cluck by instinct. But it appears truer to fact to say that sounds of that quality affect the young bird, and that the particular note to which it will respond by cowering or coming forward will depend largely on the way in which its hereditary tendencies have been modified by experience. Similarly, one would say that a lamb instinctively follows its mother. But it is truer to say that by nature it has an inclination to follow any large animal, and that experience teaches it to single out its mother as the best animal to follow. Similarly, the young orangoutang clings to its mother, but not because it is the mother, but because it has a tendency to hang on by its claws to something hairy—a tendency of which Dr. Wallace availed himself to make a dummy mother for an orphan of that species.

Summing up a mass of evidence upon this point, Mr. Lloyd Morgan says, instincts

. . . " are evoked by stimuli, the general type of which is fairly definite, and may, in some cases, be in response to particular objects. Of the latter possibility we have, however, but little satisfactory evidence." [2]

And again,

" acquired definiteness is built, through association, on the foundation of congenital responses, which are modified, under experience, to meet new circumstances." [3]

Thus the general function of experience, so far, is greatly to increase the plasticity whereby the instinctive reactions of an individual can be adjusted to his circumstances. It may be said to make possible the rise of instincts adjusted

---

[1] Wesley Mills, pp. 176 and 177.
[2] *Habit and Instinct*, p. 99.     [3] P. 100.

at birth to stimuli of a highly general instead of a definitely particularised character, and this is the first step in the conversion of an instinct into a general tendency capable of being directed by experience. The instinctive tendency as such becomes more general, and experience makes it definite.

7. *Retrogressive Assimilation.*

In the cases hitherto discussed, there was to begin with a reaction, random or instinctive, to a certain stimulus, and the effect of experience was to modify this reaction. We pass now to cases in which a reaction is acquired to which there is no initial tendency. In the former cases, the reaction had to be modified ; in these it has to be as it were created.

The sight of a man or the sound of a human voice cannot under ordinary circumstances stimulate a wild animal that does not prey upon man to expect food or prepare to receive it. But if the same animal is caught and kept in captivity, it will soon " get to know " its keeper and perhaps its feeding time. If it is an intelligent animal it may itself be readily trained to make conventional signs of its desire for food, as I have seen an elephant ringing a bell and turning a rattle, while a smaller elephant in the next stall would knock with its trunk against the sides of its cage to win back to itself the attention and the buns which were being unfairly attracted by its neighbour. But in its simpler form, this operation of experience is seen very much lower down in the intellectual scale. Fish, for example, which are accustomed to be fed, will come to the surface and be ready to snap as soon as any one approaches their tank. Mr. Bateson[1] describes a rockling which under these circumstance would lift its head above water and snap at the fingers. According to Brehm[2] tortoises and turtles in general become accustomed to men who treat them well—though it is probably the human form or voice to which they react, as it is elsewhere said that the most easily tameable of Chelonia do not distinguish individuals.[3] Watersnakes we learn on the same authority,[4] get excited when the keeper bringing food opens the door

---

[1] *Journal of Marine Biology*, p. 238.
[2] *Thierleben*, VII. p. 547.      [3] *Ib.* p. 562.      [4] *Ib.* p. 471.

(though they are often stupid enough to bite the tongs), and similar facts are recorded of frogs and toads.[1] In fact, this grade of intelligence is fairly well marked among Fish, Reptiles, and Amphibia. Similar instances among Birds are given by Mr. Lloyd Morgan.[2]

" A moorhen chick, for whose benefit we had dug up worms with a spade, and which, standing by, jumped on the first-turned sod and seized every wriggling speck which caught his keen eye, would soon run from some distance to me as soon as I took hold of the spade."

How are we to understand these cases ?

There are three possible explanations.

*a.* It may. be that the animal is aware of the connection between the object to which it is at first indifferent, and the feeding or other experience, whatever it be, in which it is interested—*i.e.*, it observes and remembers that the one leads to the other.

Without at all denying that this may be the true account of the process in certain cases, we must notice that there are two other possible explanations which do not imply so much intelligence.

*b.* The originally "indifferent" object may be directly associated with the object of interest.

The keeper brings the food, and the sight and smell thereof, which stimulate the animal to come forward eagerly and seize it, are intertwined in its perception with the sight of the keeper. The spade turns up the worms, and the moorhen picks them. The excitement of picking is thus fused with the sight of spade and digging, and this spectacle takes on permanently the character which belongs to it in certain experiences. In other words, we have a slightly modified case of assimilation. As before the sight of the black and yellow striped grub took upon itself the character of an object of aversion, so the spade or the keeper becomes an object of attraction. This explanation is at least possible wherever the perception of the object which thus acquires a power of exciting the organism can be reasonably supposed to have been, in an earlier ex-

---

[1] *Thierleben*, VII. pp. 667 and 700. Cf. Weir. *Dawn of Reason*, p. 72.
[2] *Habit and Instinct*, p. 148.

perience, an element in a state of excitement similar in its
tendency and character.

c. But it is also possible, and in some cases probable,
that more or less random movements of the animal itself
play a part. The fish that first *happens* to come near the
surface will get the pick of the crumbs, and this fact will
tend to confirm or " stamp in " the random mode of reaction. In the instance quoted above from Preyer,[1] irritation of the skin set up random reflexes, of which some
gave relief, and were accordingly preferred. Apart, however, from the simplest cases, in which the originally
random movement meets immediate " confirmation," there
remains for this explanation a certain difficulty which has
been very clearly pointed out by Mr. Thorndike,[2] who has
made much more liberal use of the explanation than any
other writer. Except in these cases, the " confirmatory "
wave must come after the initial movements of the action
leading up to it are well over. How then can it help to
establish them ? To this the first reply is, Can it do so ?
That is to say, apart from intelligence, is any complicated
or lengthy series of actions learnt in this way ? If so—
which remains to be proved—I imagine that the "confirmatory wave " must be conceived[3] as gradually spreading, as
it were, backward. We can imagine the delight of feeding
and the impulse to come to the best place for it attached,
first to the sight of the food itself, then to the keeper who
brings it, then to the sound of his approaching footsteps,
and finally, perhaps, to the click of a gate which he opens
on his way.[4] Remoter associations of this kind are un-

---

[1] P. 42.            [2] *Animal Intelligence*, pp. 103, 104.

[3] That is to say, if (1) we assume (as above, p. 122) that the primitive
form of assimilation rests on fusion of excitements through the medium of
a unitary conation, and (2) we treat these cases as mere extensions of the
primitive form.

[4] Thus, in a succession of experiments on the nymph of the mayfly,
Mr. J. E. Wodsedalek first of all by repeated efforts induced the nymph
to follow bits of food. This took several weeks. Gradually the insect
was brought to the part of the dish nearest to the operator, when it was
allowed to feed, and after about four weeks most of the specimens would
frequently swim after the food when brought near them, and would often
swim towards him when he made his experiments (J. A. B., 1912, pp. 12,
13). In organisms of very low type we can observe the spreading process
even in cases of reaction to simple sense stimuli. Messrs. Fleure and
Walton (*Zoologischer Anzeiger*, Band 31, 1907, p. 215) gave a sea
anemone scraps of filter paper, one every twenty-four hours, placing it on

doubtedly formed, and it would be interesting to get some detailed account of the way in which they are formed, particularly among animals of no very great intelligence. I do not know of any decisive evidence on this point, and I must, therefore, let this third explanation stand as a possibility, even in the case of somewhat lengthy trains of association.[1]

8. Of the three explanations offered, the second and third, though different in detail, are alike in principle. Both dispense with any intelligent apprehension of the relation between act and consequence, and trace the genesis of a response to the power of an excitation to absorb into itself or assimilate the motor tendencies or feelings with which it is intimately associated. Since this simpler explanation covers the facts, we have no right, on the strength of mere modification of response to stimulus alone, to impute the higher degree of intelligence suggested by the first explanation. It is no doubt natural to explain an alteration of behaviour towards an object by saying that the animal remembers the results of previous action, and infers that similar results will follow in a fresh case. It may seem a still more modest assumption if we explain that the ideas of two objects or two qualities—of keeper and food, or black and yellow stripes and nasty taste—have become associated in the animal's mind. But a little consideration of our own human experience will show that even this explanation goes further than is warranted by the facts. In ordinary perception we are, as a rule, in direct contact through our sense organs with only one or two qualities of the objects

the same tentacle each time. As a rule the fragment was carried to the mouth, swallowed, and then ejected. "After a few days, the number varying in different individuals from two to five days, the fragment is no longer swallowed, and in about another two days the tentacles will no longer take hold of it." Thus the inhibition first affects the mouth and spreads from it to the tentacle. But, further, though the tentacle itself with the part of the mouth attached has now learnt the lesson, other tentacles on the opposite side can still be deceived once or twice, though they learn more speedily on account of the education which the first tentacles have received. Here then we have a case of a very simple inhibition affecting different parts of the organism by successive stages.

[1] It is an obvious corollary from the third explanation that the remoter association can only be formed by slow degrees. This accords well with the facts in the lower grades of intelligence.

about us.  Experience has taught us their other qualities, and we have always at hand, ready for immediate use, the knowledge that we have gained.  But in dealing with familiar objects in practice, we seldom, unless the occasion calls for reflection, stay to form any definite idea of the unperceived qualities.  We act first as we should act if we reasoned from our idea of them, but without forming that idea.  The educated perception itself discharges the appropriate reaction.  Thus, the sight of a cab coming towards me, as I cross the street, causes me to hurry out of its way. The reason for hurrying may be formulated in the judgment, "at the speed at which that cab is coming, it will overtake me;" but if I stayed to form the judgment before beginning to quicken my pace, I should probably be run over.  What really happens is that the sight of the cab discharges the motion without the aid of any reflection. And this is due to the action of previous experiences of cabs and other moving bodies which have incorporated themselves in the perception.  The perception has assimilated them.  The experiences have endowed it with a power of awaking reactions which they have shown to be appropriate.

If it be replied that nevertheless ideas played their part in this training of the perceptions, the rejoinder is that the part played by ideas is seldom if ever exhaustive. Mill's case of the dyer who could not communicate his art is but one instance out of many.  I remember an excellent but uneducated Cornish cook who, if asked how much of a given ingredient she had put into a successful dish, would reply, "Well, as much as I thought."  Her perceptions had become insensibly adjusted to her requirements, her ideas lagged far behind.  Indeed, relatively to perceptions, ideas are of a more reflective character, and like all that is reflective, they follow and but imperfectly interpret their material.

9. We have seen that in human psychology "crude" sensation and feeling belong to the sphere of hereditary response.  That is, they may appear as the psychical side of responses made by preformed structure to stimulus.  The account now given of the earliest operations of experience

seems to corroborate this view, inasmuch as it postulates sensation and feeling as the data on which it works. Its most characteristic product in the human mind is the state often familiarly described as an act of Recognition, though it does not involve the presence of ideas. Now what is the character of an act of " Recognition " not involving ideas ? The object " recognised " is something more for the mind than that one of its qualities which happens to be present to sense. The orange is for the child more than the colour or the smell. In what way is it more ? If we attribute to the child definitely formed ideas (as of "acid," "juicy," &c.) then the orange is a possible subject for any of these ideal qualities as predicates. But these are ideas, and lie outside sense-perception. What is there then in " Recognition " of this kind more than the sense-qualities and yet less than these ideal qualities ? The answer seems to be, a character which association with the ideal qualities has lent to the presented quality. In some cases this character can be pointed out in the sense-content itself. Thus, we " see " a thing at a distance at which without previous experience we should not know it to be. The rumble that comes in at the open window " sounds " far off. If I had no experience of the effect of distance on sound, it would presumably be indistinguishable from a low rumble near by. In each instance the stimulus has " assimilated " a character, such characters having been associated with similar stimuli in past experience. In other cases we may say that the character assimilated shows itself in action. That the orange is more than a yellow ball to the child appears in the fact that the child tries to suck it. The coming tennis ball follows a path of which I have not time to form an idea, but which guides me as I spring and strike none the less. In short, in these cases of assimilative recognition, the " crude " sensation has assimilated certain characters which, if disentangled, form the contents of ideas, but which are not disentangled as long as they are assimilated. Prominent among these are motor impulses. These differ from reflex or instinctive impulses in being guided by present stimulus in accordance with the results of previous experience. We may call them acquired sense-impulses, and lay down generally that assimilative experience postulates sensations and feelings as its data, and produces modified sense-feeling and acquired sense impulse, passing into habit, as its result.[1]

10. Thus through the agency of assimilation a mass of grouped experiences—sensation, motor response, and feelings, have an effect on the organisation of such a kind that response is subsequently modified according to the nature of the feeling. There is then a certain correlation between a mass of related experiences and subsequent reactions. To the observer it is clear that the basis of this correlation is the relation of stimulus, reaction, and feeling in the primary experience, and that in the subsequent response the conation is correlated with, *i.e.*, is executed so as to produce the result. But in the type of action before us the elements are not distinguished nor the relations grasped by the agent as they are by the observer. The action of the moment is related in one sense to the past, in another to the future, but in both senses without consciousness of the relation. At no point have we successive elements of experience and action distinctly grasped and articulately correlated. We have rather the result of the earlier experiences as a whole determining the result, *i.e.*, the response, in the later experience. We may describe this as a correlation of Empirical Results, or negatively and cursorily as Inarticulate correlation.

Whether any animals other than man advance to a more articulate correlation is a question depending on the experimental application of delicate tests. To explain the nature of articulate correlation, to describe the behaviour tests from which it may be inferred, and to discuss whether there are any species of animals to which it may be attributed, will be the work of Chapters VIII–XII. For the present we are content to note that there is abundant evidence for the existence of the elementary kind of correlation, on which human perceptions and perceptual impulses are based, far down in the animal scale. Whether

[1] Except in the use of certain terms, the above is in close accord with Mr. Stout's lucid and forcible account of Acquirement of Meaning (*Manual*, pp. 84-93).

we are to attribute sensation, feeling and perception to animals as to man, may always be made a question, seeing that the consciousness of another can never be a matter of direct observation. But that animals do succeed in correlating their experiences in the sense explained is not a hypothesis, but a matter of observed fact. We regard correlation as the precise work of intelligence, and we therefore set down this elementary correlation as the first stage beyond Instinct in the Evolution of Mind, whether among animals or Man. Its operation is probably confined principally to adjusting reactions suitably to their immediate results. If more remote correlations are effected, it must be by a very slow and gradual process. The reactions effected are either those resulting from instincts of a more or less indefinite character, or are such as lead to the immediate gratification of instinctive needs. In the first case, experience tends to define, limit, and direct a more or less general instinct. In the second, it assists in the satisfaction of instinct. In either case it helps to increase the plasticity of instinct and the adaptability of the organism, while in rendering it possible for animals to thrive without highly definite instincts, it helps to bring about the substitution of more or less general tendencies and impulses for narrowly defined methods of reaction. And this, to conclude, means the rise of a fuller and more varied type, ready to respond to its surroundings in more diverse ways. Specialisation in nerve structure begins to give way to the general power of adaptation and acquisition whereby in the course of a lifetime many diverse actions may become as perfect as the two or three highly elaborated adjustments of the more mechanical type.

11. *The diffusion of the lower form of Intelligence in the animal world.*

He would be a bold man who should undertake to say where the capacity for learning by experience first appears in the animal world, or where it first begins to develop into a higher form than that described. There is, however, some reason to think that this grade of intelligence is typical of the lower classes of the animal kingdom, from many branches of which evidence, more or less abundant, has been accumulated by careful experimenters in recent years. To summarise the evidence, however imperfectly, will perhaps help us a little further towards understanding the general course of Mental Evolution.[1]

We have already quoted instances showing that among certain fish, at any rate in some individuals, the modifying influence of experience is at a minimum. Even the simplest sort of modification, the inhibition of an impulse, fails in certain cases, as in those quoted by Mr. Bateson, where after twelve months' constant experience, fish persisted in knocking their heads against the glass wall of their tank. On the other hand, there is no doubt that certain fish learn to come to the surface for food on the approach of human beings, and perhaps at the sound of a voice or of a bell. This is a simple case of an acquired reaction of the sort described in this chapter. Somewhat more difficult is the avoidance of baits. Romanes states generally that there is a marked increase of wariness in waters which are much fished, and attributes the change to "observation," on the ground that "young trout under such circumstances are less wary than old ones." If the trout really draw an inference from their observation of others being caught and dragged to the surface, they are capable of a much more complex

---

[1] It must be remembered that in the matter of intelligence there is perhaps even more difference between the individuals of a species, the species of a genus, and even between the Orders of a Class, than in the matter of physical structure. A classification of the animal kingdom based on intelligence would probably cut right across the classifications based on structure. It would probably associate the nest-building stickleback with the lower birds ; it would class the Cephalopoda with Fish and Reptiles rather than among the Molluscs ; and, whatever it did with ants and bees, it would draw a well-marked line between them and most of the insects. Intelligent acts are, above all others, "adaptive" characters—characters taken up by the organism in immediate response to its surroundings, and such characters as Darwin showed are the least to be depended on as tests of genealogical affinity. Hence any general statement as to the intelligence of, say, Fish or Birds, can only mean at the utmost that the kind of intelligence in question is very widely diffused among Fish or Birds—so widely, perhaps, that it may be regarded as representing the mean level in the Class. Some species, and perhaps whole Orders, may rise above or fall below it, while within each species the individual differences will often be much greater than they are in matters of visible structure. This qualification must be understood as applying to any general statement in the text.

mental operation than those hitherto described. But in the absence of details one would be inclined to think that in such cases the older fish are of the more wary type which under the circumstances has survived. Of each new generation, at least for a long period, a great number would always be of the less wary type, and these would be caught. The more waters are fished, the more the young are likely to preponderate among those caught. For, taking any single generation, the least wary will be most caught at each fishing, so that the more wary will preponderate more and more, whence, in subsequent fishings, that generation will have an advantage over the younger ones. At the same time fish show a good deal of " caution," *i.e.*, they examine strange objects and approach them tentatively. Schneider notes this of the mullet and parrot-fish precisely in relation to baits. There is therefore a certain basis for experience to work upon. If, in the course of such investigation, a fish is frightened, say by the shadow of the fisherman, it will be still more cautious next time. Thus the increase of wariness may be due purely to the elimination of the unwary, or it may be assisted by frightening experiences. But there seems no reason to attribute it to an articulate, analogical inference.

Many fish are, however, capable of being guided by experience in the elementary form described above (p. 111 ff.). They have the sort of instincts that must be concentrated on particular objects, and this implies that their experience in relation to those objects has some more or less persistent effect upon them. For example, they have haunts, and in some cases homes. The shark haunts places that it has found to be good hunting grounds.[1] The stickleback " knows the way " back to his nest, even if he has been absent for some hours.[2] Evidently we have here the operation of experience in some form. What sort of experience is it ? Is it accurate to attribute to the fish definite memory of the place and knowledge of its relations in space ? Or shall we be right in explaining its return to its haunts as due to those workings of experience on perception, and through perception on motor impulse, which

---

[1] Brehm, VIII. p. 440. Cf. Schneider, p. 312.     [2] *Ib.* p. 171.

have been described in this chapter ?    The same question
may be asked about other members of the animal kingdom,
of the same or perhaps of lower grade.    Thus many
Crustacea—prawns, for example[1]—have regular " homes "
or lurking places.    Even limpets[2] have been proved to have
fixed resting places to which they return, and the same is
true of snails.[3]    A little reflection will show that the power
of " homing " does not amount to that general knowledge
of locality, involving many complex relations, which we shall
see reason to ascribe to some at least among the higher
vertebrates.    It does not necessarily imply anything beyond
a tendency to go back along the trail, which may well be
heredity.    If this is so, the fixing of a home or a haunt
is in such cases an instance of the defining of an instinct
by experience—an effect of primary retentiveness.    The
homing tendency is fixed on a particular spot.    In some
instances there is direct confirmatory evidence that
this is the true explanation.    Snails leave a trail visible
to our eyes, and are known to follow it even when
it is irregular.[4]    Even if there is no trail, if a fish, for
example, is guided by the objects near its haunt, we could
not safely assume a higher process than that of association
between perception and impulse.    When the shark is
hungry the sight of the objects in the neighbourhood of
which it obtained prey attract it, and this influence might
spread to other objects on the way.    There is nothing in a
monotonous out going or home coming that might not be
built up by habituation.

Just as in "homing" or in lurking experience affixes an
instinctive tendency to one object rather than another, so
in chasing prey, fighting a rival, defending eggs, it makes
a given object a permanent source of excitability.    At this
stage of intelligence, a quarrel, for example, does not cease

[1] Bateson, *op. cit.* p. 211.    [2] Romanes, pp. 28, 29.
[3] *Cambridge Natural History*, Vol. III. p. 35.
[4] *Ib.* According to Bethe (*Ameisen*, p. 9), limpets, if moved a little
from their path, are unable to find their way.    This observation,
however, is difficult to reconcile with the results obtained by Mr. Lloyd
Morgan, who shows (*Animal Behaviour*, p. 156) that from short
distances (up to six inches) the majority of limpets find their way
back.    The successes rapidly diminish as the distance is increased to
two feet.

when the enemy is out of sight. In Brehm's *Thierleben*[1] there is a terrible account showing "*furens quid femina possit*" even among fish. Rival female Paradise fishes had to be separated by a glass partition. This would not prevent them from futile attempts to injure each other, and when a curtain was hung over the glass to hide the hated rival charms from the sight of each, they glutted their morbid feelings by getting round it so as to stare at each other. Finally, one jumped clean over the partition to resume the attack. Out of sight, it will be seen, is not altogether out of mind among fish. The hereditary tendencies to envy, hatred, malice, and all uncharitableness are definitely concentrated upon a certain object. It is not merely the sight of that object that will arouse the instinct. There is a state of permanent excitation or excitability of which the object is the centre, and under stress of which the hostile action may be continued or renewed just as though the enemy were still in sight. Of the difference between this permanence of excitability, with its renewed discharges of nervous energy and true recognition, a beautiful example is drawn from the observations of sticklebacks by Evers.[2] Sticklebacks found with their nests and transported into a tank neglected them—the moving disturbed the habitual course of action. But sticklebacks that had built in a tank would take care of eggs collected in the open like their own. The sight of the egg in the nest is enough to excite the parental tendency. But what is most significant for our purpose is the case of one stickleback in particular, which was taken from his nest to another tank. The nest was put in after him, and both he and his nest were attacked by several females, so that it became necessary to cover the nest with sand. After swimming about wildly for a time he began to recover, and appeared to be searching, and Evers, by way of helping him, brought some of the eggs to the surface as he approached. Some of the females

---

[1] *Ib.* Vol. VIII. pp. 187, 188.

[2] Brehm, VIII. pp. 171, 172. Evers justly remarks that it is impossible to decide whether he recognised the nest as his own or not. Comparison with the other cases mentioned suggests the explanation offered in the text.

pounced on the eggs.  The result was at once to reawaken
the father stickleback's protective instincts.  He attacked
the females, and then undertook the defence of the nest as
before.  The evidence when put together suggests that the
stickleback does not in our sense of the term recognise the
eggs as his own.  The truer view is that at breeding time
his parental instincts are awakened by the perception of his
eggs.  If the action of the instinct is broken off, the sight
of his own eggs may fail to renew it, while a chance
excitement may set the whole machinery in motion again.
The attachment of hereditary modes of action to certain
objects or individuals is certainly an effect of experience.
But we cannot infer from it knowledge of those objects or
individuals as objects or individuals.  It is rather a form
of the defining or particularising of instinct in which we
found the most elementary operations of experience.

According to the general account of the mental qualities
of Fish given in Brehm's *Thierleben*,[1] Fish have a certain
" understanding," but very little.  They can distinguish
enemies from those who are not hostile.  They become
wary of traps (Nachstellungen) and note places of safety.
They accustom themselves to a keeper, to feeding time,
and a signal like the sound of a bell that food is coming.
They choose suitable places for hunting, where they lie in
wait for their prey, learn to overcome obstacles, and withdraw themselves from danger, form a more or less intimate
connection with their fellows, and hunt in co-operation.
In some cases they show a measure of care for their young.
Broadly speaking, this account seems to tally well with the
elementary form of intelligence which we have described.
Both among Reptiles and Amphibia a certain capacity for
training is verified by many examples.  They "come to
know" their keepers, for example, in the sense of coming
at call or at sight of them,[2] but in this case the knowledge
often has very marked limitations.  It would seem, for

---

[1] Brehm, VIII. p. 12.  The account of reptile intelligence in the same
work (VII. pp. 24, 25) points to a similar type.

[2] Brehm, VII. p. 547, for tortoises.  The most intelligent and most
tameable kind, the fresh-water tortoises, however, do not distinguish
individuals (pp. 562, 563).  For snakes, *ib*. p. 220 ; for lizards, pp. 34, 35 ;
crocodiles, p. 525 ; toads, p. 700.

example, that they have, for the most part, little capacity for distinguishing individuals.[1] Very similar facts are established with regard to frogs and toads. Reptiles, like fish, haunt definite places. Crocodiles, for instance, haunt watering places[2] where they pick up cattle or human beings, and a tame yellow adder has been known, when let loose, to return to his cage.[3] After what has been said above, Schneider's description of a turtle persistently chasing a hermit crab will be readily understood as a cognate example of intelligence. Of direct modification by experience, the case of a Texan Snapping Turtle will serve as an example.[4] Having been caught with a bait, and having successfully resisted being dragged ashore, it afterwards avoided both the bait and the place where it was caught.

To pass to Invertebrates ; there is no doubt that in some form or other the power of learning by experience is to be found among many Insects, Spiders, and, I should say, Crustacea. Of the Hymenoptera it is needless to speak. Among insects other than the Hymenoptera, which may be classed together for our purposes as the Lower Insects, the evidence that I have seen for the power of learning by experience is not extensive. As laboratory evidence we have the case of the mayflies mentioned above, and some experiments in which Szymanski succeeded in teaching cockroaches to conquer their desire for darkness by administering electric shocks. The acquired habit persisted only for a short time, varying from about four to fifty-five minutes, but it could be re-learnt with a large reduction in the number of shocks.[5] Romanes[6] quotes a story of a fly that became tame enough to perch on its friend's thumb and eat sugar, but it is signi-

---

[1] Brehm, VII. p. 25. On the limits to the taming of snakes, see p. 220.
[2] *Ib.* p. 508.                         [3] *Ib.* p. 297.
[4] *Ib.* pp. 555, 556.
[5] J. A. B., 1912, p. 89 especially.
[6] Pp. 231 and 229. The story of a beetle that fetched a companion to move a cockchafer is beyond me. The apparent co-operation of dung beetles in rolling their balls (*ib.* pp. 236–238) is probably to be explained by the fact that to the beetle one ball is as good as another. Balls, as such, provoke the beetle to roll—even if they are quite of the wrong kind. (Schneider, p. 187.)

ficant that it finally met with its death by mistaking the thumb. The same author tells a story of an earwig that came regularly for its breakfast.

Among Cephalopoda there is good evidence of the effects of experience in the form which we are examining. The well-known story of the vengeance of an octopus on a lobster is parallel with the rivalry of the female Paradise fish showing a similar persistence of excitement.[1] It agrees with this that cephalopods should, like fish and reptiles, "know" their keepers,[2] and that they should learn to avoid the stinging sea anemones on the shell of hermit-crabs, and adopt a safer method of procuring them.[3] When we descend from cephalopods to other molluscs the evidence for any degree of learning from experience becomes much more scanty. We have seen that snails and limpets have the power of "homing;" the former, at least, are apparently guided by a trail. It is possible under the circumstances that the whole process may be instinctive. When sated with food, for example, the mollusc may feel a blind impulse to retrace its steps along its trail.[4] Dawson, however, found, among other evidences of past experience, that a snail dropped into an aquarium

---

[1] Romanes, p. 30 ; Schneider, p. 78.      [2] Schneider, *loc. cit.*

[3] But cf. J. A. B., 1911, p. 399, where some experiments by Polamanti on the cephalopod *Elebone Moschata* are summarised, which give purely negative results.

[4] There is a story (which has crossed the Atlantic) of a snail which would come at the call of a girl who had trained it to do so, while it shrank from other voices. (*Cambridge Natural History*, Vol. III. p. 35.) That oysters learn to keep their shells shut out of water for a longer and longer time is well known, but it is not clear to me whether this is due to simple practice—each time the thing is done making the next easier—or to experience of disagreeable results from opening (see *Cambridge Natural History*, Vol. III. p. 110). Mr. Lonsdale's story of the pair of snails made famous by Darwin is, at least in the interpretation given it, quite isolated. If the observation is correct, I should suppose that the first snail, after feeding, had an impulse to return on its trail to its mate, and that when they started again, the weaker mate being rested, and being also hungrier, was impelled to follow. Of failure to learn on the part of the snail, a good instance is reported by Möbius. A snail attempted to take a piece of meat from a polyp (*Actinia mesembryanthemum*), and coming into contact with the polyp's tentacles, shrank together, and turned away. It returned to the charge, with the same result. This was repeated several times over, till Möbius charitably gave the snail another piece of meat. (Brehm, 2nd edition, X. p. 479. The second half of the story is not given in Brehm's 3rd edition.)

where it had been previously kept crawled at once to the surface, while snails freshly taken from the pond wandered aimlessly.[1] Professor Yerkes has definitely shown that worms can learn a path, forming a habit as the result of from twenty to one hundred experiences, and, what is perhaps most remarkable, the habit is independent of the so-called brain, that is the ganglia situated in the anterior segments, since it persisted when these were removed.[2] Finally, with regard to protozoa, we have definite instances of selective modification, e.g., the behaviour of stentor quoted above (p. 114) has been sufficiently described. For the direct reversal of a response, due to the unsuitable character of the object, the evidence is less clear. The most definite case recorded is an experiment by Messrs. Hodge and Aiken, who gave some Vorticellæ, a "pure culture of yeast plants," in place of their normal food. "This attempt," they say, "resulted in an interesting demonstration of the educability of vorticellæ." They took greedily to the food at first, then ejected it "with volcanic energy," and afterwards " for several hours at least—how long the memory lasted was not determined—the individual could not be induced to repeat the experiment."[3] One would be glad to know whether during the same time they took any other food. It would seem possible that they were left in a state of collapse.

Metalnikow adduces a series of experiments on Paramecia, showing that at first these infusoria swallow injurious substances in large quantities, but, at the end of one or two days at most, they cease to do so while still swallowing other substances. "It seems," he said, "that the less nutritious the substance the more quickly the distinction is learnt." But it is not clear that it was the same Paramecia. Metalnikow's method of testing the condition of the Paramecia was to take a drop from the culture on successive occasions and kill the specimens,

[1] The *Biology of Physa*, summarised in J. A. B., 1912, p. 373.
[2] R. M. Yerkes, *The Intelligence of Earthworms*, J. A. B., 1912, especially pp. 351–2.
[3] Quoted by Mr. G. P. Watkins, " Psychical Life in Protozoa," *American Journal of Psychology*, Jan. 1900, pp. 179, 180.

which he examined. Thus he was dealing on each occasion with a different selection of individuals from the culture, and it is possible that those that took the harmful substance at first died of the effects, while only those that avoided it or took it in smaller quantities survived.[1] In fact, Schaeffer, repeating these experiments, obtained contrary results, and found no evidence that either stentor or paramecium can learn by experience to improve its selection of food.[2]

Whether the confirmation or inhibition of an action through experience of results is in reality a higher or more difficult form of learning by experience than selective modification is a question which I must leave undetermined. I note only that for the lowest class of organisms the former appears to be at present more definitely established than the latter. But at any rate in its most elementary forms we must apparently carry the power of learning by experience down to the lowest types of animal life. Just as we find no type of organism whose actions are purely mechanical, so it now seems probable we shall find none whose behaviour is entirely fixed by heredity in relation to present stimulus. We can at any rate say with certainty that the powers of assimilating the direct results of conation are traceable from a very low stage.

[1] *Comptes Rendus de la Société de Biologie*, Vol. LXXIV. pp. 702, 705.
[2] *Selection of Food in Stentor Caeruleus*, summarised in J. A. B., 1911, p. 400.

# CHAPTER VIII

CONCRETE EXPERIENCE AND THE PRACTICAL JUDGMENT

1. In the lowest grade of intelligence an animal learns by experience, and the experience is in a sense experience of a relation. There is a stimulus, a reaction, and a feeling, and this sequence, repeated many times over, modifies the reaction. For the observer it is clear that it is the relation between stimulus and feeling which operates, but we saw no reason to assume that the relation is grasped in the same way by the organism on which it operates. The fish or reptile may be excited by the approach of the keeper, and stimulated to come forward for their food. But we cannot infer that they correlate the perception of the keeper with an idea of food, and choose to come forward as a means towards securing that desirable end, the first and best morsel. In the present chapter we advance to the stage in which correlations of this sort are effected. We must inquire, first, what precisely the nature of such correlation is as compared with lower forms of mental adjustment; next, what kind of experience it implies, and what behaviour can be built up by its means; and lastly, whether there is any evidence that this stage is reached below the level of humanity.

I. *General character of the Practical Judgment.*

a. *Judgment and Assimilation.*

When we find that the burnt child dreads the fire, we may explain the fact in either of two ways. It may be that the child grasps and retains the relation between the flame as a bright, shining, lambent object, attractive to its eyes, and the flame as a cruel burning heat, scorching its little hand. If so, it has formed a judgment, which, when it can speak, it will express in the proposition—" fire burns," and an idea of fire as one thing with different attributes. Its experience is a whole containing elements which remain distinct. Both as such a whole, and as being concerned with a particular object, we may call it a concrete experience. Equally concrete is the idea or judgment founded thereon. But if the child is incapable of so much thought, it may still reach the same practical result by that more direct method by which the fire from being an attractive becomes a repellent object. In the one case, two terms are grasped in their relation. In the other, one term only is present, but it has for practical purposes borrowed the character of the other to which it stood related in past experience.[1] In the first case, there is judgment : in the second, assimilation.

*b. The Association of Ideas.*

Assimilation, we have seen, does not necessarily involve ideas at all. A perception which has " assimilated " the motor character of some experience to which it is related, has the power of shaping behaviour as though with a view to the repetition of that experience, yet no idea of the purpose of the adaptation comes before consciousness. In

---

[1] In ordinary phraseology the relation A—B, explicit in the one case, acts implicitly in the other. It may be asked how we can distinguish the two, when we are judging, not by our own consciousness, but by inference from behaviour. A relation is explicit in consciousness if its terms are united and yet distinct. It is implicit if it merely influences consciousness, so as, for example, to affect the way in which one of its terms is apprehended. Generalising this we may say that in consciousness the explicit is present on its own account, while the implicit is that which is present merely as qualifying or influencing something else. Extending the distinction to cases where we can judge only by behaviour, we may say that an element of experience is explicitly grasped by the mind if a distinct function in the guidance of behaviour can be assigned to it. It acts implicitly if, without having any distinctive effect of its own, it is yet a necessary part of some experience which has a function as a whole. Thus, in the case of assimilation, the experience A—B operates as a whole, and its elements have an effect only as contributing to this operation. In concrete experience, on the other hand, the relation A—B has, for example, a distinct function from that of the term A, for the reaction to A will differ according as B is or is not expected to follow. In conceptual thought, again, the relation uniting A and B acquires a function distinct from that of A and B themselves, since it may go to build up concepts with which A and B having nothing to do.

a Judgment, on the other hand, both of the related terms in their relation are presented or represented. The case of the Association of Ideas is intermediate. Here the perception does call up an idea, or one idea calls up another, but, as the associative process is generally conceived, the ideas merely succeed one another. They are not held together and formed into new judgments. It was the fundamental error of Hume's psychology—an error which also vitiated much of his logic and metaphysics—to treat associated ideas, so conceived, as equivalent to a belief in the connection of their contents. To believe that B is the effect of A is not at all the same thing as to have a lively idea of B following upon an idea of A. On the contrary, it consists in grasping the terms A and B together in a determinate relation, and asserting that relation of reality.

It may be asked whether Association as distinguished from Assimilation on the one hand and Judgment on the other is a real process at all. Is there a stage or a state in which ideas follow one another without being brought into relation ? Thought is continuous—not, as the early Associationists seemed to regard it, discrete. Perception passes into idea, and for a space they dwell together. Even in the most dreamy reverie, it may be said, continuity and connection have more to do with the line of thought than "contiguity." But this objection must not be pushed too far. It is harder to keep in mind a jangle of nonsense than a sentence with meaning in it, but it is by no means impossible.[1] The former presence of two elements in one and the same whole of consciousness is often quite sufficient to revive them in grotesque juxtaposition in a train of thought. It is to this that we owe the Miss Bateses and Mrs. Nicklebys of literature and of real life.

Ideas, then, may be associated without being logically connected. Moreover, even if they were associated so that a logician reflecting upon them could detect and expose the relation, it does not follow that that relation is itself present to the mind as the ideas float past. In a not uncommon experience, the act of "putting two and two together" follows quite clearly and distinctly as a separate act upon

[1] For some measure of the difference in labour, see below, p. 155.

the passage of the two ideas so united before consciousness. If it is argued, for contentious purposes, that mere
sequence of ideas in a continuous consciousness involves a
kind of relation, it must be replied that even so, this relation is not necessarily grasped by that consciousness. It
would be truer to the facts to urge that the relation between
juxtaposed elements of consciousness is apprehended with
varying degrees of distinctness, and if this view be adopted,
we may apply the term Associated ideas to the limiting
case in which this apprehension disappears, and the term
Judgment to the case where two or more elements are
definitely held together in some distinctive relation, making
of them a whole with a character of its own.

*c. The Practical Judgment.*

Except in one point, the Judgment as thus defined is
identical with the Judgment of Logic. In Logic, the term
is best reserved for such assertions as may be expressed
without modification in a proposition, that is, in words.[1]
But, as we shall see more fully later, the rendering
of a synthesis in words is a distinct and separate
act from that of forming the synthesis itself. A child
may be aware that fire is a bright object that
burns, without being able to form or even to understand the words. Just as I may feel or see without
naming, perhaps without being able to name what I was
feeling or seeing, so I may retain the memory of what I
have felt or seen without the aid of language, and the same
thing applies to the relation, say, of co-existence or sequence
between what I felt and saw. This relation is one thing,
its verbal expression another, involving, as we shall see
later, a distinct act of correlation. Concrete experience and
the practical thinking in which it is reproduced are so far
from being dependent on language that to the end they
cannot in all their individuality and detail be adequately
expressed in language. The proofs of this will, I hope,
accumulate as we go on. Meanwhile, we need a term to

---

[1] This, at least, seems to correspond best to general usage. See the
writer's *Theory of Knowledge*, p. 122. I need not here enter into the
question whether there is synthesis in every logical judgment—a point
which I have discussed in the same work, pp. 149-153.

distinguish a synthesis of experiences in which language is not used from the logical judgment.    Such a synthesis will deal with the particular objects and events of experience,[1] and its purpose will be to guide action in relation thereto. We may therefore call it Practical Judgment.[2]

II.  *The Conditions of the Practical Judgment in Experience.*
2.  *a.  Concrete experience.*

The character of the Practical Judgment depends in the last resort upon the experience on which it rests.    In the lower stage of Intelligence the experience throughout was of a sensori-motor character.    There was a sense-excitement giving rise to a reaction, followed by a feeling, and the feeling in turn had a motor effect.    What followed was a modified reaction, explained in popular language as due to a " revival " of the feeling, or, at least, of the motor impulse belonging to it.    Postponing for a moment further analysis of this explanation, let us first observe that the formation of judgments rests on a more concrete or articulate form of experience.    Suppose that we have an apprehension of concrete objects with their parts and qualities, their actions and changes, and suppose this apprehension to be " revived " (as the feeling impulse was revived), then we have in our revived experiences wholes consisting of distinguishable parts—that is, a synthesis of elements that remain distinct—that is the content we require for our " practical judgment."    Perception as we know it in ourselves is complex and continuous.    As we look at a house, walls, windows, and chimneys appear, forming distinct elements which are yet united in one whole.    As we attend to a series of events, listen to a speech, or watch a cricket match, a continuous stream of perceptions, distinct and yet connected, passes through our consciousness.    When we bring analysis to bear on the total impression made in

[1] For if the elements of the synthesis are recognised as general, the conditions of language are at once present.    See below, Chap. XIV., p. 321, etc.
[2] It should be noted that the limiting adjective, " practical," has been applied to animal intelligence in a somewhat different sense by other writers.    Thus, the late Dr. Mivart (*On Truth*, p. 345) speaks of animals as drawing " practical inferences," and these appear to be identical with his "sensuous inferences" (p. 145) which correspond rather with the Association of Ideas than with the " Practical Judgment " of the text.

either case, it reveals an order in the experience, a relation between part and part, which contributes as much to the total impression as the parts themselves. This relation analysis can dissect out and in a sense treat as independent of the terms which enter into it. But just because this is the work of analysis, it leads to conception, not merely to perception. What analysis reveals, however, is that, without being dissected out, the relations go to constitute perception, and are thus as truly parts of what is perceived as the terms that they unite. What is perceived is a complex of distinct but related parts. Such a complex is what we call articulate, and the terms-in-relation which it comprises may be called a perceptual relation, as against the conceptual relation which is held apart from its terms.

Let us now suppose a mind endowed with perceptions of this concrete kind, and with the power of reproducing them ideally in relation to a present perception. Thus, seeing one side of the house, I can mentally affix the unseen sides to that which I see, and recollecting, for example, on which side the door is, can direct my steps accordingly. Here the relations of unseen parts to one another and to what is seen are grasped, as before in perception, so now in idea, and this is what I mean by the Practical Judgment. It is more than Assimilation, because what is revived is an idea, a definite reference to something unperceived. It is more than Association, because the relation between the " revived " idea and the given per-ception is an essential part of it, and it is less than analytic thought, because the relations involved are not dissected out as distinct elements in consciousness.

*b. Revival.*

But we cannot pass on without dwelling on the Law of Revival (or Association, or Redintegration, as it is variously called). The broad facts, whether in this or the lower stage, are the same. There are certain experiences, A, B, C, contemporaneous or following in continuity one upon the other. Let A arise again, from whatever cause, and we say that it tends to " revive " B and C. What is the character of this revival ? Let us first remove a mis-

understanding so gross that it should never have arisen.
Neither the A nor the B nor the C of the new case is
identical with the original A, B, and C. A state of
consciousness, having once been, is gone. It has no substantial existence, as it were underground, from which it
may be brought up again. When we speak of reviving B,
we mean at most a state $B_2$, similar to an original $B_1$. An
ordinary understanding of the English language ought to
prevent any mistakes on this head.

But now comes the real difficulty. What is revived is,
after all, not $B_2$—something exactly like $B_1$—but, say, $b$,
something partially like $B_1$, but modified in some respects.
What is the nature or the condition of this modification ?
In the lower stage, taking the simplest case where an
inhibitory movement $\rho$ is revived, there is this important
difference from the original. In the first experience we
have s—R—P—$\rho$—sensation, reaction, pain, recoil. The
recoil or inhibitory movement is separated by two links
from the original stimulus. If when "revived" it remained
so separated, it would be too late to effect anything. In
being revived, it is also brought forward in time. At the
same time, the original tendency R begins to drop out.
Hence we really have not revival but modification. The
conative excitement originated by s, which gave us R, is
corrected, it may be reversed, into a different form of excitement, giving us $\rho$. In our experience the modification
goes right back to the initial step of the process. The sight
which has disgusting associations becomes itself disgusting.

Now if we turn to the revival of concrete experience we shall again find that what appears to be
" revived " is really brought up in quite a new form.
After the experience of A—B—C, A may be said to
" revive " B and C, but this does not mean that the perception of A revives the perception of B and C, but the
ideas of them. In many cases—and there is reason for
thinking that these cases are of the original type—A
excites an anticipation (or memory) of B and C. To
understand this, let us first remember that things and
events are not isolated, but connected, so that we should
symbolise the original experience not as A, B, C, but as

A—B—C. Let this whole be "revived" by A. Then, on the face of it, what A revives is not B and C each separately, but B following on A, and C on B. Certain elements in relation to A are therefore excited. Now let it be as before a condition that these elements should be excited along with A—as parts of the same state of consciousness. If they are brought before consciousness as co-present with A, the revived state will conflict with the original in which they were not co-present. If this conflict is to be avoided, they must, as excited, be elements belonging to A and yet, as "revived" from the original, they are events following on A in a definite relation. These conditions are satisfied by the transformation of the percepts B and C into elements of anticipation, which as elements we call ideas *b* and *c*. If the anticipation is made quite explicit and holds in itself several elements in definite relations, it is called a judgment. It is then the belief in or expectation of the sequence A—B—C. The unperceived elements in this sequence are known as ideas *b* and *c*. The content of these ideas and therefore of the whole judgment is determined by the elements which have been given in experience in their relation to A, and the ideas correspond to these elements of experience. It is in this sense that the whole process is one of revival, but the judgment itself is something new. It is not a repetition of a series of percepts. It is the repetition of a percept plus a reference to things as yet unperceived. The formation of such a judgment depends on the power of holding distinct experiences in a single state of consciousness without prejudice to their distinctness, and involves that distinct reference of a state to something beyond itself which we call an idea.

Experience then operates, whether in Assimilation or Judgment, by the law, as we may call it, of modified revival. The condition of revival in these cases appears to be that the revived element must enter into the same state of consciousness with that which revives it.[1] And

---

[1] A state of consciousness has duration, so that though revival takes time, A persists while it is bringing *b* into consciousness, and so with *b* and

this condition determines its change of character. The Practical Judgment "revives" experience only in the same loose sense in which it is revived in Assimilation. The judgment which we refer to a past perception as its cause is not itself a perception, but is an assertion about things that are not perceived. In the case of the Practical Judgment, it is an assertion of things that have been or will be, an assertion bringing them into relation with what is perceived. The experience on which this judgment is founded differs from the experience of the lower stage. For in the lower stage, Sensations (1) have no apparent function unless they excite a motor reaction, and (2) coalesce in subsequent experience with the feelings which modify them. In the experiences underlying the practical judgment, a sensation not itself moving a reaction may have a function as initiating ideas, which perhaps at several removes determine conduct. While secondly, it is the main point on which we have insisted that each element is kept distinct from the others that it calls up. In the lower stage it is merely necessary that there should be sense-experiences affecting the mind so as to dispose it to action. In the higher stage, there is perception of the surrounding world of objects in their manifold relations, changes, etc. Lastly, it will readily appear that in this concrete experience, any one element is a centre of many relations. A perceived object is associated not merely with some feeling, but with many other objects perceived at the same time. Any one of these it may suggest, according as a subsequent purpose marks out the lines of interest, and hence, as we shall find, "revival" in this stage is no longer necessarily dominated by association, but is free to supply means to ends as circumstances require.

3. c. *Ideas.*

The pivot upon which the practical judgment turns, as our account has shown, is the formation of the idea.

c, but A may be gone before c has come. This, of course, occurs in any long train of thought. Further, as experience grows more complex, and its results frequently conflict, beliefs are often depressed into mere suggestions or thoughts of reality. We then have " association of ideas " as ordinarily conceived.

Generically an idea is distinguished from all the modes of consciousness which we have considered hitherto, by the fact that in the scope of its reference it goes beyond what is directly present to our senses. To put the matter in its most general way, the mind, so far as it is active, is either concerned with what is immediately present to it, or is asserting, suggesting, wishing, commanding, etc., something not present. In all these cases we may distinguish the content of the act from the way in which the content is entertained (*i.e.*, by way of assertion, command, etc.). The content has always a reference beyond the present, and this is what we call an idea. [Even where an idea is applied to a present object, as when we name what we see before us, the use of the idea is either to determine the unperceived qualities of the object, or to class it, *i.e.*, bring it into relation with some general characteristic of reality.] Psychologically an idea may take the form of an image, *i.e.*, something actually *like* a percept, but with less sensational vividness and detail.[1] But we must carefully distinguish in thought between the image as something present to the mind—an object of internal consciousness—and the idea as containing a reference beyond itself. It is on this reference that the logical or practical function of the idea depends. The image is, at most, the form taken by the mental act in which that function is carried out.

How ideas first arise is a question to which only a tentative answer can be given, but in all probability their original function is to direct effort, and they may be supposed to arise in the process by which effort acquires definiteness of direction towards something unseen, unpresented to the senses. We can observe in the lower processes two elements which by their fusion would produce this result. On the one hand, in sensori-motor action we have response directed towards a given object, and as soon as the organism possesses "distance receptors," that is to say, the senses of sight, sound, and smell, the objects to which it so reacts may be remote from itself and definite in their place and motions. In the sensori-

---

[1] On this see Stout, *op. cit.* pp. 396–413.

motor visual response an animal directs its behaviour, not to the position of the object actually seen but to one toward which it is moving, but if the action is truly sensori-motor this is an effect of what is seen, discharged by pre-existing tendencies in the organism. Next, in the case of assimilation, the organism reacts to some quality of the object which is not presented to its sense, but again its action is determined by the presented object itself acting upon the structure formed by the previous experience. Let us now suppose that what is retained from a previous experience may be not a mere quality of feeling attached to the object but, say, the path on which it will move, and we then get an adjustment to this path, or rather to the position which the object will take upon it, based not on an innate tendency but on a previous experience. We thus get action directed in consequence of a past experience to something not given in the present, and here we seem to have the germ of what may be called a practical idea. The development of the idea would then depend, on the one hand upon the power of perceiving complex objects of distinct but yet related parts, and on the other hand on the power of any part to revive, not merely feelings or elements tending directly to affect conation, but elements of a perceptual character belonging to the original complex.

4. *d. Concrete Experience and Memory.*

The way in which a relation is originally experienced appears to have an important influence on its chances of revival. We all know that we can remember with more or less of accuracy, and for a greater or less period, persons or places seen only once. Similarly we remember events as having happened once. In all these cases a single experience is enough to form a basis for subsequent revival. On the other hand, if we want to learn something by rote, we repeat it over and over again, and get it perfect by degrees. In the first case the power of revival appears to be perfected by a single experience. In the second, it grows very gradually by frequent repetitions. What is the explanation of this contrast?

In the first place, we must beware of exaggerating it.

Our memory of a person or place seen once is seldom perfect. It fades with time, and is strengthened by renewal. In these respects it clearly follows the same law as memory due to repetition, and we may infer that there is no fundamental difference. The real distinction lies in connectedness of elements. If a—b—c form a rigidly and necessarily connected whole for thought, to remember a would be to remember b and c as well. If they are utterly disconnected, it requires three distinct efforts to recall them. There is an intermediate case in which they are apprehended in relation, though not in necessary relation, so that the remembrance of one naturally, though not inevitably, leads on to another. Thus I may readily remember a connected conversation or a well put argument, as each point leads naturally to the next. So again the metre as well as the thought help in the memory of verse, while in matters of simple perception, to recall one part, for example, of a once visited place is to have a beginning from which the space relations themselves help one in reconstructing the rest. In short, if instead of a, b, c, three quite separate data, we have a—b—c so related that one passes into the other or is continuous with it in perception, or leads up to it in meaning, we have quite a different groundwork to go upon. Our memory rests partly on the connection. In the alternative case it rests on association, the bringing of two things together in consciousness without any recognised connection. The difference which is made by connectedness may be estimated by comparing the number of repetitions necessary for learning (1) a series of isolated words or meaningless syllables, and (2) a connected piece of writing. Comparing words and phrases, MM. Binet and Henri estimate the advantage of phrases in one case as 25 to 1.[1] Comparing a series of meaningless syllables with a stanza of *Don Juan*, Ebbinghaus[2] found that ten times as many repetitions were necessary in the former case.

If we could say that association only acts by more or less frequent repetition, the problem of determining what

---

[1] *Année Psychologique*, 1894, p. 31.      [2] *Gedächtniss*, p. 69.

is due to connected experience, and what is not, would be immensely simplified. But we cannot deny that a single experience without any insight into relation may in some cases form a basis for memory. Thus even a series of meaningless syllables, if not too long, may be retained perfectly for a few moments, after a single hearing.[1] But the effect very speedily lapses. After twenty-four hours, the only result of a number of readings sufficient to get the syllables by heart for the moment is a certain diminution in the number required to get them perfect again. To illustrate the point, it will be enough to give one series of Ebbinghaus's experiments with twelve syllables, comparing it with his results for a stanza. The Roman numerals indicate the successive days; the Arabic figures, the number of times necessary to get the repetition perfect.

| Days | I. | II. | III. | IV. | V. | VI. |
|---|---|---|---|---|---|---|
| 12 syllables | 16·5 | 11 | 7·5 | 5 | 3 | 2·5 |
| Stanza of Don Juan | 7·75 | 3·75 | 1·75 | ·5 | 0 | 0 [2] |

I may subjoin a further table given by Mr. G. W. Smith,[3] showing the very slow improvement from repetition up to twelve times. Ten syllables were read and repeated. The table shows the number correctly given, and the number of mistakes after a given number of readings.

| Number of Readings. | Number correctly given. | Total Errors. |
|---|---|---|
| 1 | 2·2 | 22·2 |
| 3 | 2·5 | 21·4 |
| 6 | 2·8 | 20·5 |
| 9 | 3·4 | 18·9 |
| 12 | 3·9 | 17·3 |

We may conclude that as we approximate to irrational association in human experience, the number of repetitions required to fix a sequence in memory for any length of time becomes very large. Forty repetitions did not suffice to fix twelve syllables in Ebbinghaus's memory perfectly

[1] Binet and Henri, loc. cit. p. 7.    [2] Op. cit. p. 112.
[3] Psychological Review, 1896, "The Place of Repetition in Memory."

for twenty-four hours, while as many as twelve readings
fixed less than four syllables out of ten in Mr. G. W.
Smith's experiments.[1]

[1] The effective presentation of the problem of the rapidity of learning
has been the subject of several experimental studies, but the results are
not as yet as clear as might be desired. From what we know of the
definiteness of memory in the case of some particular event, we naturally
infer that a single instance should be decisive where there is a true
memory judgment. Conversely, from our common experience of the
gradualness in the formation of habit and the acquisition of skill, we
naturally take slowness of acquisition as evidence of the absence of the
true memory judgment. How far do these views stand the test of experiment? With regard to skill, Mr. E. J. Swift, in a valuable article in the
*American Journal of Psychology*, 1903, on "Studies in the Psychology
and Physiology of Learning," shows that in the practice of passing and
catching balls, progress is at first slow, and then more rapid. Where
improvement is rapid in early stages it is in relation to things which have
symbols or other devices for handling and presenting ideas. This is
precisely the contrast which we should expect, and the convex curves
which Mr. Swift presents have exactly the anticipated contrast to the con-
cave curves, with steep descents at the beginning and very gradual subsequent change, which belong to the memorising of something in which
we understand the connections. On the other hand, Mr. Hicks and
Professor Carr ("Human Reactions in a Maze," J. A. B. 1912, pp. 98–125)
have shown that the form of time curves, *i.e.*, the rate of the diminution of
the time in which an animal performs a trick, is not to be taken as a
criterion of the intelligence applied, under penalty of making rats more
intelligent than human beings. Further, Shepard and Brede (J. A. B.,
1913, pp. 274–285) have shown that the development of the pecking instinct
in chicks improves with great rapidity in the early stages, and then tails off
into a slow advance towards perfection. This is the opposite result to
those of Swift for the acquisition of skill. Again, Schaeffer, as noted
above, found inhibitions learnt by a frog in one or two instances alone,
and it would be very hard to attribute to a frog the higher order of
intelligence which we are now considering. Some other cases of inhibition by very few experiences, if not by one alone, have been recorded
among quite low animals.

I think we may find the key to these difficulties if we contrast the
rapidity with which the frog in Schaeffer's experiments learnt to reject
nauseous food with the slowness of its maze reactions as described
by Yerkes. We may suppose that the direct confirmation or inhibition of an instinctive response operates rapidly, while the building up
of habits that have no basis in instinct requires a large number of
experiments, accident probably playing a considerable part in the
process. The maturation of the pecking instinct would then follow the
law for the direct modification of response. It would advance rapidly
with the success of one type of movement and the failure of another,
and it is only the subtler adjustments which would require time. On
the other hand, the acquisition of something new, such as an acquired
art in the case of man, would be rapid only in those portions which
demand intelligence and definite memory, and would be slow on the
side of the sensori-motor adjustments. In the case of an animal learning a trick the rapid initial fall so frequently seen would probably be due
to the more intelligent elements in the process, and the slow later fall to

There is, however, another cause of retention to be considered besides frequency, namely, the vividness of an experience or the emotional interest attending it. In our own experience, we know that strong emotion lends a peculiar vividness to surrounding details so that very often trivial things that happened in a moment of great stress remain stamped in the memory for life. This vividness of irrelevant detail may be used to express a feeling which otherwise could not find utterance.

> " All's over, then—does truth sound bitter
>     As one at first believes ?
> Hark, 'tis the sparrows' goodnight twitter
>     About your cottage eaves !
>
> And the leafbuds on the vine are woolly,
>     I noticed that, to-day ;
> One day more bursts them open fully :
>     You know the red turns grey."

But cases of deep emotion stand by themselves. In a general way, it appears from a series of experiments conducted by Miss M. W. Calkins, that frequency is more powerful than vividness as a cause of association.[1] It is further clear that the influence of feeling, or other intense experience, would only extend to experiences close to it in time.[2]

the part which intelligence does not grasp. I think therefore *primâ facie* we may use rapidity of initial learning as a test of the higher processes except where we are dealing with feelings operating directly upon response.

It may be added then if a habit involving a train of connected elements is to be learnt by assimilation, numerous instances seem necessary, since at least one is required for each step. Thus chickens may respond with much excitement to the footsteps of the feeder. The excitement must have attached itself presumably first to the grain, then perhaps to the motions of scattering it, then to the feeder himself, and then to his footstep. If a connection were established between the first and last links in such a chain by a single experience it would, I think, be very strong evidence of definite memory.

[1] " Association " (*Psych. Rev.* Monograph Supplement), pp. 55, 56. Miss Calkins points out correctly that the vividness procurable in an experiment is not comparable to that of " richly emotional experiences."

[2] Two subordinate points of importance remain to be noticed. In a series of associations, A, B, C, D, E, the natural tendency is for A to excite B, B to excite C, and so forth. But A also acquires a certain power of exciting C, or even D or E, without the intermediates. This

To sum up.  In the sphere of articulate experience, a very few impressions, often a single impression, will suffice to form a permanent basis for memory.  Where the connection of elements is not apprehended, memory rests either (1) on frequent repetition, or (2) on the excitement of strong feeling.  This second influence can only extend to experiences bordering closely in time upon the moment of feeling.  In association each link normally recalls that which immediately follows, but it also has a weak tendency to recall remoter experiences.  To bear these points in mind will give us some help in deciding how to class some of the examples of the use of experience which we shall meet.

III. *The products and application of the Practical Judgment.*

4. *a.* Knowledge of objects.[1]

From what has been said of concrete experience and its revival, it follows that in this stage the mind may without impropriety be said not merely to react appropriately to objects, but to have a certain knowledge of them.  This knowledge must indeed fall short of the conceptual understanding whereby the characters of perceived objects fall into their place in a system of thought.  But still it may be called knowledge of an object as a whole consisting of distinct parts.  Such knowledge is not yielded by Assimilation alone, for here, beyond the quality perceived by the

---

power is, however, materially lower than that of normal association, and it diminishes rapidly as the links omitted are increased.  (For the evidence see Ebbinghaus, *op. cit.* pp. 130, ff., and Müller and Schumann, p. 307.)  It results that between experiences separated by an interval of time the associational tie, if there is any, must be relatively weak.

Lastly, reversed associations are not impossible.  If a series of names is learnt, we all know that we can with difficulty repeat them in reverse order.  The observations of Müller and Schumann, however, suggest that this can only happen where the previous name or syllable forms one complex state of consciousness with the later one which " revives " it.  If two syllables were grouped, they formed a well-marked backward association, but as between separate impressions they failed to establish the process with certainty (*op. cit.* p. 308).  It is safe to say that if association in this form is possible without the aid of articulate recollection—*i.e.*, remembrance of relations between elements—its effect is relatively feeble.

[1] The term is here used not in the general sense of " object of thought or of consciousness," but rather in the popular sense of a material thing with a certain individuality.  An animal would be an object in this sense.

sense organ, we have no definite reference to other
characters of the object.   It is not yielded by the Association of ideas.   To know an orange is not merely to
associate a certain colour with a certain shape, smell,
weight, softness, taste, and so forth.   If we use the word
associate at all, we must qualify it by adding "in certain
defined relations to one another."   To know that this is
an orange is to know that what I see before me will,
if I put it to my nose, emit a certain scent, if I
put my teeth into it as it is, will be unpleasantly bitter,
but if I first peel it, will reveal a pleasing juicy pulp, and
so forth.   In other words, the common object, to become
known as an object, must be understood as a kind of
structure involving related elements.   In the same way,
my knowledge of a house is not a mere association of one
room with another, but a knowledge of the relations of the
rooms, etc., in space.   While even with regard to a series
of events, though association without synthesis [1] might
reproduce the ideas in an order corresponding to that in
which the events occurred, my knowledge of the events as
a series must imply that two or more of them are held
together in their relations.

   *b. Memory and Anticipation.*

   It thus appears that knowledge of objects, and other
persons or animals, knowledge of localities, and knowledge
of occurrences depend on a more or less developed power
of grasping the elements of experience in their mutual
relations.   From this again it will be seen that both
Expectation and Memory, in the stricter sense of those
terms, rest upon the same basis.   In a loose sense the
term memory is often used to describe such permanent
influence of experience as is present in the lowest stages of
assimilation, but this is a misnomer which confuses things
essentially distinct.   What operates in assimilation we
should call retentiveness, for something is, even in that

---

[1] Such a synthesis, as I have argued elsewhere, may be given in apprehension in the simpler cases where it unites two immediately sensible
qualities through their coexistence in one point of space at one moment.
Beyond this, and thus in every case where the behaviour of an object at
different times enters into one conception of it, the synthesis acts by
bringing into relation contents of distinct perceptions.

stage, retained, and revived in relation to the present. But suppose that what is " retained " is a series of events grasped as a series, and that this series is revived in relation to present perception as its first step. We then have anticipation or expectation of the coming events. If again any connected series is grasped as a whole, there may at the end be retention in idea of the earlier stages. Such a mental reference to an experience that is past constitutes the memory-judgment in its primitive form. What is remembered or expected must be placed in some more or less defined relation to ourselves at the present moment, and conversely, where such an act of mental reference to past or future is possible, there are the conditions for the judgments of memory or expectation.

   *c. Purpose.*

   With the power of anticipation arises for the first time the possibility of purposive action in the strict sense. The paradox of organic action is that it carries out apparent purposes without purposing to do so. That is to say, it is adapted to the securing of results which we as spectators recognise as valuable to the organism, and yet we do not imagine it to be determined by any conception of those results. Just as the general bodily structure of a plant or an animal is adapted to meet the broad requirements of its mode of life, so its hereditary modes of reaction are so directed that while each is called up from hour to hour by its appropriate stimulus, and only by that stimulus, the result is to serve and to maintain the type of life peculiar to the species. The ordinary healthy animal does not eat in order to support life, but because it is hungry. It does not seek its mate in order to propagate the species, but in obedience to the sexual impulse. If the term "purposive" is claimed for these impulses on the ground that they are determined by the efforts which follow from them, the reply is that this is not literally true. There is a relation, but it is of a very indirect and circuitous kind. In the individual animal, under the sway of instinct, the impulse that appears purposive—say, the impulse to seize and devour its prey—is determined not by prevision of the beneficial effects of eating, but immediately by its

inherited structure, awakened as it is to activity by the
presence of the prey. This structure however has grown
up in the main because it did answer the requirements of
the animal's ancestors. Structures which answered those
needs less adequately have been eliminated, and through
the laws of inheritance the surviving structure has been
perfected. Thus, in an indirect and circuitous fashion,
the results of an action do go to determine what the action
shall be before the level of intelligent purpose is reached.
But this is true only in the sense that the generic results
of that sort of action have operated on the individual to
make him what he is. The particular results of this
particular action are not operative. The act is really the
result of a permanent structure acted upon by a stimulus.
It is adaptive, not purposive, its consequence in the
particular case is a result, not an end, and it should be
described as serving not a purpose but a function.

Since intelligence is above all things purposive in
character, the appearance of actions definitely directed to
and determined by the ends which they serve is perhaps
the most critical moment in the evolution of Mind. How
are we to understand this determination ? Let us first be
clear that where there is purpose there we can say that
this particular action is determined by this particular end.
Where there is adaptation without purpose, any given
action is not determined by its own end, but by a structure
which has grown up by subserving results which were
" ends " only to the onlooker. The " mechanical " reflex
is a fixed type of reaction to a stimulus of a certain kind.
Given stimulus and organism, the reaction is always the
same. We move, so to say, in a region of universals, and
action apparently purposive is in reality blind. A fish will
dart at a wriggling worm. This satisfies a need. Is it done
in order to satisfy the need ? It seems rather that the sight
of the wriggling object causes the dart, since wriggling things
that are not edible—a thread to which a button is hanging, or a curl of cigarette smoke,[1] will have the same effect.
A male frog at mating time is provided with a machinery
for grasping the female, but he will as readily grasp other

---

[1] Bateson, *loc. cit.*

M

objects of appropriate size.  In the readjustments discussed
in the last chapter, we find these types of reaction changed
by experience of results, but they are changed for fresh
types, fresh methods of reaction.   The mind in that stage
acquires new habits, but habits they are still.   Thus a
child is accustomed to drink from its special mug.
Another mug would do quite as well, but there is a
domestic storm because the proper mug cannot be found.
As long as habit is dominant, we cannot speak of purposive
action, action determined by an end, but must still call it
adaptive action, action issuing from a structure inherited or
acquired in response to a stimulus which calls it forth in
all circumstances until the structure is further modified.
Where, on the other hand, we have action not based on
habit, but on the relation between the thing done and the
result of doing it, there we have purpose.   In acquired
adaptation, though the response produces a result suited to
the organism, it is performed, not because the result will
follow in this particular case, but, in the last analysis,
because similar results have followed in previous cases, and
they have fixed the habit.   In purposive action, so far as
it is purposive, there is no habit fixed, but the response to
the surroundings is determined by the effect which it will
have in the particular case ; that is to say, by the relation
between act and consequence.   Hence we do not respond
uniformly to similar surroundings, but take into account
anything that, though outside the range of perception, is
relevant to our object.   Thus, I get up and leave the room
to fetch a book which I left upstairs, not because anything
which I see or feel moves me to rise and walk, but because
I wish to get the book ; and I direct my steps to the room
where I left it just now, and not to the bookshelf from
which I have fetched it a hundred times before.[1]   It is
clear that purposive action as thus defined will have a
much wider range and be capable of much more complex
and subtle application to varying circumstances than
adaptive action at its best.   We have already distinguished

---

[1] Unless, indeed, in a fit of absence, I relapse into a mechanical mode
of action, and then very probably my feet will carry me on the more
accustomed path.

conation from mechanism on the ground that the conative state is in some way determined by its relation to the state that comes out of it. It is not till we come to the level of purpose that the full meaning of this distinction becomes clear. A purposive act or state is a cause of events like other states of the organism, but it is a cause which knows itself, that appreciates its own tendency, direction, and probable effects. This knowledge is moreover essential to its operation and guides it. Every act which the purposive state of mind dictates is done because of its causal relation to the final result. Indeed, the bare existence of the purposive state itself is conditioned by the foresight directing the impulse which it contains. It is thus dependent for its being on its own tendency to bring other things about. We may then define purpose as a state which determines acts in accordance with the results which they tend to produce. This it effects in the human being through the medium of anticipatory ideas, and we have to ask how far and with what modifications the definition will apply to types of conation from which ideas are excluded. Of these we have seen two. Nearest to purpose stands sensori-motor action, in which response is determined by the needs of the occasion in relation to the complexity and varying movements of unique surroundings. In leaping to catch a ball the act certainly seems to be determined by what is coming out of it, but if we resolutely exclude anticipatory ideas we are denying that direct reference to the future which such determination implies. If the response is truly and exclusively sensory, we must suppose the state of excitement to be one which favours and maintains approach to the ball and suppresses adverse movements, while in so doing it adapts itself continually to the changing relations of the ball and the player. More generally, in successful sensori-motor response that selection of type movements which in fact favours the result will be maintained. If this is so the acts will be determined by relation to their results but indirectly, and this will be the point of distinction from true purpose.

Still more indirect is the relation in cases of the vague motions maintained, varied, or repeated under the influence of an uncomfortable situation or a persistent stimulus. Here the tendency of movements to give relief is quite general and uncertain, and the conative influence is seen only in the double fact that some movement is maintained while each particular movement that brings no relief is discarded, modified, or reversed. The bearing of the result upon the act is only definite so far as it is negative.

Conation in general, we may conclude, is a state which seeks to pass into some other—which is, in fact, conditioned by its tendency to do so. This other may be quite in-definite, and the acts to which the conation gives rise equally undefined and inappropriate ; or it may be definite but, as in sensori-motor action, not foreseen, so that it operates on the action only through the sense of approximation, which confirms what falls into line and eliminates the rest. Lastly, in purpose it may come before the mind as an idea, and each act and the entire movement are then determined definitely by the contribution which they make to the result.

*d. Purpose and knowledge of relations.*

Purpose, if the above account is correct, involves an idea of the end. Action can be directly based on a relation of end to means only if there is knowledge of that relation. Such knowledge, however, is in itself quite distinct from a habit of action, and is attained in a different way. It may, for example, be derived directly or indirectly from passive observation. Hence a second characteristic of purposive action. It is based on knowledge, not on habit, and conversely, if we have evidence that an act is based on knowledge, we have evidence that it is purposive. Such evidence, as has been hinted, may be derived from the nature of the experience antecedent to an action. Thus, in the example of the book, my movements are based on the knowledge of various relations derived from experience (of the house and its parts, memory of where I left the book, and so on), and in its determining factors there is nothing either in-

stinctive or habitual.[1]   The action may be so far novel that
I may never have left a book in this particular room before.
Experience gives knowledge of certain relations which are
utilised in action when they can be so applied to present
circumstances as to lead up to a desired end.   The relations
may be first perceived in circumstances in which they are
indifferent, and give rise to no reaction.   They are afterwards applied in fresh circumstances, and so become a
guide to action.   Clearly, in such instances, there is no
preformed habit.

As judged from outward action, then, the certain
signs of purposive action appear so far to be these two :
The relation upon which it is based may be experienced without leading to the formation of a habit ;[2]
and again, may be applied in circumstances differing
from those in which it was originally perceived.   Action
may often be purposive without possessing these marks,
but where we find these marks we may be sure that it
is purposive.

*e. Idea and Desire.*

The purposive act, not being guided by response to perception, is determined by reference to an end.   This act of
reference we know in the human consciousness as an idea.
We are thus brought to the primitive function that ideas
fulfil in conduct.   As long as impulses are fixed in relation to stimulus, whether by heredity or habit, action
neither requires nor tolerates any further guide.   But if
the ends of an impulse are to be served by actions varying
from case to case, a uniform reaction to uniform stimulus
will no longer do.   Minor adjustments to perceived variations are effected by present consciousness in sensori-
motor action, but if behaviour is to be suitably adapted to
remote results something more is required, and the case

---

[1] This statement applies only to the determining factors of the act, for,
just as the walking is a reflex, so my turning one way or another may be,
when once the general direction is fixed, carried out more or less
mechanically.   Conscious adjustments constantly make use of subordinate
mechanical factors.

[2] The clearest case of this is, of course, where the relation experienced
is not between the action of an organism and its effects, but between two
or more events or objects which it perceives.

is met in the human world by a formulation of the end
to which one is impelled, along with its relation to the
surrounding circumstances. The formulation of the end
constitutes an Idea, and the impulse so qualified becomes
a Desire. In the animal world, though we know nothing
of what passes in an animal's consciousness, we must yet,
if we find action similarly determined, impute to the
animal something which, if not an idea, is capable of performing an identical function. If ideas arise in this way
as a definition of impulse, it is easy to understand that
they carry a motor excitement with them. Action
would seem to be the primitive and natural accompaniment of an idea, and it is only in the course of
further evolution that ideas arise which do not prompt
to action.

5. *f. Knowledge of Objects and Analogy.*

Two further points remain in which the application of
concrete experience is contrasted with habituation. First,
since perception yields knowledge of objects as wholes
containing related elements, it makes possible inferences
concerning objects which are similar as wholes, that is in
the arrangement of their parts rather than in any special
sense-quality. Inferences of this character seem to underlie
much of our practical thinking about the common objects
of life. We may be at a loss to name any single important
sense-quality in which, say, two animals resemble each
other ; and yet we are sure that there is a real identity of
character which will make them for many purposes act
alike. Such an inference, drawn, as it continually is, without any analytical reflection, is the rudest form of analogy,
being based on what are really similarities of relation.
Such similarities may appear as an influence in practical
inference as soon as wholes of related elements are distinctly experienced—that is to say, as soon as we attain to
knowledge of concrete objects ; and unless there is such
knowledge, it is hard to see on what such an inference
could rest. Hence, conversely, inference based on such a
similarity as distinguished from identity of sense-quality
may be taken as evidence that experience is of the concrete
type.

*g. Objects as centres of relations.*

Secondly, since the relations in which objects stand are manifold, concrete experience supplies the possibility of reacting to an object in very different ways, according to the purpose in hand. Hence the comparative elasticity of the Practical Judgment in the choice of means, which we have contrasted with the rigidity of habit.

Now Association is mental habit. If one learns a string of words without meaning, like the *Ena, mena, mona, mite* of childhood, each word calls up the other, not through any appropriateness of relation, but through the influence of past sequences. In consequence association, like all other generic bases of reaction, will often act inappropriately. If a man has got into the habit of winding up his watch mechanically when he takes off his waistcoat, he will occasionally find himself doing it if he happens to change his clothes at any unusual time in the day. Similarly, if a verse is being repeated by rote, a casual association may lead to the substitution of a word or line belonging to another verse, and making nonsense. These aberrations are, of course, checked in human experience by the fact that nonsense or abnormality at once arrests attention and brings in higher processes than those of association.

Association, then, tends to form a series in which *a* calls up *b*, *b* calls up *c*, and so forth.[1] The idea which will follow on *a* or *b* is determinate, and the more so the stronger the association. If there is a well-rooted association between *a* and *b*, *b* is the only possible follower of *a*. The term *a* may stand in relation to very many other terms, but by association it will preferably excite the idea of one of them—that one with which it is most intimately associated. If more than one association has been formed, the weaker must either give way or serve merely to distract and weaken attention unless consciousness is comprehensive enough to hold both ideas before it in their distinctness. Here, then, association is at a disadvantage

---

[1] It is true that earlier antecedents have their effect. In repeating a verse by rote, it would hardly be accurate to think, for example, of each word as the sole cause determining the reproduction of the word following it. The general remembrance of the verse produces a mental atmosphere which is, no doubt, an underlying condition of correct reproduction.

as compared with the judgment. Concrete experience yields us knowledge of objects which are the meeting points of many relations. An object in space, for instance, is related to an indefinite number of surrounding objects. One of these related objects, and perhaps one only, is relevant to the purpose of the moment. To this object, whether it is that suggested by the dominant Association or not, our purpose will direct our thoughts. On another occasion, a quite different object may be the one relevant to our purpose, and the direction of our thought is altered accordingly. Thus, while association brings up the same ideas with dull uniformity, the purposive judgment selects from the material presented by experience the relation which it requires.[1]

IV. *General Character of Concrete Experience and the Practical Judgment.*

6. Concrete Experience consists in the perception of surrounding objects in their changes and relations. The elements of a percept being connected, a single experience may have a permanent effect, shown in its capacity for being revived. Such revival in relation to a present perception constitutes the Practical Judgment of which the unperceived elements are concrete ideas. An impulse directed by such an idea is purposive, and constitutes a Desire. Such is broadly the group of related psychological elements which characterise the stage of Concrete Experience and the Practical Judgment.

The use of experience in action has at this stage certain distinctive features, through which it presents a well-marked contrast with the work of Assimilation.

The basis of action consists of data of experience in their relations. Of these data, we observe that :

(1) Only one experience is required as a basis of future action. In the case of assimilation a single experience may have an enduring though seldom a permanent effect in directly checking or in forming a conative tendency. In establishing any longer or more

---

[1] *I.e.*, so far as the purpose is dominant. In the concrete the stronger association tends to conflict with the purpose, and may overwhelm it. I am again contrasting limiting cases.

complex series of actions it is only the massive effect
of repeated experience that operates.

(2) The relations given in experience, and guiding
subsequent action, may be relations between any objects
of perception, and are not (as in the case of Assimilation)
confined to those between sensations and the motor
excitements immediately attendant on them.   Hence,
further

    *a*. Inferences may be based on a general similarity
       (a similar relation of parts), and not merely on
       similarity in a distinct sense-quality.

    *b*. The same content may stand in several distinct
       relations without confusion.   In the case of
       Assimilation (and Association) one content leads
       uniformly to one other.

(3) The results of experience are applied to action in
a manner not determined by the experience itself.   In the
case of Assimilation, the application of experience is not
distinct from its acquisition, the formation of a habit
being the formation of a tendency to act.

Thus, what is effected in this stage is a correlation
between complexes which themselves involve related
elements, *i.e.*, between articulate complexes.   On the
one side we have data perceived as distinct but related,
on the other means adopted in relation to distinct ends:
the correlation consisting in the process by which the
one complex gives rise to the other.   Both complexes
belong to the perceptual order.[1]

It will be seen that the unit of this process from first to
last is the complex of related terms whether given in perception or grasped in an idea starting from a perception.   In
this complex the relation is not apprehended in abstraction
from the terms, but the terms in their relation constitute
an articulate whole.[2]   There are three stages in the ex-

---

[1] The act and its result may not in fact be perceived, but they are
particular events in time congruous with those which form the contents
of perception, *i.e.*, they are of the perceptual order.

[2] In any articulate perception the relations contained contribute to the
character of the whole as much as the elements that are related, and in
that sense the relations must be said to be perceived.   It does not follow
that the character of any of the relations concerned is analysed out and

perience of relations which should be distinguished. In the first, a relation between A and B affects the mind though A and B are never apprehended as related. This is the case of assimilation where, *e.g.*, a feeling modifies the effect of a sensation, though the sequence sensation-feeling is never grasped. In the third and highest, the relation *a* between the two terms A—B is distinguished, named, and compared with others. Thus in the same instance the relation is known as one of sequence, perhaps as one of causation. Here there is knowledge of the relation as such, and we are in the world of " universals " or general conceptions. In the second and intermediate stage the relation is not apprehended as such, but the terms in their relation are grasped together. The datum of experience is here the content A—B. In our instance the whole proceeding, feeling-following-on-sensation, is apprehended, though the relation of sequence is not dissected out and so prepared for naming and comparison with others. This I call the stage of Concrete Experience and the Practical Judgment, and its unit is an articulate complex in the perceptual order.

Apart from introspection, we may justly impute this knowledge of objects in relation when we find action based on the relation A—B as distinct from the contents A, or B, alone. The marks distinguishing action of such a character have been enumerated above.

V. *The Practical Judgment as a stage in the Correlation of Experiences.*

7. It remains to characterise in general terms the Method and Scope of the correlation effected in this stage,

---

distinguished from the terms which compose it. When I look at any complex object, as, *e.g.*, the front of a house, I am aware of a whole with many distinct parts. These parts are in definite relations to one another. I may concentrate attention on any pair ; *e.g.*, a window to the right of the door. I then not merely see the door and window, but see them in their relation to one another. By an act of analysis I can go further, and make of the relation a distinct object of thought, independent of the terms which it connects in this particular case. But in so doing I pass from perception to conception. When I speak of a relation as perceptual, or even as " perceived," I mean that it is not thus distinguished, but is an element in a perceived whole.

and to contrast it with the work of the lower stage of Assimilation.

As to scope, the first or lower stage is concerned with the correlation of sense stimuli and resulting feelings, and its function is to define and regulate instinctive and random action. The second or higher stage deals with concrete objects, and the adjustment of action to make or meet changes in the physical surroundings. Its relation to instinct will be discussed later.

As to method, we have found that the basis of the whole process is a perceived relation—in itself a correlation of distinct experiences. The terminus of the process is again what we have called a practical relation: an adjustment of means to ends ; once more an act of correlation. Further, the second act of correlation is, as we have seen, based upon the first; and there is thus a wider kind of correlation, including the two constituent relations which form the starting point and the conclusion. We have expressed this by describing this stage as a correlation of articulate complexes.

If for the word correlation we substitute inference, the process described shows a clear analogy to one familiar to logicians. It resembles, in short, the inference from particulars to particulars in which the implied universal is not made explicit. That is to say, a particular relation $A_1$—$B_1$ is perceived ; and where in a second case $A_2$ is given, the correlate $B_2$ is inferred.

This inference is equivalent to the passage in the syllogism from the minor premiss (this is $A_2$) to the conclusion (it will be $B_2$). What is called the inference from particulars to particulars then may also be described as an argument from minor to conclusion, founded on observed parallels.

We must try to understand clearly how far inference at this stage differs from the corresponding process in the lower stage.

Consider the case of the chick which learns to peck at yolk of egg. We may explain this as acquired habit or as acquired knowledge. In the former case, a series of experiences gradually remodels action. In the latter, an experienced relation is grasped and applied. If the latter explanation is adopted, we naturally express it by saying that the chick has learnt that yolk of egg is good, but it is essential to note that to express the result in general terms is precisely what the chick cannot do. The chick, we are assuming, perceives the relation in each instance in which it is given, and later on expects the coming result before it is given. The man, observing the chick's action, sees that it is working upon a principle that might be stated in general terms; but it is the man that states the principle, not the chick.

If, to carry the matter a stage further, the man were addicted to formal logic, he would express the whole process, as it goes on in his own mind, in the well-known scheme of induction and syllogism. Thus:

1. This, that, and the other yolk of egg is good.
2. Yolk of egg is good.
3. This is a piece of yolk.
4. This is good.

Now, if the chick's intelligence reaches the second stage, but no higher, it grasps the relation expressed in (1), (3), and (4) of these stages, but not that expressed in (2). At each trial it has recognised the fact that " this piece of yolk is good," and having grasped this it is at a later stage capable of forming the judgment which combines (3) and (4). That is to say, we may represent it as saying to itself: " This is a piece of yolk : it will be good." In other words, it has previously grasped the particular relations upon which its subsequent inference rests, and the inference itself consists in the grasping of a relation of which only one term is perceived. This stage is then a correlation of related elements, and if we compare it to explicit inference as analysed in syllogism, we may say that the concrete relations upon which the major premiss is based are perceived, and the relation which leads from minor to conclusion is judged, while the major premiss is represented by the psychological result of the repeated perceptions; a result shown in the power of judging the relation in a fresh case when only one term is perceived.

If now again we reverse our supposition, and reduce the

intelligence of the chick to the lower stage, we shall find that much less is explicit, and much more psychological process that we can only know by its results. We shall now have to say that the relations known to the onlooker are never perceived as such by the chick, but that each trial of the yolk goes to build up a habit (which takes the place of the major premiss), which on the perception of the yolk, issues at once in pecking. The perception of the yolk corresponds to the minor premiss, and the pecking to the conclusion of this practical syllogism ; but the chick does not, according to our analysis of this stage, grasp the relation which unites them ; he merely passes from the one to the others. In short, the minor premiss is here replaced by a perception acting upon a preformed disposition. We may express the contrast by saying that in the lower stage, at the moment of action, the conclusion alone is the explicit object of consciousness. " This is to be pecked at " expresses the chick's consciousness ; that, and no more. In the second and higher stage, the relation of minor and conclusion is explicit, " This, being yolk of egg, is to be pecked at." Thus in the lower stage, the conclusion appears as an impulse, issuing from all that has gone before as its psychological basis. There is correlation between a set of experiences on the one side, and a mode of reaction to stimulus on the other. The higher stage is essentially a process of perception and judgment—a correlation of articulate complexes each containing related elements.

Finally, the transition from the lower to the higher stage rests on the growth of experience in clearness and comprehensiveness. In the primitive experience, the feeling modifies the sensation which it follows. Let the scope of consciousness be extended so that sensation and feeling may be apprehended together while yet remaining distinct, and the content sensation-giving-place-to-feeling comes into being. This is the germ of the higher stage.

# CHAPTER IX

## LEARNING AMONG THE HIGHER ANIMALS. THE METHOD OF TRIAL AND ERROR

WE have now to ask whether there is any evidence that this stage of intelligence is attained by any animals other than man.

1. Let us begin by considering a very simple instance of the apparently purposive choice of means to an end. I once had a cat which learnt to " knock at the door " by lifting the mat outside and letting it fall.[1] The common account of this proceeding would be that the cat did it in order to get in. It assumes the cat's action to be determined by its end. Is the common account wrong ? Let us test it by trying explanations founded on the more primitive operations of experience. First, then, can we explain the cat's action by the association of ideas ? The obvious difficulty here is to find the idea or perception which sets the process going. The sight of a door or a mat was not, so far as I am aware, associated in the cat's experience with the action which it performed until it had performed it. If there were association, it must be said to work retrogressively. The cat associates the idea of getting in with that of someone coming to the door, and this again with the making of a sound to attract attention, and so forth. Those who hold language of this kind are really describing what I have called the Practical Judgment in different terms. Such a series of associations so well adjusted means in reality a set of related elements grasped

---

[1] The habit is, I believe, not uncommon among cats.

by the animal and used to determine its action. Ideas of "persons," "opening doors," "attracting attention," and so forth, would have no effect unless attached to the existing circumstances. If the cat has such abstract ideas at all, she must have something more—namely, the power of applying them to present perception. The "ideas" of calling attention and of dropping the mat must somehow be brought together. Further, if the process is one of association, it is a strange coincidence that the right associates are chosen. If the cat began on a string of associations starting from the people in the room, she might as easily go on to dwell on the pleasures of getting in, of how she would coax a morsel of fish from one or a saucerful of cream from another, and so spend her time in idle reverie. But she avoids these associations, and selects those suited to her purpose. In short, we find signs on the one hand of the application of ideas, on the other of selection. Both of these features indicate a higher stage than that of sheer association. This we shall always find, if we endeavour to apply the association of ideas regressively as explaining the apparent choice of means to a desired end.

But there is another possible line of explanation. Mr. Lloyd Morgan's dog Tony learned to open a gate by lifting the latch with his head. I do not know how my cat learnt to knock, but Mr. Lloyd Morgan tells us that Tony

" after looking out between the bars in a number of places in the railings, at length chanced to gaze out under, and at the same time inadvertently lift, the latch." [The dog then] " after a while profited by the fortunate results of an originally fortuitous experience, and now opens the gate whenever he wants to do so." [1]

Here, then, is a way back to association. It is of course still possible on the facts before us that Tony grasped the relation which he had once experienced—saw, however vaguely, that pushing in his head at a particular point and then lifting it would get the gate open, and that he afterwards applied this knowledge. But it is also possible that the pleasure of getting through became associated with

[1] *Habit and Instinct*, p. 154.

that method of action and "stamped it in"—in other words, that the action assimilated the character of its result and became in itself attractive to the dog.

2. *Mr. Thorndike's Experiments.*

This method of explanation, which, it will be seen, virtually dispenses not only with a knowledge of relations, but with association of ideas, and carries us back to the stage of assimilation,[1] has been applied as a sort of universal solvent by Mr. Thorndike.[2] Mr. Thorndike's view, based upon a number of ingenious experiments with cats, dogs, and chicken, is, roughly, that the acquired actions of all animals below the primates are to be explained upon that principle of the selection of the successful act and elimination of failures which we applied in Chapter VII. to explain retrogressive associations. Mr. Thorndike does not go quite as far as to deny animals all images or ideas whatever, but his general position and tendency are not unfairly represented by the following passage.

"The possibility is that animals may have *no images or memories at all, no ideas to associate.* Perhaps the entire fact of association in animals is the presence of sense-impressions with which are associated, by resultant pleasure, certain impulses, and that therefore, and therefore only, a certain situation brings forth a certain act."[3]

In any case, he seems pretty clear that the association of ideas is not the important point, but rather the impulse-feeling association.

"The groundwork of animal associations is not the association of *ideas,* but the association of idea or sense-impression with *impulse.*"[4]

The general conception of the life of the higher animals that results is so interesting as to deserve quotation in full.

"One who had seen the phenomena so far described, who has watched the life of a cat or dog for a month or more under test conditions, gets, or fancies he gets, a fairly definite idea of what

---

[1] This method of learning, depending on repeated blundering efforts with fortuitous successes that are gradually selected, has been called by Mr. Lloyd Morgan the Method of Trial and Error.

[2] "Animal Intelligence," *Psych. Rev.* Mon. Supp., Vol. II. No. 4.

[3] P. 73.

[4] P. 71.

the intellectual life of a cat or dog feels like. It is most like what we feel when consciousness contains little thought about anything, when we feel the sense-impressions in their first intention, so to speak, when we feel our own body, and the impulses we give to it. Sometimes one gets this animal consciousness while in swimming, for example. One feels the water, the sky, the birds above, but with no thoughts *about* them or memories of how they looked at other times, or æsthetic judgments about their beauty; one feels no *ideas* about what movements he will make, but feels himself make them, feels his body throughout. Self-consciousness dies away. Social consciousness dies away. The meanings, and values, and connections of things die away. One feels sense-impressions, has impulses, feels the movements he makes; that is all.

This pictorial description may be supplemented by an account of some associations in human life which are learned in the same way as are animal associations; associations, therefore, where the process of formation is possibly homologous with that in animals. When a man learns to swim, to play tennis or billiards, or to juggle, the process is something like what happens when the cat learns to pull the string to get out of the box, provided, of course, we remove, in the man's case, all the accompanying mentality which is not directly concerned in learning the feat. Like the latter, the former contains desire, sense-impression, impulse, act and possible representations. Like it, the former is learned gradually. Moreover, the associations concerned cannot be formed by imitation. One does not know how to dive just by seeing another man dive. You cannot form them from being put through them, though, of course, this helps indirectly, in a way that it does not with animals. One makes use of no feelings of a common element, no perceptions of similarity. The tennis player does not feel, "This ball coming at this angle and with this speed is similar in angle, though not in speed, to that other ball of an hour ago, therefore I will hit it in a similar way." He simply feels an impulse from the sense-impression. Finally, the elements of the associations are not isolated. No tennis-player's stream of thought is filled with free-floating representations of any of the tens of thousands of sense-impressions of movements he has seen and made on the tennis-court. Yet there is consciousness enough at the time, keen consciousness of the sense-impressions, impulses, feelings of one's bodily acts. So with the animals. There is consciousness enough, but of this kind." [1]

It would be out of place to examine Mr. Thorndike's interesting paper in full detail, but we may consider

[1] Pp. 83, 84.

the main reasons which lead him to this remarkable conclusion.

Mr. Thorndike's principal experiments consisted in placing cats, dogs, and chickens in a variety of cages so contrived that they could be opened by means well within the animal's physical powers, yet quite outside the range of its ordinary experience. Thus clawing at a string, depressing a lever, pushing aside a swing door and so forth enabled the prisoner to escape. It was found that the cat or dog—we may confine our attention to them—at first clawed and scratched more or less indiscriminately ; in so doing it would in course of time give, by accident, the required push or pull, and so obtain its freedom. After a certain number of repetitions, the animal would acquire the power of doing what was needed more and more quickly, until at last the trick was properly learnt. The right action was " stamped in " by success, while the indiscriminate pawing was stamped out. As a measure of the perfection of the habit, the *time* required to achieve freedom is taken practically as the sole test. The results are exhibited graphically in " time curves," falling with more or less marked fluctuations from the maximum point of several minutes, to the minimum of a few seconds. Some of the tricks, it may be mentioned, were decidedly complex. One was a " thumb latch " complicated by the fact that after the latch was lifted the door still required a force of 400 grammes to open it, and still more by the fact that the latch would " fall back into place again unless the door were pushed out at least a little." Another, called Box J, required two separate movements to open it ; others called K and L required three such movements. Bearing in mind that the result in these movements would be something utterly foreign to the initial experiences of the cats, and would to the end remain connected only by the observed fact of sequence and not by any perceived continuity, one is somewhat surprised at the measure of success which the animals achieved. All the cats learned some of the tricks, and all the tricks appear to have been learnt by some. The dogs were not so uniformly successful. Let us then examine the grounds on which Mr. Thorndike uses observations which some writers might have taken as a proof of high intelligence, as proving precisely the contrary.

3. *a. Habituation and number of instances.*

Explicit memory, as we have seen, serves as a basis for inference from a single experience. If we could convert the proposition and be assured that inferences from a single experience imply explicit memory, then we could without further difficulty assign memory and the type of inference based on it to many animals. The elephant or the dog that long cherish vindictiveness for a single injury, the horse which knows better than its rider the road they have once traversed, and that perhaps in a contrary direction, could be said without more ado to draw inferences of this type. We must return to this point later. It is enough for the present to remark that while habits are, as every one knows, generally formed gradually by many repetitions, explicit memory is due to a single experience.

Mr. Thorndike's first argument is based upon this contrast.

"The gradual slope of the time-curve, then, shows the absence of reasoning. They represent the wearing smooth of a path in the brain, not the decisions of a rational consciousness." [1]

But is the slope gradual ? Turning to the actual curves (p. 18, ff.) there seem to be many cases in which it is not so by any means. Thus in box D, which was opened by pulling a string at the top of the box, one cat appears to have learnt the way of escape after four *successful* trials (the failures clearly would have no direct influence), another after two trials, another after one only. That is to say, after the trials mentioned, the time taken, though slightly fluctuating, did not exceed half a minute. Another cat appears to have learnt the trick in one trial—though its time afterwards rose in two cases to about a minute, and after many experiments it became so well versed in the matter that a lapse of seventy-two days only raised its time to a little over a minute again.[2]

---

[1] P. 45.

[2] I speak with some diffidence as to the exact numbers, as the curves are not so drawn as to be particularly easy to measure. On this point,

Take Box E again, where the cats had to put out a paw and claw a string outside the box—a thing that would hardly be done accidentally in many minutes of random clawing, and would, one would say, not be done twice over in such a manner within twenty experiments. One cat (No. 6) after one success reduced its time to about ninety seconds, and after the third trial to fifty seconds. It had a few more trials, and after fourteen days its first experiment took about one minute. These figures surely suggest partial recollection rapidly becoming perfect, rather than a slowly ingrained habit. Box I, which was opened by a lever, appears to have been mastered by cat No. 3 in *one* instance, while Nos. 4 and 5 seem to have had no difficulty with it from the beginning—their time never rising much beyond half a minute, and remaining at a minimum after the lapse of many days.

In many cases no doubt the fluctuations persist longer and the instances approximate more closely to the type required by Mr. Thorndike's argument. But a few instances to the contrary are sufficient to disprove his sweeping general statement. It is quite possible that some of the cats learnt the tricks more intelligently than others, just as some failed to learn many tricks altogether. These differences are still more marked in the case of the few dogs experimented on. Hardly any of their time curves can be called gradual—unless the slope of a church steeple is gradual. In the lever box, one dog's time curve came down from several minutes to fifty seconds after a single success. Another *began* with a time of some forty seconds only, which he reduced in three experiments to eight or ten. A third seems to have got the trick nearly perfect after one success, and quite so after two. It seems

---

and in the whole examination of Mr. Thorndike's important monograph, I have been specially helped by Mr. A. E. Taylor.

As to the fluctuations, it must be observed that the time taken can only be a very rough and imperfect measure of the perfection of the cat's habit or understanding as the case may be. Alterations in degree of liveliness, accidental failures to clutch properly, and a dozen other causes, would produce delays, and various fluctuations occurring in cases where habits were well established seem to indicate that this occurred. Mr. Thorndike does not seem to realise at all adequately the very rough and ready character of his statistical methods.

superfluous to quote further examples. Mr. Thorndike himself would probably have been impressed by those referred to if he had not entertained an exaggerated conception of the "perfection" of what we have called explicit memory, or memory in its stricter sense.

. . . "Real memory is an absolute thing, including everything but forgetfulness. If the cat had real memory it would, when after an interval dropped into a box, remember that from this box it escaped by doing this or that and consequently, either immediately or after a time of recollection, go do it, or else it would not remember and would fail utterly to do it." [1]

The statement is so astonishing that one would take it for a mere slip, but that much of Mr. Thorndike's argument is founded upon it. A moment's self-recollection is enough to show that memories of past events or of things learnt are of all degrees of completeness. That it should take four or five trials to teach a cat a novel sort of trick is certainly no more than one would expect on the hypothesis that a clear grasp of the relations involved was being gradually formed and fixed in memory. What Mr. Thorndike's experiments prove, so far, is not that cats and dogs are invariably educated by the association process, *i.e.*, by habituation alone, but, on the contrary, that at least some cats and dogs conform in at least one point to the methods of acquisition by concrete experience—they learn in a very few instances. [2]

4. *Failure to learn by being put through an action.*

What we may call the sense-impulse theory of association implies that an animal can only learn to do a thing by doing it, and so getting the pleasure of success associated with the doing. Now, if one puts an animal through an act to show him how it is done, and if he can learn in this way, the theory breaks down. For to have his limbs mechanically moved by the hand is quite a different thing from moving them himself. The set of sensations involved would be, *apart from the perception of the movement*, in the main different. In particular, the impulse to move would be absent. This case therefore is critical for the sense-

---

[1] P. 98.
[2] On the question of the value of time-curves see above, p. 156, note.

impulse theory.    Mr. Thorndike himself obtained negative results from his experiments, which he generalises.
But here again his experience is surely at variance with
common knowledge.    I have seen dogs in process of learning tricks by being held in position.    Wundt [1] explains
that he taught his poodle to shut the door in that fashion
—in four or five lessons moreover ; and my wife, who had
a pug which shut the door to admiration, tells me that she
taught it in the same way.    The regular method of teaching elephants is, as I am informed by the experienced
elephant trainer at the Belle Vue Gardens, Manchester, for
the keeper to guide the trunk from point to point.[2]    To
test Mr. Thorndike's assertion, I myself made a little experiment with a kitten, which seems clear enough.    I
showed the kitten some food, fish or milk, and then, setting
the dish for a moment on another table near, I lifted the
kitten on to a desk, and handed it the food.    I did this
six times without result, the kitten merely mewing and
begging in its own fashion.    The seventh time the kitten
jumped on to the desk of itself.[3]    After this I left home,
and it had no more lessons for a fortnight.    On my return
I found that it jumped on to the desk at the first trial, and
after that the act became habitual.    In this case the kitten
did the thing regularly after doing it once ; and it never
had any inducement to get on to the table, such as might
produce a nascent impulse, in seeing the food there while
it was below.    It saw the food in my hand, near but not
on the desk, or else, as I bent to pick it up, on the table
near.

No doubt cats and dogs differ, and so do their trainers,
but even a few positive instances are sufficient to destroy
Mr. Thorndike's generalisation.[4]

[1] *Lectures on Human and Animal Psychology*, p. 360.
[2] See below, p. 198.
[3] On the sixth trial, the kitten got on to a chair as if to get up, but
went down again.    Except on one day, when I gave it two lessons, the
experiments were, roughly, at intervals of twenty-four hours.
[4] Mr. Small, whose remarks (*American Journal of Psychology*, Jan.
1900) go to the root of the matter, points out that any "Attempt . . . to
restrain or constrain the animal would defeat the desired end—attention
would assuredly be diverted from the objective point to the restraining
conditions—would be lost in the affective absorption induced by them"
(p. 163).    And commenting on Mr. Thorndike's experiments, he says :

## 5. *Failure to imitate.*

A more serious negative result was reached by Mr. Thorndike on another point. He found reason to think that imitation in the sense of "transferred association" does not exist among mammals below the primates. That is to say, that animals never will do a thing because they see others obtain their ends by so doing. Cats and dogs were shut up in boxes, and allowed to watch the method by which another cat or dog escaped from another compartment of the box. To this compartment they were afterwards admitted, and it was found that they had learnt nothing. These experiments are of somewhat doubtful value.[1] So far as they go, they fall in with the view to which I have been led independently, that an animal makes no intellectual provision for the future. If the cat could say to itself, " There is my friend Tom in the outer compartment. I shall be let in there in a minute, so I will watch, and see how Tom gets out;" it would doubtless watch Tom's proceedings with care, but it would also be a much more reflective animal than it is. The probability is rather that its attention is aroused only as a rule by the act or object that leads up to or is connected with the end to which it is itself striving. Other things may strike it by chance, but its interest is not directed to them. Thus it would be more likely that one animal would imitate another if both were trying to escape or to get fed at the same time.[2] Whether under these conditions

" This method manifestly disregards the factor of attention above adverted to, and consequently fails to demonstrate the absence in animals of those higher associative processes involved in inferential imitation " (p. 164). It follows that the method would be much less likely to succeed with a cat, which resents being held, than with the obedient elephant or the trustful dog. I failed in my attempt to use it with a Rhesus monkey (see below, p. 284).

[1] Mr. Thorndike says that the cats watched their instructors "more or less," and afterwards reckons up the number of times which a cat " probably saw " or " certainly saw." My own experience in experimenting convinces me so strongly of the difficulty of judging what a cat or dog really sees—even when I am making a direct effort to get its attention—that I am surprised that so experienced an investigator should speak of certainty in connection with the question whether one cat saw another perform a seemingly trivial operation on the other side of a grating.

[2] Mr. Thorndike tried this experiment with two cats, of which, one, in fact, succeeded. Mr. Thorndike, however, states that it acted just like

there might be reflective imitation—imitation based on the perception of another's act and its result to that other—remains uncertain.

What has first to be settled is the possibility of a still simpler mental act—learning by the perception of an event and its consequence—when that consequence directly affects the learner. If an animal sees something done which has the immediate effect of giving it what it wants, then the something done falls within the sphere of interest as above

the others who formed the association by accident. But I notice in Mr. Thorndike's table that this particular cat only succeeded in one other box ; we are not told in how many it failed. In any case, Mr. Thorndike seems to be in error in arguing that there was no imitation because the one cat used its teeth to pull the string, and the other its claw. In my experiments I found that animals frequently varied their own method in this fashion. Mr. Thorndike's argument would only hold against a purely mechanical and unintelligent theory of imitation.

Another cat failed to climb up netting, though eighty times it saw other cats climb up and get fed ; but as Mr. Thorndike tells us that even when a piece of fish was held out through the netting he would not climb after it, this result is not very surprising. If the cat would not climb to get fish which he saw before him, it is not likely that he would climb because he saw others do so.

In the remaining experiment mentioned by Mr. Thorndike, two cats learned to do as a third, but they did not " form the association more quickly than they would have done alone." But how quickly would they have formed it alone ? One could only judge from the speed of other cats, and nothing is more unsafe than to infer from the performance of one animal to that of another.

Mr. W. S. Small's experiments with rats (*American Journal of Psychology*, Jan. 1900) are more satisfactory on this point. They go to show—(a) that when two or more rats are confronted with a difficulty (*e.g.*, to find their way into a box to get food) one will overcome it first, and there will be no tendency on the part of the others to learn from him as long as he is there. They will follow him, and very likely rob him, but they will leave him to do the work. But (b) if the pioneer rat is removed, the effect is not uniform. In several instances the remaining rats seemed to have learned nothing ; but in the case of four young rats called A, B, C, and D, the results seemed to favour imitation. Here rat A learnt the trick first in an hour and a quarter. As long as he remained in the box, no other rat seems to have made any attempt to help or learn from him, but on his removal, rat B made the attempt, and succeeded in two and a half minutes. Again, when B was removed, C succeeded in the same time. D was not tried alone. This does, I think, suggest that both B and C had learnt something from A, but Mr. Small seems to think that what they learnt was merely to attack the door and not waste time on the rest of the box. What is most instructive in aiding us to judge the value of negative results is the total change in the behaviour of these rats as soon as the pioneer is removed. If a rat finds that stealing is easier than work, he will leave his friend to work, and for his own part will adhere to his stealing. There is evidently a good deal of human nature in rats.

defined. Do animals profit by experience of this kind ? If so, their action falls outside the category of habituation. If an animal pulls a string because having done so before it has given him pleasure, it is possible to regard his education as the gradual growth of a random way of acting into a habit. But if he pulls it because he has seen it pulled, and then got the pleasant result, his act appears rather as a practical application of what he has seen—a perceptual relation converted into a practical adjustment. It is quite possible that an animal should get to this point without being capable of the slightly more complex act of applying to himself what another does on his own account.[1]

---

[1] Mr. Thorndike's experiments have given rise to voluminous discussion and a long series of experiments in American laboratories designed to confirm or refute his results. Meanwhile he has reprinted his original monograph without substantial alteration, and I think that it is on the whole best to leave the criticisms contained in this chapter in their original form.

# CHAPTER X

## SOME EXPERIMENTAL RESULTS

1. In the hope of deciding whether animals can learn by perception of results (as distinct from " imitation " in the usual sense), I made a number of experiments on a variety of animals. I have not been able to carry the experiments as far as I could wish, but they seem to me to be suggestive of certain results both in regard to the special point which I had in view, and in relation to the broader question of the part played by accident and habituation on the one hand, and by the " intelligent " apprehension of means and ends on the other. My experiments were begun with my own dog and cat. They were afterwards, by the courtesy of Messrs. Jennison,[1] extended to several animals in their great collection at the Belle Vue Gardens, Manchester, including monkeys of several species, a young female elephant, and an otter. It seemed to me that interesting analogies and contrasts might be drawn by confronting different animals with the same or similar problems, and so, I think, it turned out.

I must say a word about the methods used. Of the character of the individual animals, a most important point, I will speak as I come to each. Essentially, each experiment consisted in setting the animal the task of obtaining food by some method presumably strange to it. For example, food was put into a box, which was then shut, and left for the animal to open, or it was

[1] I must particularly thank Mr. George Jennison for many hours of helpful collaboration.

placed out of reach, yet so that it could be obtained by pulling a string, or pushing a door. The animal was first allowed time to discover the method of obtaining it for itself. If after a little while it showed no sign of hitting on the right method, it was shown, and allowed to get the food.[1] Fresh food was then placed as before, and a new trial began. It was of course necessary that the experiments should be tried before the animal's ordinary meal, but there seems to be an immense difference in the effort which different animals will make to satisfy their hunger, and this difference has to be kept carefully in mind in weighing results.

2. The original object being to discover whether what an animal sees done will have any effect, the first thing was to secure that it should see. This can only be done by gaining its attention, and I do not think that any one who has experienced the difficulty of getting an animal to attend to what is going on before his nose, will be surprised at any number of failures to learn by perception of results. In every case the animal is taken up, on the one hand with its desire for the food, on the other with its own instinctive or habitual method of dealing with the obstacle before it. One's dog will momentarily attend out of politeness to his master, but a cat is moved by no such considerations, nor is an elephant, nor a monkey. A mere mechanical performance of the act before the animal, which it may or may not see, has no effect whatever. I therefore always endeavoured to call attention to what I was doing.

It must be added here that as with a human being, so with an animal, attentive perception is something different from mere perception. I will not attempt to determine in what psychologically the difference consists, but there is in some animals a certain obvious difference of expression which strikes the observer. The pricked ears, fixed gaze, and strained, tense, alert attitude of the attentive dog are

---

[1] It might be thought that to withhold the food is the better plan. Sometimes I did this, but never for many trials together. It discourages the animal, and makes him think (I speak popularly) that he is being fooled. The opposite danger—very marked with some dogs—is that he may simply wait, or beg his master to do the thing for him again.

unmistakable. When one says that the dog attends, one means that he assumes an attitude of this kind, and where there is attention, there seems to be a mental digestion of the fact attended to, a working of it into the mass of experience so that it becomes available as a guide to action. Whatever else may be said of human attention, this will, I imagine, be allowed to be its normal effect, and this is, I think, also its normal effect in the animal world.

3. Besides showing the thing to be done, then, I also tried to attract attention. Further, after the trick was shown, in case of failure on the part of the animal, I used two supplementary methods. The first, which I call Suggestion, consisted in pointing to the object to be attacked by way of reminder. It was used rarely.[1] The second, which I call Encouragement, was used habitually, and consists in stimulating the animal to persevere by a " good dog " or a " get it, pussy," or by pointing, not to the object to be seized, but to the place where the food is. Encouragement is distinct from Suggestion as merely stimulating the animal to effort, and not helping in any way to direct its efforts. I also used Discouragement, when an animal became rough in his excitement.

The time of each trial was not regularly taken. Times are apt to be quite as misleading as instructive. Suppose, for example, that a cat begins without any delay to pull out a bolt which sticks a little. It is an open question whether she will persist or not. If not, she will probably take to her ablutions, and after washing her face with great elaboration while the experimenter waits with what patience he can command, will deign to return to the

---

[1] Suggestion is to be distinguished from inducement. I might teach my dog to bite at a string by waving my hand with a piece of meat towards it so that he would jump after my hand and accidentally catch the string. I might get him to raise a catch by smearing the box below and at the side of it with meat, so that in smelling at it he would knock the catch up. Then, if he discovered that to bite the string or raise the catch gained him meat, he would, of course, repeat the act. This would be a simple case of learning the thing by doing it, and bears no relation to learning by seeing. Mere pointing could only be an inducement if there were a previous association through which an animal had learnt to interpret the sign. Apart from such association its function is to direct attention to the proper object, and so revive the " ideas " associated therewith.

business in hand, and perhaps with one strong pull get the bolt out. In this way the time may suddenly rise from twenty seconds to five or six minutes, and the rise really signifies nothing but a slight failure in persistence. Nevertheless, I generally took the time when I could get a time keeper, as there are cases, particularly where " trial and error " play a large part, in which it can be made instructive. In the main, I relied on taking notes of everything that seemed essential at the moment. What an animal does is far more important for our purposes than the time which it takes to do it.

My original aim being to measure the influence of perceptual acquisition (learning by perception of results) as distinct from motor acquisition (learning an act by doing it) I tried to find things for the animals to do in which accidental success was improbable. It is no easy matter to devise problems which combine this feature with that of being clearly within the competence of the animal physically and mentally. Some experiments I discarded when I found them opening a door to accidental success. Others I went on with for the sake of collateral problems, without regarding them as instances of learning by perception. Those which do seem to indicate perceptual acquisition are of unequal value, some being more and others less open to the suggestion that the success may have been accidental.[1]

4. Description of experiments.

(1) Pulling string.

My first experiment was with my cat Tim, a small black tom, rather more than a year old. It was repeated with my dog, Jack.

Tim is a sociable creature, who follows his friends about in the half dog-like way that some cats have, but as a psychologist he has two great defects. His attention is of the most fickle order, and what is even worse, he gets his meals at the most irregular times, and by methods known only to himself. It is therefore impossible to say beforehand whether he will take any sustained interest in the proceedings at all. He will not put himself out

---

[1] I was throughout trying to find methods quite as much as results, and I have given a somewhat full account, even of experiments which prove little, in the hope that the methods used may be suggestive to others.

much even for fish, and five or six mouthfuls seem always to take the edge off his appetite. Jack, on the other hand—my dog, who may be introduced at the same time—has two great merits. He is always anxious to oblige, and he is quite unfailingly ready to eat. In other respects, I should not have regarded Jack as a favourable subject for experiments designed to test the higher limits of animal intelligence. His moral qualities—if psychologists will allow me to speak of such a thing in connection with a dog—have endeared him to a large circle of friends, but his stoutest champions have admitted that his virtues were of the heart rather than the head. At the same time, after comparing his performances with those of other dogs, I think we underrated Jack. It remains, however, that his manners are rough and boisterous. He is very strong, and claws things to pieces if he does not get what he wants.[1] But, as I soon found out, the essential difference between Jack and the cat is that Jack's attention is concentrated, and Tim's dissipated. The cat is the finer workman, doing things scientifically if he does them at all, but he seldom makes a real effort to overcome a difficulty. Jack bounces and blunders into everything, is apt, if the right method fails, to get excited and try his strength, yet by continuity of effort learns more rapidly and learns more.

In this particular experiment, Jack showed to great advantage as compared with Tim, and indeed, with all other animals on whom I have tried it, except the elephant and the monkeys. A piece of meat was placed on a card to which a string was tied, and then placed on a shelf beyond reach of the animal with the string dangling down. After long delay the trick seemed to " come " to the cat almost on a sudden.

I first tried this with Tim, thinking that a young cat would very likely pull the string in play. I was surprised to find that he took no notice of it. I showed him seven times, pulling the string down before his eyes, and letting him get the meat. Neither this, nor a series of trials in which the card was placed on the table barely out of the cat's reach, had the slightest effect. The kitten once grabbed at the string as I was arranging the card, probably in play, and brought the card down without the meat. For the rest, he either made no attempt at all,

---

[1] In this connection it would be natural to mention Jack's breed, but this is a point on which I hope nobody will inquire. I could not bring myself to call Jack a mongrel. I may say that some have thought him more of a fox-terrier than anything else. If so, he is on an unusually large scale with broad brawny chest, and mighty claws.

or tried to claw at the meat directly.  About a fortnight afterwards I began a long series of trials in which the string was tied
to a chair leg to make it more conspicuous.  Sometimes I let
Jack pull the food down—when the kitten frequently stole it—
sometimes I pulled it myself.  Fourteen trials gave no result.
Next day, eight trials passed without result, but at the ninth, the
cat bit slightly at the string close by my fingers as I adjusted it,
and as soon as I had got it right, pawed the string down.  The
biting was doubtless due to the string being slightly smeared with
fish, but the effect was apparently to call the cat's attention to
the string for the first time in all this long series.  It is clear
that in pawing it his aim was to get the fish on the table.  If he
had merely been attracted by the smear on the string, he would
have used his mouth.  At the next trial, he sat still for a while,
and then pawed the string again.  At the next, he took to washing himself, and I gave up for a time ; but on replacing the string
I saw him watching me, and he pulled it down at once.  In the
next trial he did the same.  Next day he appeared to have forgotten, but walked under the string and knocked it down with
his tail.  At the second trial, he slightly brushed against the
string, but walked away.  I had to rearrange it.  He watched
me doing so, and pawed it down at once.  He then pulled it five
times running without hesitation.

I have described this experiment at length because,
putting all the facts together, they seem to show the
effect of attention in a very remarkable way.  It really
seemed that though the string was constantly before its
eyes, the cat never took notice of it till the incident of
the biting,[1] and from its single success on this occasion the trick—in spite of one lapse later in the series,
and temporary forgetfulness on the following day—was
substantially learnt.

The experiment was tried with two other cats.  Teufel,
a four-year-old half-Persian, belonging to Miss G. Thring,
who kindly made several experiments for me, only succeeded after his attention was called to the string by its

[1] It is possible that in the case mentioned in the earlier series the cat
did turn its attention once to the string, but as it acted prematurely, and
failed to get the food, this would disappoint it, and account for its not
attempting the same method again.  That the cat should fail to take any
note of a string just before its eyes will surprise no one who has watched
cats attentively.  I have known this same cat seize my fingers instead of
a piece of fish which I held out.  Cats frequently have great difficulty in
finding food that lies just before them on the ground.

being moved about. On the other hand, Miss M. V. Vernon, who also kindly made some observations for me, found that her cat Balbus pulled the string without being shown at all.[1] The individual differences among dogs in this experiment are not less striking. Two collies and a fox-terrier which I tried failed to learn it in several trials. One collie brushed the string down four times in roaming about, and still showed no sign of learning the trick. Jack, on the other hand, was present while I was teaching the kitten one day. He saw me pull it down once, and the next time took the string neatly in his teeth and pulled it down. Oddly enough, he did not repeat this success at once, but for several trials would stand and bark stupidly for two or three minutes until I pointed towards the string, or lightly touched it.

Sometimes I had to point two or three times. He began in the same way next day, so at the second trial I changed my tactics, pointing to the card. Jack then jumped up towards it and scrambled it down. At his next trial—the eighth all told from the beginning—he pulled the string without being shown, and never failed again. As soon as he was perfect in it, I stretched the string across from the chimney-piece to a chair-back, and found that Jack jumped at it at once. He began by aiming too high, and while still on his hind legs, edged away sideways till he came to a point which he could reach.

In this experiment, anything like accident seems ruled out. The very first success was a quite definite act, with every appearance of deliberateness, and opposed in character to the jumping up and "scrabbling" which occurred at his first trial. Jack saw the thing done, and then did it. He was not, however, established in the trick by the success, but needed "suggestion." Now, it is possible that the mere pointing to the string might induce a dog to seize and pull it independently of any special association,

---

[1] The card was placed on a table, and the string tied to a chair. The experimenter prevented the cat from jumping at the table, and pointed to the string, which he then pawed. The card was then moved to a (higher) sideboard, and the string left to dangle. After a long delay, Balbus's attention was attracted to the string, and he pawed it. Next day he failed in this once, and was shown. He also failed several times when the food was placed still higher, and this notwithstanding two successes.

but I cannot think of anything in Jack's previous behaviour which would suggest that it would have had this effect on him.   My lightly touching the string might, I think, have led him to smell at it, and possibly to paw at it.   I know nothing to suggest that it would have led him to bite it, and it therefore seems to me to have acted as a suggestion or reminder of what he had just done.   On the whole, the impression left on me is that Jack learnt this trick by perception of result plus suggestion.

(2). String on banisters.

After teaching Jack the previous experiment, I tied a string to the banisters of the landing, and hung to it a little tin toy bucket containing meat.   I passed the string round the next banister to the one to which it was tied, so that by pulling the string between the two, he could get the bucket up.   I will give Jack's full record for this experiment, as it is a little interesting.

1. In showing Jack the arrangement his paw got twisted in the sting.   I notice this point as possibly helping to suggest pulling to him.   As soon as I put meat in, and dropped bucket, Jack ran downstairs to see if he could get it from there.   He then came back and tugged at string, but, taking it near the place where it is tied, he only pulls at the post, so to say, and there is no tendency to pull bucket up.   I encourage him a little, but without result.   I then alter string by passing it over three or four posts, so that if he seizes it at the further end from place where it is tied, and then backs away from banisters, he can get it.   Having altered it, I partly pull it up from right place, whereupon Jack seizes string and gets food.

2. He pulled at once, but string slipped, and he failed.   I then pointed to right place, whereupon he pulled again.   Bucket stuck just at top ; I pulled it in, and meat had tumbled out, so I gave him a piece.   (The bucket was very apt to catch in ledge made by floor ; it was not very easy to get meat out.)

3. Jack again pulls, without waiting for a sign, but fails to back far enough, and bucket slips down.   He tries again and fails.   I pull it up for him.

4. After some delay Jack succeeds, backing better this time.

5. Slight delay ; then success.

6. First trial—pulls it nearly up, and then misses.   After some encouragement, tries again, and succeeds.

Next day.

1. Jack makes two or three attempts ; is uncertain as to right

place, finally gets bucket up to top, but knocks it back in trying to seize it. I then show him.

2. Does not get string well at right place, but backs well, and so manages to pull bucket up.

3. Took right place, helped self with paw, and got it.

4. Does not go at right point first, but gets towards it, and rapidly gets meat.

Two days' interval.

1. Jack gets it without difficulty.

It will be seen that Jack did not require to be taught to pull at the string. This might be explained by saying that Jack had come by this time to pull at strings as such. This, however, would be to pass over the fact that he first ran downstairs, trying to get the meat there. I think, therefore, we ought to call it an adaptive use of the experience previously gained with the string. Next, Jack had to learn the right place to pull at. Pointing did not teach him this, as the record shows. He learnt it apparently from seeing how the meat was pulled up ; and by the same method, also no doubt aided by his own failures and successes, he learnt to back properly, at the same time letting the string run through his teeth. On the whole, the experiment is rather a complicated one. It does not succeed unless the animal takes the string, backs away from the banisters, and lets the string run through his teeth as he does so without letting go. Yet Jack practically learnt it at the fourth trial, and only wanted to be shown once on the following day. I should ascribe this success to a fusion of the method of perception of results with that of experience of success and failure.[1]

(3). Lever.

I took an old bird-cage, and passed the pole laterally through the wires of the door, weaving them in and out.

---

[1] Since writing the above, I have been shown an interesting account of a similar performance by a bird, in *Our Bird Friends*, by R. Kearton. For the benefit of some blue tits, Mr. Kearton hung the kernel of a Barcelona nut from a stump. The little birds could hang on to it with their feet and peck at it. " Great Tits tried time after time to imitate their lighter brethren, but never once succeeded in maintaining their hold upon the kernel. But one, wiser than the rest, did a much cleverer thing one day. He stood on the stump, and, seizing the thread, hauled it in reef by reef with his bill and feet until he got the kernel to the top, when he held it down and chipped his well-deserved reward off it " (p. 11).

The pole ran out along and beyond the side of the cage, so that by pressing it, the door, which otherwise shut with a spring, could be opened. I held the cage above Jack's head, in such a position that the door would open downwards, and a piece of meat placed inside would then fall out. For six trials (after each of which he was shown) Jack merely jumped up and " scrabbled " at the cage. He then pulled the lever but did not get " fixed " in the habit immediately.

There were three or four more failures out of eleven trials in this series, and he had to be shown three times the next day. He then became perfect in it, and when for the cage I substituted a box which could only be opened by a projecting lever, he soon went at the lever after a little preliminary scratching at the box, and without being shown.

It is clear that accident might easily enter into this experiment, especially in the case of the box. Jack, however, did not seem to learn it by any accidental clawing. He naturally aimed straight at the food, and he had to learn to claw or bite (he used both methods) at a bar some inches away. He seemed to do this quite definitely all of a sudden,[1] though he sometimes forgot it afterwards.

Tim failed to learn this trick in three trials with the bird-cage, but acquired it at the third trial with the box, and did not afterwards fail.[2]

Of other animals, the otter learnt to use the lever by being first accustomed to open the door, which for his benefit was left with a crevice afterwards filled up. The elephant had no difficulty with it. One collie, Rose, absolutely failed, or perhaps refused [3] to open a box thus by lifting the lid. Her son opened it after being shown three times.[4]

---

[1] The notes show that he *once* before nearly pawed the lever—in his first trial.

[2] When a general statement of this kind is made it refers only to the same experiment under the same conditions. Sometimes an acquired trick enters as an element into a more complicated experiment, and then failure in that experiment would put the animal off its simpler performance. This occurred in the present case.

[3] After showing her several times, her master arranged so that she began pushing her nose in as he lifted. Even this had no effect.

[4] He failed several times the same night, but I found afterwards that the lever would rub uncomfortably against his nose. I altered this, and next night he succeeded.

(4). Pull-bolt.

The same and similar boxes were fastened by a loose bolt which could be drawn right out.    I call this the pull-bolt.

I first showed this box to Jack placed on a chair in such a way that the bolt being drawn the lid would fall.    He pulled the bolt out at once with his teeth.    This was not extraordinary cleverness, but rather a "false analogy" from the lever experiment.    He had been accustomed to seize the lever in his mouth and pull, and he now treated the bolt in the same way.    To determine how far he could discriminate the two things, I gave him the two boxes alternately, and found that he got on very well as long as one box was on the floor and the other on the chair so arranged that the bolt was end on to him as he approached it.    But next day I placed both boxes on the floor, and much confusion resulted.    Four times Jack pulled the bolt as though it were the lever, at right angles, and had to be shown.    The fifth time he got it roughly out, helping himself at the end with his paw.

I subjoin the rest of his "record" under this head.

Same afternoon (this from imperfect notes jotted after series was over) he had to be shown the lever *once*, and was then successful.    (His experience with the bolt would of course put him off the lever.)    Then was thrice shown bolt.    Then succeeded twice.

Next day the bolt and bar are put on the same box, which is now slightly tilted so that it is necessary to paw bar (after the bolt is drawn out) to open it.

1.  Pulls out bolt, but puzzled because door does not open. Shown.

2.  Scrabbles and pulls more or less in right direction, but has to be shown—and also have door opened for him.

3.  Gets bolt out, and opens door half by accident.

4.  Pulls out bolt very awkwardly, and after delay, opens door.

I now give him the bar alone.

1.  He takes it in his teeth, but has his paw against the door, and gets violent.    I have to set the box to rights and give it him again, when he opens it.

2 and 3.  Opens bar *upwards*.

We return again to bolt, which he pulls out better, but he scrabbles so hard at door that it breaks.

Two or three days after, pulls out bolt and opens box three times, though coming up from off side and from behind.    Also twice pulls out bolt by string attached to it.

Many days later I gave him thirteen trials with the bolt again, in all of which he succeeded in both movements (bolt and lever). The average time of the second to the seventh trials being, roughly, 29″, of the last six, 23″.

This success was a case of acquired discrimination. Jack had to learn that one sort of projection had to be pulled out, while another had to be pulled at right angles. This was perhaps rendered more rather than less difficult by his spurious success at first. There was the further difficulty, that, by using his strength, Jack could get out the bolt, or possibly break it when pulling at a considerable angle. This was much against rapidity and neatness of learning.

This was the first experiment in which a *double action* was made necessary. The bolt and lever being learnt separately, the box was so arranged as to combine them. Jack was baffled by this until twice shown.

The cat learnt the bolt rapidly, and soon came to pull it out scientifically, curling his claw round, and working by a series of pulls.

His record is as follows :—

1 and 2. Shown.

3. I now place box on floor. He claws bolt out. I put it back, holding door firm, thinking he has done it accidentally. He does it again, and gets meat.

4 to 9. Pulls bolt out. N.B. Once in 5 after bolt is out, does not see door is open, until I swing it for him. Afterwards opens door himself. In 8, tries to open the door before bolt is properly out.

Next day. (Box tilted, so that door must definitely be opened by cat after bolt is drawn.)

1. Claws about, has to be shown.

2. After hesitation, pulls out awkwardly. Door not opening, cat is puzzled, and I have to do it.

3. Pulls out better, and opens.

4. Same. ✳

After two days—new smooth bolt.

1. Several times tries bolt, but it is too slippery. I put in a rough one. He refuses to try. I pull it out, and he opens door by the bolt-catch.

2. Pulls it out after two or three efforts. Opens.

3. Same.

Box turned with lid up.

After some exploring of side, kitten pushes lid up.

It will be seen that the cat also acquired the double movement (clawing door open after pulling out bolt) after two trials.

The bolt trick seems important. In Jack's case it could be done by blundering strength, but it would seem that the cat had to know pretty clearly what to do, and how to do it, before he could succeed.

The bolt trick was also taught to two elephants. The box used was broadly similar, except that the bolt was made of iron and the lid of the box was opened with a knob. The first elephant, an old female named Sally, was taught in my presence by the keeper. As the box was placed for the lid to open upwards, three movements were necessary—(1) to pull out the bolt ; (2) to pull up the lid by the knob ; (3) to get the trunk under the lid to prevent it falling again. This last was physically no easy matter. The method used by the very experienced keeper, Mr. Lawrence, was that of taking the trunk in his hand and guiding it, teaching his elephant the whole trick stage by stage.

The bolt was virtually learnt at the seventh trial, but the combined movement was not perfect till after the fortieth trial on the third day. Sally showed some intelligence in trying to meet the difficulty of the falling lid—trying, for example, to throw it right back, but I doubt if she would have had the patience to get it perfect without guidance.

I now began to teach a young elephant inappropriately called Lily.

Lily is ten years old, and not much taller than I am. In teaching her, two or three points have to be kept in mind. Her trunk is ceaselessly in motion, groping about everything outside her cage, frequently about the pockets of her teacher. There is therefore a large proportion of random movement which sometimes contributed to success, and sometimes to failure, and in any case leaves a large field open for accident. Again, her eyes are a long way off, and one cannot tell what she is looking at. She is, I regret to say, a very impatient pupil, and apt to get excessively annoyed when she fails in an experiment. On these occasions, like a monkey, but unlike other animals that I have taught, she seems to get angry with her tools, and, if she can, gets hold of them and smashes them.

I first showed Lily the box unbolted, and she quickly learnt to open it by the knob.[1] I then put in the bolt, and she pushed it out by a random movement. That it was random was proved by the two following trials in which she failed and was shown. At the fourth trial she succeeded, and here she seems to have learnt the trick, for three more successes followed, and no failure.[2] The next day, however, she was awkward about it, and I showed her twice.[3] Some days later she pulled out the bolt at the first trial, though she failed to get the lid open until I turned it conveniently for her.

I do not think there is any doubt that the elephant learnt the trick substantially at the fourth trial. How she learnt it is another question which I cannot decide. The first—purely random—success apparently gave her no help; and, indeed, my observations suggest that, as a general rule, the more a success appears to be purely accidental, the less it is likely to be repeated. The same tendency to random movement caused her partial failures (trying the knob first, and pulling the bolt the wrong way) later on. It is to be observed that this was a double movement learnt *regressively*—i.e., the act to be done last was learnt first. Having learnt to open the door by the knob, she had then to learn that it was useless to pull the knob till the bolt was out. To learn this without getting disgusted implies a certain measure of articulateness in experience. Two things must be, in some sense, known, and their order kept in mind.

Billy, the otter, a most mercurial little animal, was now taught to bolt.

---

[1] I kept the box sideways to avoid the complication of raising the lid. Even so, the opening was not easy, as the bars of the cage would get in the way.

[2] After the seventh trial I turned the box up. This baffled her at first, and she kept fumbling about the side where the bolt had been. (This suggests that she goes more by feeling than by sight.) However, she succeeded in the end.

[3] In her first trial she tried the handle before the bolt, and also tried to pull the bolt the wrong way. She then took to knocking the bolt out. I replaced it, and showed her. After this she got vexed, and tried to confiscate the box. I rescued it, and showed her. Two or three times this day she was awkward and uncertain in her actions.

Billy's method of solving a problem is quite distinctive. His principle is never to stay still. He slips all over and round the box like a drop of quicksilver, sniffing and pawing and gnawing with a vast amount of superfluous energy, and greatly delaying himself thereby.[1] He was but a young thing, however, and rather like a kitten in his ways, mewing with excitement while the box was being adjusted. He learnt the bolt after seeing it done twelve times, but how far *by* seeing it done, I am unable to judge. Billy was taught by his keeper. When I visited him he showed a distinct inclination to increase his meal at the expense of my legs. At the same time, by an odd coincidence, I found that a better view of the proceedings could be obtained from *outside* the bars. So Billy's education was left to Mr. Craythorn, who has taken great interest in his development, and has frequently assisted me by taking notes in my absence.

The bolt was pulled out twelve times, the otter being left each time to open the box by the lever. The otter then pulled out the bolt three times running, with some delay. The next day he had to be shown the first time, but after that he always succeeded, though by no means always with equal neatness. He would often bite at the bolt a good deal, and sometimes on the wrong side of the staple, but he would soon correct himself. Sometimes, too, he would pull the bolt half out, leave it hanging, and then try the lever. After a struggle with it, he would go back, and finish with the bolt.[2] At times he would take a run round after pulling out the bolt, or gnaw irrelevantly at the lever or the extracted bolt itself. At other times, when the door was swollen with damp, and would not open easily, his persistence in pushing at the lever was really remarkable. On the whole Billy's behaviour may be understood best by regarding the proper plan of action as a kind of centre from which he kept deviating always to return again.

(5).   Push-back bolt.

A similar box was fastened by a bolt furnished with a knob. It could not be pulled out, but had to be pushed back. This turned out to be much harder for the

[1] Mr. Small's description of his rats ("An Experimental Study of the Mental Processes of the Rat," W. S. Small, *American Journal of Psychology*, Jan. 1900) often reminds me of Billy. Superfluous movements of the kind make it difficult to measure intelligence, especially when they intervene between two actions. Mr. Small rightly remarks (p. 142) that extra hunger sometimes increases rather than diminishes the useless movements, which, of course, come nearer to the normal methods by which hunger is satisfied.

[2] He is now, I am told, very perfect with the bolt, but he has been used to it for between two and three months.

animals, principally, I think, because they got no definite
impression of the thing to be done.   The other bolt was
pulled out.   There was a definite change, which the
animal soon learnt was a necessary preliminary to the
opening of the box.   The cat altogether failed with this
trick, trying to draw the bolt out like the other one.
Even the chimpanzee failed, though repeatedly shown.
The little Rhesus monkey, Jimmy, of whom I shall have
to say more, dealt with the difficulty by turning the box
over and over, till presently the bolt fell.[1]   Afterwards, I
kept my foot on the box, and he gradually learnt how to
deal with the bolt by constantly experimenting with it.
A similar box with an ordinary iron bolt fitted with a
catch was placed in a cage with three large Drills.   The
bolt was drawn several times in their presence, but they
were far too wild to be systematically shown.   They made
no attempt at it, and it was not till two days after that
the box was first found open.

That day, it was opened twice.   Three days later it was again
found open, and the next day it was opened half a dozen times.
The next day I saw it done for the first time.   At the first trial
two of the three still bit at the box, but the third pulled the bolt.
At the second trial a second[2] monkey attacked the bolt, which
was now placed with the catch down.   He took the handle,
raised it out of the catch by an up and down movement, and continuing the same movement, gradually worked it back.   Evidently
he had learnt to free the bolt from the catch by repeatedly working the handle up and down, and he kept up this movement when
there was no need for it.

The monkeys, when they did learn this trick, learnt it
properly.   The case was different with Jack and the
elephant.   In all, I gave Jack about ninety lessons, and at
the end I do not think he clearly appreciated what he had
to do.   The reason probably is that the staples hid the

[1] On the other hand, a little female monkey did it at sight.   She had
lived in a house before, and must, I think, have had experience with
bolts.
[2] I wish I could be quite sure that it was not the same monkey, as it
would throw light on the question of imitation ; but the truth is that the
three were so much alike and so wild in their movements that it was
difficult to tell.   Both Mr. Craythorn and I were under the impression
that it was not the same monkey.

bolt, and the dog never clearly saw the difference between pushing it back all the way and part of the way.

A special source of confusion on this head would be that if the bolt were nearly but not quite back, an extra strong pull and a vigorous shake of the box would shake it back and open the box. Hence Jack was tempted to trust to strength rather than art. Hence, also, he never quite perfectly learnt that the bolt must be pushed before the lever was pulled,[1] though he seemed to get nearly right on this point in the first ten trials.

Upon the whole, whether by his own attempts or by watching me, or by both methods combined, Jack learnt that he had to push the bolt and then paw the lever, but exactly how, or how far the bolt was to be pushed, he did not understand. His perceptions, as indicated by his method of dealing with the bolt, were, to use Mr. Small's expression, " crass." He knew that a lot of pulling with the teeth or pushing with the paw at the bolt was the thing wanted, but he had no "idea" of the object of the pushing and pulling—*i.e.*, he did not seem to *direct it definitely to the effecting of a particular physical change as a step towards his desire.* In this respect his action contrasted with, for example, the behaviour of the cat in pulling out the other bolt, and with his own behaviour in pulling up the string, and in other experiments to be mentioned later.

A further point of interest in this experiment was the impotence of a casual success.

Jack actually succeeded at the third trial, but clearly without understanding how, for at the next attempt he tried to pull the bolt the wrong way. A second sporadic success occurred much later, and at the forty-fourth trial[2] came a third success, after which there were few complete failures,[3] but the work remained

---

[1] In the last fifty-eight trials he tried the lever first seven times, three at the beginning of one day's series, two at the beginning of another, and the remaining two quite sporadically.

[2] There was a gap of two or three days after the first fourteen trials, as Jack in his efforts with the lever broke it.

[3] Three or four times I showed him without waiting to see if he would manage it himself—the main interest being to see whether he would get really perfect. His average time during the last three days was, roughly, 37″, 29″, and 32″. The time frequently fell to 5″, and sometimes rose to 70 or 80″.

very rough, and the average time nearly constant from day to day. Such seems the typical character of a trick in which the *point* is not clearly apprehended, and all the animal knows is, roughly, that a certain sort of action is required.

The elephant learnt this trick better than Jack, but, on the whole, in the same way

After leaving her to fumble with the bolt and bar for a long time, I showed her both movements. After this, she twice succeeded in a fumbling way. She seemed to learn from this that both bolt and lever had to be used, and that the bolt came first. (She only three times afterwards made a mistake on this point, and only once seriously.) At the eighth and ninth trials she succeeded again,[1] and the next day was successful, though in a fumbling way, throughout. I only once noticed her definitely trying to push the bolt the wrong way, and when once I turned the box round (so that to pull in the same direction as before would be wrong), she tried to push instead of pull, and then, after a little fumbling in the wrong direction, moved round in her stall so as to get in the right position for pulling.[2]

On the whole, we may say that the elephant learnt that the bolt must be pushed inwards, and the lever then pulled. She nearly learnt this from seeing it done two or three times, and had it practically perfect after eight trials, in which she had herself done it three times. She failed to learn that the bolt must be pushed quite back.

(6). Catch.

I had a box made for Jack, closed with an ordinary window-catch. He could lift it with his nose, and then open the box by pulling at the catch with his paw. This second movement, unless skilfully applied, was apt to close the catch again ; and this difficulty entirely baffled the cat, who never tried to lift the catch, but failed in this preliminary. Tim, I must say, showed great stupidity in this experiment. He never grasped that by merely changing his position he would avoid the hitch, but would

---

[1] The experiment ended for the day at this point, because Lily succeeded in getting hold of the box, with which she was obviously annoyed, and leant her chin on it. It was a very strong box, but an adjournment for repairs was at once necessary.

[2] When I reversed the box again, she was not so successful, fumbling a bit, but presently she seemed to get accidentally into a better position, and then opened the box easily.

sit in the same place, pawing the catch down two or three times running. At the same time he generally modified the act in some slight way so as to get it open in the end.

Jack, on the other hand, found out the whole process for himself in one trial. He had by this time had a considerable experience of boxes, and he went straight for the latch. His record is as follows :—

1. Not shown. After a little scrabbling, raises latch with nose, scrabbles at it, and knocks it down two or three times. Tries to pull it with mouth. At length opens. N.B. He attacked fastening immediately.

2. Begins scrabbling. Soon lifts with nose, and after an unsuccessful attempt, opens with paw. 15".

3. Lifts latch at once, and scrabbles at it with paw, but knocks it down again. Then takes it in mouth, lifts, and opens. 24".

4. Lifts at once ; scratches open. 9".

5. 5".

6. 4".

Next evening—runs at box arranged for cat, lifts twice with nose, each time knocking down again with paw ; lifts again, and opens with paw.

I cannot regard any part of Jack's behaviour on this occasion as a wholly random act. He selected the catch for attack, soon found that something was movable, and moved it. He would then feel that the door was free, and would try to scratch it open. That, notwithstanding initial failures in the scratching—suitably varied once by pulling with the teeth—he should have virtually learnt the whole business in one trial, indicates something more like appreciation of the actual thing that needed doing, and the dependence of one point on another, than anything else that I have seen in Jack's behaviour.

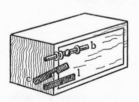

*b*, bolt, drawn ; *c*, catch, raised ; *l*, lever.

For the otter I had a different kind of catch. The projecting wooden lever of the lid had a notch cut in it, into which another wooden lever, pivoted on the side, descended. Once raised, the catch did not fall again, as

it worked stiffly, and the box was opened by the lever.
This is his record:—

December 6th.—1. First tried lever itself, next lifted catch by
pushing nose under, but did not understand it. Seized catch by
teeth, pushing it down again. Pushed head under catch, raising
it, pulled lever, and opened. Time about 50″.
December 7th. Morning.
Did it immediately (keeper's statement).
Afternoon (own observation).
1. Raised catch quickly ; did not pull lever at once ; bit at
catch ; then pulled.
2. In interval he has done a " string " trick.[1]  In doing that,
he tried unsuccessfully putting head under lever. This now puts
him off. He gnaws and pulls at both lever and catch for some
time, but presently lifts with head and opens.
December 8th. Morning. Pull bolt added.
(Keeper reports) raised catch and pulled bolt together three
times rapidly.
Afternoon (own observation).
1. Bolt and catch. Knocks up catch, but gets excited, and bites
and pulls at right angles at bolt instead of pulling it out. Then
bites and struggles all about.
Catch taken off. Half pulls out bolt, but leaves it hanging,
and rampages again. Bolt replaced. Pulls it out up to outer staple
and opens.
2. Does both actions pretty rapidly, lifting catch, then drawing
bolt and again lifting catch, which has fallen, and opens.
3. Keeps on at lever and catch. Pulls bolt half out. Gnaws
again. At last opens. Time about 2′ 35″.

Subsequent experiments showed that the trick was
learnt.

There was much more of accident in this than in Jack's
success, as the detail of the first trial shows. Nevertheless,
the otter showed great alertness in taking advantage of an
accidental success.

A second box was then given him, similar to the first,
except that the catch had to be depressed instead of raised.
Result:—

1. Otter quite baffled—all over place ; presently gets chin over
catch ; depresses it ; at once puts head under and *raises* it again.

---

[1] In this the lever was tied by a string. The experiment failed through
difficulties of arrangement.

This done twice.  At length depresses further by double movement, and, after a little scrabbling, opens.  Time over 2′.
    2. Similar.  Thrice pulls down lever and raises again, once
without raising again.  After some minutes, shown two or three
times.  But does not try.  Gives up.
    Next day—
    1. Pushes down catch twice and raises again.  At length pulls
it down and opens door by lever.  Time 30″ to 40″.
    2. 10″.  Tries at once this time, pushing at lever as soon as
catch is depressed.
    3. 16″.  Pushes down and does not raise again, but quits for
a while and smells round.  Comes back and at lever.
    4. 10″.  Would be immediate, but did not clear catch of lever
at first.
    5. 12″.  Sniffs about a bit.  Then both movements at once.

Next day, the two boxes were alternated, and he did
both without difficulty and no sign of confusion.

With this second box it is clear that the first trial of the
second day was the *critical* success.  The showing had
apparently no effect.  It was a random success properly
utilised.

I gave the same box to the elephant.

After accustoming her to the lever, I put on the catch.  She
pulled violently at the catch and lever, nearly thrusting the catch
down.  I had to take the box away in fear of consequences.
When I gave it back, she showed no improvement.  I then
showed her twice, once opening the box, but not letting her get
the bread.  Again she got violent, and I had to rescue the box.
After this, however, she began fumbling at the catch, pulling it
down and up again, and then pulling at the lever.  She was
beginning to learn.  I now showed her the whole process twice,
and thereafter she managed to do it, though she had a way of
catching the tip of the trunk in the end of the catch after she
had depressed it, whereby she kept raising it again.  At the twelfth
trial she was perfect, her times for this and the four remaining
trials of the day being roughly 3″, 2″, 5″, 6″, 3″.
    Next day her times were about 12″, 30″, and 5 to 7″.  There
was some fumbling in the first two, but the clear downward
thrust was unmistakable.

This experiment is perhaps more distinctly suggestive
of learning by perception than any other of Lily's
performances.  At any rate, it was a rapid piece of

learning. There was only one occasion after her first success in which she so far forgot herself as to try the lever first.

(7.) (Loop).

As already mentioned, Jack's box had an iron lever projecting from the lid by which it was opened. I drove a gimlet into the side of the box parallel with the lever, and placed a brass loop over it and the lever. As I placed the box for Jack, the loop had to be pushed up in order to open the box. Jack learnt this after being shown twice.

During the first two trials Jack " scrabbled " a good deal, once or twice nearly knocking the loop up with his nose in the course of his random movements. The loop was twice pulled off, and he was left to open the box. The third time he knocked up the loop with his nose, and with some difficulty opened the box. He did not fail again, though for three or four trials there was some useless preliminary scrabbling.[1] Sometimes the loop stuck a little, and he would then push hard and repeatedly. Next day, there was a little scrabbling at the first trial, but no failure.

There may have been an element of accident in the first success. It was within the scope of a random movement. The dog seemed quite clear in this instance as to what had to be done. The persistence and gradual dying away of useless scrabbling is noteworthy.

The cat did this trick at sight.

No doubt attracted by the novelty of the loop (which for his benefit was put sideways), he began clawing at it at once, and in about 90 seconds got it off and opened the box. He repeated this eight times, but showed a tendency to claw at the gimlet (also a novelty) before the lever. The total times varied from 60″ to 15″. The next night he refused to try, but the next he succeeded, awkwardly, three times.

This was a clear case of a single random success having a permanent effect.

(8.) Spike.

Taking out the gimlet I put a small chain over the lever, and, stretching it tight, stuck a skewer through a

---

[1] From the seventh to eleventh trials inclusive, his average time for the whole process was under 14″.

link and into the hole. The chain was too tight for Jack to get at it with his teeth, and the only resource was to pull out the skewer.

During five trials Jack[1] bit and pulled indiscriminately at lever, chain, and skewer. At the sixth trial he pulled skewer out awkwardly.[2]

At the seventh he pulled it half out with an effort, and then gave up, returning after an interval, and pulling it out. There was then an interval, after which his record is as follows :—

8. Scratches long time at chain ; does not try to pull skewer out with teeth.

9. Half pulls out with teeth ; tries to scratch out rest of the

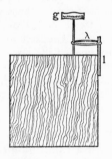

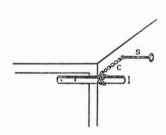

BOX ARRANGED WITH LOOP.

*l*, lever ; *λ*, loop ; *g*, gimlet.

BOX ARRANGED WITH SPIKE.

*l*, lever ; *c*, chain ; *s*, spike.

way and to push his nose through the door. Shown. Time 3 minutes.

10. Half pulls skewer, gets it out at last ; declines to open for some time, at last opens.

11. Knocked skewer further in with nose, scrabbled, barked, gave up. I put skewer so as to project beyond bar ; he opened. Time, little over 1 minute.

12. Pulls it out and opens with very little scrabbling.

13. Reluctant, little scrabbling, opens. Time 30″.

14. Pulling at skewer nearly all time ; skewer-head in beyond bolt. 35″.

15. Does not try to bite skewer for long time, but pushes at lever and chain. I pull skewer out beyond bolt, thinking he

---

[1] In the first trial I had used a string, which he managed to get off (he had had a previous experiment of this kind which failed owing to defective mechanism). I then substituted the chain. At the fourth trial he took the skewer in his teeth as I was pulling it out.

[2] I left it projecting further, so that it was more easily grasped.

could not get at it, but he accidentally knocks it in ; then deliberately pulls skewer out and opens. Time 1' 20".

16. Barks, slowly pulls out, skewer sticks a good deal, opens. Time, 1' 5".

Next day, I alternated the loop and spike experiments. Result:—

Loop.

1. 12". Pushes from beginning with nose.
2. 7". Does it at once.

Skewer immediately afterwards substituted.

1. 1' 11". Gets it out gradually, pulling at it practically whole of time ; some difficulty in grasping, as skewer pushed in up to head. Began at skewer at once.

2. 16". Skewer a little further out, more easily grasped.

The cat, oddly enough, pulled out the skewer at sight as he had done with the loop, but in a casual fashion. In this case the random success left no impression. The cat had three more trials, in which he utterly failed, never even trying the skewer again, though I showed him each time, and finally used suggestion, pulling the skewer half out.

A comparison of the two experiments of the loop and skewer is instructive. They show, first, how much a young cat may do as the result of random exploration. In this respect the elephant, monkey, and cat resemble each other for experimental purposes. All fiddle with things, especially new things, examine them and pull them about. In this, they differ, if not from puppies, at any rate from older dogs, which investigate things, not by picking them to pieces, but by smelling at them. To avoid accidental success with a dog, he must be given something that he will not effect either by smelling about in the neighbourhood or by random scratching. For this reason, notwithstanding the case of the cat, I cannot think Jack's success with the skewer was in any way accidental. The act was for him a very awkward one, and at best he had a great struggle with it.[1] In some cases he had to make more

---

[1] I believe that I spoke encouragingly once or twice during these struggles. The adjustment of the skewer might also have been suggestive as a reminder in some of the later trials. I mention these as the only possible aids to him, other than perception and his own efforts.

than one distinct effort. Altogether it seemed very clear to me in this case that he saw what had to be done, and did it. The cat's two performances, on the other hand, are instructive as a contrast. In both cases it led off with a random success. In the one case this success was immediately utilised; in the other it had no effect at all.

(9). Upsetting jug or tumbler.

One knows how a cat will get milk out of a jug, which it cannot reach with its tongue, by dipping in the paw, and licking it. Would a cat learn to turn a jug over and pour the milk out, a thing which a monkey does as a matter of course? Or, conversely, if a tumbler or vase were inverted over a piece of food, would it turn it over to get the food? With the jug, Miss G. Thring made a series of experiments with her cat Teufel, the result of which was somewhat anomalous.

After experiments on five successive evenings, which had resulted in complete failure, some scraps of meat were put into the jug instead of milk. The cat turned the jug over accidentally with his hind leg, but was not allowed to pick up the meat. He then put his paw in, and turned the jug over four times in ten minutes. On the third occasion, the jug being more full, he fished out the meat with his paw twice, but then, not getting any more turned it over. He still refused to turn it over when filled with milk instead of meat, until the ninth night, when it happened that the jug was placed on a newspaper instead of a plate. The cat, for some reason best known to himself, seemed to think that this made an essential difference, overturned the jug at once, and lapped up the milk. This was done several times. After a week's interval the cat was given the jug on a plate as at first, but overturned it without any hesitation.

The interpretation of this very interesting experiment is not easy. The first success with the meat may have been due to the accidental overturning. If so, it was a singularly intelligent application of an accident, since the cat was not allowed to get the meat. From what I saw of the cat, I am more inclined to think that there was not much discrimination between clawing at the meat, and clawing the jug over. The other question suggested is why the substitution of the newspaper should make any difference. I cannot pretend to answer this question; but it seems clear, for whatever reason, that the cat had originally some reluctance to upsetting the milk, which was overcome when he once accomplished it without untoward results.

I tried my cat with the milk jug once or twice only, but without effect. I then gave him several lessons with a tumbler, inverted over meat, also without effect. He persistently tried to claw at the carpet, or to smell at the bottom of the tumbler. Miss Vernon's cat Balbus behaved in the same way.

I now substituted for the tumbler a little bronze tripod, which was more easily upset because it stuck in the carpet. The cat soon learned to upset this, apparently by seeing it done, and afterwards extended the act to other objects.

I upset it, by pushing at the top, six times. The seventh time [1] the cat turned it over deliberately with its paw at the top, and repeated this six times.

The next day, the cat still failed with the glass, but repeated its success with the tripod.[2] A tall vase was then substituted. The cat put its paw round, and moved the vase, finally managing to push it away from the meat. A short silver candlestick was then substituted, being inverted over the meat. This the cat pushed with paw or nose, either pulling it away or knocking it over, seven times in succession. But when the candlestick was set upright, and the meat put under its broad, flat bottom, the cat failed to turn it over. Next day, he turned the candlestick over twice, and when set upright managed to move it away. I now took a china vase again, and first gave it him upright ; he put his paw right down, and managed to reach the fish, at the same time upsetting the vase. I then reversed the vase. He tried to get the fish by moving it along, so I lightly held the vase over it, whereupon he put his paw round it higher up, and turned it over. At the next trial, he repeated this at once.

This success seemed to be originally due to perception of results. There was no movement in the original efforts of the cat at all resembling those which I showed him. There was the tentative pawing of the fifth trial, which suggested that the " idea " was half formed. Then came the definite success of the seventh trial, followed by an unbroken series of successes.

In strong contrast with the performance of Tim was

[1] At the fifth trial, the cat put its paw gently to the top and side of the tripod, as though half making up its mind to give a push. Otherwise it merely smelt about, and made no effort.

[2] It knocked it down first with its head, but the tripod being replaced, knocked it down again with paw.

the success of two older cats, Teufel and a Persian living in the same house, who turned tumblers over without being shown.

I tried Jack with this experiment, but it was of no avail, for he applied his nose so vigorously to the bottom of the tumbler, that he knocked it over or pushed it away without the slightest difficulty. On the other hand, a little fox-terrier who visited me one evening behaved in a manner strikingly recalling Tim's performance.

During three trials, he merely smelt about, or stared in a sur-prised fashion at the vase. At the fourth, he knocked it over. At the fifth, after staring and smelling, he very hesitatingly pawed the top and sides. He then seemed to abandon the enter-prise as too bold, but presently plucked up heart, put his paw out again, and knocked it over. The sixth time, after pawing in-effectually at the side, he knocked it over with a push of his nose near the bottom. The seventh and eighth times he knocked it clean over with his paw, each time after a short pause. The dog's behaviour suggested that he had seen something very sur-prising ; and though he had seen it, did not quite believe in it. It was not the hesitation of an imperfectly formed habit, but—at least in appearance—rather that of an imperfectly grasped idea.

(10). Cover.

A very simple experiment was to see whether a cat would lift a lid to get at food beneath it. Tim learnt this on being shown five times.

I took a little china tea-pot, and dropped some fish inside before Tim's eyes. At first he pawed hard at it, chiefly at the spout. I lifted the lid, and he clawed out the fish. At the next trial, he pawed at the cover, and pushed with his nose, but had to be shown again. At the next, he made a dash at it as I put the meat in, and helped by this, pawed the cover off. However, at the fourth and fifth trials he failed. At the sixth, I took the cover off two or three times, replacing it. He then pushed it off, and repeated this three times without failure. The next day he seemed at first to have forgotten, but presently succeeded without being shown. When I substituted a larger tea-pot of wholly different appearance, he got off the top at once, and got the meat out without turning it over.

Jack did this trick without being shown.

He was in the room while I was teaching the kitten. Whether he was watching, or merely used his common sense, I do not know ; but he lifted the cover with his nose at once.   He could not, however, get the fish out, and I upset the tea-pot for him. Next time he pulled off the lid and upset the pot at once.   The food unfortunately stuck in it, and I pulled it out.   The third time he turned it completely upside down ; and when, after an interval, I gave him the large tea-pot, he first, after removing the cover, turned it on its side ; then, as the fish was still unattainable, turned it completely over, and pulled it away from the food.

After being once shown Jack learnt to pull a stopper out of a jar with his teeth.

The stopper fitted into a large round glass jar, and could be lifted with the teeth by a projecting peg.   I lifted it out for him once, and left him to deal with the jar, which he did by knocking it over, and rolling it all about the room until the meat was jerked out.   At the second trial he pulled at the stopper himself with his teeth ; and he repeated this many times.   As to the other part of the experiment : if I left the bottle to Jack, he found no better method than that of rolling it about.   Another way was for me to hold the bottle, when he could get his paw in. I took his paw, and pulled the biscuit out with it twice ; and after this he used the paw himself when I held the bottle.   The first time that he did so, however, seemed to be in the course of general scrabbling, so that an accidental success may have combined with the effect of my teaching to influence him.

The first part of this experiment seemed to me strongly suggestive of perceptual learning.

(11).  Drawers.

I used a small cabinet of four drawers for the instruction of Jack and three cats.   The cats could open the drawers easily by clawing the loops.   Jack could not get hold of the loops well, and had to do it by hard scratching.   In this way, whether by watching me, or by random efforts, he learned the trick substantially in seven trials.

During four trials, there was no result beyond smelling about, and once a little scratching near the handle.   At the fifth and sixth trials, he scrabbled wildly at the handle (and the one right handle out of four).   The seventh time he scrabbled hard at the top of the drawer, and apparently in the crevice between the drawer and the chest.   In this way he somehow got the drawer open.   There was then an interval, after which he failed once, and then succeeded five times.   I afterwards tried his power of discriminating the drawers, in which he failed signally ; and owing to his disappointments, he twice failed or refused to open at all.   Nevertheless, I think it may fairly be said that the trick of opening, as distinct from discriminating, was definitely acquired.   It is hard in this case to say how much was accident, and how much perception of results.

Some time later, I tried Jack with a drawer more suited to his capacities.   It was a drawer in the sideboard, a little above his head, with a brass handle which I stuck out for him to take in the teeth.   If he pawed at it the handle fell, and he frustrated himself, so he could only pull quite deliberately with his teeth.   From the result it appeared that he rapidly learnt what he ought to do, but for a long time failed, owing to a curious reluctance to pull the metal handle.

For five trials Jack clawed indiscriminately ; for three more he clawed at or about the handle ; at the ninth and tenth he took the handle gently in his teeth, but did not pull, and refused any further attempt.   The next day, after twice refusing any attempt, he again took the handle gently in his teeth without pulling, and again refused further attempt.   After two days' persistently showing him, I tried holding him up to it, and pointing, without result.   I then took his head in my hands, and tried to put the handle in his teeth, but he merely resisted.   By this time I was convinced that it was not stupidity, but reluctance to pull the handle, which he probably felt hard to his gums.   I therefore lashed a short stick (previously used in the bolt and lever experiments) to the handle.   He at once, without any showing or pointing, took the stick in his mouth near the end, and pulled.   The pull being a little sideways, the drawer jammed, and I helped him.   The rest of his record (from the 4th trial of that day) is as follows :—

4. Same—again drawer jams, and I have to help.

5. He manages it alone.

6. I now take stick off handle.   He again barks as before, and refuses for some time, but finally, being encouraged, takes handle in teeth, and after hesitation, pulls.

7. Pulls it out, but not far enough, and in scrabbling to get his nose in, shuts it again.   Then baffled.   Knocks handle up with his nose.   I put it out for him, and he pulls drawer out again, further this time.

8. Same thing happens.

9. This time he pulls it farther out.   Nevertheless, as he rises to take food, his weight somehow shoves drawer back, and it

catches his paw.   He naturally refuses to try again for some time, but I encourage him a good deal, and at length he opens.

10. Opens more carefully, using nose instead of claw, when drawer is opened a little way.   Then uses paw.

I can hardly doubt that Jack really understood this trick from an early stage, but was afraid of it.   When he found that the drawer opened so easily, he got over his objection to the handle.   The minor adjustments, in particular the avoidance of shutting the drawer upon his paw a second time, are interesting, and show a very clear appreciation of what had to be done.

About three weeks later I gave Jack another little cabinet of drawers, hanging a button-hook on to the handle so that he could get hold of it.   This he very rapidly dealt with.   As he was smelling about, the drawer shook a little bit open, and I shut it again.   This seemed to stimulate his attention, and he at once opened it, repeating his success three or four times.

The cats dealt with the cabinet of drawers in a much more scientific fashion than Jack.

My cat was encouraged by the drawer being left slightly open at first, but two other cats, Teufel and his companion, a two year old Persian, learnt it without any such adventitious aids. Teufel was shown it three times, and then opened with the handle.   At the next attempt he failed at first, tried again, and succeeded.   After this he did not fail again.   The Persian was shown twice only, and then opened without fail.[1]

The discrimination of the drawers was quite another matter.   Jack failed in this hopelessly ; so, at first, did Tim.   I have seen the cat open the bottom drawer when the food was placed in the top.   The failure seems due entirely to inattention.

In a long series of experiments, the cat was right three times out of six—and in the remaining trials, hesitated twice at the right drawer—when allowed to stand just in front of the drawers. When held further away while the meat was put in, he became confused, and in the next six trials was only right twice.   In the next six he was right three times ; in the next, twice ; but counting from the last trial of that six, he was right four times

[1] The experiment was repeated with Teufel the next evening without failure, but apparently not with the other cat.

running, which suggests that, if I had continued the experiment, there would have been an improvement.

The older cats did better. Teufel, in the first series, was right four times out of six ; in the second series was wrong once only, and right three or four times running.[1] The two year old Persian was right three times out of five.

The little Rhesus monkey, Jimmy, who was kindly lent to me by Messrs. Jennison for some days, also failed signally in this experiment.

He was generally right if I let him sit in front of the drawers while I put the food in ; but if I banished him to a chair, he got quite wrong, and by degrees I noticed that he was elaborating a method of his own to save him the trouble of attention. To make quite sure, he would open the drawers systematically, from the bottom upwards.[2]

Success or failure, in an experiment of this kind, seems to be a matter principally of attention, partly of retentiveness.[3]

[1] In this series bread and butter were used instead of meat, to avoid guidance by smell, if possible. This, however, is hardly a danger in this experiment, as the cat opens with its claw, and at that distance the smell could hardly guide it as between one drawer and another.

[2] He did not, indeed, get this system perfect, as he often forgot the bottom drawer ; but it seemed to be growing as he went on. The point of it was that when an upper drawer was pulled out, the one below was difficult to reach, so Jimmy made sure of avoiding this difficulty. In quite a similar way the chimpanzee, who had to identify two boxes out of seven (marked B and containing banana), frankly gave up the attempt, and took them quite systematically in order, sometimes finishing the row after he had secured two pieces of banana, and sometimes leaving it. In discrimination experiments of this kind the penalty of failure is not sufficient to stir the animal's attention. Somebody unkindly suggested that if we put a live wasp in each of the blank boxes, we should soon teach the chimpanzee his alphabet.

[3] Some further experiments confirming this view will be mentioned lower down.

Mr. G. V. Hamilton (J. A. B., 1911, pp. 33 ff.) has described a series of experiments with human beings, monkeys, dogs, cats, and a horse, where the problem was to open one of four closed doors. The rule was simply that the same door was never locked twice. Only the human beings showed by their behaviour that they grasped the relation. But some of the animals, particularly the monkeys, took to opening all the doors in succession either in regular or irregular order. This is precisely the behaviour to be expected of a semi-intelligent animal. Mr. Hamilton's trick would be more baffling to such an animal than to one that was quite stupid, for it would always tend to be guided by the result of the last experiment, which would always be wrong. It gets out of this by the simple process of trying all four doors in succession, the best thing it can do in the circumstances.

(12). Sliding lid.

I taught Jack to open a child's toy box, the lid of which slid out in one direction only.

During three trials he clawed promiscuously.  At the fourth he pawed the top half open, but not seeing that he had succeeded lay down dejectedly.  I pointed at the top, and he jumped up and finished his work.  He repeated this four times, the last three without any delay.  The next day he had to be shown twice, and after this he sometimes clawed from the side or at random at first ; but he always got it right in the end.  In the fourth trial, for example, he came round, and clawed from the end.  In one case he tried to finish the work with his teeth.

Clearly it would be possible to learn this by random clawing, and I will not undertake to discriminate the factors in Jack's success.  Some of the details that I have mentioned, however, show that, by whatever means, he had acquired a pretty clear appreciation of what was to be done ; that is to say, that the lid had to be pulled, and pulled in a particular direction.  My cat wholly failed in this trick because he sat at the end where the meat was put in, *i.e.*, the blind end of the box ; and persistently scratched in that direction.  Teufel, on the other hand, learnt the trick in almost the same way as Jack.  He is described as watching anxiously during four trials.  At the fifth he scraped the lid, slightly opened it, and then was helped.  He did not fail again that night or the next, but required a hint once on the third night.

(13). Pushing of door.

After Jack had learnt to pull the string, I put the card with the meat on a high shelf, and tied the string to a tack stuck into the top of a cupboard door, near by.  The door swung open so as to bring the tack near to the shelf. When pushed away from that position, it would pull the string, and with it the card and food, down to the floor. Jack never showed any appreciation of the mechanism of this arrangement, for after he had learnt to push at the door, he frequently came to the wrong side.  I must admit, however, that by pushing hard enough on the wrong side, he caused the door to rebound, and so several times obtained his desire.

I did not begin by showing him how to do this, as I wanted to see whether he could puzzle it out for himself. At the first trial the door was pushed accidentally, but it is not likely that Jack saw how it happened. At the second, Jack managed by an extra high jump to catch the string. At the third, I called attention to the door, and he pushed it. At the fourth, he pushed the door on the wrong side, without result. I pointed to the door again, and he stood up to it, so moving it; whether intentionally or not was not clear. He then twice got the meat by knocking the door with his back as he jumped up towards the string; but at the seventh time he failed altogether, and I showed him the whole process. After this, he never failed to respond to the pointing,[1] which I made slighter and slighter till, on the third day, and twenty-third trial in all, I dispensed with it.

This series was abnormal in the number of trials requiring suggestion after the first success. It may be noted, however, that while there was one complete failure after the first success, there was no such failure after he had once been shown. This experiment is mainly interesting as illustrating what Mr. Small calls crassness. The dog learns quickly that he is to push a door; but which way he is to push it is a point which he treats as more or less immaterial.

(14). Weight.

I arranged the box already described on a table, with the projecting bar pointing upwards. In this position, if the lid were not held, the door would fall open of its own weight, and a biscuit would fall out. I then tied a string to the lever, and passed it over the back of the box nearly to the floor. A flat iron placed on a hook at the end of the string held the lid closed. If the flat iron was knocked off the lid fell.

Jack pretty quickly learned to knock it off. I showed him four times without success, the mechanism being defective.[2] After the mechanism was put right, I showed him three times. The third time he tugged hard at the string. The fourth time he stared hard at the iron, and then retired. I said to him, " Get it." He whined, and went towards the box. I said to him,

---

[1] At the first trial next day he showed no remembrance when I touched the door. He then put his paws up, but it was not quite clear that he pushed with intention.

[2] For the same reason two previous trials had been without result.

"No."    He then came to me, knocked the iron off with his paw, and got the biscuit.    Next time he did this almost at once. Next time he began by biting at the string.    The iron fell off, but I prevented the lid from falling, and replaced the weight. He then began jumping on the box, but, being restrained, looked carefully at the iron and pawed it off.    Next time I had to restrain him from pulling the table cloth, and he then pawed off the iron.    Next time he knocked it off without hesitation.    The next day he first bit at the string, and the iron tumbled off, and he got the biscuit.    In the next trial he repeated this, but I cheated him by keeping my fingers on the lid, and replaced the iron.    He then pawed it off the hook, and repeated this four times in succession.

This experiment seemed to me strongly suggestive of learning by perception of results.    I cannot think that any accident would have led Jack to pay the slightest attention to the weight.

*Failures of Jack.*

(*a*) I tried without success to arrange a converse experiment to that of the weight.

A basket was hung by a string from the door of the box, and the plan was to balance it so that when a weight was put into the basket, it would weigh the lid down.    Unfortunately my arrangement was very defective ; and furthermore, Jack soon found out that to put his own paw in the basket was quite as effective as putting the weight in it.    I tried to defeat him by frankly holding the lid in place when he used his foot, and I gradually got him to the point of knocking down and pawing the piece of wood which I used as a weight, and which was placed near the basket.    At other times he would take the wood in his teeth, and three or four times he knocked the wood on to the basket.    The failure may be ascribed partly to the complexity of the task ; but equally, I think, to the knowledge of another and simpler method.

(*b*) Hook.

The same explanation applies to an experiment in which I tied the latch of a box by a string to a hook, which was then fastened to a nail, first, on the box itself ; later, at a distance of about a yard from the box.[1]    The string held the latch in place, and to free it, it was necessary either to break the string or remove the hook.    I began by testing whether Jack would learn this without

[1] See diagram, p. 280.

seeing it done. I kept putting the hook on, and removing it while his attention was distracted by something else. This had no effect ; he merely bit and clawed at the string, and at times succeeded in biting it through. When I substituted wire, he would still pull so hard that the wire sometimes broke. After an interval of some days, I tried the same trick, only showing him. Unfortunately, the hook several times gave, which encouraged him in pulling hard at the wire. It was not until the twentieth trial that he made any attempt at the hook, though he had twice before come to look at it, probably because I called his attention to what I was doing. He then pawed at it a little, but failed to get it off. This seemed to discourage him. He tried at the hook vaguely two or three times afterwards, but never succeeded.

It seemed indeed that an accidental failure, when the trick was attempted in the way shown, was abnormally discouraging. Thus, I tried Jack with the simple trick of opening a cupboard door by pulling a key arranged so that he could easily get hold of it. He was so quick about this that at the first trial he jumped up to help me to pull, and at the second he began to pull at once. Unfortunately, to reach the key he had to put his forepaws on the ledge below the door, and they rested against the door itself, neutralising his efforts to open it.[1] After this failure, though several times shown, he refused to make the slightest effort—surely a suggestive result.[2]

5. *Habit and Discrimination.*

To these experiments, in so far as they may be offered in proof of learning by perception of results, two objections may be raised. The first is that, after all, each trick might have been performed in the first instance in a more or less random way, and that such an accidental success, not the sight of what the teacher did, would be really responsible for the establishment of the trick.

[1] Instances of animals thus hindering their own actions are fairly common, but both Jack and the elephant frequently showed some adroitness in overcoming that kind of hindrance. I thought my Rhesus, Jimmy, very stupid for trying to open his box upward while he sat on the lid, but my respect for him increased when, after many trials, he managed it—by sidling to the edge of the hinges.

[2] I mean that the effect was more marked than that of an ordinary failure, and points to more subtle psychological forces than that of bare perception and its application—namely, to the dog's confidence in his master and what he points out to him.

This objection I will deal with later. It will be most convenient to consider, first, another line of criticism which allows " imitation," but holds that, at least below the apes, it is of the sensori-motor kind. This kind of imitation Mr. Small found well-marked among his rats,[1] leading one to dig or scratch where another was digging or scratching, and, indeed, it is matter of common observation. The question, then, is this : does my dog pull a string or a lever merely because he sees me doing so, or because he has just seen the results which followed when I did so ? In the first alternative, the imitation is sensori-motor—that is, the perception of what is done discharges a motor impulse to do the same thing, quite apart from any purpose to be served by doing it. Of such a character, to quote Mr. Small again, is the frown of the baby which answers the frown of the nurse.

In an extreme form, this interpretation would be quite inapplicable to the animals observed by me. The interpretation would require that the animal should be influenced by the perception at the time when it perceives it. Thus the rat, I suppose, runs to dig or gnaw where and while the other is digging or gnawing. My animals, on the other hand, normally repeated my performance only after it was all over and the result had accrued. Jack did not, for example, rush forward to help me to drag down the string, but watched me as I dragged it down, searched for the meat, ate it up, waited while I replaced meat and card, and then dragged it down again. The opposite cases[2] were quite exceptional, and I think confined to Jack, who was always the most eager of my pupils.[3]

---

[1] *Op. cit.* p. 102.

[2] Such were his actions in one trial of the spike experiment, and in the cupboard-door experiment.

[3] By way of testing this irrational suggestibility, I did one or two " control" experiments. I took a little ivory box, and solemnly opened it before Jack. There was nothing inside. I then gave it him to play with, and he pawed it about and chewed it. This was repeated four or five times, after which Jack would not touch it unless bidden. He never tried to lift the lid off, though it came off several times as he played with the box. A day or two afterwards I put an empty paper-rack before the cat, who was at once very much interested. The rack consisted of three or four brass leaves or sides. One of these was loose, and I pulled it out. The cat began at once to claw the rack, and presently pulled the loose

The theory may, however, be reconstructed in a more plausible form. It may be said that the animal never perceived the relation between one act and another, but that when his attention was called to the act, he acquired a slight impulse to do it, which was speedily confirmed by the satisfactory results. There are not wanting facts in favour of this theory. Jack, for example, undoubtedly acquired a taste for hanging strings, and would pull at them frequently with no result. Similarly, the elephant, who would pull in a basket containing bread by means of a cord, would also pull dummy cords arranged for the purpose. I have seen the cat sitting up before the cabinet of drawers systematically pulling out one after another when there was nothing in them at all, and what is more, I have seen him pull out the same drawer three or four times in succession. Such cases suggest at least that the action tends to become habitual or sensori-motor. That is to say, it tends to become attached to the perception itself. And so far as it is attached to the perception, the relation between the act and its apparent end ceases to be operative.

How far, then, does this tendency go, and how far can we still trace the direct influence of the end upon the act? The simplest method of determining this question is by a

piece out, but sideways, not lengthwise as I had done. Nothing happened. I showed him again several times, and as nothing happened, his interest speedily drooped, and he departed, probably in some dudgeon.

Meanwhile, Jack was watching the proceedings. He now came up, and pawed all about, getting out the loose piece first sideways, and after a time, during which he was not shown again, lengthwise. I then showed him once or twice, and at length he pulled it out more or less deliberately. When he found that nothing happened, and I replaced the piece, he took no notice of it at all. I showed him again, and he knocked the piece out sideways, and bit it. After this he refused to take any notice till I had shown him three times, when he pawed at the side, and knocked the whole thing over. After this he absolutely refused to take any notice until he was ordered to pull it out, when he again got up and knocked the whole rack over.

Both animals began with every appearance of expectation that this was to be another of the now familiar tricks, which, according to experience, resulted in a tit-bit for them. Both showed interest in the proceedings, and an attempt to follow what I was doing at first; and both, when they found there was no result, abandoned their efforts. It would, of course, be possible to get the dog to persist through the motive of obedience, but this would be quite a different thing from mechanical imitation. Of this there seemed to be no trace.

discrimination test. An animal is accustomed to react to a particular object, and by so doing gets food. We wish to decide whether the reaction is determined by the sight of the object, or the desire for the food. Let us then multiply the object by two or three, and arrange so that the food is connected with one only. If the animal has means of knowing this, and—the food of course being out of sight at the time of action—prefers the appropriate object, the motive seems sufficiently clear. I have already mentioned some of the experiments which I made in this connection. The behaviour of the cats to the drawers showed in two cases a decided, in the third case a slighter, preference for the right one. The otter showed no hesitation or confusion at all between the two similar boxes, in one of which the catch had to be lifted, and in the other, depressed. But as a special test of this question, I made some experiments with Jack and his strings.

In the first series,[1] I put a paper on the projection over a door, carried the string over a neighbouring picture, and. dangled a dummy string down from the upper hinge of the door, so that the two strings hung at an interval of about a yard. The dummy was the nearest to Jack. As I was arranging this, Jack tugged at the wrong string, and I drove him away. When I put the biscuit up, and called him, he ran up, and pulled the right string. Next time he pulled the wrong string.

His whole series is as follows.

1. Right string first.
2. Wrong first.
3. Right first (seeing me put it up).
4. Right first (seeing put up).
5. Wrong first ; not seeing put up.
6. Right first ; ditto.
7. Right approached, not pulled ; pulled wrong, then right (ditto).
8. Right first.
9. Right first.
10. String shortened (to obviate difficulty of his seizing it too

---

[1] I had previously made an experiment with four strings attached to his box. Three were dummies, and one pulled the lever which opened the box. Jack virtually failed in this. I kept turning the box about, and his tendency was to take the string nearest him. He was right first seven times out of twenty. The strings swung about near together, and this and the movement of the box made matters too puzzling for him.

low to pull efficiently). Fails to find right string ; pulls wrong one ; back, and looks for right, but does not see it till I point repeatedly.

11. Right first.

12. Right attempted ; misses seizing it. Pulls wrong, chews it, and goes back to right.

Next day.

Right five times running. He only pulled at wrong string at beginning, while I was arranging experiment, and before I put right string up. (N.B. wrong string *once* pulled down after biscuit eaten.)

In this series ;

(*a*) He was right from the first when he saw process of arrangement.

(*b*) When not seeing it, his first record was wrong, right, wrong, right, right.

(*c*) Then came shortening of string, and he failed to see it. That twice put him wrong. But that he had really learnt the right string is shown by his behaviour next day, when the string was made more easy to see, and he made no mistake. He therefore certainly learnt to discriminate strings in eight experiments without seeing the biscuit put up ; and probably three trials would have been enough, but for the difficulty of sight.

I now reversed the strings, making the arrangement before his eyes. We will call the string which was formerly right and now wrong, *the old string*, and the other the *new string*.

1. Pulls the old string first, then new.

2. New.

3. New.

He is now taken away, so that he cannot see biscuit put up. Result :

11 times pulls old string first, each time passing the new string to get to it.

12. Stops at right, with claw on it ; hesitates, looking towards old ; biscuit falls down.

| | |
|---|---|
| 13. Old again. | After three-quarters of an hour :— |
| 14. Old. | 24. Old ; hesitation. |
| 15. New. | 25. Old. |
| 16. Old. | 26. New. |
| 17. Old. | 27. New. |
| 18. New. | 28. New. |
| 19. Old. | 29. New. |
| 20. New. | 30. New. |
| 21. Old. | 31. New. |
| 22. Old. | Next day. |
| 23. New. | New, five times running. |

This was a case of sheer mechanical habit, gradually overcome. The seizing of the wrong string became more and more mechanical, so that after pulling it the dog would not wait to see whether the biscuit had fallen down but would go to the new string at once, even with the old string still in his mouth.

It must be remembered, however, that the penalty of mistake was a very slight one ; he always pulled the right string immediately after the wrong one—therefore virtually lost nothing by it.

So far the experiments were not decisive. The first series showed that Jack could discriminate the strings, and preferred that which he learnt to be connected with the food. The second series, on the other hand, testifies forcibly to the strength of habit. Later on therefore I made a second series of experiments in which he saw the biscuit put up, but could not see it after it was put up. Three strings hung down side by side, at intervals of about a foot ; and I put the food first on one card, and then on another, varying them quite irregularly. The result showed a rapid growth of discrimination, which soon became nearly perfect.

Jack, who had not had the string experiment for some time, was very much excited, and at first kept pulling down the strings before I had time to put the meat up. He then began pulling in very random fashion, and only chose the right one first three times in the first fifteen trials. Soon, however, he became more attentive. In the next fifteen trials he was right seven times, and seven times also in the next ten. The experiment was resumed in the afternoon under stricter conditions. He was held back a yard or two, and I counted three after the biscuit was placed, and before he was let go. In the first four experiments he was right twice, but had some difficulty at the beginning in seeing the strings. In the next ten, he was right seven times, and one trial was doubtful.[1] During the course of these trials he gave up pulling down the remaining strings after getting the biscuit.

I now made a further experiment to test the effect of irrational imitation. Putting the biscuit on one of the cards, I pulled it down, and let him take it. I then placed a biscuit on another card, to see whether he would be guided by what he now saw, or by what I had just done. The case was closely analogous to the ordinary experi-

---

[1] He jumped between two strings, but caught the right one.

ments, in which he had learnt to get food by the method by which I had previously got it for him ; and the question therefore seemed here to come to a head. If he was influenced by what he saw me do, there would be some tendency to pull the string which I had pulled. But if this influence was subordinate to the desire of getting the biscuit, he would soon learn that for once he was wrong in following me ; and he would as before take to watching where the biscuit was put, and pulling the string that led to that place. This is in fact what fell out. In the first four trials, he three times pulled the string which I had pulled previously.[1] After this, he six times in succession pulled the right one, to the neglect of that which I had pulled before.

This experiment seemed to me to show at once the influence of previous perception, and its subordination to the results connected with it. The experiment also illustrated once more the function of attention. Comparing its earlier and later stages, it would seem that Jack's attention was rapidly cultivated. He began with great carelessness ; and his successes were actually below the average of pure chance. By the end of the day, he had improved so much as to be nearly always right.

Tied cord.

I was struck by a performance of the chimpanzee with a cord which I had knotted round a bar outside his cage. He was accustomed to pulling in food by means of this cord, and I wished to see how he would act if I tied the cord round a staple, so that the end in his possession became inoperative. I found that without any hesitation, he "made a long arm," and reached beyond the knot; and I thought it would be interesting to compare the action of other animals on this point. I therefore arranged a cord for Jack's benefit, which passed from the leg of a table diagonally upwards, round a support of the sideboard at about three feet from the ground, and from there up to a

---

[1] At the first trial he nearly pulled the right one, but passed to mine. Both strings fell. In the third trial he pulled neither the right string nor mine. It must be added that each time, after having pulled down the card, I replaced it immediately before placing the biscuit on another card, so that his attention to the wrong card was maintained.

high shelf where a little basket was placed. The result showed that Jack had no appreciation of the knot, and did not find the right place for himself, but learnt it rapidly from my suggestion.

The string was first made loose, and Jack got the basket by pulling the lower portion. I then knotted it round the support, but, as it happened, I did not make the knot tight enough ; and by biting persistently at the lower string Jack got the biscuit again. At the third trial, Jack pulled the lower string till it broke, when he got some satisfaction in chewing it. He then pulled slightly at the short hanging end of it, and then pulled above the knot. I now substituted a stout cord, and first made it loose. Jack pulled from below as before. I then tied it again, and the rest of his record is as follows.

5. He pulls hard at wrong place. Then higher up, close to the knot but not above, which involves his coming round leg of sideboard. Sits watching. Goes away. Comes back. Just nips at cord in wrong place, but gives no real pull, and sits still again.

I say, " Good dog ;" he pulls at wrong part again. I point to basket. Again at wrong ; now jumps up and at knot. I point to basket again—similar result. I point to string—similar result. *I point to right spot of string.* Same, only tries to get paw up on to sideboard.

*I point again.* He comes round under string and to right place, and pulls successfully.

6. Wrong again. Then waits. I say, " Good dog ;" no result. Then he comes round, bites just by knot, but gets right side, and so succeeds.

7. Right at once (both these times he started from same corner where he had sat at first, and had to come round corner of sideboard).

8. Comes round at once, but at first takes string just below knot. Quickly drops it, and pulls right.

9. Pulls wrong hard. Then jumps at sideboard. Pulls, not seriously, at wrong again. Pause. At last comes round as before from corner, and yet pulls *wrong,* near knot. He lies still a long time. At last I say, " Go on, Jack." He goes to right place, pulls wrong slightly, then right.

10. To right place at once (from old corner). Pulls wrong slightly. Then right.

11. Wrong slightly, but quickly to right.

12. Barely mouths wrong string. Then right.

13. Right at once.

14. Same (makes a sort of feint at wrong).

**Next day.**
1. Wrong first. Then quickly round, and pulls right.
2. Right at once.
3. Same.
4. Same.

This really resolved itself into a discrimination experiment, in which Jack learnt the right part of the string by my pointing to it twice in one trial,[1] after which he never altogether failed, though he once temporarily forgot.[2]

Teufel also did an experiment of this kind, in which the right part of the string was at first distinguished by some wool. The right string was pointed at the first time and once later. The whole record is as follows.

RECORD IN BRIEF.

(Right or wrong at *first* trial.)

| First night. | Second night. | Third night. |
|---|---|---|
| 1. Right (pointed to). | Right. | Wrong. |
| 2. Wrong. | Right. | Right. |
| 3. Wrong. | Right. | Right. |
| 4. Right. | Right. | Right. |
| 5. Wrong. | Wrong. | Right. |
| 6. Right. | | Right. |
| 7. Wrong. | | |
| 8. Right (pointed). | | |
| 9. Right. | | |
| 10. Right. | | |
| 11. Right. | | |
| 12. Right. | | |

Finally, I arranged a similar experiment for the elephant, with similar results.

---

[1] His success in No. 3 may have helped him, but it would probably be neutralised by my leaving the string slack again in No. 4.

[2] This was a particularly instructive case of temporary failure. I did not give him the slightest hint or reminder, but after he had waited stupidly for a long time, I told him to go on, in the reproachful tone which one might use to a person who really knows a thing, but is suffering from some inhibition which prevents his using it. In Jack's case my remark seemed precisely to have this effect of removing the inhibition, or perhaps of supplying the needed stimulus to set the machinery to work.

A cord started from the bottom of her stall and was passed over the railing above her head. From there it descended diagonally, and was tied to a basket placed out of sight, two or three yards away. She pulled it in six times by means of the near portion of the cord, showing by the way some ingenuity in so doing, either helping herself with her foot, or turning her head right away. The cord was now tied round the railing, and the elephant was at first baffled. In despair she opened her mouth wide for the food to be thrown in, and having raised her trunk for the purpose, brought it down with a swish over the outer portion of the cord, and secured the basket. This was clearly an accident, and at the second trial she was quite baffled again. At length the keeper, who was present, pointed to the right cord, and she pulled it. At the third trial, however, she again pulled the wrong part hard at first, but at length, in again putting her trunk up to open her mouth, she put it round the outer cord, and pulled. This time it did not seem to be altogether an accident, for she curled the trunk about the cord ; and in fact, in the next trial, she pulled the right almost at once. In the next trial again, after slightly trying the wrong part, she pulled right. She was then three times right in succession. Two days later she began by pulling at the right cord, but the basket caught in some rails over which she had to pull it. This led her to try the wrong part for a while, but she reverted to the right portion, and got the bread. At the next trial she tried the wrong part for a moment, and then was right ; after this she was right four times in succession. Six days later she always pulled the right cord, though generally with a slight preliminary pull at the wrong one. On the knot being loosened, however, she pulled the downward string.

*Result of the Discrimination experiments—Instinct, Habit, and Intelligence.*

Taken together, the discrimination experiments go to show that whatever the force of habit, and whatever the feebleness and uncertainty of attention, the animals are on the whole aware of what they are about, and able at need to correct their errors by results. Their behaviour is most easily understood if we conceive the more intelligent act as overlaying habitual action, which in its turn overlays the actions of instinct and impulse. Mr. Small notes the inveterate tendency of his rats to " fool." They run about, smell, dig, or gnaw, without real reference to the business in hand. In the same way Jack scrabbles and jumps, the kitten wanders and picks, the otter slips about everywhere like ground lightning, the elephant fumbles ceaselessly, the monkey pulls things about. This is, as it were, the basal behaviour : the matrix out of which more adaptive action is hewn. But it tends to persist, even when the intelligent mode of conduct is fully formed. Still more does the animal tend to relapse into it when his intelligence fails. Under the pressure of desire he must do something ; and he falls back on the action that is native to him. Upon this tendency are superimposed the results of experience. Experience selects some of these actions, and applies them to this or that object. So selected or applied, the acts tend to become habitual, and are performed apart from those results which brought them into being. They become in this way incorporated, though less intimately, in the life of the animal, and serve him as a form of play or recreation. But once more, they give place on occasion to the actual desires of the animal, and the thing necessary for their attainment. We must take habit into account as a disturbing influence in the work of intelligence, but we must not attribute to it all that intelligence does.

6. *Probable reasons for imputing perceptual Learning.*

The question remains, whether, after all, any of the tricks were learnt by perception. I have admitted, as the detailed account shows, that other elements may in some cases have entered in, and may not this be true even when appearances suggested the contrary ? Is it not possible that in each case, after a certain amount of random endeavour, the animal hit by chance upon the appropriate movement, and finding that successful, repeated it ? If this were so, to show the method would be superfluous, and an animal should learn on the average as quickly if left to itself as upon the method adopted by me. I may say at once that the influence of imitation cannot be finally established until comparative experiments on a large scale have been conducted upon this point.[1]

---

[1] As a beginning I myself borrowed two collies, mother and son, for the purpose. My intention was to proceed as follows :—Taking experiment *a*, to show the method to the mother, and leave the son to discover

My experiments gave the affirmative instance, and the negative is required. But the reasons for holding as a probable inference that my animals were guided by what they saw are briefly these. There was in nearly all the experiments which succeeded (and most did succeed) a certain point at which a well marked change of attitude took place. This point varied, from the second trial to the seventh or eighth, and once or twice it was still longer delayed. Before this point, the efforts were of a random character ; not purposeless, indeed, but directed towards getting the foods by the methods natural or habitual to the animal. At a certain point it became clear that the animal was abandoning these methods, and adopting mine. The transition was more or less clearly marked, in accordance with the nature of the thing to be done. Where that was something very definite, the transition was striking and conspicuous. Such, for example, was Jack's first experiment with the string, where he began by leaping up and pawing wildly, and after once seeing the card pulled, took the string neatly in his teeth, and pulled it down. Other conspicuous instances with Jack were the spike experiment, in which, from general biting at spike,

it. Then, taking *b*, to reverse the process, showing it to the son, and leaving the mother to find it out. For both dogs, each trial was to be limited to 30 seconds, and, upon a series of experiments, it would appear whether the tricks shown were upon the average learnt in fewer trials than the tricks not shown. By this method of alternation I hoped to eliminate the differences of quality between the two animals. My experiment failed, because neither animal was sufficiently successful to give tangible results. The older collie would pay no attention at all to what she was shown, but merely looked to her master, and begged him to do the thing for her. I only succeeded in teaching her (by showing) to scratch open a lid ; and I am bound to say that, having once got the method, she applied it to a quite different box intelligently enough, always turning the box rapidly round till she found her scratching succeeding. In fact, she was not wanting in intelligence, but in initiative. So marked was this that when, in despair, I gave her a tin, which, as I held it, could not fail to open if once scratched at, and which the young dog accordingly scratched open at once, she made no effort till shown it several times. It was after learning this that she was taught to scratch open the lid of the other two boxes. The young dog was much more lively, and inclined to attempt things. He learnt rapidly (by showing) to open a box by the lever, throwing it upwards with his nose ; and also more slowly (when shown) to push back a lid with his nose. But the matter could not finally be decided without employing at least a dozen dogs or cats. At best, I do not think that perception of results would, except in difficult tricks, counterbalance any marked difference in intelligence or initiative.

chain, or lever, he passed in one trial[1] to the deliberate attempt to pull out a skewer somewhat tightly rammed in, and four or five inches long—an action which required definite and sustained effort. Another case was that of the weight, where, from biting at a string and jumping up at the box, Jack after having steadily looked at the weight, came up and knocked it off. Equally definite was the removal of the stopper, done neatly with the teeth after the operation had once been seen. No less definite was the pulling out of the sideboard drawer by the handle, though this experiment was marred by the reluctance described above. There is no sort of gradual transition from a general scrabble of the paws about a drawer, to the act of quietly seizing the handle with the teeth. Similarly, the opening of the drawer by Teufel and the Persian ; the drawing of a bolt by my cat ; the upsetting of the tripod and the pulling down of the string by the same animal, were very definite actions, not emerging from a general scratch, but, from the first, to all appearance definite in their aim. The little fox-terrier's action with the tripod, like the cat's, seemed to be a quite definite act, emerging as it were out of pure nothingness, *i.e.*, out of mere absence of effort. It must be added that as the table (p. 246) shows, both in these instances and in others, what was once acquired was very rarely lost. In many cases there was no complete failure after the first success. In others, there were none in the same series. Where there were failures, they were generally few, suggesting a momentary forgetfulness rather than an imperfectly formed habit.

7. *Evidence of guidance by "Ideas."*

Nor is this all. In some cases there were indications that the animal was learning not merely to execute a certain movement, but to do a certain thing : to move a certain object in the way in which it had been shown. Such, at least, was the impression left on my mind. When the cat, for example, learnt to pull out a bolt, it learnt not merely to paw, nor to paw at a particular thing, but to pull that bolt right out, a thing requiring a certain

---

[1] After one preliminary effort, in which he joined me in pulling.

combination or repetition of minor movements.[1] I have already referred once or twice to Jack's efforts with the skewer. Even more remarkable was the combination of efforts by which he pulled the string up through the banisters. We cannot in such a case apply the conception of a perceived object discharging a uniform motor reaction. There is rather a combination of movements which are not always the same except in this, that they are so adjusted as to produce a certain perceptible change in the external world. The string is seized in the place learnt through two or three experiences to be best ; the dog backs, and lets the string run through his teeth without letting go, or perhaps helps himself with his paw ; and finally darts forward for the bucket, all as the needs of the moment dictate.[2] So again in opening the sideboard drawer : Jack not merely pulls, but learns for himself how to get his head into the drawer without shutting it again, altering the method when he once hurts himself, and finding another. So again I have seen him, when standing up to pull open the door of his box by means of a wire, accidentally pushing it with his paws again as he let go. At a second trial he was careful to avoid this, dropping the wire, and pushing his nose in as soon as there was room. Similarly, I have seen the elephant shift the box that she was opening when she had found that in a certain position the door would slam to again before she could get her trunk in. I have mentioned how well she would pull in the rope by successive stages, and in the same way, in an experiment in pulling a stick, which will be referred

---

[1] This at least is true of his action at its best. It was not always equally decisive, and once at least the cat pulled at the door before the bolt was properly out.

[2] Thinking memory might have exaggerated Jack's performance in this trick I tried it again after writing the above. In the first trial he succeeded with some difficulty by backing, and letting the string run through his teeth as he pulled. At the second he tried another method. Having pulled the string in a little way, he dropped it, and tried by darting forward to catch it further on. In this he was defeated, because the string slipped away more quickly than he could get forward. He then put his paw on the string, holding it while he darted his mouth forward. Repeating this once or twice he succeeded in getting the bucket up—on the whole perhaps his most intelligent performance, and in detail quite novel.

to lower down, I noticed her "shortening," slipping her trunk along the stick as she got the end nearer towards her. These minor adjustments suggest the dominance of an effort to effect a certain external change : to pull in a stick, pull out a bolt, open a door. They thus correspond to what in human experience we know as ideomotor action—action in which we deal with the objects of perception not in accordance with a fixed habitual response, but in such a manner as to produce in them a certain change which we desire.

These indications, slight as they may be,[1] suggest—and the result would hold, apart from the question of imitation —that what the animals learnt was not merely to respond in a particular way to a particular object, but to produce a certain change in that object as a means to securing their food. If this view is correct we have here in an elementary form the equivalent in action of the practical judgment—or idea. That is to say, we have a series of muscular movements directed towards a certain proximate end, which end is supported and made valuable by the fact that it is a means to something further. Action is directed towards the end A. A is in itself indifferent, but is valuable to the animal as a means to B. This relation, A—B, the animal has had opportunities of perceiving. We have, therefore, if the observations are correctly analysed, the clearest evidence that it is the knowledge of this sequence applied by the animal which determines its behaviour. In human experience the means and the end in such a case form the content of ideas, and their combination would be called a judgment. The above observations suggest that, if animals have not such ideas, they have something which can perform an equivalent function. To put it differently, I would define a practical idea as the function which directs action, not necessarily in accordance with habit or instinct, to the production of a certain perceptible result. It is, further, a necessary part of such an idea that it rests on a

---

[1] I much regret that I did not make more frequent notes on points of this kind, the significance of which did not occur to me at first. I have tried in the text to render fairly the impression left on my memory by many of the experiments, in the hope that in future experiments special attention may be given to this point.

perceptual basis, and is capable of being brought into relation with another such idea, for example, as means to end.[1]

*Absence of analysis.*

At the same time it must be understood that, if we attribute ideas to an animal, they are not ideas arrived at by any breaking-up, analysis, or other elaboration of what is given in perception. None of my animals (with the possible exception now and again of the monkeys) showed the least understanding of the how or why of their actions, as distinct from the crude fact that to do such and such a thing produced the result they required. It is this want of what one may call analysis that made, for example, the push-back bolt such a difficulty. What Jack or the elephant knew was, crudely, that they had to push this bolt. That the reason why they had to push it was to get it clear of the staple they obviously never grasped.[2]

Similarly, Jack learnt to push a door, but which side he was to push it he did not know. Clearly he did not realise that to push the door would pull the string, and so drag down the card. All he knew was that a push on either side might get him the meat.[3] If, then, positively,

---

[1] The practical ideas which I would attribute to animals, therefore, correspond with the explicit ideas of Dr. Stout. Ideas in Dr. Stout's terminology may be either tied, explicit, or free. Tied ideas are those "complicated" with perception, the elements which, in the terminology here used, have been assimilated by a sense datum. They are not separable elements in a mental state (*Manual*, pp. 191 following). Explicit ideas "extend and supplement present sense perception." Such an idea is a distinguishable element in consciousness but it does not arise except in relation to a percept (p. 196). Free ideas, on the other hand, have an individuality of their own and can exist apart from that which originally revives them (*ibid.*). Explicit ideas correspond precisely to those which I impute to the stage of the practical judgment. Free ideas, I think, belong only to that more reflective consciousness which we presume to be the exclusive attribute of man.

[2] It may have been mere chance, but I did observe the monkey Jimmy at times fingering the space between the two staples. Here at least was a datum out of which understanding of the bolt might come.

[3] I therefore fully agree with Mr. Small's meaning, though I should employ a slightly different terminology, when he says :—"It is also clear, I think, that, what properly may be called ideas, find slight place in the associative process. Crass images—visual, olfactory, motor—organic conditions, and instinctive activities are assuredly the main elements.

the experiments suggest "practical ideas" negatively, they strongly suggest absence of any sort of analysis in the genesis of those ideas. An animal can shift its attention to this or that object or change within the sphere of perception ; but it cannot apparently follow out the structure of any complex object with any minuteness and accuracy.

8. *Further evidence as to perceptual learning.*

To return to perceptual learning. If we allow ourselves to go outside the region of experiment we find plenty of instances of it in the observations of psychologists and others. Of these the ordinary case of the cat and the thumb-latch will serve, as an example, as well as another. Writers like Mr. Thorndike, who deny imitation, have to fall back on the theory that the cat learns this, in the first instance, by some lucky combination of random jumpings and clutchings and scratchings and pushings. This would only be possible, to begin with, if cats habitually jumped about and clutched and scratched in such a manner when they wanted to leave a room. Mr. Thorndike has experimented so much with cats shut up in cages that he seems to think this a possible explanation. If three cats out of eight learnt, by scrabbling all round their pens, to open their latches, why, he asks,[1] should not three cats in a thousand learn to open a thumb-latch "in the same way"? —*i.e.*, I suppose, by jumping and scratching all round the room. But the reply is that a thousand cats do not spend their time jumping and scratching round rooms. Such behaviour is, no doubt, natural to cats confined in a cage, but ordinary observation of cats under normal conditions is enough to show that this explanation is purely imaginary.

*Comparative unimportance of accident.*

I must add here that, so far as I could judge, the more a success was accidental the less likely were the animals

That these elements may bleach out and attenuate into ideas is not impossible " (*op. cit.*, p. 155.)

As I use it, the term *idea* means any mental state, however little analysed, the function of which is to refer to something not actually perceived (see above, Ch. VIII., p. 151).

[1] *Op. cit.*, p. 44.

to take advantage of it.   The elephant, for example, who succeeded by a random pull in getting out the bolt at the first trial, failed immediately afterwards.   But when, after being twice shown, it succeeded again, the trick was established.   Jack seldom failed more than once or twice after learning apparently by perception.   But consider the case of the push-back bolt, which Jack learnt principally by trial and error.   Here there was a random success at the third trial, followed by no less than twenty-nine failures.   A second success later on was also isolated, and it was not till the forty-fourth trial that a third success practically established the trick.   I have referred above to the collie, which no less than four times knocked the string down by roaming about, but showed no inclination whatever to pull it down by a deliberate act.   In short, these experiments seem to suggest that recent writers have over-estimated the effect of pure accident.   In any case it would seem that, whether accidental or not, the success is only effective if attended to.   When due to some chance movement disconnected with the efforts of the animal,[1] it seemed, as a rule, to leave no impression.[2]

----

[1] As, *e.g.*, the knocking down of the string by the cat with his tail.

[2] So far as they go the "double movement" tricks, if properly arranged, tell in favour of learning by attention to the changes rather than by association of movements.   The most instructive of these experiments are those in which an animal first learns an act A, and then learns that B must be done to make A possible.   Thus, the otter first learns to pull a lever, then to draw a bolt or raise a catch in order that the pulling of the lever may be effective.   If this be explained as regressive association it must be borne in mind that first the association of success with the act A has to be dissolved—the animal pulls at the lever and finds it of no use.   Then the association has to be reconstituted for A-in-the-circumstances-created-by-the-performance-of-B, and then B has to be learnt.   Now, all this is accomplished by the animals in some cases in a very few trials.

Instances of double movements learnt by Jack were the "loop" and "skewer" and "pull-out bolt."   It is noteworthy that where, as in the "push-back bolt," he had great difficulty in learning the preliminary movement, he would every now and then try the other out of its place.

The cat got the order right in the "loop" experiment, but wrong in the "skewer."   He also got disheartened with the lever in the "push-back bolt" experiment, and refused to try it.

The elephant learnt bolt and knob, and gradually got perfect about the order (see table).   After learning the catch she was only once wrong as to the order, but in the "push-back bolt" did not properly acquire it.

The otter learnt some highly complex movements rapidly, but was never "safe" as to the order.   Subject to that limitation it may be said to have learnt the bolt and lever in thirteen trials, catch and lever in one.

*Attention not natural but acquired.*

Nor had the animals—and this is a further negative result of some importance—any natural impulse to attend to what they were shown. There is no instinct to learn by perception. So far as my own experience goes, indeed, the absence of this instinct is as strongly marked among apes as among lower mammals. I found the Rhesus monkey less attentive than my dog, and certainly not more attentive than the cat.[1] To learn new methods of action by watching an external process is certainly not a part of an average animal's normal life. On the other hand, attention can be cultivated. Jack showed a very marked improvement in this respect, so that I was able to lead him on step by step to more difficult things ; and both he and my cat showed what may be called a general appreciation of what was to be done. They became excited when I

It did the catch and bolt together, with only one failure, though with much delay. Later it was given a box with two levers to be raised running at right angles with each other. It took five minutes over this at the first trial, and two minutes at the second. When I saw it a fortnight later it bungled the first trial rather, but did the second in thirty-five seconds. It then tried a box with one catch to raise, another at right angles to depress, and a bolt to draw. It failed in the first two trials because it knocked one catch up so as to interfere with the other. This being prevented with a nail it succeeded, though with a good deal of bungling, but in the second trial it seemed clear about the two catches. The Rhesus monkey, Jimmy, learnt several double movements. Thus, I taught him first to push back one bolt, then to pull at a wedge which prevented the bolt from going back, then to remove a spike which prevented him from pulling at the wedge, and, in addition, to pull out a loose bolt by which the box was also guarded. Jimmy, when interested, would go through the whole performance, every part of which, except the pushing of the bolt, he learnt for himself, with great rapidity. But I am bound to add that he would also pull at the spike when I so arranged it as to have no function. Playful pulling at things is the basis of Jimmy's learning.

Further experiments are wanted on this head, particularly with regard to the rapidity with which the order is learnt before any safe inference can be drawn from them.

[1] Hence he utterly failed, though repeatedly shown, to learn to open a cupboard door by turning a button. For another conspicuous failure see p. 284. I also tried in vain to teach him to use a hammer to break walnuts. Miss Romanes succeeded in this with her Cebus, but it was already accustomed to use a metal plate for this purpose, and merely learnt to substitute the hammer. I do not wish to generalise from a slender experience, but I am bound to say that the monkeys I observed scarcely showed a trace of "mechanical" imitation in their behaviour, and generally learnt much less by being shown than from their own experimentation.

made preparations for an experiment, even though it was of a new kind. This was very plainly marked in their disappointment with the "control" experiment which I tried without food.

9. *The normal process of learning.*

Whatever the basis of learning, whether accident, imitation, or other, the normal process was clear enough. In each case the central point was what I have called the critical success. In nearly all cases this was also the first success. Sometimes, indeed, success was arrived at in stages. The animal would fairly attempt the right method without succeeding ; or perhaps, though having once succeeded, it would require a reminder before succeeding again. But seldom would it fall back from partial success to complete failure. In other cases success was heralded by a kind of tentative action, as when the fox-terrier or the cat slightly pawed the vase without seriously trying to overturn it. Finally, after success, it was not uncommon to have a break-down in one, and, more rarely, two trials of the same series. Generally this happened when the series had been prolonged, and it gave the impression that the animal's powers of concentration had been exhausted by its successful effort. There is no doubt that the process of learning what to us appears so simple is to them attended with great effort. It was seldom of any use to prolong a lesson beyond a dozen, or, at most, twenty trials ; and the dog and cat in particular would seem, at the end of such a series, quite exhausted, and would stretch themselves out for a good sleep, after half-an-hour of which they would wake up, and do very much better.

Many observers credit animals with apparent "memory" of particular events, and, rightly understood, this view coincides with the conception to which we have been led of the learning process. We cannot, indeed, from any external action infer that an animal makes a memory-judgment in the strict sense, *i.e.*, is aware of an event as having taken place at a certain time in the past. In this sense the possession of memory by animals is at least unprovable. What we can say is that a single occurrence often has a permanent effect upon the animal, as shown by its actions after perhaps considerable lapse of time. With the higher animals this effect is not confined to cases in which a simple reaction is encouraged or inhibited by the immediately attendant pleasure or pain.[1] It is seen equally in the speedy and long-retained recognition of places and persons. The power of cats and dogs to find their way home over a route once traversed, even among all the turnings of a big town, is too familiar to need remark. Similarly, Romanes correctly writes :—

" The memory of the horse is remarkably good, as almost every one must have had occasion to observe who has driven one over roads which the animal may have only once traversed a long time before." [2]

A comparatively trivial event may also be " fixed " by a single occurrence.

" When I was at the Cape I used to take my two dogs up the Devil's Peak, an outlying point of Table Mountain. There were several places at which it was necessary that I should lift them from ledge to ledge since they could not scramble up by themselves. After the first ascent they always remembered these places and waited patiently to be lifted up." [3]

It would be useless to multiply instances. The question is, how to interpret a familiar observation. In that interpretation we cannot, if we go solely by the actions of the animal, attribute to it a memory-judgment in the sense of an act of thought about the past. But we can fairly say that one condition of the memory-judgment is present, *i.e.*, the animal takes note of a single occurrence and guides his conduct thereby on subsequent occasions.

[1] Inhibition is, of course, the least definite, and in that way the easiest lesson that experience can teach. A case of inhibition by one experience is alleged by Bingley (quoted by Romanes, p. 25) from the Mollusca. I should like to see it tested. It is also possible that in the matter of the signs of approaching prey or danger, heredity prepares a machinery with which the appropriate sound or sight fits not congenitally, but after a minimum of practice. In these cases there may be rapid learning, and yet the operation of experience may be only of the mechanical, inarticulate kind. But where a poodle remembers his way to any house where he has once been, we have to do with an appreciation of space relations probably very complex, which, one would say, must either be retained in an articulate form, or not at all (see Brehm's *Thierleben*, 3rd ed., Vol. II., p. 157).

[2] *Animal Intelligence*, p. 330.

[3] Lloyd Morgan, *Comparative Psychology*, p. 118.

## SUMMARY.

To put these points briefly together, the experiments suggest :—

1. That animals learn by attention to a simple sequence of events. It is easiest for them to learn if the first event is an act of their own, and the second a result of that act, which gratifies or hurts them. But even in those cases, their method of learning does not ordinarily, in the instances which I have observed, conform to the notion of the gradual growth or inhibition of a habit. It conforms rather to the rise of an idea, at first perhaps dimly grasped; then clearly seen ; for a while waveringly held, but soon definitely established.

2. For reasons that have been given, the basis of what was learnt was, in several cases, most probably the perception of what was done by the experimenter, and its result. This, however, requires further proof.

3. Whether by perception of what was done by another, or by noting the results of their own actions, it seems fair to say—though on this point, also, further evidence is required—that what the animal learnt to do was, in some instances, though not in all, to effect a certain perceptual change as a step to securing food. Their behaviour cannot be described in all cases as a uniform motor reaction to a perception but rather suggested a combination of efforts to effect a definite change in the perceived object. Such a direction of action to an external change, I call a practical idea. And the correlation of such an idea with a remoter end, I call a practical judgment.

4. This "idea," however, does not represent any analysis of what is perceived. Animal perception as compared with human perception would seem, by the use of it, to be crude; and the ideas derived from it are no less crude.

5. There is no natural tendency to learn by perception; still less to " reflective " as distinct from " simple " imitation.[1]

---

[1] Mr. Small says, "It is not impossible that a form of imitation, involving the higher associative processes, might be demonstrated if it were possible to direct the attention of the rat to the actions of the other rat, while retaining undiminished the affective basis for action" (p. 163, op. cit.). Except that the animals used to watch, not the actions of another,

It may be added that in spite of much difference in the way of going about a thing, there appeared to be no essential difference in capacity to learn between the dogs, elephants, cats, and otter. The difference between individual dogs, for example, appeared much more marked that those beween the dog Jack and the elephant Lily.[1]

but my motions, this sentence expresses in a few words the point on which success or failure in the above experiments appeared to turn.

[1] The problem of perceptual learning has been the subject of a large number of laboratory experiments since the above was written, many of which gave negative results. It must be remarked, however, that the question is not whether the lower animals in general can learn through perception, nor whether the higher animals normally use this form of intelligence, but whether some of them are on occasion capable of so doing. It is therefore a case in which the affirmative instances are decisive as against the negative, and in a number of cases the affirmative appears to be clearly made out. To begin with monkeys, Kinnaman ("Mental Life of Two Macacus Rhesus Monkeys in Captivity," *American Journal of Psychology*, Vol. XIII.), while associating his general account of their methods with that of Thorndike's cats, shows clearly that the female learnt from her male companion to pull out a plug in which she had failed when by herself, and Dr. Haggerty ("Imitation in Monkeys," *J.C.N.*, Vol. XIX.) showed that of eleven monkeys which she used all but two exhibited imitative behaviour (p. 434). Her remarks upon the nature and stimulus of imitation are very instructive. In the first place she points out that in the most successful cases the imitator responds "by attacking a particular object." He does not necessarily repeat the "movements of the imitatee in detail. The impulse seemed to be to do something to the object, and the imitating animal used his hands and teeth interchangeably" (p. 439). This accords with my experience. It is against a mechanical interpretation of the imitative act and favours its purposive character. Further, "there is evidence to show that in certain cases the behaviour of the animal, unaccompanied by any profitable result, is not sufficient to produce imitation." Our author concludes : "Thus the facts would indicate that not only the act of the animal but also the profitable result of that act was a necessary feature in producing imitation" (p. 441).

Rapidity of learning comes out markedly in Kinnaman's experiments in relation to complex acts such as opening a door by turning a button, lifting a lever, and so on. In several of these cases the time falls plumply after the first trial in a relation of ten to one or more.

Coming lower than monkeys, we have Mr. C. S. Berry's studies of rats and cats. In the case of rats Mr. Berry concludes, like Dr. Haggerty, that the result is of importance. The untrained rat learnt the way out from the trained one, but "it was not until the trained rat had got out a few times that the untrained rat began to follow him." At the beginning they showed "no particular tendency to take note of each other's moves." ("The Imitative Tendency of White Rats," *J.C.N.P.*, Vol. XVI., especially p. 359). His experiments on cats ("An Experimental Study of Imitation in Cats," *J.C.N.P.*, Vol. XVIII.) gave very similar results. Imitation occurred and once again Mr. Berry interpreted it as due to the perception of the result rather than to the perception of the performance of the act itself by the trained animal. "In many cases I think it is not so much the association of the trained-animal-performing-the-act with the getting-of-food as it is an association of the act-being-performed with the getting-of-food" (p. 20). It may be remarked that Mr. Berry found evidence of imitation where both the imitator obtained food each time that the trained animal performed the act and also where the imitator was not fed at the moment but was free to imitate. He found no cases of imitation where the imitator observed a performance of the act from another compartment. This again coincides precisely with the view taken in the text of the limits of possible learning by perception of results.

With regard to dogs, Mr. Jennings ("Animal Behaviour," reprinted from the *American Naturalist*, Vol. XLII.) quotes a paper by Mr. G. van T. Hamilton, which unfortunately I have not been able to obtain, describing an experiment in which a dog had to learn that in order to escape from a pen he must select for pressing a lever bearing the same sign as one that he could observe on a sign-board elsewhere in the pen. The dog succeeded in this, but unfortunately "discovered a much simpler method of action that accomplished the same results. He merely began at one end of the series and pressed the levers in order till he came to the one that worked." When electric shocks were attached to the wrong levers he decided that he did not care to play that game any longer and the experiments had to end. The dog's method was in fact the same as that described by Mr. Hamilton as used by animals of various species in learning to escape from a room, and by my monkey in opening drawers. It is one in which the animal experimented on at least shows enough intelligence to outwit the psychologist.

Lastly, Mr. L. W. Cole made some remarkable experiments with raccoons that have been already referred to. Three signals of different colours were shown to the raccoons in a certain order. Upon the appearance of the third they had to mount some steps in order to obtain food. The order could be varied and they had to learn to discriminate between the series which meant and the series which did not mean food. The raccoons achieved this rather complicated result (Jennings, *loc. cit.*, cf. Gregg and McPheeters, "Behaviour of Raccoons to a Temporal Series of Stimuli," *J.A.B.*, 1913, p. 241. I regret that I have not been able to lay hands on Mr. Cole's first paper) and would themselves claw up the signals and, as will be mentioned elsewhere, tore down the wrong one. Whether this remarkable result can be quoted as proof of the existence of images of the unseen signals in the mind of the raccoons I will not pretend to determine, but that it involved actions directed by relation to that which was not present on the basis of past experiences in which the object had been presented I am clear, and so to direct action is the function which practical ideas perform. Mr. Cole, in his reply to Dr. Hunter and Messrs. Gregg and McPheeters ("Chicago Experiments with Raccoons," *J.A.B.*, 1915, pp. 158, etc.), points out that the explanations to which his critics are driven come by a roundabout process to the admission of a function identical with that which he supposes. Thus he quotes Dr. Hunter as writing : "Some intra-organic (non-orientation) factor not visible to the experimenter must be assumed in order to explain a number of the correct reactions of the raccoons and all of the successful reactions of the children. These cues fulfil an ideational function." And again : "By applying the term ideas to these cues, I mean that they are similar to the memory idea of human experience so far as function and mechanism are concerned" This really admits all that is here required. Of what passes within another organism we can know nothing but the nature of its functions and its origin. In full logical strictness this applies to every human being as it does to animals.

# APPENDIX TO CHAPTER X

THE object of the subjoined tables is to exhibit some of the main results of the above experiments in summary form. They must be taken rather as a rough aid to the formation of a judgment than as an exact statement of results possessing equal numerical value. Different experiments were directed towards different objects, and none were performed with a view to tabulation. Hence, for example, the number of failures after first success depends largely on the interest which the experimenter had in getting his animal perfect by showing it repeatedly. There was no time-limit for successes. These defects are, it is hoped, partly remedied by the appended notes and partly by the full preceding description. In the first tables, only experiments in which success was established are reckoned—the test of success being, unless otherwise stated, at least four successes—whether on the same or different days—after the last failure. In Table IV. is given a list of definite failures. Table I. illustrates the process of acquisition—especially the effect of the first success. Before the first complete success there was often an act which might on various grounds be termed a partial success. There must be something arbitrary in the nature of such successes, but it would be more misleading to ignore them, and, when necessary, their character is briefly explained in the "Remarks." Only complete failures are reckoned under the heading so named, mere mistakes or blundering being passed over.

Table II. arranges the experiments with the elephant somewhat differently, distinguishing the apparently random successes before the trick had been shown from those achieved afterwards. The result is to suggest that the showing had a material effect. As the elephant was a great fumbler, columns are added for her partial failures—in which are reckoned not mere mistakes of execution, but failures indicating misapprehension or forgetfulness of the right method.

Table III. deals with the Method of Acquisition. It is confined to the cats and dogs, and to those experiments in which there was some suggestion of perceptual learning. It states the method used by the experimenter (in which connection see the general account, pp. 186-189), and compares the behaviour of the animal at the first trial with the behaviour necessary for success. When there was a distinct suggestion of some other influence guiding the animal, that is noted.

Table IV. notes the definite cases of failure where the experiment was fairly tried. Twelve trials distributed over more than one day are taken as establishing a fair trial. In some cases I have entered failures of special interest not fulfilling this condition. Only animals appearing in the other tables are entered.

## TABLE I.—PROCESS OF ACQUISITION (EFFECTS OF CRITICAL SUCCESS).

| Animal. | Experiment. | First partial success. Trial No. | Complete failures after partial and before complete success. | First complete success. Series. | First complete success. Trial. | Complete failures after complete success. Same series. | Complete failures after complete success. Later series. | Complete failures after complete success. Total. | Remarks. |
|---|---|---|---|---|---|---|---|---|---|
| | **DOGS.** | | | | | | | | |
| Jack . | Pulling string . . . . | 2 | 0 | III. | 8 | 0 | 0 | 0 | Partial success = pulling string on my pointing ; complete success = without pointing. Strictly, trial No. 2 was a complete success, but is ranked as partial because subsequent trials showed complete success not established. |
| ,, | Pushing door . . . . | 3 | 3 | III. | 23 | 0 | 0 | 0 | Partial success = pushing door on pointing. Complete success, same without pointing. Side of door not discriminated. |
| ,, | String on banisters . | I | 0 | I. | 4 | 0 | 0 | 0 | Partial success = making fair trial. Complete success = succeeding without help. |
| ,, | Drawers . . . . . | 7 ᵃ | 0 | II. | 9 ᵇ | 0 ᶜ | no trials ᶜ | 0 ᶜ | ᵃ Serious attempts at handle in fifth and sixth trial. ᵇ Complete success = pulling by handle. See note 3. ᶜ After some discrimination experiments he refused to try, and also two or three times reverted to scrabbling. |
| ,, | Lever . . . . . . | | | I. | 7 | 3 | 3 ᵃ | 6 ᵃ | ᵃ One partial—lever has tendency to slip out. In later trials, box substituted for bird cage. |
| ,, | Sliding lid . . . . . | 4 | 0 | I. | 5 | 0 | 2 | 2 | |

| | Object | nth | 0 | I. | nth+2 | | | | Remarks |
|---|---|---|---|---|---|---|---|---|---|
| ,, | Sideboard drawer | | 0 | I. | 3 | 0 | 0 | 0 | Took handle in teeth at ninth trial. |
| ,, | Push bolt | | | | 2 | 11 | many | many | Learnt principally by trial and error. |
| ,, | Stopper | | | I. | 15 | 0 | 0 | 5 | |
| ,, | Two strings | | | I. | 3 | 3 | 2 | 0 | |
| ,, | Loop | | 1 | | 6 | 0 | 0 | 2 | Case in which he did not see food put up. |
| ,, | Skewer | $4^a$ | | | | 0 | $2^b$ | 2 | $^a$ *i.e.*, helped me pull. $^b$ In one makes a good attempt. In some trials, readjustment of spike may have had suggestive value. |
| ,, | Weight | | | III. | 8 | 1 (?) | 1 (+1?) | 1 (+2?) | In cases queried he bit at string first. In one case this resulted in box opening, and failure of the experiment. This is the case of failure noted. In the other cases he pawed the iron afterwards. |
| ,, | Tied string | $1^a$ | | | $2^b$ | $0^c$ | 0 | 0 | $^a$ = with pointing. $^b$ = without pointing; not immediate. $^c$ twice appeared to have forgotten, but ultimately succeeded. |
| ,, | Lifting catch | | | | 1 | 0 | | | |
| Tiny . | Upsetting vase | | | I. | 4 | 0 | | 0 | |

### CATS.

| | Object | nth | 0 | I. | nth+2 | | | | Remarks |
|---|---|---|---|---|---|---|---|---|---|
| Tim . | Tripod | $3^a$ | | | 7 | 0 | 0 | 0 | |
| ,, | Drawers | | 3 | | 6 | 0 | 2 | 2 | $^a$ Drawer left slightly open. |
| Teufel | ,, | | | | 4 | 0 | 0 | 0 | |
| Persian | Lever | | | | 3 | 0 | | 0 | |
| Tim . | | $3^a$ | | | 6 | 0 | $0^a$ | 0 | $^a$ Claws feebly at the bar. |
| ,, | Bolt | | 2 | | 3 | 0 | $2^a$ | 2 | $^a$ Could not get bolt out, and when easier one substituted, refused to try. Only two trials after this, both successful. |

TABLE I.—*Continued.*

| Animal. | Experiment. | First partial success. Trial No. | Complete failures after partial and before complete success. | First complete success. | | Complete failures after complete success. | | | Remarks. |
|---|---|---|---|---|---|---|---|---|---|
| | | | | Series. | Trial. | Same series. | Later series. | Total. | |
| **CATS.** | | | | | | | | | |
| Tim . | Loop . . . . . . | | | | 1 | 0 | 1 [a] | 1 | [a] Total record; first day, nine successes; second day, one trial, failure, little effort; third day, three successes. |
| Teufel | Lid . . . . . . | 5 [a] | | | 6 | 0 | 1 [b] | 1 | [a] = opens slightly. [b] = does it on pointing. In this case there was only one trial after last partial failure, but there had been many previous successes. |
| Tim . | String . . . . . | | | | n [a] | 1 | 2 [b] | 3 | [a] Much earlier string was once pulled down (? playfully) before meat was put on end. [b] At next trial required suggestion. |
| ,, | Lid . . . . . . | | | | 3 [a] | 3 | 0 | 3 | [a] First success due to his dashing at food. No failures after deliberate success in No. 6. |
| Teufel | Hanging string . . | | | | nth | several | 1 + 1 ? | several | ? = attention had twice to be called to string. |
| ,, | Tied string . . . . | 1 [a] | 0 | | 4 [b] | 2 | 2 | 4 | [a] = with pointing. [b] = without pointing. Trick practically learnt after second pointing. |
| ,, | Upsetting tumbler | | | | 1 | 0 | 0 | 0 | |

| | | | V. IX. | | | | | Notes |
|---|---|---|---|---|---|---|---|---|
| ,, Upsetting jug— (a) With meat | | | | | 0 | 0 a | 0 | *a* But sometimes long hesitation. *b* Jug for first time placed on paper. |
| (b) With milk | | | | | 0 | 0 | 0 | |
| **OTTER.** | | | | | | | | |
| Otter. Bolt | | | — | 13 | 0 | 1 | 1 | Shown twelve times; each time left to open. |
| ,, Catch, to raise | 0 | 0 a | | 1 | 0 | 0 | 0 | Learnt by own effort first time. |
| ,, Catch and bolt | | | | 1 | 0 | 1 | 0 | Tendency to alternate before either action is successful. |
| ,, To depress catch | 1 a | 1 | | 4 b | 0 | 0 | 0 | Begins with clear confusion with raising. This persists through two trials first day, and one next day; then disappears. *a* i.e., raised lever after depressing it, but finally opened. *b* Depressed lever without raising again. |
| **ELEPHANT.** | | | | | | | | |
| Lily . Pulling out bolt | — | — | I. | 1 | 2 | 1 a | 3 | *a* And one doubtful. Defect in the record. |
| ,, Cord | | | I. | 1 | 2 | 0 | | Slight pull at wrong part first not reckoned as constituting failure. |
| ,, Push-back bolt | | | I. | 1 a | 4 b | 0 | 4 | *a* After being shown. *b* i.e., I showed her four times. It is not clear that she would have failed if given longer, but twice she pulled obstinately at lever. |
| ,, Catch | — | — | I. | 3 | 0 | 0 | 0 | |

## TABLE II.—ELEPHANT. EFFECT OF PERCEPTION.

| Animal (elephant). | Experiment. | First success without being shown. | First complete success after being shown. | Failures after complete success on being shown. | | | | | Total (partial and complete). | Remarks. |
|---|---|---|---|---|---|---|---|---|---|---|
| | | | | Complete. | | Partial. | | | | |
| | | | | Same series. | Later. | Same series. | Next. | Later. | | |
| Lily | Bolt . . . . . . | 1 | 4 | 0 | 1 + 1?a | 1b | 3 | 1 | 6 | a Defect in note. b Partial failure = attempting knob before bolt is drawn. |
| ,, | Cord . . . . . | 1 | 3a | 0 | 0 | 0b | 0 | 0 | 0 | a Pulled right on keeper's pointing at No. 2. Success in 3 semi-accidental. b Slight preliminary pull at wrong cord not reckoned as partial failure. |
| ,, | Push bolt . . . . | — | 1 | 4a | 0 | 0 | 2b | — | 6 | a i.e., four times shown. b i.e., lever attempted before bolt. |
| ,, | Catch . . . . . | — | 3 | 0 | 0 | 1a | 0 | 0 | 1 | a i.e., tries lever first. |

It will be seen that while the two successes without being shown were not followed up, those subsequent to the showing were maintained in 3 cases out of 4 almost without failure.

## TABLE III.—METHOD OF ACQUISITION.

| 1 Method used by experimenter before first success. | 2 Experiments. | 3 Animal. | 4 Supplementary methods after first success. | 5 Behaviour of animal at first trial. | 6 Method used by animal with success. | 7 Evidence of processes guiding animal independent of experimenter. | 8 Remarks. |
|---|---|---|---|---|---|---|---|
| Showing | Push-back bolt | Jack | None | Pulling lever . . . . | Pawing or pushing bolt with nose | Trial and error | Trial and error apparently the main factor. |
| ,, | Stopper | ,, | ,, | Not noted . . . | Pulling out stopper with teeth | None | |
| ,, | Loop | ,, | ,, | General scrabbling, nearly knocking loop | Lifting loop with nose | ,, | |
| ,, | Skewer | ,, | ,, | Scrabbling, and biting at lever, chain, and skewer | Long pull at lever with teeth | ,, | Some encouragement possibly given to animal when skewer stuck. |
| ,, | Weight | ,, | Discouragement from scrabbling | Jumping at box and pulling string | Pawing iron off hook | — | Iron once or twice tumbled off when he was pawing at string. |
| ,, | Pulling string | ,, | Suggestion | Jumping up and scrabbling | Pulling string with teeth | | |
| ,, | Opening small drawers | ,, | — | Smelling about and very little scratching | Scrabbling at handle and top of chest | | Tendency to revert from use of handle to scrabbling at chest, which would effect opening, but not so well. |

TABLE III.—*Continued.*

| 1<br>Method used by experimenter before first success. | 2<br>Experiments. | 3<br>Animal. | 4<br>Supplementary methods after first success. | 5<br>Behaviour of animal at first trial. | 6<br>Method used by animal with success. | 7<br>Evidence of processes guiding animal independent of experimenter. | 8<br>Remarks. |
|---|---|---|---|---|---|---|---|
| Showing. | Lever | Jack | —$^a$ | Pawing generally, once nearly pulling lever — mainly at cage itself | Pulling lever sometimes with teeth, also with paw | | $^a$Once in second series cage was slightly tilted to help him in depressing lever. Box being substituted for cage, there was some scrabbling at first. Lever then opened with teeth. |
| Showing, with suggestion | Pushing door | ,, | — | Jumping up at food—back to door | Standing up with paws against door | Accident in 3rd and 4th trials | Suggestion (pointing at door) might in this case act as inducement to put up paws. |
| ,, | String on banisters | ,, | — | Pulling at wrong point of string | Pulling at right point, backing, and letting string run through teeth | Previous experience with string | |
| Showing, with help | Sliding lid | ,, | — | Noses box all round, and some scratching | Clawing in one direction | — | Help given consisted in showing animal that lid was open. |
| ,, | Sideboard drawer | ,, | Help | General scrabbling | Pulling handle with teeth | Previous experiment with drawers; use of a stick familiar in other experiments | Pulling of handle apparently learnt from showing alone. See text. |

| Showing alone | Upsetting vase | Dog (Tiny) | None | Smelling about | Knocking over with paw | | |
|---|---|---|---|---|---|---|---|
| Showing | Lifting lid | Cat (Tim) | None | Pawing indiscriminately | Pawing cover . . . | First success perhaps accidental | Two failures after quasi-accidental success. |
| ,, | Upsetting tripod | ,, | ,, | Smelling about . . . | Putting paw to top of tripod, and over-turning | — | — |
| ,, | Lever . . . | ,, | — | Clawing at cage or box | Clawing at lever, or pushing it with head | | He sometimes clawed *between* lever and box. |
| ,, | Bolt . . . | ,, | — | Not specially noted . | [a]Curling claw round bolt and pulling | | [a]Clawing not always equally good. |
| ,, | String . . . | ,, | — | In general no attention to string | Clawing string . . | | Very large number of failures before first success, in course of which he once gets paw over string and once pulls it down prematurely. |
| Showing | Opening small drawers | Cat (Teufel) | — | Purring, and walking about box | Inserting claw in handle and pulling . | — | Drawer not always opened by handle. |
| Showing with help | Sliding lid . . | ,, | —[a] | Watching . . . . | Scraping along lid . | | [a]Slight suggestion once on third day. Help consisted in finishing opening lid once after the cat had partially opened it. |
| Showing | Opening small drawers | Persian cat | — | Not stated . . . . | Scratched drawer open from side . . . . . | | |

## TABLE IV.—DEFINITE FAILURES (AFTER AT LEAST TWELVE TRIALS ON MORE THAN ONE DAY.)

| Animal. | Experiment. | Character of movement. Simple. | Character of movement. Double or complex. | In learning by perception. | In learning from own success. | In analogy. | In discrimination. | Remarks. |
|---|---|---|---|---|---|---|---|---|
| Jack . . . . | Putting weight into basket . . | | 1 | | | | | |
| " . . . . | Taking off hook . . . | | 1 | 1 | | | | |
| " . . . . | Using stick as rake a . . | | 1 | 1 | | | | a Ten trials. |
| " . . . . | Drawers a . . . . | | | | | | | a Eight trials. |
| Fox terrier (Tiny) . | Pulling string a . . . | 1 | | 1 b | 1 | | 1 | a Nine trials in one series. b Suggestion also used fruitlessly. |
| Cat (Tim) . . . | Upsetting tumbler . . . | 1 | | 1 | | | | |
| " . . . . | Raising catch . . . | | 1 | 1 | | 1 | | Does not properly learn to open when catch is raised for him. |
| " . . . . | Skewer a . . . . | | 1 | 1 | | | | a Four trials only. |
| " . . . . | Sliding lid . . . . | | 1 | 1 | | | | |
| " . . . . | Push-back bolt . . . | | 1 | 1 | 1 | | | |
| Elephant (Lily) . | Stick . . . . . | | 1 | | | | | |

# CHAPTER XI

## THE KNOWLEDGE OF CONCRETE OBJECTS

1. So far, the results of experiment indicate that the higher animals can learn, not merely by the mechanical repetition of experiences, but by careful attention to one or more instances, the number being really irrelevant, provided that attention is once seized. Further they appear to learn by the perception of concrete facts in their relations, *i.e.*, in their order as experienced. This order they are capable of " reproducing," in the sense that they can apply the results of perception to guide their future action. This does not mean that they are aware of relations as such, or order as such, or qualities as such, but that they are aware of the concrete whole, which the qualities in their relations build up ; and that when the whole is familiar to them, they can proceed inferentially, from the part or state which they see, to the part or state which they do not see. This view is corroborated by certain general considerations and by evidence outside the region of experiment.

*a. Class Inferences.*

The more intelligent animals not merely learn to react appropriately to a certain kind of sense stimulus, but from knowledge of one concrete and perhaps highly complex object, they learn to deal suitably with another object of the same class. Thus, a dog that is accustomed to one house readily familiarises himself with another. In the course of some observations which I made on the power

of dogs to find their way about a new place, I carried a
fox-terrier in a box into a room on the first floor of my
house, and asked her master to call her from outside.
After being let out from the box, and going to the
window, she appeared for a short time to be puzzled, but
soon started off, and went steadily out of the door, downstairs, out of the house door, and round the corner to her
master. Her total time was 27 seconds. This dog was
not in the least infallible, for in the very next experiment
she missed her way to begin with. But apparently she was
guided by what in a human being we should call common-
sense. Familiar with houses, staircases, rooms, and doors,
she would understand that to reach her master, she must
get out of the room and out of the house. She would be
familiar with stairs as leading her to the ground floor.
She would judge that, though leaving the house in the
opposite direction, she would be able to get round to
where her master stood.[1] None of the dogs which I
observed in this connection, with the exception of one
puppy,[2] showed any hesitation in endeavouring to get out
of the house, by however roundabout a way, if their
master was outside, or to run round to some door which
they had before passed through, if he was inside.[3] That
is to say, the full-grown dogs, though in different degrees,
could use their experience of houses as structures that
have passages and doors and staircases by means of which
you can reach your object through roundabout paths, as a
guide in my house, which was strange to them. In the
same way, an animal's attitude to strange men is determined by his dealings with the men he knows ; if he is
guided by resemblance, it is certainly not because he fails
in discriminating one individual from another. The little
monkey Jimmy was respectful and even friendly to all
men, and flew quite systematically at all women and

---

[1] From the front door onwards, she may very possibly have been influenced by previous experience, as she had come in that direction from
her home. In fact, she took the same turning wrongly in the next experiment. She had not, however, been brought in through the front door, but
by another way ; nor had her master been in the house at all.

[2] Another young dog failed at first to go down the stairs.

[3] On the other hand, they had considerable difficulty in locating a room
from outside, particularly if it was upstairs.

children. Whether this was due to a generalisation from teasing boys, and the nurses who accompany them, I do not know. The point remains, that Jimmy was guided by a general, or, as it might be called, a class resemblance, and this again not to the detriment of his knowledge of individuals,[1] for I have seen him get into a state of wild excitement on merely hearing the footsteps of his former keeper.

Little facts of this kind suggest that the assemblage of qualities which constitute an individual make a certain impression upon the animal mind,[2] and prepare it to deal with objects presenting a general similarity to those with which it is familiar. In short, an animal reacts, not only to resemblances of simple sense quality, but to the more general similarities which unite the individuals of a class. Such similarity is notoriously difficult to analyse ; but it seems to be a similarity in which many elements are concerned, and in which the relation between the elements is perhaps the determining feature. I one day gave Jack his box with a footstool in front, which prevented the door from opening. After very little hesitation, Jack scratched away the stool and got at the door ; and he repeated this action when for the wooden footstool I substituted a large hassock. Now, Jack would be of course accustomed to scratch at things, and in particular to scratch away earth to find a buried bone. It is extremely unlikely that he ever before had to scratch away a similar object under similar circumstances. It was again an act of common sense, the application by a kind of analogy to a new object of an action familiar under other circumstances. The similarity connecting this action with Jack's ordinary experience would be a similarity in the relation between the thing desired and the obstacle hindering access to it. Similarly, when I gave Jack a box with a new sort of fastening (the catch), he attacked it at once and persistently. Though he did not know what was to be

[1] At the same time his memory is very short. He clearly did not recognise me at first after a few days' absence.
[2] On this point see some good remarks in Mr. Schaler's *Domesticated Animals*, p. 39, on a dog's knowledge of the boundaries of his master's property.

done to it, he saw that this was the thing to attack and explore.

On the whole, then, it would seem that animals are influenced by similarity of relations. Not that they dissect out the common element which constitutes a class identity ; they have not solved the problem which has baffled logicians. It is rather that they have a concrete perception of the man or animal, house or locality with which they are familiar ; that such an object contains many elements in various relations ; and that when they meet another object similar in general character, *i.e.*, really in its constitutive relations, to the first, they know how to deal with it. This implies that they have the power of grasping an object as a whole including distinct elements which I have called Concrete Experience, and the power of applying this experience which I have called Practical Judgment.

2. *b. The object as centre of relations.*

A further point distinguishing the knowledge of objects lies in the use made of it. To perception, as already pointed out, any object is a centre of many relations. And if there is knowledge of objects, any one of these relations should be available to serve whatever happens to be the purpose of the moment. Here again is a marked difference from the habituation in accordance with which an animal learns to react in a uniform manner to a given stimulus. Thus one can understand that by habit or association, an animal should always resort to a particular spot as his home or his feeding place, or that he should follow—as our own feet often mechanically follow—a well-known path. But if applied to explain a dog or cat's acquaintance with locality, the habituation theory seems to break down. Thus, on this theory, when a dog, hearing the dinner-bell, rushes down to the dining-room from a distant part of the house, we should have to explain its action somewhat after this fashion. The sound of the bell impels it to rise : the sight of the door, to open it and pass through ; the sight of the passage, to turn to the right, go downstairs, turn to the left, and so forth. Each new motion must on this theory be due to an impulse arising out of a similar reaction in the past, with which a satisfactory result s associated. It is, on the surface, an argument against this theory, that if the direct or customary way into a room is barred, a dog or cat will at once [1] betake itself to any other route that there may be. This adoption of alternatives suggests that their action is to be referred, not to an impulse urging them to move in a particular direction, but rather to a desire to be in a particular place, the road to which is indifferent, so long as it is passable.

By way of testing the point, I made a number of experiments with dogs about the house in which I live, to which all of them were strange. Like most houses that go back for four centuries, this house is full of turnings and windings, and afforded opportunities for devising on a small scale intricate and alternative routes. My method was to get the dog's master to stay outside the house, while I took the dog in, and brought it to the window, whence it could see its master, who would then call it. Afterwards I would reverse the process, the master going inside, while the dog remained outside. In all cases, the use of scent was prevented, by taking care that the master did not go over the track which the dog would have to follow. The dog, it will be observed, had to respond to its master's call in quite unfamiliar circumstances. It has no association between taking this turn or that turn, and the satisfaction of rejoining its master.

In these as in other experiments the dogs showed a great variation in intelligence, initiative, and persistence.[2] The most noticeable defect was a failure in "orientation," the result of which was that on getting out of the house, for example, the dog would turn towards the spot where his master had last been found instead of towards that in which he had last been seen.[3] In such cases, the dog would as a rule rapidly return, and either go back into the house, and perhaps to the window again, or (as

---

[1] As a rule. I confess I have seen dogs fail in this respect.

[2] Putting aside the case of the puppy mentioned above, there were comparatively few complete failures (though there were often initial mistakes) when the master was outside. The dogs were also very fairly successful in finding their master in a ground floor room, but uniformly failed when he called to them from upstairs. This may be attributed partly to greater complexity, but mainly to the impossibility for a dog of identifying an upstair room by its window. The ground floor room the dog could look into and recognise.

[3] I only noted one clear case in which the more familiar route was at once rejected for the right one, against many in which a mistake was made at this point.

in at least one case) at once try the other direction.[1] In these cases, no doubt, previous experience has an undue influence, i.e., we get incipient habit, but the habit explains only the wrong part of the act, not the effort to correct it.

Neither impulse guided by habit nor random searching seem adequately to explain the way in which a dog looks for his master. Thus, in one of my experiments, a dog is held at the back of the house, and sees his master go in through the back door and re-appear at the dining-room window, which looks in that direction. After trying to follow his master through the back—unsuccess-fully, because the door is shut—he makes off round two corners to the front door, and so into the dining-room. He had never been in this room before, but has once been from the back into the house by the front door.[2] The experiment is once repeated, and the dog remembers this route five days later. On arriving at the house on this occasion, he is taken through a side door into the dining-room, and then out at the back. He first finds his way in through the front as mentioned, and then for a further trial both front and back door are shut. The dog goes to and fro from one to the other,[3] and then suddenly goes right off round the house and in by the side door—a route which he had never taken before. There may have been an element of chance in this success,[4] but, on the whole, we seem to have a series of acts dictated by the *desire* to find the master operating on the remem-brance of the modes of entrance. The same interpretation seems to apply to one more instance which may be given.

A little fox-terrier had once found her way from the back of the house through the front door into the dining-room to her master. I then took her out again, the master remaining where he was, to the same place outside, closing the front door behind me. After trying the front door several times, she at last set off round a further corner of the house, and found the side door, through which she got into the house, and found her master. The total time was 2 minutes 20 seconds. She had indeed traversed the whole of this route before, but under quite different circum-stances, for she had come round from the back to find her master in the garden outside the side door, and from thence I had taken her away from him through the side door to show her the dining-room, upon which followed the two experiments that I have mentioned.

---

[1] This part of the experiment was unfortunately spoilt in several instances by masters calling their dogs prematurely.

[2] The room itself he may have found by scent, chance, or possibly "direction sense."

[3] For some reason he did not go the whole way to the back door.

[4] But it was repeated immediately afterwards without any hesita-tion.

In this matter of searching for a lost object, the contrast between desire and impulse seems to be presented in a very simple form. By impulse, I understand response uninfluenced by an anticipatory idea. Such a response would explain a dog's running straight to his master on hearing his voice. A series of such responses might explain its following a route of which every portion was familiar, and each turn associated with the satisfaction of the impulse. But I do not see how it can be made to explain the traversing of a route not associated with such satisfaction,[1] nor the rapid choice of an alternative route, nor the return, which I have seen in the case of a puzzled dog, to the point of departure to seek further assurance. These appear rather as a series of actions dictated not merely by the perception of each object on the dog's path, but by the constant pressure of a desire, the determining factor in which is the remembrance of the master as seen at a certain spot, the relations of which to the place in which the animal finds itself determine its motions from moment to moment.

3. *c. Knowledge of individuals.*

It will now be understood that what has been called above[2] the knowledge of localities, objects, or individuals, makes its appearance in this stage of intelligence. That is to say, there is something more than acquired appropriate reaction to a perceived quality. There is an appreciation of an object, as a whole, to which many parts and many qualities belong ; and there is a capacity for definite reference to those of the parts or qualities which are not perceived. A toad, a snake, or even a fish, is said to know its keeper. What this usually means is, in fact, that the animal comes at the sound of his voice, or perhaps at the sight of him. There are two or three kinds of reaction which the presence of the keeper excites. This is no more knowing a person than to put down so many shillings on demand is to know the clerk at a booking office. It is merely appropriate reaction to certain

---

[1] Except, perhaps, where an animal has only to retrace a path just traversed.

[2] P. 158.

qualities of a person.　We human beings know our friends
in a very different way.　A man is many-sided, and to
know him is to respond to him with a many-sided understanding.　In their degree the higher animals have this
knowledge of their masters.　The ape, the dog, and the
elephant—in a lesser degree the horse, and even the cat—
notoriously " understand one."　The dog follows with
anxious sympathy the subtlest variations of mood.
" Knowledge " of this kind makes attachment possible
as an emotion.　It may be said that in attributing emotions
of this kind to the higher animals, we base ourselves, after
all, on certain modes of reaction.　But, if we do, our
interpretation is borne out by agreement with the facts.
The cat that looks angry also acts like an angry being,
and scepticism on this point may prove practically
dangerous.　On the whole, we may say that knowledge
of individuals becomes possible at the level of intelligence
which we are discussing, and that the appropriate emotions
of attachment, dislike, jealousy, and so forth, are to all
appearance expressed at this stage.

A certain mutual understanding seems also to be implied
in many features of animal play.　No doubt play is
instinctive, and the activities of play are often called
forth by a stimulus acting upon hereditary structure ; but
observers tell us of many instances in which animals of
different species, even where one might naturally be the
prey of the other, learn to play fearlessly together.[1]　It
is difficult to think that a game could arise under these
circumstances, or be maintained without degenerating into
a serious fight or hunt, unless each animal takes what the
other does as meant in play, and not as meant in earnest.
It must know, that is to say, that the threat to bite is not
going to be followed by a real bite.　In a word, each
animal must judge of what the other is going to do.[2]

The view that an animal not merely reacts to objects,
but knows them, is thus confirmed by evidence from more
than one source.　We have seen some ground for thinking

[1] See Groos, pp. 128, 143.
[2] For the degree of mutual understanding in courtship, see Groos,
p. 253.

that it perceives changes in outer objects, and bases its action thereupon, or adapts it to the production of such changes as it desires. It appears to be guided not only by the simple resemblances of sense-qualities, but by the similarities of relation which constitute the bond of identity between complex objects. And now, lastly, we have seen that it is not tied to one uniform type of reaction in response to a perceived object, but forms its behaviour in accordance with the relation in which the object stands to the goal of its desire for the moment.

4. *d. The application of experience.*

These results are corroborated by observers who report cases in which the behaviour of an animal is devised to meet the behaviour which he has learnt to expect from other animals, or from men.

In these cases, the experience may be said to be applied with a certain amount of originality, which puts the behaviour observed out of the category of habituation. A certain event is anticipated, and, without instruction or suggestion, preparation is made to meet it. Or, perhaps, a situation has been found advantageous, and a spontaneous effort is made to bring such a situation into being again. Or, lastly, unique circumstances occur, in which knowledge is applied in a manner appropriate to those circumstances alone. In all of these cases, we have behaviour indicating not merely knowledge of objects, but also power of applying that knowledge with a certain spontaneity. Now, are these cases authentic? Does such behaviour exist? I know of no experimental evidence of it below the level of monkeys.[1] There is, however, a considerable body of casual observation,[2] tending to show that be-

---

[1] The evidence with regard to monkeys will be referred to in the next chapter. By experimental evidence I mean cases in which the circumstances and antecedents of the act have been systematically traced.

Mr. Cole's raccoons (cited by Jennings. *Animal Behaviour—American Naturalist*, March, 1908, pp. 213, 214) afford an exception to the remark in the text. They learned not only to react to signals (as described above, p. 243), but to claw them up themselves. They could not see which they were getting up beforehand, but if the red one came up, which was wrong, they clawed it down again, raised the green one and prepared to receive food.

[2] The value of evidence of this kind is briefly considered in Chapter XII., p. 296 *et seq.*

haviour of this kind is not uncommon, at least among the more intelligent mammals. It will be worth our while to analyse a few instances.

If it is true that a pointer will sometimes adopt, untaught, the plan of running round cover so that he drives the game towards his master, he evidently acts on the basis of a familiar experience.[1] He knows how his action will affect the birds, and he knows what his master wants. Granted this knowledge, it is very easy to understand how he applies it to the circumstances before him, and so forms his plan. If we refuse to grant it, the whole proceeding becomes unintelligible. There is no habit in the matter, for the dog is adapting his action newly to meet a difficulty ; while, if we call it association of ideas, then, the idea of the birds rising must be an idea of them rising at a given moment in a given direction as the result of his action—*i.e.*, it is equivalent to an anticipation. In such cases it makes little difference whether we speak of association of ideas or of inference, provided always that it is understood that an idea definitely applied to perception is equivalent to a judgment. There are other cases, however, in which the term Association becomes altogether inappropriate. Mr. Lloyd Morgan, in discussing whether animals can reason, quotes[2] a story contributed by Mr. Stone to *Animal Intelligence* of two dogs.

"One of them, the larger, had a bone, and when he had left it the smaller dog went to take it ; the larger one growled, and the other retired to a corner. Shortly afterwards the larger dog went out ; but the other did not appear to notice this, and, at any rate, did not move. A few minutes later the large dog was heard to bark out of doors ; the little dog then, without a moment's hesitation, went straight to the bone and took it."

On this, Mr. Stone comments :—

"It thus appears quite evident that she reasoned—That dog is barking out of doors, therefore he is not in this room, therefore it is safe for me to take the bone. The action was so rapid as to be clearly a consequence of the other dog's barking."

[1] See Hutchinson, pp. 51 and 289, and compare Schaler, *Domesticated Animals*, p. 28 (a more complicated device).
[2] *Comparative Psychology*, p. 300.

Upon this interpretation Mr. Lloyd Morgan remarks:—

"Now, here a course of action, which is quite readily interpreted on the hypothesis of sense-experience through association,
is explained in rational terms, and the dog is supposed to think the
*therefore*. But on similar principles every case of association may
be thus interpreted." [1]

He proceeds to show how the refusal of a cinnabar
caterpillar by a chick may be interpreted as a rational act,
and thrown into syllogistic form.

"Nothing is easier than to interpret this intelligent course of
action in rational and logical terms : Black and gold caterpillars
are nasty ; that is a black and gold caterpillar ; therefore it is nasty.
This does not seem to me to be at all more far-fetched than the
suggestion of Mr. Stone's that his dog reasoned :—That dog is
barking out of doors, therefore he is not in this room." [2]

I quite agree with Mr. Lloyd Morgan that there is no
evidence that a dog can " think the therefore." That is
to say, it has no explicit consciousness of the thought-
connection uniting one stage of the inference to the next.
I see nothing whatever to suggest that an animal can
analyse out this element in its own mental processes as a
man does when he uses an illative particle. But this does
not seem a sufficient ground for denying to the operation
the title of inference.[3] To the animal much less is explicit
than to the man, but to the man much less is explicit than
to the philosopher, and to the philosopher much less is
explicit than he could wish. Inference is essentially one
function, from the simplest case quoted by Mr. Morgan
of the chick, up to the highest elaboration of experience
by the human intellect. The differences are differences in
articulateness on the one side, and comprehensiveness on
the other ; and the question is, precisely what point in the

---

[1] *Comparative Psychology*, p. 300.     [2] *Ib.* p. 301.
[3] It is no doubt in part a question of terms. I have used the term
inference in a very wide sense to express a certain generic unity of
function exercised with very different degrees of articulateness. It is, of
course, possible for any writer, while recognising this generic unity, to
prefer to keep the term inference for the higher grades. This difference
of usage is, as I gather, responsible for making the divergence between
Mr. Lloyd Morgan's views and mine appear much greater than it
really is.

scale of ascending clearness is occupied by such an inference as that attributed in this story to the dog. Admitting that it falls below the stage in which inference is expressible in general terms, and the connection of one proposition with another by an appropriate particle, must we say that it falls to the stage represented by association? If we contrast the use made of experience by the dog and the chick respectively, we shall see that there is a very material difference. The chick's response to a certain stimulus is guided by the feeling experienced in immediate relation to a precisely similar stimulus. We may, therefore, fairly speak of an association [1] between the stimulus and that feeling. The dog, on the other hand, in this story, has to make a sort of construction of several different elements of experience. Mr. Lloyd Morgan would not suggest that the sound of a bark outside would naturally impel the little dog in the room to jump up and seize a bone. It has this effect only as applied to the particular circumstances; and one does not see how the little dog could apply it except by going through a process corresponding to that attributed to him by Mr. Stone. The bark operates on him only as suggesting that the big dog is out of the room; and being out of the room, cannot prevent him from taking the bone. Past experience suggests each stage in this argument, but the dog has to put them together for himself. His action, taken as a whole, is not based on the association of a feeling with a stimulus, but on a judgment resting on experience as to where another dog is, and what it can or cannot do.

Under the same head fall cases in which a cat or dog gets a man to do for him what he cannot do himself. A good instance is narrated by Péréz,[2] whose dog, a puppy of six months, having been punished for not going out of doors when it was desirable that he should have done so, wakened M. Péréz at nights by scratching at his door, or howling. The same writer a little lower down [3] describes how M. Marion's cat, as soon as dinner was served, would

---

[1] In a loose sense. More strictly as we have seen it is a case of Assimilation.
[2] *Les Trois Premières Années de l'Enfant*, p. 263.     [3] P. 272

go to and fro between the table and his master, inviting him by *mines persuasives* to come to the joint feast. Every one knows, or ought to know, that cat.

Closely connected with these are the many instances of apparent deceit which give animal psychologists some trouble to explain.[1] It is not necessary to suppose that an animal thinks out a lie, as a deliberately treacherous human being would do ; but an animal does know what it is told to do and what it is forbidden to do. It knows what the consequences of disobedience will be ; and it knows when its master's eye is on it, and when it is not. If it is very acute, it may further recognise some of the signs by which its master will gather what it has done in his absence ; and it may seek to remove them. All this follows very simply from the attribution to an animal of a judgment based on experience as to the way in which its master will behave. No higher faculty is required, but we cannot, unless we wholly reject or painfully distort evidence of the kind under consideration, do with anything lower.

The distinctive feature of the cases dealt with in this section is that if they are correctly reported and interpreted, they are cases of the application of experience with a certain originality or spontaneity. In its lowest form, the application of experience is not distinguishable from its acquisition. Habit is built up out of action, or the refraining from action ; and it issues in similar actions or similar refrainings. The formation of the habit is the tendency to act (or refrain). Nothing need be added to the habit in order to produce the action. In the higher forms of experience, there is a change in this point. Experience is acquired in order that it may be used in practice, but its acquisition and its application fall apart into two clearly distinguishable acts. In its most elementary form, this distinction appears even in cases of learning by direct perception of results. An animal desiring B, observes

---

[1] For instances, see Schneider, p. 355; K. and O. Müller, p. 13, and Lloyd Morgan, *Comparative Psychology*, p. 371  (The story of the Maltese terrier which was supposed to dance round the table on two legs ; but dropped on to four at the end where it could not be seen.)

the sequence AB. It applies this by setting to work to produce A. It sees food placed in a box, it sees the door shut and bolted ; then again it sees the bolt withdrawn, and finds that it can open the door and get the food. Its attention once clearly awakened to this sequence, it draws the bolt for itself, opens the door, and gets fed. There is here, first, the perception of a sequence of events ; and then, a second stage, in which the perception has to be worked into the effort of desire, and the motor impulses necessary to the act. This second stage sometimes fails, as when my dog refused to pull the drawer, the working of which, as his actions seemed to show, he had perfectly learnt. When it succeeds, it is a kind of synthesis of the result of perception with the motor impulse effected by the organism itself. This, then, is the simplest case of the application of experience. Much more distinctive and decisive are the cases referred to immediately above, in which, on the strength of past experience, a certain event is anticipated, and without any instruction or suggestion, preparations are made to meet it. A few demonstrated cases of this, which we may distinguish as spontaneous application, would be sufficient to decide the whole question before us ; but for animals below monkeys evidence on the point is, as we have hinted, not wholly satisfactory.

5. However this may be, we have seen some ground for thinking that the more intelligent animals have knowledge of surrounding objects which they apply in action ; that they are capable of learning to act in accordance with physical changes which they witness ; that they can be influenced by the general similarities which unite individuals of the same class, and can guide their action in dealing with any object by the relation in which it stands to that which they desire. Further, evidence has been brought that in the process by which they learn, not repetition of instances, but concentration of attention is the important point. Lastly, it is suggested that in some cases, they not merely learn to meet a given perception with a certain motor reaction, but also to combine and adapt their actions so as to effect physical changes which, as they have learnt, aid them in

gaining their ends. We have thus gone through all the points enumerated on p. 168 as distinctive of Concrete Experience and the Practical Judgment, and have seen some ground for imputing each and all to the higher animals. At no one point, perhaps, is the evidence conclusive ; but it is to be remembered that these functions are interconnected, so that evidence of capacity for one is indirect evidence of capacity for another. We have, therefore, a set of independent arguments all pointing in the same direction, and it is on this convergence of evidence, rather than on decisive proof at any one point, that our hypothesis must rest.

# CHAPTER XII

1. WE have seen evidence in animal behaviour for the operation of what we called practical ideas, but they were ideas of a very crude and unanalysed character. Evidence of more articulate ideas is much more restricted, and so far as decisive experimental tests are concerned, confined, I believe, to monkeys. By a more articulate idea, is meant one in which comparatively distinct elements are held in a comparatively distinct relation. Thus, that a bolt must be pushed back is a crude idea ; that it must be pushed back so as to clear a staple, a relatively articulate one, implying a distinction between the parts of the object perceived (the bolt and its staples), and an appreciation of the relation between them. As ideas become more articulate, the results of experience are more freely combined or modified to suit practical needs. Something like originality begins to show itself, and we have instances of what we have called "spontaneous application." Of this also, it is difficult to find experimental evidence for animals lower than the monkeys. Whether this is because the intelligence of all other mammals is lower, or because monkey intelligence lends itself more readily to the kind of experiment which human intelligence most readily devises, is not so clear. There is, in fact, a good deal of evidence of the anecdotal kind suggesting the existence of intelligence of this grade below the Primates. Before considering the value of such evidence, I may illustrate the kind of

articulateness and originality of which I speak from some experiments which I made with the monkeys at Belle Vue.

My principal dealings were with two monkeys. One was the little Rhesus Jimmy, which has already been mentioned more than once, and which came to stay with me for several days. Jimmy was not altogether a hopeful subject for experiments. His attention was terribly dissipated. In the monkey house, every noise distracted him, and he would break off in the middle of a most promising experiment to run backwards and forwards in his cage, in sympathy with the monkeys in the large cage opposite. He seldom appeared to be hungry ; but I found at last that he would do almost anything for a baked potato. After that discovery, we got on better.[1]   Nor can I praise Jimmy's temper. I have already mentioned that he flew at all women and children ; and though he tolerated me, and would climb about me as if I were a piece of furniture, he never showed a trace of affection. In my house, I found that his chief passion was for the fire. He would sit on the edge of the fender, or stand on his hind legs, close to the high, old-fashioned grate, with scarcely two inches between his chest and the flames. But though I once noticed him touch a bar, and draw his hand quickly away, he never burnt himself with the hot cinders. The black cinders he ate freely, and packed his cheek pouches with them.

The other monkey of which I saw most was the chimpanzee, which for reasons of my own I called the Professor. The difficulty with the Professor is his extremely retiring and unsociable disposition. No one can approach him with whom he is not quite familiar ; and after an acquaintance of two months, he will only take a banana from my hand at arm's length, amid great trepidation. It is therefore very difficult to show the Professor anything. When, for instance, I tried to instruct him in the push bolt, I had always to leave the box in the cage, and retire myself, before he would come near it.

2. When I first saw the Professor, he had already elaborated a somewhat remarkable performance. He lives for warmth in a cage enclosed within a larger cage or house. Passers by threw nuts and other gratifying objects

---

[1] In this want of persistence, Jimmy contrasts strongly with the Cebus described by Miss Romanes. Nor did Jimmy show any of that "tireless spirit of investigation" which Dr. Romanes found in the same animal. The only thing Jimmy investigated was his own person, and in this he certainly did seem absolutely tireless. But he showed extremely little curiosity, and no persistence in working at anything, except for the sake of food.

into the house, which would often fall too far from his cage to be within reach of his arm. To deal with this difficulty, he would retire to his bed, pull from it his rug, stuff the rug with considerable effort, bit by bit, through the narrow rails, and proceed to throw it like a net over the desired object, which he would thus work towards him. It was noticeable that he was always careful to pull the rug in again. The first thing I taught the Professor was to substitute a stick for the cumbrous rug.

I cut a small stick from a tree, pulled a bit of banana about with it, and gave it to him. He tried to use it, though ineffectually. The next day, I brought him up a stout walking-stick with a crook, which he used awkwardly, and nearly succeeded in his object. He then used his rug instead, with success. I then put a piece of banana in a box. He tried ineffectually to reach it with his rug, but did not use the stick. I pulled the box a little about with the stick, and left it with him. When I came back, he had got the box, and opened it. Next day, he used the stick at once to get a lump of sugar. At first, he knocked it away, but soon got the stick round, used the crook, and pulled it in. I found, however, that he never really learned the use of the crook. He would use either end indiscriminately. This, I think, was not altogether due to stupidity. It must be remembered that he had to work the stick with his hands through narrow bars. He was awkward with it at the best of times, and when the heavy crook was at the remote end, he could not place it accurately enough to be of real use to him.

Next day, the chimpanzee learnt to use a short stick in order to reach a larger one, with which in turn he could reach the banana.

I put my stick out of his reach, and a piece of banana beyond it again, while I gave him a short stick. He did not, however, use it until I first pushed the big stick about with it. He then made an attempt to reach my stick with the short one, but without success. I gave him rather a larger stick, with which he at once tried to reach mine ; but instead of getting hold of it, he knocked it slantwise, so that one end was further off from him than before, and one end nearer. He now directed his stick to the nearer end, pulled mine in, and with its aid reached the banana. Another day, he was given a big broom handle to use. As he drew the banana in, the end of the handle knocked against the partition door of his cage, which was behind him. He at once shifted it so as to clear the door.

In general, he had two chief movements with his stick. The banana was generally given him inside a cigar box. He would reach out with his stick at the box, and sweep it round by a radial motion, so that it came up to the side of his cage. It will be observed that in so doing he was not obeying the natural impulse to draw it straight towards him, but merely was bringing it to a point to which he could afterwards go and get it. One half of his cage, however, was covered with plate glass, so that if in describing a quarter circle he swept the box up against the glass, he could not reach it at once with his arm. He would then alter the motion, and rake with the point of the stick, drawing the box in in a straight line. When he had to fish for a box close by the wall, he would take trouble to get his stick in between the wall and the box, showing that he was quite aware of the way in which he had to push it. On the other hand, he not only, as I have mentioned, failed to learn the use of the crook ; but I have seen him sweep at the box with the crook downwards, so that the stick passed over the top.

On one occasion, when I borrowed a child's hoop, and gave it him in place of a stick, he used it very unintelligently. Instead of getting the hoop round the banana, he made sweeps with it, so that the curvature kept driving the fruit away. I should like to have made further experiments to see how he would have learnt the proper use of the hoop, but its small owner became alarmed for its safety. The Professor sometimes tried to find remarkable substitutes for a stick. On one occasion, when he was trying an experiment with a rope, which he could not understand, he spied a long, heavy iron bar lying by his cage. He dragged this up, and it came over the rope, of which he had one end in his cage, while the other end was fastened to the box outside. He tried to push the bar out towards the box, and failing, tugged at the rope, lifting it up, and the bar with it. The bar of course ran down the rope, and nearly reached the box. How much of this was intentional, the reader may determine for himself. In any case, I am not going to infer that the chimpanzee understood the principle of the inclined plane.

One day I gave him a rope with a noose to throw over the box in place of his stick. I did not give him any hint, but he soon tried it in a vague way. He did not, how-

T

ever, understand the matter very well, for when he succeeded in getting the rope round the box, he did not seem
aware of his advantage, flung it away, went off for his
shawl, and used it very sucessfully. I then tied a block
of wood to the rope to assist in throwing it. He attempted
this spontaneously, at first without success. Presently,
however, he happened to pitch the block right into the
box, which to-day was open, pulled it in, and got the
banana. Notwithstanding this signal success, he never
took to this trick.

At the next trial, he tried to use his rug, until I confiscated it ;
but after one or two unsuccessful trials, he succeeded in throwing
the block beyond the box, and roping it in. At the next trial he
failed again, and tried a smaller shawl, which I was also compelled
to confiscate. Bereft of all other means, he threw the block once
more, but hit the wrong side. One more failure stirred my com-
punction, and I gave him the banana, and restored his confiscated
property. The next day he would not throw the block, but used
the rope with success. At length, however, he refused to go on
with this method. Evidently he had considerable physical difficulty in throwing at all well.[1]

In another connection, however, he would also use the
rope with some ingenuity. In the experiment to which I
have already referred, when the box was tied to a rope,
the further end of which was passed over a stanchion
several feet from the cage, he failed, as I shall mention
later, to find the right method, but was fertile in devising
wrong ones. He would shake the rope violently, so that
the banana would fall out of the box. He would then
swing the rope to and fro, swishing the banana about from
side to side, until by degrees it would come within his
reach, in a way which I should have thought beforehand
to be quite impossible.

Jimmy was much slower in learning the use of the stick,
but he had probably had no previous experience like that
with the rug. I began by placing a nut in the crook of a

[1] Pechuel-Lösche (Brehm's *Thierleben*, I., p. 50) has given reasons
for repudiating the common view that many monkeys in the natural state
use stones, nuts, etc., as missiles. Miss Romanes' observations, however,
show beyond doubt that her Cebus threw things at people deliberately.
(*Animal Intelligence*, p. 485, etc.)

little stick, the whole resting on a board which I arranged outside Jimmy's cage at Belle Vue. He at once pulled the nut in, but made no attempt that day to get the stick into position for himself. The next day I arranged it again, and also dragged the nut about outside. At the fourth trial on that day, he waved the stick about as if vaguely trying to hit the nut. I append the remainder of the notes taken on that day, and the next.

4. Stick being placed near nut, he swishes it sideways, and gets nut.

5. Swishes about persistently with stick. Knocks nut away once, and we replace. Then by deliberate casts gets it.

6. Pushes stick out from cage. Hits nut away. Sulks.

7. Great struggle to get it. Throws stick and picks it up again. At last gets nut.

8. No effort, till we go away. Then at once tries, but knocks nut away.

Next day.

1. Swishes stick about vaguely. Swipes at nut. Vexed, and throws stick away. Gets stick over nut, and pulls a little. Gives up again. Throws stick over it, and pulls by crook. At last gets it.

2. Swipes about, knocks nut further away. New stick substituted—T shape. Examines and bites at it. Gets it into cage. Apple substituted for nut. Stick lies near. He gets apple at once.

3. After long time with no effort, makes awkward casts at apple, handle of stick getting mixed up with netting. Throws stick away again in vexation. Does not understand drawing it in like Professor. I give it back, putting it under bar. Tries to throw it over apple sideways; fails.

4. After an interval, I shorten stick. He fishes about for small pieces, and gets them.

5. Gets a big bit better.

As long as he was in his cage, Jimmy showed himself much less handy with the stick than the Professor. He had to operate through a wire netting, which however did not reach to the floor by an interval of more than an inch. He seldom made use of this interval for getting the stick in and out, though it was much handier than working through the railing. If the stick was put inside the netting, he had great difficulty in getting it out. The crosspiece with which the stick was fitted was too long to go through the mesh of the net without a little manœuvring; and in this, he very often failed. He would push it so violently that the stick would get through and fall out of his reach; and once he bit the cross off, probably out of annoyance. Nor did he manage the pulling in as well as the chimpanzee, frequently getting the end of the stick involved with the meshes of the net. In fact, in the whole matter of manipulation, the chimpanzee is the more dexterous of the two. In handling the boxes, for example, in which his fruit was placed, he always turned them edgewise if he wanted to get them through the bars. Similarly, the child's hoop mentioned above was passed by him in and out of the bars edgewise without difficulty. Jimmy's comparative failure in this respect must be ascribed largely to impatience. To say the truth, if he did not succeed at once, he lost his temper.

Jimmy pretty soon learnt to use a short stick in order to reach the longer one. If stick and fruit were both too far from him, he would try to help himself by pulling the whole board on which they lay towards him ; and he seemed quite clear as to the necessity of getting the stick beyond the thing that he was pulling. If it lay just on his side of the apple or nut, he would be careful not to knock the apple away, but to get the stick well beyond it. When Jimmy was staying in my house, he was kept on the cord ; and, being unembarrassed with netting, would use a stick very freely. It is also interesting that without any instruction he rapidly learnt to use substitutes.

I first gave him a child's skipping-rope. He took no notice to begin with, but when I placed the rope suggestively near the bread, which was out of his reach, he made a cast at it with the wooden handle. At first he lost the rope. I returned it to him, when he threw it again, and worked the bread within his reach. After this, he would use a cord ; and, after some hesitation, a wire. If other things failed, he would pull off the large dust sheet which covered his chair, and use that, as the Professor did his rug. Here is one note which shows his resourcefulness in trying one thing after another. I put a piece of onion in a basket within reach of his stick. After first refusing any effort, he tried to reach it with the stick, and failed. In reaching towards it, he found the big box (one of Jack's boxes, which he also used) lying across his chain, and preventing his reaching forward. He threw the box off. Having failed with the stick, he will not try it again, but makes wild efforts to throw the rope. Then he actually rolls his box at the food ; then goes off and gets down the dust sheet from the chair, and tries unskilfully to sweep at it ; finally, makes a longer stretch, and just reaches it with his own claw (his elasticity was really remarkable).

Both these monkeys, then, clearly learnt to use sticks, ropes, or anything else that came handy, to reach at things outside the range of their claws.[1] It is instructive to compare their behaviour with that of the dog and the elephant. I chained Jack up, put a biscuit out of his reach in the crook of a stick, and he rapidly learnt to pull it in. But of any attempt to get the stick into the position in which he could use it, I never saw a sign.[2] It was the same with the elephant, who time after time would pull the stick in to her, getting the bun if it happened to be placed exactly right, and missing it if it was possible to do so.[3] Thus, the elephant and the dog remained in the first stage of the trick. It would of course have been far less easy for them to have got the stick into the right position, but for the elephant, at least, it would not have been impossible. She confined herself, however, to repeating what she had done herself with success, or seen done for her. But to get the stick into position, and use it with effect, involved rather more than this. It is true that the monkeys had seen me use it, and that Jimmy had also seen me place it in the right position for him to use ; but it was no mechanical imitation by which they learnt to use the stick for themselves. It was necessary that they should grasp how the stick and the food stood in relation to them ; that they should get the stick at the food and beyond it. If we regard imitation as the basis of this performance, it is imitation of the higher order, that we have called Reflective or Analogical. A form of " analogical extension " is also strongly marked in the use of substitutes differing very widely in appearance and the manner of use from the

[1] Mr. Bates's Cebus also used a stick for similar purposes, and on one occasion is recorded to have flung a swing at some skins which he wanted so as to get them on the return of the swing (Romanes, p. 480). Miss Romanes records similar facts. Two other monkeys at Belle Vue failed to learn the use of the stick in the few lessons which I gave them. It would seem to be a feat which must be *learnt* by the animals.

[2] I did not, I must admit, repeat the experiment many times, because Jack strained at the chain so much in his excitement, that I was afraid of his hurting himself.

[3] When she missed it, she got excessively annoyed with the stick, and would try to break it by stamping on it, or would throw it away into her cage, if I did not intercept her. On such an occasion she returned it to me on being ordered, with a very bad grace.

object first employed. Another point illustrated besides the " articulateness " dwelt on above, is the combination of movements frequently observed,—a good case of the sort of adaptation of one act to another in a series which we have taken as differentiating Desire from Impulse. There was indeed in their whole proceeding a degree of articulateness which I have not seen in experiments with any other animals. Mr. Small's epithet " crass " would have to be modified before it was applied to the perceptions or ideas of monkeys. Their handling is indeed much less dexterous, and—if I may use the expression—refined, than one would suppose an untaught man's to be, but far more discriminating than that of any other animal that I have seen. Perpetually exploring objects, pulling them to pieces, and pushing them about, they get to understand better than any other animal how things will act, and what they can do to things. Their hands are far finer organs of tactual discrimination than anything which lower animals possess; but equally, they seem inferior in this point to the human finger ; and with this tactual discrimination, the degree of their appreciation of objects, their behaviour and relations, seems to be closely correlated.

3. Tied rope. (See above p. 192.)

The elephant, dog and cat were easily taught to pull beyond the knot of a tied rope. The monkeys may be said rather to have shown an appreciation of the knot.

The Professor was enclosed in his inner cage, as shown in the diagram. I tied a box to a rope, passing one end straight through both bars to him, while the other was passed round beyond the bars, and also given to him. It was natural that he should pull the straight rope, and this he did, reaching through both bars to get at the box. I then twisted the straight rope round one of the bars. He at once put his hand beyond the bar, and pulled the rope in.[1]  I then moved the knot to a remoter bar. After once pulling on his side of the knot, he again reached beyond, and I found the next day that he would either claw beyond the

---

[1] Mr. George Jennison, an experienced and very judicious observer, who was with me, thought this attributable merely to the effort to reach as far as possible. The subsequent trials, however, suggest that the chimpanzee recognised the knot as the critical point.

knot at first, or after one trial at his end of the rope.  He would
also sometimes claw slightly at the knot itself.  When, finally,
I moved the knot to a bar beyond his reach, after a slight trial at
the straight cord, he would pull the other.[1]  For Jimmy, I arranged a cord knotted to the handle of a writing-desk.  He was
tied to a heavy chair, by moving which I could let him reach
beyond the knot, or prevent him, at pleasure.  When I let him
do so, he at once reached beyond the knot, even if he had to
make a great stretch for it.  When I put the chair back, he did
not try to use a stick to rake in the free cord, but at first pulled
the tied part fruitlessly, and then taking it in both hands, pulled
so hard as to drag his chair forward, whereupon he immediately

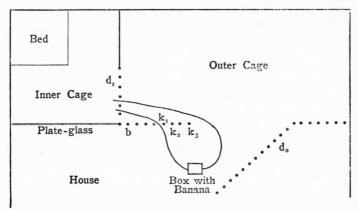

$d_1$, inner railed door ; $d_2$, outer door ; $k_1$, $k_2$, $k_3$, knot in different positions.

reached out, and caught the cord beyond the knot.  This was
repeated, and if at first accidental, certainly became deliberate.
On the other hand, if the chair was held fast, he would not at
first try to use the stick to fish for the string, but would pull
irrationally at the tied string.[2]  The next day, however, he took
to the stick, and thereafter used it freely.  He would now wholly
disregard the tied string, unless he wished to pull himself forward
by means of it.

---

[1] There followed two trials in which he attempted the wrong rope first
and then pulled the right.  He then pulled the right five times running.
The ends of the rope lay close together, and were indistinguishable in
appearance.
[2] The stick was placed in position for him several times, and then he
used it, but he only once that day made an effort to get it into position
himself.

### 4. Bolt fastened by hook.

I took the box with the push-back bolt, tied a string to the knob, and, passing it round the box, fastened it by a hook to a nail at the back. The string now held the bolt forward in the staple, so that unless the hook was removed, the bolt could not be pushed back. Jimmy at first failed to find out how to open this box, but one day appeared to learn it, as it were, in a flash.

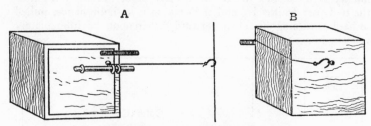

A. Diagram showing box with hook fastened to wire netting.
B. Diagram showing hook fastened to nail at back of box.

At the first trial, he worked a good deal at the bolt, bit the string a little, and after a time, took the hook off. He then began to work at the bolt, and might have found it all out, but that his attention was suddenly distracted. After this, though he two or three times took the hook off, the action was purposeless, as he would go away again, and perhaps not try the bolt until a minute had passed, or perhaps not at all. Two or three days afterwards, however, I was putting my hand to the hook, meaning to take it off without letting him see. Apparently this called his attention to the hook. He at once took it off, and almost immediately, came round the box, pushed back the bolt, and opened it. He repeated this five times, and when the hook was too tight to come off, he would pull the string till it slackened. To baffle him, I now turned the box up so that the hook was underneath. At first, not finding the hook, he pulled at the string and worked at the bolt; but at length he turned the box over, the hook fell off, and he opened.

I then further varied the experiment by fastening the hook to the netting of his cage, pulling the box away from it so that the string was taut. After trying the bolt a little, he attacked the hook; but it was too tight to come off. He then threw the box about, until he turned it into a position in which the bolt fell.[1] After another trial, in which he failed to remove the hook, I

[1] He had an amusing struggle to keep the lid up while he got underneath it. Finally he threw the lid right back.

fastened it again so that the string was slack. He then quickly
pulled the hook off. His record for the rest of the day is as
follows :—
12. I re-fasten tight. He tries bolt, works to and fro, and
leaves it more forward, so that string is slacker. Then at hook.
Gets it off and opens.
13. Slightly at bolt ; then at hook. String works slack, and
he opens.
14. String too tight for movement of bolt to let it slacken.
He tries hook hard, finally gets bodily on to string, so as to pull
box in towards fastening and make string slack. Then gets
hook off, and opens.
15. After trying hook, pulls string down hard at once. Tries
bolt slightly, which nearly goes back. Then takes off hook.
Then opens.
16. Same. Tries hook well. Then bodily on to string.
Pulls in. Then gets hook off, and opens.

The next day he was indifferent, and I did not try him again
till ten days after, when I tied back the catch of the other box
in a similar manner, fastening the hook first to a chain. He appeared at first to have forgotten this experiment, and began by
biting through the string ; and when I replaced the string by
wire, he pushed the box about until he got it into a position
where it could be opened. I then fastened the hook on to the
box itself again. He watched me doing this, and attacked the
hook at once, but it was too tight for him. I then gave him six
more trials with the hook on the chain, each time taking it off as far
as possible without letting him see me do so.[1] It was not, however,
till the sixth trial that he made any attempt at the hook.[2] So I
took the hook off, and put it on to the fender. After this he
succeeded at once, and repeated his old performance of jumping
on the string, or giving it a vigorous pull if it was too tight for
the hook to come off.

Taking this experiment as a whole, three things are
noteworthy.

(1) First, the monkey showed no systematic endeavour
to trace out the nature of the obstacle to his
pulling the bolt. He did not follow the string round, and
get the hook off, but

[1] He may have seen me at the third trial.
[2] Instead of trying the hook, he bit the string through once, and another
time broke it in jumping on the box, the cord by which he was held
catching in the string and pulling it violently. It was noteworthy that he
repeated this jump, which he had found successful.

(2) He did recognise obstacles when, so to say, they stared him in the face ; and then devised means of his own for dealing with them.   This was particularly noticeable in the slackening of the string.   He must in some obscure fashion have felt that the string was pulling against him when he tried to unfasten the hook ; and for this he found the appropriate remedy.   This was therefore a good case of " original application."

(3) His first success was one of the most striking examples that I have seen of the effect of a sudden turn of attention.   Though he had pulled off the hook before, and also pushed back the bolt, he had clearly never put two and two together.   For some inscrutable reason, the movement of my hand suddenly seemed to bring the whole thing into his mind.   He at once took off the hook, pulled back the bolt, opened the box, and did not fail again.

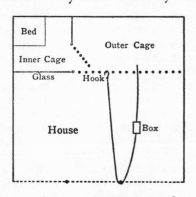

5. On the other hand, both monkeys failed in another experiment with a hooked rope.   I passed a rope round a stanchion outside the chimpanzee's cage, tied a box to one part of it, and gave the free end to the chimpanzee. The other end I hooked to a bar of his cage.   The result was that he could pull the free end as hard as he pleased, but it would have no effect unless he took the hook off. In this he failed, though I repeatedly took the hook off myself, thinking that he might learn to see the difference which it made.   Jimmy failed equally in a similar experiment which I arranged for him.   Both monkeys, after trying one rope, would try the other ; and it was interesting to note how, on at least one occasion, the chimpanzee, after having lost the free end of the rope by pulling hard at the other, kept both ropes in his hands while he pulled.   The same monkey showed considerable, but from the experimenter's point of view perverted,

ingenuity in getting the box within his reach by switching the rope about from side to side. Why did neither of them learn to take off the hook ? Imitation was excluded, because I concealed the operation as much as possible, and it would seem that they failed to compare the two situations (hook off and hook on) so as to draw an inference. This failure is to be connected with the very short-sighted want of attention to my operations while adjusting the experiment. Such attention was rare. Had the monkeys any degree of forethought going beyond the satisfaction of their felt desire, one would suppose that they would take note of what passed in one experiment with a view to success in the next. They would therefore fix their minds on the nature of that change in the situation which enabled them to get the coveted prize. I never saw in a monkey any trace of a prevision of this kind.

6. Working stick within tube.

I noticed the Professor one day trying very ineffectually to use a small stick as a lever to open a box. I did not further test his powers in this direction, but thought of a slightly different experiment. There was a large iron pipe lying in the cage, into which I stuffed a piece of banana, and gave the monkey his little stick with a tin tack at the end, by which I thought he might fish it out. I did not show him this at all ; but he at once used the stick, working it in with ease, and though he failed to get the banana out bodily, he seemed to derive satisfaction from sucking the end of the stick each time he drew it out. As I thought this was meagre sustenance for him, and a poor reward for so much merit, I secured a shorter piece of piping, and a long iron rod, one end of which would pass easily into the pipe, while it was long enough to go right through. The Professor meant to use this in the same way as the stick, but he very soon found that he pushed the banana right out at the other end. He then always looked for it at that end, and moreover, finding that it was apt to get lost in his hay, he transferred his operations to the part of his floor which was covered with sawdust. Moreover, one trial was enough to show him that only one end of the rod could be used.[1]   I wondered whether anything could have suggested this operation to the chimpanzee, and I found afterwards that when drinking his water at lunch, he had a way of dipping straws in and then sucking them.   This, or the use of his finger in searching, would perhaps be the point of departure for this burrowing in a hole with a stick.   But the analogy seems somewhat remote.   For the rest, the degree of exactitude required in the execution was the most interesting feature of this performance.

Jimmy, on the other hand, absolutely failed to learn this trick.   Though repeatedly shown it with a hollow bamboo, and either a stick to push the food out, or a wire to fish it up with, he never made the slightest effort to push the food out for himself.   If I gave him the tube with the stick inside it, he would pull it back instead of pushing, though if the next moment I took it in my own hands, he would look anxiously at the opposite end to see the potato come out.   It was a remarkable and by no means isolated case of failure in imitation.[2]

7. Use of stool.

The first evening that Jimmy was with me, I observed him pull a box towards him, climb on the top of it, and thence jump to the top of the table.   This can hardly have been by design, as he could climb the table without such aid with the greatest ease.   But the next day I made a series of experiments to see whether he would learn to place a box or chair for himself, with a view to standing on it.

The experiment was not very easy to arrange for so agile a climber, but I managed it by putting a piece of potato on a table at such a distance from the point to which his cord was fastened that he could just reach it if

---

[1] If he made a mistake on the point on subsequent days, he speedily corrected himself.

[2] Mr. Shepherd also obtained negative results in this case with his monkeys (*Some Mental Processes of the Rhesus Monkey*, p. 35. Mr. Shepherd, apparently by an oversight, speaks of his results as differing from mine.   With regard to the Rhesus they agree.   My positive result was obtained with the chimpanzee only).

his body and the cord [1] made as nearly as possible a straight line. Thus he had not law enough to climb the table, nor to reach to the top as he stood on the ground ; but if he stood on the  stool and stretched forward, he could just reach it.   I did not, to the best of  my remembrance, let him see me bring the box to the table for him, but rather brought the table and adjusted it to the box.  After he had got it in this fashion, I moved the box away.   He did not try to move it back, but began exploring the box, and threw it open.   The lid, being thrown back, came near to the table, and after a little time spent in  investigating the box and himself, he

jumped on to the lid and got the food.   When I put another piece of bread on the table, he did not try to repeat this performance, but tried to pull the table towards him.   He then jumped on to the box, and tried to open it in a futile way while sitting on the lid.   After a long interval, I attracted his attention to the bread again, and he once more opened the door of the box ; but this time it opened at right angles to the direction required, and so did not help him.   He pushed the box a little towards the table, but did not persist.   After another trial, in which he circumvented me, by extraordinary litheness of body, he began pulling a chair towards the table, but found it too hard work, and gave up.   I then noted as follows :—

Pulls at box.   Takes up brush and makes a vague lunge with it, then takes rope, and similarly half tries to throw it.

[1] The cord was tied to a belt of sacking, which went round the narrowest part of his body above the thighs.

I put a lighter chair within his reach. He tumbles it over box, and finally down by table—it lies lengthwise. He then climbs on it and tries to reach biscuit, but his rope has got twisted, and is too short. I lengthen it, and push table nearer. He gets biscuit.

I now put chair in another place, upright again. He climbs about it, but instead of using it, pulls table near him. Ultimately gets food by reaching from chair.

Food replaced. Fairly pulls box to within reach of table—gets on to it and reaches food. Replaced. Tries to reach from chair as it stands, and to pull table. Gets on to chair through back, so that rope is passed through, and will get twisted unless he goes back. I show him a bigger piece. He jumps down *through back of chair*, goes to box, opens it, and pulls it a little way towards table, then jumps on top and gives up again. Finally, through my moving biscuit a little nearer to encourage him he gets it. I now place it on top of high chair. He tries to climb chair, but fails. He catches curtain, and swings by it to chair, and gets biscuit.

After lunch, I place potato in basket hung from ceiling. He gets it by jumping, and reaching from screen which he climbs up and along. At length, other things being made impossible, I put chair near. He pulls at this, and finally turns it over so that it falls underneath. He then climbs on it and gets potato.

Replaced. He does not try to use chair, but after some efforts by other means, drags box underneath, jumps on it, and gets part. As I write above, he tried to draw box towards table where bulk of potato is left. It is too far. He also tries to throw rope. Finally I move table a little nearer, and he gets potato, standing on box. Replaced, and box put out of way. He lugs it up. Pushes it too far. Then brings it back, opens lid. Stands on it, and tries to reach. I push table nearer him, and he gets potato.

I now put box so that by opening lid and throwing it back he can reach. He gets on top, and so prevents himself from opening until he gets near hinge. He then opens, tumbling right over. He climbs on lid to reach, but the whole thing overbalances. The same evening he pushed the box towards the table, but rolled it over too far. Tries to reach and fails. Sits on box and opens lid (at side) quite uselessly. Apparently tries to get it to stand out at right angles.[1] No further effort though I draw table a little nearer. On my going out of door, reaches food from corner of box.

---

[1] I mention this as suggesting that he had a confused remembrance of getting the food before by opening the lid, which he now applies quite absurdly. He seemed to try to make the lid stick out at right angles, as it does when thrown back from the top.

The next day, he failed to use the box as a stool. The day after, I placed the box in its old position while his back was turned. The result was as follows :—

No notice till I go out of room. He struggles as I watch behind door. Chain is too short, and box is only in his way. He removes it. I lengthen chain, and move table slightly and raise onion, placing it on a piece of bamboo rested on some object on the table. He goes at it, fails to reach, pulls oak chair towards him, gets on it, reaches out, drags at corner of oak table so that onion, which is on bamboo, swings round over chair ; then just manages to knock it over on to floor, jumps down and gets it. After two miscalculations of mine, in which he gets it without chair, he again pulls chair into line, and gets food, reaching over it with great stretch, and knocking onion down.

His success in this experiment indicates a power of fairly precise adjustment of one thing to another ; and it is one in which neither accident nor imitation can be supposed to have played much part. I do not think that he ever saw me adjust the stool to the table,[1] nor could chance play much part in aiding him to place a thing which, if to be used at all, had to be brought into one particular position and no other. I only once saw him make a complete mistake upon this point ;[2] when he dragged a large basket into the line between his fastening and the food, but much too near to the fastening. One must admit that in this case the animal judged, from memory or otherwise, that a certain arrangement would help him, and set about to make that arrangement. What is principally remarkable is that the arrangement involved a certain adjustment of one thing in relation to another. If we explain it by reference to an idea, we must conceive the idea as having much less of that " crassness," of which we have spoken.[3]

[1] Nor, if he did, did he begin by a similar movement, but by throwing open the lid.

[2] *I.e.*, as to the direction in which the stool had to be moved. It sometimes happened that the heavy box would roll too far or not far enough.

[3] Cuvier's Orang would place a chair for himself to stand on, according to Romanes. (*Animal Intelligence*, p. 481.) Mr. Shepherd's monkeys, on the other hand, failed completely in this test (*op. cit.*, p. 53.)

8. Removing obstacle from chain.

I arranged matters so that the monkey's chain was shortened for effective purposes by passing round a corner of his box.

I then put a piece of potato on the floor, just beyond his reach. After a little hesitation, he came back, moved the box out of the way, and after a little fiddling with it, went back and got the potato. This was repeated a second and third time without hesitation.[1] The next day, he pushed the box, and later, the fender, out of the way of his chain ; and when, later, I put the fender right over his chain so as to shorten it to two or three inches, he pushed it back, gaining a foot, and then turned it completely over, thereby freeing himself.   I do not infer that Jimmy knows that the diagonal is shorter than two sides of an oblong, but I think that he did clearly appreciate that the box prevented his chain from running out, and this is what I mean by an articulate idea of concrete objects in their relations.  The same may be said of Miss Romanes' Cebus, which would take great pains to push the marble slab to which his chain was fastened nearer to the object desired.

"It is too heavy for him to pull along by his chain without hurting himself, so when he desires to do any mischief which is beyond the reach of his chain, he deliberately goes to the marble and pushes an arm down between an upright part of it and the wall, until he has moved the whole slab sufficiently far from the wall to admit of his slipping down behind the upright part himself.   He then places his back against the wall and his four hands against the upright part of the marble, and pushes the slab as far as he can stretch his long legs." [2]

A still higher perception of " concrete relations " is implied in the account of a Barbary ape in Brehm's *Thierleben*,[3] which found a niche into which it could squeeze its

---

[1] Each time he acted furtively, apparently fearing that I should prevent him.  This, I think, accounts for the fiddling with the box in the first trial—a characteristic performance when he meant to do something which he thought forbidden.     [2] Romanes, p. 487.     [3] I. p. 147.

rope and so fasten it. The rope thus became a swing, and if it was either too short or too long, the monkey is said to have climbed up and altered the fastening.

9. Unwinding chain.

In dealing with his chain generally, Jimmy was far less clever than Miss Romanes' Cebus. He could never be relied on to undo any serious tangle ;[1] and he constantly got himself twisted by wandering to and fro. He would, however, as a rule, undo a single twist by retracing his steps ; and sometimes would undo a more complicated one by a developed form of the method of trial and error, which consisted in this: that each time he felt the cord shortening on him, he would go back the way he had come. In this way, by successive trials, he was likely to get free. He did not, however, improve in this respect in the course of a considerable number of experiments. It would take up too much space to relate the whole of this series. I will mention one or two points that seem significant. After the knotted string experiment, when I had the potato in a basket attached by a cord to a handle of the bureau, which he could reach by a stick if he had the full length of his chain, I passed the chain round an oak table,[2] thereby shortening it for practical purposes. (Fig. 1.) The first result was as follows :—

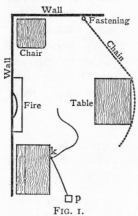

FIG. 1.

*k*, knot ; *p*, basket with potato.

[1] Contrast Miss Romanes : " When his chain becomes twisted round the bars of a ' clothes-horse' (which is given him to run about upon), and thus too short for his comfort, he looks at it intently and pulls it with his fingers this way and that, and when he sees how the turns are taken he deliberately goes round and round the bars, first this way, then that, until the chain is quite disentangled " (p. 486). From what Jimmy did, I think he could have learnt this if he were a little more persistent and attentive, but after seeing his failures, I can realise better the high degree of " articulateness," both of perception and purpose, implied in the description given by Miss Romanes.

[2] There had previously been two or three untwisting experiments.

He darts at tied end, and tries to pull himself up by it ; does move table in this way and gets nearer. Tries to grab at string beyond knot. Tries wildly. Tries to catch it by throwing other string over it, and nearly succeeds. *Never* attempts to come back and walk round table, nor to move table out of way, nor to use stick. Finally, being encouraged by extra hard pull at tied string, manages to shift table and so reach. No mistake about his going for string beyond knot.

In the second trial, he used the stick ; in the third, he gave up. I then picked him up, and took him round the table to untwist him, but he was much frightened, and presently got twisted again. I soon found that he was really after the remainder of the potato, which had been left carelessly in another part of the room. At length, in the course of his wanderings, he got free from the legs of the table. I quote the following from my notes :—

He still does not think of going *round* table, but makes another fainthearted attempt to reach the food directly. Presently wanders round to fire, and then sees strings ; goes at string beyond knot, and gets.

I again put cord round table. He tries to reach ; then comes slowly but steadily round table, and back to fire. Then goes and gets.

Food, etc., replaced. After once straining towards string, goes round table, straight to string, and gets food.

Replaced. Same ; but cord has got twisted round foot of table, so he pulls at tied string, pulls table nearer, and gets food by pulling string beyond knot.

After lunch, replaced. After short pull, *i.e.*, straining at his cord, goes round at once.

I now pass chain *through* legs of table. He goes back through and round at once.

It will be seen (1) that it did not occur to him to go round the table at the first trial, but (2) that having once done so in casual fashion with satisfactory results he repeated the process.

After this, I tried the more complicated untwisting experiments to which I have referred. The next day, I

varied the experiment by passing the chain round a
high "grandfather's chair," standing in the corner of
the room. (Fig. 1.) The way round would be quite
dark and unobvious, but I wished to see whether he
would draw the analogy from the table. The result was
as follows :—

He makes great effort to reach potato, tries to use hammer as
stick to reach it, tries to move chair, turns and pulls with hands
at rope, makes (for first time that I have seen him do it) a sort of
dash at a point where his chain is fastened, but does not think of
going round chair.

I take chain from chair and put it round table. As I arrange,
he is excited, wanders, and gets entangled. Cannot disentangle
himself. I do so, and let him have some potato. Then I replace
round table. After trying straight at potato, he at once darts
back, but instead of going outside, leaves one leg to the right,
table standing thus :

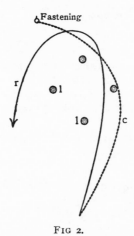

FIG 2.

*r*, route : *c*, chain ; *l*, legs.

He then gets entangled, but disentangles himself by stages, and,
getting free, goes somewhat hesitatingly round table and gets
potato.

Replaced. He makes exactly same mistake, but rapidly
disentangles himself through three or four turnings, runs round
table and gets.

Total time can only have been a few seconds.

Replaced.  He rushes round right way before I have time to put potato down.  I give him some bread.
Replaced.  No hesitation.
I now placed chain thus :

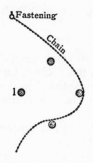

FIG 3.

He starts wrong, but rapidly gets out between legs, perhaps by chance, then goes round table and gets.
Replaced.  He untwists himself (though starting wrong) while I am placing bread.  Then comes round table and gets food.

These experiments give a fair measure of his accuracy in disentangling himself.

Some more untwisting experiments followed, and then I placed the chain round the high chair again.
He tries a little at potato (*i.e.*, to reach it directly), but does not attempt to go round chair.  Jumps on it once.  Very little effort.  After interval, tries again, wanders a little.  The clank of his chain seems to strike him, and he starts off, goes round chair deliberately, and gets potato.
Replaced.  Tries (direct method), then back, and after one false start, goes round at once.
Replaced.  Does not even try to go straight, but goes round at once.

In this experiment again, the thing seemed to strike him all of a sudden.  Just as in the hook experiment, the movement of my hand, so, in this, the clank of the chain seemed suddenly to set the whole thing before him. For the rest, one may regard his getting round the chair as a kind of analogy from his experience with the table, and one not so easy to draw in fact as it may seem from its description upon paper. For round the table the lie of the chain when once attended to was obvious ; round the chair it was hidden in the darkness of the corner.

10. Attempted theft.

My reasons for suspecting Jimmy of trying to deceive me are not only a certain furtiveness of manner that came over him at times; but the use of methods the object of which was unmistakable. It often happened that when I was giving him bits of potato, I would leave the bulk of the potato carelessly somewhere within his reach. On such an occasion the first symptom I noticed of anything wrong was a loss of interest in the experiment. I would then see him wandering off to perch on some table or chair, or investigate some harmless object. Looking for a reason, I would see that he was almost within striking distance of my potato, and then, a stern, " No, Jimmy, no !" would send him scuttling back to the fire, and to the investigation of his person. On one occasion in particular, as I was going out of the room, having left the potato on a table, as I thought, out of his reach, I saw him walking quietly, not to the table, but towards a box near by. As I looked back, I saw him sliding from the box to the table, and I stopped him just on the spring.[1]

People ask whether animals use deception. I do not for a moment suppose that Jimmy has any clear conception of a lie. I do not suppose that he troubles himself about my mental state. But I do think that he could form a pretty shrewd estimate of the way in which I was likely to act under given circumstances. He was perfectly certain that if I saw him making a dive for the whole potato, I should stop him ; and I do attribute to him, further, the idea—I do not know how else to express it—that if he avoided going straight at the prize, he

[1] Of a baboon described in Brehm's *Thierleben* (I. p. 177) it is said that she "stahl meisterhaft."

might get near enough to it for a spring. I doubt whether Jimmy's state of mind can, with due allowance for the facts, be reasonably analysed into simpler terms than these ; and the use of these terms clearly implies both an " original " application of experience, and a fairly complex adjustment of one consideration to another.

11. I have imputed " practical ideas " to animals lower than the monkeys, to express the fact that they not merely respond in a uniform manner to a certain physical situation, but appear to direct their actions to the production of a certain physical change. Keeping to the same terminology, I should say that what distinguishes the ideas of monkeys from those of other animals in so far as experiments like mine can measure them, is an increase in elaboration and articulateness. By increased elaboration, I mean that in experiments of this kind, the monkey is less the slave of the perceptual order. There is more work of the mind in the plans which he lays on the basis of his experience. And this is principally shown in the increased articulateness of the plan itself. The monkey can apply one object to another ; that is why he can use a stick, a stool, a poker.[1] It may be said, so could the dog, if he had a hand. I am not prepared to deny this hypothetical statement ; but I would rejoin that if the dog had a hand, his intelligence would be developed in a different way. He has not the empirical data at the disposal of the monkey ; and therefore, in experiments of the kind which one can institute in a house or a laboratory, experiments depending principally upon the manipulation of objects, the ape appears head and shoulders above other animals. Whether we speak of ideas or not, we cannot refuse to allow to the ape actions

[1] The reasons why animals do not use tools are partly physical, partly mental, and the two reasons are correlated. The use of tools implies a certain articulateness of ideas—the grasping of different objects in relations not given by perception. This articulateness again implies a power of tactual discrimination only to be gained by the use of the hand. Hence the employment of tools is almost unknown below the apes, and rare among them. Of the *making* of a tool, I only know one authentic instance. A chimpanzee formerly at Belle Vue would not only pick the key of its cage out of a bunch, but could make itself a key out of a piece of wood. This is less marvellous than it sounds. The key was a simple square (like a railway key), and the monkey had only to bite the wood till it would fit into the square hole.

in which one point is correlated with another, and this perhaps with a third or fourth, on the basis of past experience and present perception, yet without being dominated by either, with a certain degree of precision, in such a way as to bring about the gratification of an impulse. The empirical basis of such a plan is often more or less indirect. In the use of the stick as a rake, there was for the chimpanzee his own experience with the rug, and the hint which I gave him by using the stick myself. To transfer the act, and apply it to himself and his own needs, was, at lowest, a strong case of "reflective imitation." But the use of the term *imitation* in this connection is really misleading. At most, my act served as a hint. It would be impossible to use a stick under such circumstances with success merely from seeing another do it, and without grasping for one's self the way in which it is to be done. And all the detailed adjustments by which the use of the stick was perfected, were worked out by the monkey for himself. The same animal's use of the stick, and afterwards the iron rod, in the pipe, is another example of a very accurate adjustment of means to ends, to the latter of which it is difficult to think that there could have been any close parallel in his previous experience. One must rather imagine his general knowledge of objects reacting on his immediate perception and desire, and together engendering an essentially novel kind of act.[1]

In the case of the little monkey, the adjustment of the footstool, and the removal of obstacles from his chain, seem again to rest rather on a kind of common sense than on any specific experience, and to imply a tolerably accurate judgment of the spatial relations of the objects concerned. The furtiveness which I have discussed above suggests similarly a certain power of combining inferences as to how I should act, and how he could act, and how the potato might be the result.

[1] Cf. Kinnaman. As his experiments proceeded "it appears that there was improvement in dealing with fastenings in general. All locks towards the last were attacked with definiteness, and as if the animals had a dim realisation that they were the proper objects for attack, a thing which was not true at first (*Amer. Journ. Psych.*, XIII. 122). Cf. his account, too long to quote, of the plan by which a monkey obtained a piece of apple in a difficult position (*op. cit.*, p. 208).

Does a similar power of selecting and combining results of experience under the stimulus of desire exist among other mammals, or is it confined to monkeys? Systematic observation and experiment, of which in comparative psychology there is a plentiful lack,[1] does not enable us to answer this question decisively. In my own experiments, the difference between monkeys and other animals appeared strongly marked. But I was experimenting in a field much more suited to the ways of a monkey than to those of other animals. Suppose one were to take a dog, for example, on his own ground; in a hunting problem, for instance. Is it not possible that he would show an equal power of applying the results of experience in a novel manner? If we are to trust to ordinary observation, and "anecdotal evidence," the answer is undoubtedly in the affirmative. The question for psychology is as to the value of such evidence. Much of it, everybody knows, is consciously or unconsciously invented or exaggerated. And even where the facts are faithfully reported, we can never be sure that we know all the circumstances. What appears when complete to be an act of great sagacity, may, when its genesis is carefully traced, reveal itself as the outcome of accident, or perhaps of training.[2]

---

[1] Notwithstanding the body of laboratory experiments which has grown up since this was written. Such experiments give very little scope for anything like originality on the part of an animal. Till this defect is overcome anecdotal evidence cannot be wholly ruled out of our subject.

[2] See, for example, the delightful and instructive story of Mr. Lloyd Morgan's fox-terrier Tony, and the crooked stick, with the passing remarks thereon of the countryman who had watched the proceedings for two minutes. It is superfluous to add that a trained animal may exhibit apparently marvellous intelligence, with a very moderate amount of the real article. There was formerly an elephant at Belle Vue which would take a penny from a bystander, put it into the slot of an automatic machine, and get a biscuit from the other end of the machine. If a halfpenny were offered instead of a penny, the elephant would fling it back angrily. "Marvellous intelligence!" is the enthusiast's comment. "Rather too tall a story," is the sceptic's. The simple truth is, that every stage in the performance was a matter of careful training. The elephant, as the keeper explained to me, was taught the use of the machine by having its trunk guided; and, having learnt this, was taught, by between two and three months' labour, to distinguish between the penny which would and the halfpenny which would not set it working. A modicum of intelligence remains when the explanation is given in full, but nothing beyond the ordinary performance of an elephant.

On the other hand, comparative psychology cannot afford altogether to neglect the casual observation. It must be borne in mind that the little combinations of experience which are in question, are, to the animal, if they exist at all, what a new invention is to the human being. When sufficiently clear and pronounced to strike the observer, they would naturally be rarities, occurring only now and then under favourable conditions, internal and external. Such conditions are likely to occur only when the animal is at work on its own ground. They are less probable when we set the animal to work at a task of our choosing. Lastly, it must be added that the body of evidence of this kind is too considerable to be altogether ignored. There appear to be in the ordinary works on natural history and animal psychology, a great number of instances of " animal sagacity " which are impossible if we suppose the learning of animals limited to the formation of habits or associations, but are readily intelligible if we grant them the power of forming practical ideas on the basis of experience, and of appropriately selecting and combining such ideas to meet the pressure of practical needs in the circumstances of the moment.

I will not go through the mass of this evidence, but may take one or two cases as typical. I have referred above to stories such as those given in General Hutchinson's book *Dog Breaking*,[1] of dogs running round game when they found that the game, instead of rising, ran before them. Clearly, this is a violation of habit, and is unintelligible if we suppose the dog to act without the purpose of making the birds rise. On the other hand, no abstract idea: no general plan: no universal conception is required. Grant that the dog wants to get these birds up, and that past experience will enable him to form a concrete judgment as to how they will act, and we have all the conditions that we need. What is postulated is, concrete experience, present purpose, and the interaction of the results of experience with present perception to form a combination or adaptation of actions suitable to the needs of the moment.

[1] See p. 264.

To recognise what I have called the practical judgment
as something not identical with the association of ideas,
but as intermediate between habituation on the one side,
and general reasoning on the other, is, as it seems to me,
to find the key not only to the ordinary behaviour of the
higher animals, which we witness from day to day, but
also to those little acts of invention and ingenuity which
occasional observers recount.  The observer who is not a
psychologist is apt to translate the animal's action into
abstract terms, as if it were the animal who made the
abstraction, and not the observer.  The psychologist,
whose duty it is to prune the exuberance of imagination,
resolves the proceeding into an instance of association,
where it may be that association, if the term is to remain
distinct from what I have called the Practical Judgment,
cannot be made to cover all the facts.  Thus Mr. Lloyd
Morgan writes as follows:—

" A well-known writer, Dr. Andrew Wilson, describes the case
of a dog which used to hunt a rabbit nearly every morning down
a curved shrubbery, and each time ran it into a drain at the end.
'The dog then appears to have come to the conclusion'—I quote
Dr. Wilson's words—'that the chord of a circle is shorter than
its arc, for he raised the rabbit again, and, instead of following him
through the shrubbery as usual, he took the short cut to the drain,
and was ready and in waiting on the rabbit when he arrived, and
caught him.'  It is here assumed that the dog perceived the
relation between a chord and its arc.  I do not myself believe that
he did ;—but that is not the question ; it is merely an expression of individual opinion.  The question is :—Can we or can
we not explain the dog's action as the outcome of sense-experience,
as indicative of intelligence profiting by association ?  I do not see
how this can be denied.  The terrier used to start the rabbit
nearly every morning, and each time saw it escape into the old
drain.  There were thus ample opportunities for establishing an
association between rabbit and drain.  That the sight of the
rabbit should suggest the drain into which it daily escaped, and
that when the idea was suggested, the dog should run there
directly, is a sequence not impossible, one would think, to sense-
experience."

[1] *Comparative Psychology*, pp. 301, 302.  It should be said that Mr.
Lloyd Morgan has in his latest work, *Animal Behaviour*, practically
given up the use of the term Association from a sense, as I gather, of its
ambiguity.

I do not, any more than Mr. Lloyd Morgan, suppose a dog to know that a chord is shorter than its arc, but neither do I think an association of the idea of the drain with that of the rabbit adequate or even relevant to the case. Why should an " idea of the drain " cause the dog to run to it ? The dog does not want to catch a drain, but a rabbit. What is needed is the idea of the "rabbit at the drain," and that, moreover, as an event that will shortly take place. In fact, as we analyse the idea, it turns into the judgment, " The rabbit will run to the drain " as it did yesterday, and then it becomes an intelligible basis for the dog's action in taking the nearest course. In any case, whether we call it association or judgment, we have to admit that the dog acted, not as he acted before, but with a difference, and this difference is explained if we conceive him as applying the results won from previous experience to present circumstances in subservience to his desire. I do not suppose that the little monkey Jimmy is aware that a straight line is the shortest between any two points. What I imagine is, that he found that if he had something to stand on at a particular point, he could reach the potato ; and he therefore brought things to stand on at that point.[1]

I will add one more dog story, which seems to me to indicate the intelligent use of experience as distinguished from mere association, on the authority of Mr. Lloyd Morgan himself.

---

[1] Many stories are told by animal psychologists, and referred to association, when the whole point of the story is that the ordinary associations of the act are not present, that is to say, the act is performed under new circumstances, or in a new form, where everything but that which is essential to the purpose is altered. Thus Wundt, who refers everything to association, tells a story of his poodle, which frequently crossed a river with his master, and if left behind, was compelled to swim. The poodle much preferred going dryshod, and on one occasion, after running up and down the bank "whining dismally," he suddenly saw a strange boat pushing off to cross, jumped in, and crossed without wetting himself. In joining the strangers, the dog was of course violating his habits, and if we say that he had an association between boats putting off, and crossing the river, we tend to overlook the central fact, that it is not the idea of crossing the river that he needs, but the idea of getting into the boat. This idea is associated with the presence of his master or his friends, and the event shows that instead of being at the mercy of his associations, he picks out what is essential, and drops the rest.

"When I was at the Diocesan College near Capetown, a retriever, Scamp, used to come and sit with the lecturers at supper. He despised bread, but used to get an occasional bone, which he was not, however, allowed to eat in the hall. He took it to the door and stood there till it was opened for him. On one occasion he heard outside the excited barking of the other dogs. He ran round the hall, picked up a piece of bread which one of the boys had dropped, and stood with it in his mouth at the door. When it was opened, he dropped the bread and raced off into the darkness to join the other dogs."[1]

The associationist's explanation of this piece of craft must evidently be cumbrous. He must plead that the dog had got accustomed to connect being let out with having something in his mouth, and that now, wanting to be let out, the familiar associate turned up. But in ordinary circumstances, the dog had a bone, and not bread ; he wanted to eat, and not to get out ; he did not drop his food ; and so forth. In short, the circumstances are as different as possible, except in regard to the *particular relation* between taking food in his mouth and getting out, which happens to serve the dog's purpose. The ordinary associations were not present. But out of past experience, the animal picks a way of satisfying its desires. The practical judgment is not independent of associations, for association supplies the whole of its material. But out of that material, it selects what it wants, and shapes it as required.

As more observers and experimentalists enter the field, it should be possible to cover the ground now left to casual observation in a more systematic manner. In the meantime, if by a self-denying ordinance we restrict ourselves entirely to laboratory experiments and to the comparatively few observations which have been made consecutively, like those of Dr. Wesley Mills, we shall have to draw a marked line between the apes and the lower mammals,[2] allowing to the former a power of combining the results of experience which is not provable for the latter. If, however, taking the whole evidence

---

[1] Lloyd Morgan, *Comparative Psychology*, p. 95.
[2] Though even here we should not forget Mr. Cole's raccoons.

now available, we ask what is the conclusion pointed to with the greatest probability, it is, that on their own lines, and in their own way, some at least of the more intelligent mammals have powers equivalent to those of the ape.

Intelligence, we shall recognise, develops in different forms, and in divers directions. It originates within the sphere of instinct, and in its earlier stages is shaped by the instinct which it subserves and expands. We must not expect to find dog intelligence to be quite the same thing as cat intelligence or ape intelligence. It is not only a question of difference in degree, but also, in a sense, of difference in quality, arising from difference in origin. Among men, we know that A, who is clever at languages, is incredibly stupid at mathematics, while with B, it is just the opposite. So, a dog may show not merely a highly developed hunting instinct, but real cleverness in the adaptation of past experiences, when it is a question of catching a hare, but he may be also an intolerable dullard about opening a box.[1]

---

[1] We must guard against the assumption that every novel adaptation to special circumstances implies a knowledge of means and ends. What looks ingenious and original may involve only a slight variation of pre-existing impulse in response to a unique stimulus. *E.g.*, Dahl observed a spider, which habitually cut the thread holding its fly when carrying the fly off to the hole, fighting with another spider over a prey which was claimed by both. Both spiders were fastened by threads to their own point of support, and the first spider won the victory by severing the thread of the other. If this was not merely a happy blunder, we may regard it as a modified application of a habitual impulse. The rival spider's thread occupied the place ordinarily taken by the meshes entangling the fly, and being so far similar, awakes the cutting impulse.

Perhaps a similar explanation may be applied to the action of a caterpillar which tried to mount three different sides of a pit in succession (Weir, *Dawn of Reason*, p. 206). Here, and in a somewhat similar application of the method of exhaustions by a snail (Romanes, p. 26), we shall probably find the key in the habitual moving of the head for purposes of exploration. The animal is accustomed to try different directions in succession and adapts the habit very neatly to its special difficulty.

In some cases selective modification may be at work. Thus an octopus, having been stung by the anemones with which hermit-crabs arm their shells (with an eye to this very result) will cease to seize the shells but will feel inside them instead, and draw the victim out with its tentacles. The same impulse is at work, and its first line of discharge being blocked, it finds another. But it is, of course, possible that the action belongs to the higher type.

The beetle seen by Mr. Lloyd Morgan (*Animal Life and Intelligence*,

SUMMARY AND CONCLUSION

12. The question with which we set out at Chapter VII. was, whether the second grade of intelligence was realised in the animal world. That grade of intelligence we called the grade of Concrete Experience and the Practical Judgment. It was marked by the appearance of several functions in close interconnection. The primary function is that of concrete experience itself; *i.e.*, the power of perceiving surrounding objects or passing events as wholes of distinguishable parts. Where such an experience exists, and is "reproducible" in the form of ideas guiding action, we have all the characteristics of the second stage. We have memory, in the form of the idea of a past event; anticipation, in the form of an idea of something about to come attached to present circumstances through the relation suggested from the past. Anticipation, with the impulse to avoid or attain, is again Desire. Where there is desire, *i.e.*, the idea of the end, there may also be an idea of the means, and choice of means with a view to the end. Such a choice from the material presented by reproduced experience, is the Practical Judgment. Lastly, out of the combined results of perceptions and the concrete ideas reproduced in connection with them, is built up the knowledge of individuals, localities, and the whole concrete surroundings of the organism : surroundings including a multitude of related facts, any one of which relations is at the disposal of the practical judgment to serve its ends.

p. 368), which could not lift its ball out of a hole, and butted down the side so that he could roll it up, was perhaps less intelligent than it looked. To us it was converting a perpendicular wall into an inclined plane. To its own consciousness perhaps it was merely butting away an obstacle.

Lastly, one impulse impinging on another may result in a happy compromise by which both are satisfied—in the manner discussed in relation to instinctive adjustments (above, Ch. VI).

It remains that in many of these cases, we must end for the present with a confession of ignorance. We cannot understand them until more is known of the whole life and character of the animals concerned. What is important for the present is that we should not impute a knowledge of the relation of means and ends unless we see action resulting from an experience of that relation, and then only under the conditions and with the limitations that have been discussed in the last two chapters.

In a word, concrete objects are known in their relations, and the knowledge is applied in action.

These functions being thus closely interconnected, the possession of any one makes the possession of others a matter of some probability. And if there is independent evidence, of some probability, for the possession of each function by the higher mammals, the probabilities stand to strengthen one another. Now, the only evidence to be found for the performance of these or any other functions by animal intelligence, is evidence derived from animal behaviour. Having this in view, we laid down certain points of behaviour by which the practical judgment might be distinguished from the lower stage of intelligence in which action passes out of the control of instinct to come under that of habit. These points were as follows :—

(1). *The single Instance.*

Habit except in the direct modification of an impulse is built up by a large number of repetitions. One clear perception of a relation should have a permanent effect.

On this head, we found abundant evidence that the higher animals frequently learn by a single instance, and normally by what I have called a critical instance, in which their attention seems to be for the first time definitely directed to the facts.

(2). *The Perception of objects in their relations.*

The relations given in concrete experience and guiding subsequent actions may be relations between any objects of perception—and are not (as in the case of Assimilation) confined to those between sensation and the motor excitements immediately attendant upon them.

The simplest evidence of the appreciation of such relations is Learning by Perception of Results. A habit can only be acquired by previous action. The practical judgment can be formed on the basis of a perception that the change A leads to the desired result B.

Of the power of animals to learn in this way, probable though not conclusive evidence has been given. In many cases in which accidental success seems improbable, animals repeated what they had seen done, and in some instances, actions were so co-ordinated as to bring about the physical or external change A, which the animal had observed to lead to the end B. This implies a function coinciding with that of a practical idea A, the essential features of which would be, on the one hand, its power to direct the minor adjustments of action towards the production of a physical event, and on the other, of being correlated with and subordinate to another idea.

Further evidence tending in the same direction is to be found :

*a*. In the appreciation of that general similarity of relations in which objects of a class resemble one another. We saw reason to think that in inferring from one person, animal, or complex inanimate object to another of the same class, an animal shows itself to be guided by similarity of this kind.

*b*. In the absence of a uniform reaction to a known object, and the choice on the contrary of a reaction determined by the relation in which the object may stand to the thing desired. On this head, we brought evidence to show that an animal's knowledge of locality could not be resolved into a series of motor reactions to the things which surround it, but that its movements may be guided by Desire to find what is out of the range of perception.

(3). *Application of Experience.*

The results of experience are applied in action in a manner not predetermined by the experience itself.

Such application appears in an elementary form even in "perceptual learning," where what is first a passive observation is utilised as a guide to action. A much higher case, in which the contrast with habit and association is decisive, is that of "spontaneous application," in which an inference is drawn from experience, and an act not done or seen before is performed to meet the case.

Of such use of experience there seems to be sufficient evidence in the behaviour of apes.[1] Among lower animals, the evidence at present is sporadic and "anecdotal."

---

[1] I would refer to the action of the Rhesus in loosening the string which held the hook, in its attempts at "theft," and as a probable case in the use of the footstool. The use by both chimpanzee and Rhesus of one stick to reach another seems a slightly more complex case of "application."

With the higher forms of application, we must class " reflective imitation," in which the act of another, which produced no direct result to the observing animal, is by it copied and applied to its own ends. Of this there is also sufficient evidence among monkeys, and some evidence, though less copious, among other animals.

Lastly, greater freedom in the application of the results of experience to one another, combined with more nicety of perception and clearness of reproduction, yield results of which we have found experimental evidence in the behaviour of monkeys. Such are the relatively articulate Ideas, involving a relatively accurate and detailed appreciation of the relations of objects (as in the use of the stick, the stool, the removal of obstacles from the chain, the insertion of a stick into a tube). Such are again the intelligent combination of distinct methods of effecting a purpose, seen, for example, in the efforts of the chimpanzee to swing a banana out of its box, and then swish it in by lateral movements of the rope. The same thing appears in many details of its use of the stick. To the same mental factors we may refer such analogical extension of experience as the use by the Rhesus of a rope or a sheet instead of the stick which it had learnt to handle.[1]

It thus appears that so far as experimental evidence is concerned, both the *Application* of experience in its higher forms, and the power of forming and combining ideas of a fairly articulate type appear in the behaviour of apes, but not of lower animals ; but the tendency of a mass of anecdotal evidence would suggest that in a different sphere corresponding powers might be found among the more intelligent mammals below the primates.

Putting all the evidence under these heads together, I think it may be held that the cluster of functions here grouped together under the head of the Practical Judgment, are to be found in the animal world below man. That is to say, that animal intelligence at its highest point

---

[1] Mr. Shepherd, summing up on his Rhesus monkey, writes : "Of the higher powers of the mind the monkey has only rudiments. He has a something which corresponds in function to ideas of a low order and which serves practical purposes. This something we call, with Hobhouse, practical ideas." *Op. cit.* p. 60.

of development effects a correlation between related elements of experience and action. As applied to the apes, this conclusion appears very probable indeed ; and as applied to some other mammals, it is, I think, a better provisional hypothesis than any other that I know. As a provisional hypothesis, its truth will be assumed in the rest of this work.[1]

[1] The considerable body of investigation undertaken in America since the above was written by such observers as Yerkes, Watson, Haggerty, Berry, Cole, and many others, has yielded very diverse results in different cases, but as a whole has tended to confirm the hypothesis here put forward, with the limitation that intelligence on the higher level is the exception, so that only the most alert individuals will give clear signs of it, and that only under favourable circumstances. With the questions raised by accounts of the Elberfeld horses I deal in the Appendix.

# CHAPTER XIII

## INTELLIGENCE AND THE SOCIAL INSTINCTS

1. WE have already seen that instinct and intelligence, though opposed in idea, are so far from being incompatible in fact, that it is within the sphere of instinct that intelligence first arises. The first function of intelligence is to define the proximate ends of instinct, and thereby to render experience available in the choice or revision of means. Hence, the higher the intelligence, the greater the complexity of which instincts are capable, and the more readily are they adaptable to meet a novel situation, and the individuality of changing circumstances. We have, unfortunately, no means of precisely measuring the complexity of which pure instinct is capable. But about the higher instincts, two things are noteworthy.

(1) It is in those Orders or Classes where we find most evidence of intelligence, that instincts chiefly arise which are adaptable to very complex conditions. It is here, for example, that we find attention to the young, the rudiments of social life, and of mutual help ; the provision of a temporary or permanent home.

(2) We have direct evidence that operations of which the basis is instinctive are modified in detail according to experience of results. It is to be inferred that instinct, at least among the higher animals, is not wholly blind. There must be some consciousness of the purpose, where, as the result of experience, means are taken to avoid its frustration. Thus the foundation of mutual help is no doubt instinctive. The cry of the young excites the mother to come to it, or to hunt for food for it, as the

case may be.  The mother cat is moved to lick and clean
her kittens as unthinkingly as they are moved to suck her.
When they pair, birds doubtless feel an impulse to build,
which the sudden gift of language would no more enable
them to explain than it would help to teach them the art
of nest-building.  Nest-making, complex as it is, is mainly
the result of instinct.[1]  Yet in these matters experience
also plays a part.  Whether it is experience of the higher
or lower grade is difficult to determine.  But when we find
that birds which have built their nests on the ground learn
on the introduction of cats into their island to move house
to the more salubrious quarters of the tree tops, we must
recognise that in animal behaviour there are well-developed
schemes of action in which intelligence has its share.
They are frequently modified by experience, and suitably
adapted to peculiar or to changed circumstances.  They
are not instincts of the complex-mechanical type.  Though
certainly not due to intelligence alone, they are not executed
altogether without intelligence.  The adaptability of behaviour in the main based on heredity is well illustrated
in the case of nest-building.  The oriole, according to Dr.
A. R. Wallace,[2] endeavours ordinarily to conceal its nest
from snakes and hawks, but in villages where it does not
fear these enemies, it builds openly.  The orchard oriole
builds a shallow nest upon the stiffer branches, but upon
the slender twigs of the weeping willow builds deep, so
that the young may not be thrown out by the swaying of
the nest.  The house sparrow, which makes a domed nest
in a tree, is content with loose building in a hole in thatch.
Schneider[3] states on the authority of Brehm that a tame
Cardinal finch which was bringing up a Cowbird, brought
it a cricket to eat.  The nestling finding the insect too big,
the nurse tore and chewed the prey, and gave the softened
pieces to its charge.  Many habits, which seem too complex
to be wholly due to intelligence, are nevertheless gradually
learnt.  Thus, though the basis of nest-building is indubit-

[1] Dr. A. R. Wallace maintained the contrary view (*Natural Selection*,
p. 10 *et seq.*), but the evidence given by Mr. Lloyd Morgan (*Habit and
Instinct*, p. 232 *et seq.*) appears conclusive.
[2] *Natural Selection*, pp. 114, 115.  Cf. Romanes, *M.E.A.*, p. 210.
[3] P. 374 ; Brehm, IV. p. 373.

ably hereditary, perfection in the art is acquired by practice. One might, as Schneider says,[2] attribute the opening of fir cones by the woodpecker to get at the seeds inside, to an inherited method of reaction to a certain perception ; but, in point of fact, it appears that the old birds bring the young, first the seed itself, then partly opened cones, and then the complete cones. Thus the method of preparing the family dinner is at least as much a tradition as an instinct.

Such instances suggest that in the higher instincts, while the ground plan is no doubt determined by heredity, many of its points are grasped by intelligence. Instinct prompts the building of the nest, but intelligence notices a casual defect, and makes it good. There is hereditary impulse to feed, clean, and protect the young, but there is a sufficiently clear understanding of what the young wants at any given moment—sufficiently clear to enable a special need to be met by methods not provided for by heredity. Thus, at this stage, pure instinct tends to disappear, or, more strictly, to become suffused with intelligence. Intelligence grows in power of grasping the purposes which instinct sets before the individual, and in carrying them into effect by means suggested by experience or the perception of special circumstances.

The use of " sentinels," which is widely diffused among birds and mammals, is another practice which, though perhaps more uniform in its working, is very difficult to understand, without allowing a measure of intelligence to eke out habit and instinct. Mr. Cornish (pp. 48, 49) quotes from Mr. St. John a vivid description of the manner in which a flock of wild geese coming to a field of newly sown grain " make numerous circling flights " before alighting, " and the least suspicious object prevents them from pitching." If they do alight they remain motionless a minute or two with head erect reconnoitring. They then leave a sentry who " either stands on some elevated part of the field, or walks slowly with the rest—never, however, venturing to pick up a single grain

---

[1] Wallace, *loc. cit.*; Lloyd Morgan, *Habit and Instinct*, pp. 234 ff. ; Romanes, *M.E.A.* pp. 209–212.          [2] P. 298.

of corn, his whole energies being employed in watching."
Mr. St. John says : " When the sentry thinks that he has
performed a fair share of duty, he gives the nearest
bird to him a sharp peck. I have seen him sometimes pull out a bunch of feathers if the first hint is not
immediately attended to, and at the same time uttering
a querulous kind of cry." Mr. St. John was constantly
baulked by sentinel geese, and found that whole flocks of
swans would have their heads in the water except one—
" who was relieved from time to time." Sentinels have
an alarm note. " Ibex, marmots, and mountain-sheep
whistle, prairie dogs bark, elephants trumpet, wild geese
and swans have a kind of bugle call, rabbits stamp on
the ground, sheep do the same, and wild ducks, as the
writer has noticed, utter a very low caution quack to
signal ' The enemy in sight.' "

The response to the alarm cry is no doubt an ordinary
case of an instinctive method of reaction perfected by experience, but the position and behaviour of the sentinel,
and in particular, the change of sentinels, are difficult to
explain without crediting the birds or beasts concerned with
some power of understanding one another and the purpose
they are fulfilling. Moreover, according to Brehm,[1] at
least one case has been observed in which the sentinels were
set as the direct result of experience. A marabout having
been shot in visiting a slaughter house, the survivors thereafter instituted a guard. There is surely a marked contrast
between such a use of experience and the mere pruning of
impulsive tendencies by pleasure and pain. In the latter
case a reaction is checked or encouraged by what an animal
has itself felt. In the former, a special contrivance is
adopted to avoid a fate which it has witnessed in the case
of another.

2. The appearance of sympathy and attachment between
the higher animals may doubtless, in many cases, be explicable as the effect of hereditary methods of response to
stimulus as perfected by experience. Just as the smell may
direct the young to the udder, so the sight of the calf may
stimulate the cow to go towards it, or run after the cart

[1] Quoted by Schneider, p. 352 ; Brehm, VI, p. 522.

which is carrying it away, and the cry of the young bird may stimulate the parent to go worm-hunting. But here again we find a " particularity " in the behaviour of animals which could not be provided for beforehand by a class-response. When a monkey—and a male, moreover—comes back from a general flight to rescue a young one which has been cut off by dogs,[1] the notion of an instinctive adjustment, or an action acquired gradually by practice, is ludicrously out of place. We are forced to speak of the ape as acting with a purpose, and if we allow it purpose in this case, we must grant it sympathy or fellow feeling of some kind. It is not merely mothers that feed their young, but companions or " friends " that upon occasion feed others in distress.[2] A cat no doubt suckles its young by instinct, but it is not by instinct that when her milk has run dry, she will coax her mistress to the hayloft where the kittens are, and bring them to her.[3] A young mammal will doubtless follow an older one more or less blindly and uniformly, but what can we say of the following incident described by Mr. Cornish[4] on the authority of Lord Lovat ?

"Three stags had been moved in a young plantation. The two best jumped the three ft. wire fence, but a third, a two year old stag, got frightened, and refused. The two waited for him for some time, while he walked and ran up and down ; at last the larger of the two—a good royal—came back to the fence. The little one ran towards him and the royal trotted away ; but no, the little one could not make up his mind to jump. Back came the royal over the fence, went close up to the little fellow, and actually *kissed him* several times. With the glass not 500 yards away, we could see them rub their noses together. Then the royal led down to the fence, but still the little stag would not have it. At last the royal tossed his head in the air, and seeming to say " Well, you are a fool," went off up the hill to join his companion. When out of sight the little one took courage, got over the fence in a scramble, and followed."

The ordinary reader would infer from this that the

---

[1] See Brehm's *Thierleben*, I. p. 186.
[2] See Darwin, *Descent of Man*, I. p. 77 ; and Lloyd Morgan, *Animal Life and Intelligence*, pp. 397, 398. Cf. Romanes, p. 473.
[3] Brehm, *Thierleben*, I. p. 438.
[4] *Animals at Work and at Play*, p. 26.

older stag wanted to encourage the young one and get him
across the fence, and substantially, the ordinary reader is
right. The stag cannot analyse or describe his own
actions, and it would be a fallacy to impute the description to him. Nevertheless, it may be, and I think is as
nearly as possible the right description as given by a
looker on. It is of some interest in this connection to
contrast the abundant *prima facie* evidence of attachment
and affection among Birds and Mammals with the comparatively rare cases among the Lower Vertebrates. Apart
from one or two isolated stories of snakes, the evidence
for attachment to individuals among these classes is in
fact somewhat dim. Many that can be tamed—tortoises,
for example—do not appear to distinguish individuals, and
according to the statement already quoted from Brehm's
*Thierleben*, the crocodile does not distinguish between the
white man who shoots him and the black man who does
not.[1] Yet the distinction, if difficult, is material. In care
for the young, reptiles and amphibia appear for the most
part to be on a level with the higher Fish. The majority
of fish pay no attention to their very immature ova, and
accordingly enormous numbers are spawned to maintain the equilibrium of the species.[2] The most rudimentary form of attention is shown, for example, by the
female Aspredo, which sticks the eggs to her, and so
carries them about. She hatches two thousand annually,
as against sixty thousand in the nearest species.[3]
Similarly the females of Solenostomata and Doryrhamphus
carry their eggs in pouches. In other cases the male
carries the fertilised eggs in his mouth or in a pouch.
The dump-fish, again (*Cyclopterus lumpus*), carries
its young, which adhere to it, into places of safety, and
the Angel-fish (Squatina) takes them if threatened into
its mouth.[4] Without fuller information than I have
found, it is very difficult to judge whether there is any-

---

[1] Brehm, VII. p. 24.
[2] According to Mr. Sutherland (Vol. I. p. 27), in 75 species representing 8 out of the 10 orders, the yearly average is 646,000 per female. It must
be remembered, however, that these are unfertilised ova, and are scarcely
comparable to the fertilised and well-protected egg of higher vertebrates.
[3] *Loc. cit.* p. 31.                          [4] Schneider, p. 379.

thing more than instinct in these actions, which, if
effective, must at any rate be fairly well adjusted to
the presence of real danger. The semi-intelligent Para-
dise-fish makes a rude nest of bubbles, and is said to make
a special provision for the weakly, yet when its young are
old enough to fend for themselves it frequently eats
them.[1] The highest development of nest-building is
found among sticklebacks, to which we have already
referred,[2] and we must not forget the conscientious care
shown by some species of sharks in fixing their eggs in a
safe position. Careful choice of place for oviposition is
indeed characteristic of this grade, and some rough
preparation may go along with it. Among reptiles,
tortoises scrape holes for their eggs, and some measure
of care for them is shown by crocodiles, lizards and
snakes. All these actions, however, along with the nicely
adapted oviposition of many insects, and the choice of
suitable spots by cephalopods, we must set down to
instinct. More interesting are cases of protection attributed to parents in this grade. Thus the cayman is said
to defend its young,[3] and the guana to defend its
mate.[4] Upon the whole, the parental behaviour in
these classes is no higher than we should expect from
the general level of their intelligence. The gregarious-
ness of fish and other animals in this stage would seem
to be purely instinctive, and the alleged instances of
attachment too few to lay stress upon. There is little
if anything of that close attachment to individuals and
many-sided attention to their needs that we find so
conspicuously among birds and mammals.[5]

A broad comparison of the different forms of parental
care, from its germ to its highest development in the
animal world, is given by Schneider.[6] From this it

---

[1] Brehm, VIII. pp. 187, 188.
[2] See Sutherland, I. p. 36, and a good description in Romanes, p. 243
et seq.
[3] Brehm, II. p. 536. [4] Romanes, p. 255.
[5] The summary account of reptile intelligence in Brehm's *Thierleben*
(VII. pp. 24, 25) states explicitly that their care for the young is not
to be compared with that displayed by birds and mammals. It is "meist
wohl nur Folge eines mit der Geschlechtsthätigkeit zusammenhangendes
Reizes"—a significant description. [6] *Op. cit.* p. 372 *et seq.*

would appear that the operations implying attachment
to the young as an individual are peculiar to classes
of animals in which there is independent evidence of the
higher grade of intelligence, *i.e.*, the higher insects, birds,
and mammals. In the lower grades, as among some
molluscs, the eggs are so far attended to as to be
fastened to an appropriate spot.[1] And among some
fish, there are cases in which this is done with a
certain adaptive skill and care.[2] But the feeding of the
living young is confined to the higher classes mentioned ;
and in these classes, and in these exclusively, are found
instances of the more complicated parental care implied
in the training of the young, and their protection at
the risk of the parent.

These facts when put together appear significant. It
is in the classes which appear most intelligent, and therefore most capable of recognising the young, and of
understanding their needs, that we find the rudiments
of an individual attention first appearing ; and we know
that this individual attention, though instinctive in its
basis, is not wholly blind in its operation. Is it too
much to infer that the working of the parental instinct
implies a recognition of the young which is something
more than an automatic reaction, and a desire to satisfy
them which is not wholly blind ?

3. *Animal morality.*

The higher animals lead a social life, not only in the
sense that they congregate together like swarms of
gnats or shoals of fish, but in the sense that they have
social or family relations with one another. In these
relations, acts of mutual help or forbearance are involved,
and it is out of acts of mutual help and forbearance
that morality as we know it among men is built up.
Are we then to attribute morality to animals ? Have
we a right to praise or blame them, to apply to them
epithets carrying a moral significance ? This question, so
far as it is not a question of words, will be found to
resolve itself into the question of the degree of intelligence which we impute to animals. Their behaviour

---

[1] *Op. cit.* p. 267.     [2] *E.g.* sharks ; *op. cit.* p. 273.

has frequently the external character of an act of sympathy, forbearance, courage, self-restraint. The question whether these terms are rightly applicable depends on the question, how much the animals know of what they are about. If we decide to apply them, we do not mean that animals act in obedience to any conception of right or any principle of duty. We mean in final analysis this—that the apparent end of the " social " action for the sake of which we human beings give it its name and assign its character is also its real end. This end of course is concrete and particular, not abstract and universal. The animal shows sympathy not because sympathy is a virtue, but because it sympathises. On the other hand, the show of sympathy is not merely an inherited or habitual method of reaction to a certain kind of stimulus. It is not merely an unthinking response to the cry of a hungry animal or the sight of one that is in distress. It is directed to the relief of the distress, and guided accordingly by what is required therefor. The little monkey, famous through Darwin's description, that rescued its keeper, is justly called brave, for it knew the danger, and overcame its fear. Such bravery requires no knowledge of general principles to make it admirable.

We move in this matter between two sources of fallacy. If we say that consciousness of its purpose is not necessary to make an act praiseworthy, we end by making praise and blame meaningless. If we praise a fly for the unselfishness which it shows in providing for young which it will never see, and of which it cannot be supposed to have the most rudimentary idea[1] we must end by lauding the self-sacrifice of the microbe which ends its own existence by splitting into two or four young microbes. What an excess of parental devotion ! May we not even, while we are about it, call it rather devotion to the welfare of the species and the interests of posterity ? Clearly the purpose must govern praise and blame, or the attribution of any of those qualities which carry a note of praise or blame. We must not go by the result which

---

[1] See Weir, *The Dawn of Reason*, p. 104.

the action is adapted to produce, but by the psychological nature of the adaptation.

But here an opposite fallacy awaits us. If there is to be consciousness of purpose, can moral purpose be something attributed to any animal? Does an animal do a brave or kindly act because it is brave or kindly? The difficulty in this form arises from a misconception of the purpose of an act. A kind act is one that is done for the sake, say, of relieving suffering. It is not one done for the sake of being kindly. That would be a quite different purpose, implying a general principle of action, and the act which it dictates would rather be an act of duty than of kindness. A kindly act in the strictest and most direct sense is one which purposes the help that it gives. It may well be that even of this end the animal has a much less clear conception than the man. He probably cannot realise the feeling of the sufferer, but he sees him in want or danger, and purposes to see him safe or satisfied. There is a distinction of degree here, not of kind. The distinction of kind arises, as we shall see, when in the human world emotions and impulses are named, and their actions and objects generalised into rules, while the rules in turn are subordinated to principles. The man may then act by rule or on principle, and if this is essential to morality, then morality is rightly confined to man. But the rules of human conduct are in turn based on purposes which they do not create, but rather systematise, and thus in a measure remodel. The moral judgment is a reflection on the purpose, and the higher animal, if the view of the preceding chapters is correct, has the purpose, though it has not the judgment upon it. The lower animal, on the contrary, has neither the judgment nor the purpose, but merely the impulse to react which heredity or experience has shaped in a fashion which simulates purpose. If this is granted, it becomes a matter of words where we shall draw the line of " morality."

Perhaps the strongest reason for so drawing it as to include the higher animals is to be derived from the facts of self-control. In lower stages, one instinctive impulse may inhibit another,—fear, for example, may overcome hunger, or, as in the case of Mr. Lloyd Morgan's chicks, the experience of a repulsive taste may operate so as to overcome subsequently the general tendency to peck.   In the higher stage we find action dictated by purposes.   We also find the natural reaction to a sensory stimulus subordinated to some remoter end in which the animal's general habits of life are concerned.   That is to say, we have purpose controlling impulse, and such a form of control is the germ which, as purposes are widened and systematised, develops into the rational self control of human morality. Pathetic stories are well known of dogs impelled to bite under the extreme pain of the dressing of a wound, and checking the impulse, or converting it into a caress.   The self-restraint of a pointer is the result of severe training, but we must not regard it as the work of mere blind habit superseding blind impulse, for as Diezel remarks,[1] the same dog that will refrain from following a hare in his master's presence, will eagerly chase it if unobserved.   The impulse is not extinct, but is controlled by knowledge of results.   There is no need to multiply instances, as the broad fact is generally admitted, and the only question is as to its proper analysis.   I will not here discuss whether the appearance of self-control in the observed instances is itself enough to prove the higher degree of intelligence of which we have been speaking.   It is at least something of a corroboration.

[1] In Brehm's *Thierleben*, II. pp. 144, 145.

# CHAPTER XIV

## THE CONCEPT

1. If the conclusions reached in the preceding chapters are sound, the highest animals have as much capacity for dealing with the practical exigencies of their surroundings as can be attained by an intelligence limited in its scope to the concrete and the practical. Intelligence as we conceive it in this stage is capable of forming what we have called Practical Judgments. Its Impulses are transformed into Desires by consciousness of their objects, and are regulated in action by the perceived relation of means to end. Its experience is no longer of the dim, semi-conscious kind which slowly remodels impulse by inhibiting one tendency and augmenting another. It is an explicit experience of concrete objects with their attributes, and of events in their relations. There is no reason for denying it a certain memory of the past, and there is strong ground for granting it anticipation of the future. In short, at this stage intelligence grasps events in concrete series so far as they are relevant to immediate practical interests.

To understand the next stage of mental evolution, we must inquire in what ascertainable way such an intelligence falls short of ordinary human achievement. We may suitably attack this problem by inquiring first, what precisely the use of language adds to the practical intelligence which we have described. An intelligent dog or ape can, if the evidence which we have quoted is sound, use experience intelligently, and even plan an adjustment of means to ends with a certain measure of inventiveness.

But it cannot describe what it does to us, nor, so far as we know, to another individual of its own species. In many respects, a child of three shows less practical capacity and intelligence than a dog, but it has one great advantage : that it can describe what it is doing, or what it wants, and can learn to do fresh things, not only by imitation, but by having them explained to it. Now, the description of a concrete fact or action proceeds, as we all know, by combinations of simple words each expressing a general idea. The free use of language supposes a stock of general ideas, and description of particular facts is a means whereby those facts are brought into relation with the store of ideas. It is in the existence of such a store at its disposal for use in practice that human intelligence is broadly distinguished from that of the highest animals.

If we grant the highest animals concrete experience, the power of grasping perceived relations and applying them afresh to new and different circumstances, we grant, I believe, enough to explain the most intelligent action which can be attributed to them on any substantial authority. Caution, cunning, and sagacity of the kind of which " animal stories " are so full do not as a rule imply anything more or less than the " concrete experience " that we have described. How much readiness may be shown in the use of past experience, how much cleverness and originality in the adaptation of means to ends, is a question purely of degree. How much of these qualities we are to grant to animals is a question of fact. The evidence by which it is to be decided is at present in a very unsatisfactory condition. But the same general powers with which we have credited the higher animals would explain alleged instances of sagacity and cunning which one would certainly not rely upon to prove the possession of such powers. Nor by going further in this direction, and attributing to animals more of the kind of intelligence in question, do we bring them sensibly nearer to the distinctively human intelligence the specific character of which consists, as we have hinted, in a distinct method of organising or correlating its experiences.

To take an illustration. I have referred to the chimpanzee Consul, at Belle Vue, which made a key for itself by biting a piece of wood till it would fit into the square keyhole. The animal had been taught to use the key. It found that some pieces of wood would act instead, and then, when a piece was of the wrong shape, it bit off the excrescence which hindered it. There is here a clear appreciation based on experience of the relations of one object to another, and what we have called a " spontaneous application " of this experience prompting an act which is in no way imitation, but is cleverly adjusted to overcoming a practical difficulty. All this falls readily within the lines already laid down. But supposing that we could find a monkey that had never seen a key used, and supposing that the circumstances forced us to infer that he had been told all about keys, and how to use them, by a companion; then we should have to revise our view altogether, and admit that monkeys, like men, can forms ideas which are communicable in the absence of the sense impressions to which they relate.

2. If we consider how such communication is effected by human language, we shall be able to measure the difference. If the key were used, not by a man to confine an ape, but by a white man to confine a savage, any savage who had seen it work would be able to make the matter sufficiently clear to his friends by the use of words drawn from the common objects of their experience. If keys were unknown in the tribe, the narrator would fall back on simpler and more general ideas, which he would combine so as to convey a description accurate enough for the purpose, and the white man would soon have to fall back on some more recondite device for the "benevolent" control of his " contract labour."

Now much controversy may be raised on the question whether animals can have " ideas." We have attributed to the higher animals " practical ideas " in the sense of a function which does for them that which practical ideas do for human behaviour. The nature of the inner consciousness that we impute to them cannot of course be matter of direct observation, and our conception of it rests on an analogy which is admittedly not perfect in all respects.

Our present point, however, is that whatever ideas we attribute to an animal, they are ideas of the concrete, the particular object of desire, the relation impressed by past experience. Thus, the chimpanzee may have an idea of the key and the door, and the fruit that he will steal if he can escape. Our difficulty in representing, or at any rate in trying to set forth his presumed state of mind in words, is precisely that in clothing it in words we do what he cannot do. We put it into general terms—rendering the content of a consciousness which is concrete and particular in terms of its elements, which are general and common to many experiences. If the chimpanzee could so break up his perception, analysing it into elements common to the experience of other monkeys which knew nothing of keys, if he could re-combine the several elements as we put general terms together to form the unique meaning of a sentence, and if his companions could follow such a combination—then he would be able to communicate to them the precise nature of an operation which they had never witnessed. He would be able to speak.

3. Language rests on the combination of general terms,[1] and its use therefore implies at least two things. First, the general content, idea, meaning, or whatever we may call it, which the term expresses, must be analysed out of the perceptions of experience ; and secondly, it must be capable of combination, performed apart from the compulsion of perception, with other and similar ideas. In his dealings with the key we have attributed to the monkey a clear consciousness of distinct elements—the key, the hole, the opening of the door, and so forth. These elements and their relations he recognises clearly in the particular case. He has seen them, and in some form he retains the impression. But to be able to communicate the impression, he would have to do something more first. He would have to be able to single out the elements and identify each of them with its class. This could only be done if

---

[1] More strictly, of terms expressing elements common to the experience of speaker and listener. The same individual object may present itself in many experiences and in the experience of many people. The proper name which denotes it is then intelligible to them. But it is not a general term since it refers to a single object, not to a character common to many.

some conception of the class, a conception operating independently of present perception, were already formed, and expressed by a class name. This brings us to the first stage in the formation of language. The process of naming implies, first, that the common elements in different experiences are attended to. There is not very much in this as it stands, because in the lowest types of inference, the common element in different cases is what is operative. If a child calls out " Mam-mie " at sight of its mother, this is a simple reaction to a familiar percept not differing in principle from other reactions, such as that of running towards the mother, or smiling in response to her. The action of the common character or the " universal " is no peculiarity of human intelligence. It begins with intelligence itself.

What is new is perhaps better seen when we turn to the second element in the use of language. If language consisted of baby talk—of exclamations Dad-da! Gee-gee! Puff-puff! at the sight of the appropriate objects—it would not serve as a basis of communication. Baby talk in its first stage has only an element of language, viz., the word. It is a second stage, and in the case of infantile development distinctly later and more difficult to compass, when distinct words are put together, especially when they are put together to express something which is not present to perception. When this can be done, even in the simplest way, it shows that ideas can be detached from their context, and pieced together newly. Even in the narration of an event, this is true of the hearer, though not perhaps necessarily of the narrator. When a child of two comes in and relates some little event of its walk, it may be regarded as merely reviving the impression. But when the child itself understands a story, the higher stage is clearly reached. The different words must each carry a meaning. It is the word which gives rise to the idea, which must therefore be independent of perception. If the monkey could communicate the secret of the key, not only would it have to possess a set of terms to express each point in the description, but the other monkeys would have to be endowed with an intelligence in which each of these words would give rise to a definite idea which they could combine as they followed the story into an intelligible whole. It seems to be this use of the elements of experience as ideas that can be detached[1] from the perceptions in which they are first given, and in their detached state brought at will into any sort of combination which is the psychological basis of language.

4. It may serve to make some of these points clearer if we examine the analogies or approaches to language that we find in the animal world. First of all, then, the cries and other sounds made by animals under the influence of various feelings and emotions are significant in two ways. They express the feelings of the animal in the sense of being physiological results, responses produced by or attendant on those feelings. In this sense they are no more and no less expressive than tears or laughter, or the arching of a cat's back, or the stiffening of her hair. But they are also expressive in a sense which brings them much closer to language. They are "understood" by other members of the same or it may be of other species, in the sense that they act upon other individuals in a determinate manner, which we may presume moreover to be the manner desired by the animal who utters the sounds. Thus the love call of bird or mammal acts as invitation to the opposite sex, the " danger-cluck " of a hen calls the chicks under her wings, and the angry barking of a dog frightens away an intruder. There seems no reason to deny that sounds of this kind are uttered not merely as the reflex effect of the emotional situation, but with intention, as they certainly are uttered with effect. The cries of animals form a true rudimentary language, in so far that they are sounds uttered in order to affect the behaviour of others, and successful in their object. The limitation of this sort of language is that it is concerned with immediate feeling and the appropriate action, expressing the one, and inciting to the other. It is in no way disengaged from the concrete experience of which we have spoken. Its utterances are indeed in a sense " universals." The " danger-cluck," for instance, is a sound uniformly evoked by circumstances differing in-

---

[1] Or, as psychologists call them, "free" ideas.

definitely in detail, but agreeing in that they are terrifying.
But they are utterances which only concern the present,
the objects or circumstances immediately perceived or
desired.

The function of the instinctive cry may be performed
among domestic animals by the spoken word. The dog's
name called out in a tone of reproof, approval, or
exhortation, as the case may be, excites him to appropriate
actions. The parrot goes a step further, and undoubtedly
uses words with intention. Of a learned grey parrot, it
is said :—

> "As soon as the dinner bell rang he called the waitress louder
> and louder until she appeared. If a knock came at the door, he
> said, 'Come in,' but was never deceived by any one in the room.
> If he saw preparation made for uncorking a bottle, he made the
> noise long before the cork was out. . . . When the green parrot
> standing near him screamed, he first tried to quiet her with a
> reproving 'Pst!' but if that did not avail he called out in a loud
> voice, 'Hush, hush, you!' He loved to talk to himself late in
> the evening, and regularly closed his monologue with the words,
> 'Good night, good night, Jacky.'"[1]

In one sense, probably the parrot does not understand
the meaning of what he says. He knows "good night"
or "come in" as sounds appropriate to certain occasions,
and, it may be, as producing certain effects on others.
But there is, I imagine, no reason to suppose that he can
analyse, that he knows the meanings of good and of night
taken severally, so that he might at need construct such a
phrase for himself. Without such knowledge, it seems
clear that the words are only a more refined and subtle
development due to education of the cry or scream, which
also is a definite sound used appropriately and with
effect.

Closely analogous to parrot talk is the speech of a child
about, and for some time after, the close of the first year.
Before that time, syllables really meaningless are uttered
often with many vain repetitions. This babblement
seems to represent the really instinctive element in language.
Darwin noted the syllable "Da" pronounced clearly but

[1] Groos, *Play of Animals*, p. 204.

without meaning by his child at five months.[1] The same child, like other children at a later date, invented words to express his wants.[2] Indeed, Darwin places the invention of words before the imitation of words spoken by others in the development of speech. I have noticed that the sounds " Dad, dad, dad," " Mam, mam, mam," are often repeated long before they are used with any meaning, but how far this is due to the child's hearing the sounds, it is impossible to say.[3] Preyer[4] gives a very clear account of the linguistic powers of his child at this age.

" Of these syllables [a number of meaningless sounds already used by the child], *na-na* regularly denotes a desire, and the arms are stretched out in connection with it ; *mama* is referred to the mother perhaps in the fifty-fourth week, on account of the pleasure she shows at the utterance of these syllables, but they are also repeated mechanically without any reference to her ; *atta* is uttered now and then at going away, but at other times also. His joy—*e.g.*, at recognising his mother at a distance—the child expresses by crowing sounds, which have become stronger and higher than they were, but which cannot be clearly designated ; the nearest approach to representation of them is *ăhijă*. Affirmation and negation may already be recognised by the tone of voice alone. The signification of the cooing and the grunting sounds remains the same. The former indicates desire of food ; the latter the need of relieving the bowels. As if to exercise the vocal cords, extraordinarily high tones are now produced, which may be regarded as signs of pleasure in his own power. An imperfect language has thus already been formed imperceptibly, although no single object is as yet designated by a sound assigned to it *alone*."

The understanding of words was somewhat more advanced, but Preyer notes that the word " give," for example, " operates almost like a reflex stimulus, ' mechanically.' "[5] He taught his child some little tricks in response to certain questions, etc., and just like a dog, whose education is imperfect, the little fellow would

---

[1] *Mind*, Vol. II. p. 292.

[2] *Ib.* p. 293. Taine (*Mind*, Vol. I. p. 253) also suggests that the effect of example and education is to call a child's attention to the sounds it has already made, *i.e.*, so that it selects sounds appropriately.

[3] Taine (*loc. cit.* p. 254) notices that " papa " is used without meaning at first, and is associated with the father later.

[4] Preyer, II. p. 114.    [5] P. 120.

occasionally get confused, and substitute one response for another. On the whole, we may say that there is a well-marked stage in a child's development, falling roughly between the twelfth and eighteenth months, in which it responds to certain. perceptions with a word, and to certain words with an act. At this stage it cannot be placed above the parrot, nor on the side of understanding above the dog. It is well to mark out this stage in which isolated words are clearly developed from the later stage in which words are put together to form language proper.

The use of language at the level which we have been considering does not as such rise above the stage in which, whether by inheritance, or as the result of experience, a sound or a sign produces a certain reaction. It becomes Purposive only when used with intention and even this would not raise it above the level of the Practical Judgment. It may be strongly questioned whether there is any evidence of the communication of complex facts among animals. Thus, there is a well-known class of dog-stories in which, for example, a little dog is mauled by an enemy, and gets his big friend to come and avenge him. Mr. Lloyd Morgan[1] relates such a story of a little dog and his big friend Boxer. As the story is told, it gives the impression that the little dog must have given a dramatic recital of his wrongs, but Mr. Lloyd Morgan thinks, I have no doubt rightly, that all the little dog said was "Come!" In other words, the little dog was able to incite Boxer to follow him, and then to attack the enemy. Mr. Romanes[2] directly observed a similar communication between two Skye terriers, and interprets it in the same way. Similarly, in the numerous games of animals in which somewhat subtle and complex mutual understanding is involved,[3] we need not postulate any explicit interchange of ideas. One dog will entice another to play by taking up the appropriate attitude ;[4] one action leads to another; the playful mood

---

[1] *Animal Life and Intelligence*, p. 344.
[2] *Animal Intelligence*, p. 445.
[3] See Groos, *op. cit.*, p. 124 *et seq ;* also 225, 245, 253, for numerous instances among birds and mammals.
[4] See, for instance, a good description in Groos, p. 124.

is readily aroused by the appropriate stimulus, and partly by instinct, partly by training, the young animals scuffle and race and make pretended bites, according to the rules of the game. Finally, a cat or a dog can make us understand well enough within certain limits what it wants. Without saying, " I want to go out," a cat will make it quite clear by stages. She will attract attention by mewing and rubbing against one's legs. Then, looking up, one sees from her face that she wants something. As soon as she sees that her master is attentive, she will stroll in a delicately insinuating manner towards the door, looking round to see if she is followed, and, if not, coming back again, and going to and fro from the door to her master. Finally, if she does not get her way at once, she will sit before the door with a gaze half reproachful and half resigned, but wholly suggestive, towards the handle. And as soon as she gets the door opened, she darts out without the " thank you " which a good-natured dog would be sure to express.

We shall probably not be far wrong if we take this proceeding as typical of animal language. The cat knows in the concrete what she wants, but she has no terms common to her and her master into which she can reduce it, and so make it clear in its completeness at once. What she can do is to impel her master to take the successive steps required, one by one. Her " language " is thus an adaptation or employment of concrete experience and the practical judgment. It is not an analysis of the concrete into its elements whereby it is brought into connection with a world of ideas common to two interlocutors.[1]

---

[1] It is possible that by a combination of sensori-motor suggestions a specially intelligent animal might be made virtually to understand a complex situation. Such, for example, would be the case with the dog which, according to Dr. Wesley Mills (*op. cit.* p. 33) would fetch at command any one of six different articles. A still stronger case is that of the dog which, on the authority of Mr. Bastian (*The Brain as an Organ of Mind*, p. 315), would fetch home the particular cow named to it, or keep cattle in an assigned part of a field. These cases seem to illustrate the beginnings of a transition to a higher stage, but they are clearly developments of the process already described. The order to fetch, *e.g.*, excites a set of motor impulses which the name " hat " or " stick " defines by attaching it to a familiar object.

If higher developments of communication are to be found in the animal

5. The same results may be put in a slightly different way by saying that language among animals, so far as is known, and among children at the word-reflex stage, does not assert facts, but is either exclamatory or hortatory. With children, the word which is at first an exclamation or a call becomes converted into a word-sentence during, we may perhaps say, the latter half of the second year. Preyer recognised the first spoken judgment in the case of his child in the twenty-third month. The judgment referred to the milk which the child was drinking, and consisted of the word *Heiss!* That this was a judgment meaning "The milk is too hot," rather than an exclamation, could of course only be determined by the circumstances and manner of the child. But the circumstances are often such as to leave no doubt upon the matter. Thus, I have seen a little girl come down stairs, display a new dress, and say, "Nannie," by way of conveying that Nannie (nurse) had put it on. But a decided advance in articulation, mental as well as verbal, is shown when two or more words are for the first time put together.[1] Preyer [2] found the first significant combination during the twenty-fourth month, in the command or wish, "Haim, mimi," which is nursery-German for "I would like to go home and drink milk." A month later, the same child

world, it will probably be among apes. Their chatter is said to contain more distinct sounds than that of any other animals, if we except the artificial case of birds trained to talk ; but, apart from the question of intelligence, it may be doubted if they have sufficient nicety of perception to found a language. Indeed, Mr. George Jennison writes me : "In four years' work with chimpanzees we could never notice any sounds not marking distinct emotions,—pleasure, pain, anger. Almost any chimpanzee will respond to the 'pleasure' cry."

As to the social Hymenoptera, Lubbock's experiments (*Ants, Bees and Wasps*, pp. 275-8, and 311, 312) are unfavourable to communication among Bees and Wasps, while with regard to Ants, they appear to indicate the kind of communication we have described as sensori-motor (see p. 164). The further experiments described (pp. 172-177) do not really seem to modify this result. Bethe (*Ameisen*, pp. 51-54) throws doubt even on Lubbock's somewhat modest inferences, and attributes all the apparent communication of ants to a marvellous co-ordination of smells with motor impulses. But Bethe is defending a thesis.

[1] I mean, of course, words that already have a separate use. An independent-minded little girl of my acquaintance used the phrase Pitda (put me down) almost before any other, but this was of course a mere imitation of the total sound, not a combination made by the child herself.        [2] *Op. cit.* p. 151.

attained the dignity of a five-word sentence, exhibiting its
" first attempt to relate a personal experience—" mimi
atta teppa, papa oï (Milk gone [on] carpet, Papa [said]
Fie).[1] It was in the eleventh month that this child first
clearly used a word (*atta*, which appears to be the German
equivalent of the English nursery *ta-ta*) with significance.
It is in the twenty-fifth that it first puts as many as five
words together to describe a past event.  The length of
the interval, during which the child is rapidly developing
in every way, may serve to indicate the difficulty and importance of the transition from appropriate exclamation to
articulate assertion of fact.

Listening to a little boy in the stage to which we have
now traced Preyer's child, chattering happily to himself as
he played, I have often noticed how his talk consisted of a
running commentary on what he was doing.  For example,
if he was building a station, he would be saying, " Now
put dat dar, man go dar, puff puff come in dar," and so
on, suiting in each case the word to the act, as though he
were practising the art of simple description, which indeed,
in an unconscious way no doubt, he was doing.  As this
process advances, the child gradually builds up a true
world of " detachable " ideas, detachable because they are
applied in all manner of combinations, and serve as a link
between one percept and another, and between himself and
his hearer.

6. When an element common to many experiences is
not merely recognised when it appears, but (1) is thought
of without being perceived, and (2) is capable of being
combined in thought with other elements, it becomes a
concept of general meaning and application.  To be a
general concept, the element must be something for consciousness apart from its perceptual setting, and it must be
applicable to a different setting.  The concept grows up
by a movement in which synthesis and analysis interact.
The most important form of synthesis concerned is
comparison by which analysis is guided.  Now, analysis
of a kind may be imputed to the practical judgment, in
which there is undoubtedly a certain selection of the

[1] *Op. cit.* p. 155.

related elements within the complex situation of an experience. If a cat, for example, sees that the lifting of a latch has to do with the opening of a door, it is clear that it has singled out certain elements in the perception, it has distinguished the latch from the rest of the door. There is, however, no reason to think that analysis in this stage goes beyond the point of distinguishing one concrete object or actual event from other objects or events. The handle is still an object of perception : it might theoretically occupy the whole of a perception. Its movement is an event seen, and seen to be followed by another event, the opening of the door. So far as it singles out objects or events in this way, analysis seems to consist in a movement of attention towards one percept rather than others that are within the range of the organs of sense at a certain time.

In the formation of general conceptions, on the other hand, analysis breaks up perception in a different manner. It not merely isolates one object or one series of events from others, but dissects an object or event into component elements. The child, for example, as it examines the latch, might measure its length and breadth, or learn that it was a lever moving on a fulcrum in accordance with certain mechanical laws. These properties of the latch are no longer concrete percepts. They are certainly elements in a perception, but unlike the latch, which conceivably might fill perceptual consciousness to the exclusion of anything else, they cannot any one of them be given in perception except as elements in or attributes of the whole which they characterise. When analysis breaks up a percept in this manner, it follows a new line of cleavage. In the previous case it merely divided a complex set of percepts into components, each of which was as good a percept as the whole. Now it breaks up the percept into elements which in perception are mere attributes of the whole, and dependent thereon. The object is always concrete. It is the attribute of the object or a relation in which it stands that is general. To distinguish such an aspect or relation as a quality of the concrete whole is to form a concept applicable equally to other concrete objects. In other words, generality rests on the attributive relation, the fact that concrete wholes are qualified by attributes. The concept is the thought-function which has mastered this attributive relation, and therefore can construct what is not perceived, nor ever has been perceived, as a whole. The analytic movement which we have thus traced is under another aspect also a movement of synthesis. Analysis rests on comparison, which is an act of synthesis, since it brings different experiences into relation ; and gains in explicitness, *pari passu* with the common character on which the comparison turns. And not only does the concept rest on a synthesis, but its essential function is to make a further synthesis possible. It must not be regarded as a kind of mechanical abstraction which takes an attribute out of its surroundings and hangs it up alone in mid air. The general attribute is nothing if it is not understood as qualifying objects, and in its use in thought—and explicitly so in the universal judgment— it must be recombined with other elements of reality. It is the power of entering into diverse combinations while still recognised as the same content that constitutes generality. And recombination does not mean that the two elements are placed side by side, but that they are fused or applied to one another in a certain definite manner. The new combination, in short, is in a general way parallel to that from which the elements were originally taken by analysis. There is thus in the free usage of detached concepts a synthetic process always at work articulating what has been disarticulated by analysis. To make the general concept a reality, the mind must be able not merely to detach fragments of its experience, but to follow that articulation of reality whereby attributes qualify substances, enter into relations, are resolvable in turn into more elementary attributes, and are united by manifold and interwoven affinities. This articulation is the broad basis of the conception and the judgment, and analysis and synthesis are the processes by which the mind comes to understand and track it out.

When we say that analysis is guided by comparison, we do not mean that there is always an explicit mental synthesis of two distinct cases before the common element can be selected and named. Such synthesis certainly exists, and is expressed in the Comparative Judgment (Jem is as tall as Jack. These two ribbons do not match). But explicit comparison is not essential in the lowest stages of the evolution of the concept. It is enough that similarity is operative. Now similarity, the presence of a common element in several experiences, is also operative in the stage of concrete experience. The difference is that, not necessarily the similarity relation, but the common element which is the basis of the similarity is in this higher stage made explicit. Here, as throughout mental evolution, what is before operative without being recognised is now recognised, and is more effectively operative than before. The practical experience of the lower stage is really a form of argument from particulars to particulars. Based on a resemblance, the foundation of which is not clearly brought before consciousness, it is loosely and unsystematically applied according as the resemblance happens or does not happen to strike the mind. When the point of resemblance is analysed out, and a general proposition is founded thereon, we get, in substitution for this loose and haphazard procedure, a fixed rule, stating what we can and what we cannot infer from our data. As the "major premiss" becomes explicit, inference becomes exact.

It will be seen that the formation of the general concept implies no new "faculty." It merely brings into clear consciousness the common element in diverse experiences which was already at work in guiding practical inference. And in so doing it relies on the analytic movements of attention which were equally necessary at the earlier stage. But it does imply that analysis has taken a new turn, that it is applied to distinguishing the qualities or attributes of things, and it does bring into consciousness a new kind of relation. The characteristic affinities of things form the basis of the whole world of ideas, with its generalisations, qualifications, definitions, and classifications. These affinities in a humble sphere are operative in guiding practical inference. But that stage is most easily understood if we conceive the mind as actively occupied with the concrete circumstances in which it is placed, and the series of events with which it has to deal. Affinities between this series and others influence the mind in its choice of means to the practical end, but the affinities are operative without being brought before consciousness. It is this cross-relation between the different series of events, the affinities and differences which unite and separate them, that the general conception and the universal judgment bring out. In other words, we have reached a higher stage of correlation, in which a new relation is brought into consciousness, and one more of the operative factors no longer merely influences the mind, but is recognised as an influence. We are a step further on in bringing the factors of knowledge into an articulate system.

7. The general meaning—the reference to a class or to Reality at large—is potential rather than explicit in the Concept. It is made explicit in the Universal Judgment. The function of this judgment is to bring the contents of two general conceptions into relation with each other, whether as substance and attribute, cause and effect, or in any other way. " Animal " is a general conception. "All animals possess consciousness," a Universal Judgment, true or false. The universal relation is asserted as holding good apart from any special circumstances or any particular perception. Its reference is to Reality at large, and it asserts that wherever we find the one term there we shall find the other which is predicated of it. This is often expressed by saying that it attributes one thing to another " as such." In our example, the fact that an organism is an animal is taken to be of itself, or " as such," a sufficient ground for crediting it with con- sciousness. The universal deals with general terms, and attributes one to the other without taking anything else into account. It thus enables us to go beyond our own experience, and build up a " world of ideas." [1]

---

[1] We are not of course to suppose the rigidly defined universal of science common to all human thought. The universal begins in the form of the rough and ready rule of common sense, to which common sense itself tacitly allows many exceptions and limiting conditions. But from the first rough rule onwards, the assumption is the same, that one general term may be used as a basis for inferring another. The conditions

8. It follows that the true universal is a relation which is not merely actual, but necessary.    At least, it is grounded on necessity.    We may say that a thing is so because we see it, or because it must be so.    In the first case our judgment is based on perception, and ought not to go beyond perception.    If we go beyond perception legitimately, it is because of some connection that we have reason to suppose between the terms of our judgment, some necessity which brings them into relation.    Hence we can always convert the universal into a hypothetical judgment, and instead of All a is b, All murderers are hanged, say, If a thing is a, then it is b—if a man commits a murder, he is hanged.

This necessity is clearly recognised in human thought where two or more propositions are connected by means of a "then," "therefore," "because," or whatever it may be.    The ordinary combination of a single premiss (the minor premiss of formal logic) and a conclusion is, in fact, a sort of translation of the universal into the particular case. The universal All sugar is sweet, is, so to say, incarnate in the inference "I have put plenty of sugar into this, so you will find it sweet."    The Syllogism of formal logic writes down the universal in its abstract dress as its "major premiss," and follows it up with a minor and conclusion which merely repeat it in its concrete form.    It thus achieves a wholly unreal form of thought, a form corresponding to no actual process.    None the less, it sets out what is implied in the actual process in which consciousness advances from a single premiss to the conclusion.

This advance, which we now see to be the application of the necessity contained in the universal judgment, has its verbal expression in a connecting particle.    Here again we find a process operative at an earlier stage becoming recognised in consciousness.    From the first germ of intelligence onwards, the mind is of course influenced

---

limiting a universal truth are themselves universals.    The ideal universal takes all these conditions into its scope, thereby evolving from a single judgment into what is really a system of judgments.    Common sense is apt to leave the conditions unexpressed, and scarcely distinguishes the strict from the Approximate Universal—the judgment of general validity. Its "General truths" rest on the same principle as the scientific Universal but carry out its conditions less fully.

by the connection between one experience and another. The necessity whereby A follows upon B leads it when it perceives B to prepare for A. But in the stage of concrete experience, this, we may believe, is an influence which operates without being formed into an object of consciousness. In the stage now under consideration, this influence, always operative, becomes a sufficiently clear content of consciousness to be expressed by a word. Thus in the recognition of necessary connection by the Universal Judgment, we have once more a mental achievement which consists in forming into a distinct content of consciousness an element which at an earlier stage is operative without apparently being understood by the mind on which it operates.

9. A no less important aspect of the Universal Judgment is its reference to an indefinite number of cases, or, if we prefer so to put it, to reality and experience as a whole. This aspect of the universal has indeed been something of a stumbling block to logicians from Aristotle downwards. There is something of a paradox in a form of thought taken to refer to a number of cases of which no one is specified, and the vast majority may be utterly unknown. A sense of the paradox has led many writers to refuse any meaning to the universal as " taken in extension."[1] They have failed to allow for a certain unavoidable artificiality in the distinctions of Logic which seeks to appraise functions of thought that cannot wholly be understood in isolation from other functions to which they are related. The universal judgment is not so much a reference to an indefinite number of particulars as a rule of reference. As a thought-function, it needs, in this respect, completion by the " minor premiss," or again, it forms the keystone of the arch in Judgments of Comparison and Classification. But however incomplete in isolation, its function in thought is (*a*) to sum up the result of a mass of experience in the shape of that which pervades the whole whether as a continuous identity or as

[1] This is the point common to Aristotle, *Post Anal.*, I. 1, and Mill, *Logic*, II. ch. 3. It led Mr. Bradley (*Logic*, p. 228) and Hegel (*Wiss. der Log.* Part II. Werke, Bd. V. p. 146) to find a contradiction in the Syllogism " taken in extension."

a common character, and (*b*) thereby to form a guide in dealing with a further mass of experience to come. Under both aspects it brings the action of the moment into explicit relation not merely with the immediate circumstances or the particular end, but with that which is of enduring significance in the order of the world.

Under this aspect, once again, we find the universal rendering explicit influences which have already been operative without being expressly formulated. In both the lower stages of intelligence, the influence of often repeated experience appears in ways too manifold and too obvious to need mentioning in detail. Indirectly the same influence may be traced even in pre-intelligent organic reaction—since even if we exclude any direct transmission of "acquired qualities," it is the broad average result of ancestral experience that goes to determine the constitution of the individual, and his reflexes and instincts thereby. Thus, in an indirect, cumbersome, and imperfect manner, with much loss of life and efficiency, the actions of animals in the lower stages become shaped by the preponderant results of great masses of experience, and fitted to conform roughly not merely to momentary ends, but to the general plan of their lives. When the results of experience can be succinctly summed up and communicated, it would seem that this process should become far more speedy and effective. There is evidently more scope for tradition and training ; less necessity for perfection of instinct ; less elimination ; less waste of life ; less time and energy lost in learning. One sees how it is that with the growth of intelligence in human life, the ready-made perfect instinct tends to disappear, while yet the power of maintaining life increases.

10. Thus the " world of ideas " or of universals, which is generally, and I believe rightly, taken as the distinctive property of humanity, is built up by a special application of that power of correlating its experiences which is the universal property of mind. But the correlation follows a different line and rests on a more articulate form of experience. Experiences are now correlated not merely in

their order of time or space, and in subservience to immediate practical interests, but upon the basis of their affinities, and the more remote connections that follow therefrom. To arrive at these affinities involves a measure of analysis and comparison whereby the character of an experience, or any portion of its character, is detached from its setting or surroundings, and becomes free to enter into new combinations, or conceptions. The combinations so formed may be taken as mere products of the imagination, or they may be held to express general truths, or they may form rules of conduct. In any case, they go to make up the world of ideas. In the second case—we need not here discuss the difficult logical implications of the third—they form judgments held to be possibly, probably, or certainly true, and affirming relations as actual, contingent, or intrinsically necessary. Such judgments sum up in general terms the results of experience, and apply to the future with a reference that is no less general. By tracing back experiences to their underlying affinities, human thought is made capable of grasping what is permanent and common to masses of experience, and of ordering action towards comprehensive ends. It is set free from the limitation of immediate surroundings and the pressure of felt wants, and there is no longer any permanent limit to the scope of its reference, or to the field within which it is able to bring the chaos of experience into harmony and co-ordination.

# CHAPTER XV

## THE PRODUCTS OF CONCEPTUAL THOUGHT

1. *The Self.*

The universal is not the only form in which experiences can be massed. Its function in this respect is fulfilled, and fulfilled more definitely, by the Collective Concept—which unites many individuals into a whole, and less obviously, but no less certainly, by the Individual concept, as distinguished from the Particular. The Individual person and even the Individual thing is an object not confined to a single experience, but common to many, and probably not even exhibiting its whole character until a long series of experiences is accomplished. To have a conception of one's own Self, one must be aware of a certain identity running through the mass of past experiences, and inferentially prolonged into the future. The genesis of such a conception seems therefore to depend on the capacity for organising experiences in the mass on the basis of their relations and affinities, the particular relation which is the basis of this conception being that of permanence or persistent identity. And the case of the Self is typical. Generally, the Individual and the Collective Concept resemble the true Universal in detachment from any single sense experience, and in that they group together a mass of experiences on the basis of a common element pervading them all. This element, which in the true universal is a common quality or character, is in the individual or collective concept rather some kind of persistent identity, or causal interconnection.

Concepts of all these kinds, therefore, are formed by the same methods of correlation applied to different material, and are thus to be referred to one and the same stage in the growth of mind.    Viewed as a correlation of life's experiences, it will appear that the conception of self must always be in varying degrees incomplete.    " Know thyself " was a precept of the gods, a precept therefore which man cannot adequately fulfil.    It might be regarded as fulfilled sufficiently for human purposes if we had a clear grasp of the essential structure of that being that unrolls itself in the personal actions and experiences, and true self-interest would be to act conformably to the permanent requirements of that structure.[1]    In actual life this is not realised.    Indeed, at first sight, the actual man is so inconsistent in his different capacities that we often speak of him as having two or more personalities— and psychology gives to popular language a certain sanction.    In a sense, it is scientifically true that the business man, who has spent the day in besting a rival, is not the same person as the father who comes home to romp with his children.    The outward and visible semblance is the same, but within it there are two quite different masses of thought, emotion, and will, each forming an interconnected system by itself, yet standing in no logical or moral relation with the other.    When the cleavage becomes extreme, we speak of " double personality," of alienation or insanity.    But the germ of this sort of madness is in all of us.

If we could carry psycho-physical research far enough, we should presumably find an ultimate unity in which even these extreme differences come together.    Meanwhile it remains true for practical purposes, that is to say, for the scientific evaluation of self-knowledge, that the practical self, the self which a man considers when he is thinking about his " interest," is rather a great fragment of his being than his being's whole.    A business man in his office has nothing to do with " sentiment," but looks at things " as a business man."    At home he may be entirely swayed by the

---

[1] Cf. the famous description of true and false self love in Aristotle, *Ethics*, IX. ch. 8.

"sentiment" that elsewhere he disparages. Between his home and his business there is probably the ultimate bond of connection that the one is maintained by the other, but this does not mean that the principles or ideas of the one in any great degree dominate the details of the other. Practically a man's action in any capacity is guided mainly not by what he is in other respects, but by what he is in that capacity.

What is true of self-knowledge applies of course equally to self-interest. The self-interest which guides a man's action can only be the interest of the self as the man conceives it at the time. A man might act in the interest of his true self, if he knew his true self. But for practical purposes "enlightened self-interest" ordinarily means the subordination of momentary considerations to the broad ends or the general plan by which a man is dominated in one or other of his different capacities. It seems necessary to say this much in order to avoid exaggerating the co-ordination of conduct which the conception of the self may be held to introduce into life. In its theoretical completeness, enlightened self-interest would mean the subordination of each action to the whole system of purposes that make up the self. This would also of course involve that the experiences and the impulses of the personality were brought into a system. To understand how far self-knowledge would take us in the intelligent co-ordination of action, we may usefully throw this ideal or "limiting conception" into contrast with the fragmentary co-ordinations of the "practical judgment." Here there is combination of means to an immediate end. There may even be the preference of one "end" over another, as when a dog, after wavering between the principles of obedience and the impulse to hunt, comes at last reluctantly to his master's call. In this case of "self-control" we see the dog's permanent habits overcoming a momentary impulse based on a deep-seated instinct, and we might say without much straining that the dog's "truer nature," founded on his fidelity, conquers the mutinous impulse which threatens its harmony. But it would be a long step from this admission to the suggestion that the dog on his part has any concept of the self, any broad principles or any conception of his own permanent welfare to the test of which he brings his action. No doubt the broad tendencies of his nature operate unconsciously within the dog as they operate for the most part unconsciously within us. But we can also, with varying degrees of accuracy, understand and formulate them, and this there is no evidence that the dog can do. Thus, so far as the conscious co-ordination of action is concerned, the Practical Judgment, resting on concrete experience alone without the power of summing up masses of experience into general conceptions, is limited to the adjustment of means to a desired end, or the preference of one end over another. The judgment of Enlightened Self-Interest in its theoretical perfection would subordinate all immediate and even remoter ends to the requirements of the self as a whole. In actual life, it guides its action rather by certain broad purposes, each of which fills a great part of life, but which are not brought into such systematic harmony with one another that we can speak of the whole life as forming a rational unity.[1] Just as masses of past experience are summed up in the form of universal judgments, so the broad purposes of life, masses as we may say of future experiences, are summed up in the conception of the self and of the various broad ends of life that fall within it ; and actual conduct is correlated with both.

2. With the conception of Self comes the conception of other Selves. Indeed, as many thinkers have been fond of insisting, the two conceptions are in constant interaction. We form our conceptions of others from ourselves, and of ourselves from others. It follows that the conception of Personality in another will tend to be of the same broken and partial character as the conception of Self. We know one person merely as. a " good fellow " at the club, another purely as a professional colleague. Even our nearest and dearest, whom we think we know through and through, we find, tragically, to be " strangers yet." As are the

---

[1] It is perhaps superfluous to point out the obverse truth, that the cheapest way of approaching unity is to starve the self by suppressing all sides of it save one, as, *e.g.*, by consistent asceticism, or sensualism, or even professionalism.

limitations of self-interest as a practical guide, so are the limitations of interest in others.  The unity of the species, of society within the species, and of many closer organisations, of which the family is the chief, within society imply a varying measure of interest benevolent or malevolent in others.  Confining ourselves to benevolence —a serious restriction in the world as we know it—we might repeat all that we have said of the direction of conduct by and towards the interest of Self, substituting for self another or others.  Action may be guided by the requirements of another personality as well as our own, and is so in the case of all actions of affection, benevolence, and social duty other than those which spring from the impulse of the moment.  The relatively permanent happiness as distinguished from the temporary needs or pleasure of another is the end of sympathetic or social action at this stage of intelligence.

This development of "altruism" is an elaboration of impulses which are already well developed among the higher animals.  In one sense indeed many birds and mammals recognise the personality of others in a very thoroughgoing manner, since they give undoubted signs of permanent and deep-seated attachment to individuals.  This does not necessarily imply, however, that they conceive the individual as a personality in the sense explained above in dealing with the self.  It means that the sight of the beloved mate or child or master rejoices them, that absence of the loved one depresses them, and stimulates them to find him.  If we were to look for a conception of personality as something that persists and develops, we should look for it first, perhaps, in the training of the young.  Such training undoubtedly appears among the more intelligent birds and mammals, but it would seem to be limited to three methods.  There is first, punishment, the slap which a mother ape or even a cat gives to the young one which transgresses.  This, if not merely impulsive, is sufficiently explained by the desire of the mother to check the young one in doing something immediately harmful. There is secondly the method of stimulating the young to exercise its faculties, as by bringing it its natural prey to play with, and there is, thirdly, the method of example which the young is encouraged to imitate, as seen in the practice of those Divers which hold a fish before their young and then dive with it.[1] These methods seem to follow very naturally from the parental instincts as developed by concrete experience. The direct delight[2] in seeing the young ones do things may as readily be conceived to be a part of the parental instinct among animals as it certainly is among men. The means used are simple adaptation to immediate practical ends all working on an instinctive basis. We can hardly credit the mother-cat with a conception of the future career of her kitten as a famous mouser or as a household pet. Nor can we legitimately impute to her that vicarious self-control which would subordinate the immediate gratification of the kitten to the training of its character. It is to be feared that whenever the mother-cat's action has the appearance of such a refinement, it is rather to her own comfort than to her ideas of moral training that we must look for explanation. But these conceptions of permanent welfare and character are the root ideas of human education, and follow naturally from the conception of personality.[3]

3. If the conception of personality in Self and others is dependent on the power of grasping masses of experience in comprehensive and inter-related conceptions, it seems hardly necessary to argue that the same thing is true of organised political society. Human society probably in all forms, and certainly in the most primitive known, rests on a mass of observances based on tradition, and providing rules of conduct that continually thwart hereditary impulse or instinct. Rights and duties in relation to property, to sex, to a parent, to a chief, form a system, and, as social life develops, a system so complex as to be difficult even for the trained reasoner to apply consistently. The finer differentiation of duty in the several relations of

---

[1] See Schneider, p. 375.     [2] *Ib.*, p. 376.
[3] Whether such a conception and the type of education founded on it is universal among mankind, we do not here inquire. The foundation is laid in the power of forming conceptions. What is built on it may vary indefinitely, and extreme cases may vary down to zero. The savage conception of personality is no doubt extremely rude and confused.

life, though inherited tendency is its foundation throughout, far outruns in subtle complexity any possible achievement of instinct.

One hesitates to dogmatise about animal societies until
they have been more thoroughly studied, but what we know
of them goes to show that the division of labour—the
most notable form of social differentiation in the animal
world—is based, in the cases where it is most elaborate,
on differences of structure. This is conspicuously the
case with the Social Hymenoptera, where the distribution
of functions between fertile females, infertile females, and
males is the basis of the whole order. The further
differentiations which appear among ants as between
" workers " and " warriors," " mistresses " and " slaves,"
are also directly correlated with differences of physical
structure. The division of labour in these cases would
thus seem in its main lines to follow rather than to over-
ride the inherited tendencies to which physical structures
give rise. On the other hand, the rudimentary division
that we find among the higher vertebrates is not sufficient
to justify us in speaking of a social " system " at all.
The habit of fixing sentinels is the typical case. Probably
we must ascribe this to a kind of tradition as much as to
heredity, the habit once formed being kept up in each
flock or herd from generation to generation, by the simple
practice of forcing the younger members as they grow up
to take their turn at watching while the others feed. It
is a special adjustment to the needs of a gregarious life,
part instinctive, part traditional, part, very likely, intelligent. One such adjustment, however, does not make a
system with a complex ramification of duties. Lastly, the
submission to a chief, which we find conspicuous among
apes, seems to be of the same habitual character. The
most active and capable member of a troop tends to
acquire a certain primacy. Here again there seems to be
something of habit, and perhaps something of intelligence,
operating on the hereditary tendency to follow and
imitate. If there were evidence that the chieftainship
became hereditary, and that apes would tolerate and
grovel before a *roi fainéant*, we should have to consider

anew whether the ape should not be put on a level with *Homo sapiens*.

Human beings, from the lowest known levels upwards, live in organised societies, resting on a complexity of relations maintained from generation to generation by oral or written tradition. It is this complexity of organisation in which many distinct and on the surface conflicting obligations can be held together, which appear to distinguish human society and human morality from the social life and morality of animals. It would be superfluous to dwell on the way in which this complexity increases in civilised and particularly in modern civilised life. The relations of a man to his family, his neighbours, his town, his profession, class, country, church, his own moral consciousness, and his duty to humanity, involve him in a network of obligations about which the surprising thing is that the cases of conflicting duty are so few. Among the higher animals we seem to find traces of the personal, family, and social impulses which form the basis of human life and society. But to work these out into an elaborate system in which every instinct is pruned and reshaped by a mass of social observances, customs or laws, would seem impossible without the machinery of general rules, definitions, and exceptions provided by conceptual thought. If moral impulse exists among the higher animals, morality as a rule of life comes into being only with the conceptual order of thought, and hand in hand with a regular political society.

4. It should be added that with the power of working with detached ideas the whole world of imagination may be said to come into being. There is, if not art, at least the potentiality of art as soon as there is free play of ideas in detachment from practical interests. So certain does this seem to be, that the existence of anything resembling Art among any species of animals might of itself be taken as sufficient evidence of the capacity of that species for conceptual thinking.[1] Science and the technical arts rest

---

[1] The analogue of Art among the lower animals is play in which imagination, if it can be said to exist, takes the concrete form of immediate frolicsome action.

on the same basis. Though science arises out of and remains indirectly connected with practical interests, these are of course not the interests of immediate action to which the "practical judgment" is limited. It is only when men get interested in needs that go beyond the particular purpose in hand, and begin to generalise and reflect upon them, that they evolve out of their practical skill a body of technical rules that can be handed on and developed. Finally, like art and science, religion is a system of conceptions built up by the aid of imagination out of inward and outward experiences. We do not here inquire into the historical origin of religion. It is sufficient to note that in all its forms its practical efficacy and real meaning in the life of a people rest on the adequacy and faithfulness with which it clothes, in a form which appeals to the feelings, the experience, particularly the moral experience, of the people who profess it. Religion is one form in which experience, taking the word in its most comprehensive sense, is organised. All true revelation is from within. The only Sinai is a fresh height of man's spiritual nature, and the missionary attempts to preach religion can only succeed in so far as an equation, so to say, establishes itself between the doctrine taught and the minds of those who learn. Thus it is the perpetual tragedy of the higher religions to be vulgarised as they become popular, and to be ruined by success. When the apostle has converted the crowd, he becomes a bishop.

In the different forms thus cursorily enumerated,—in traditional morality, custom, and law, in social organisation, in the technical arts, in science, in religion, and even indirectly in imaginative art—human experience organises itself into systems governing human conduct. Past experience, including now the accumulated tradition of the race, is used in an organised form in guiding conduct. Action is shaped and determined by some conception of the permanent good of self, the family, society, and possibly the species. The same factors have been present all along, even before the germ of intelligence appears. For instinct is shaped under the laws of heredity by the past experience of the species, and it is so shaped as to contribute indirectly to the permanent maintenance of the species. But in this early stage the process of shaping is extremely slow, cumbersome, and wasteful, and it is only in the course of a geological period that it can bring forth a more many-sided, fuller life, that is, a higher organisation. For the combination of many higher qualities in one individual can only be a comparatively rare occurrence, and even then, the survival of that individual, and the preponderance of his descendants, is exposed to all the accidents of untoward outward circumstances. Hence it is that orthogenic evolution—the development of higher types—is of geological slowness, and is only one course out of many that evolution may take. At its best, biological evolution finds the right path only by being constantly turned back from the wrong one. Only when experience is so far systematised that the future is read in the light of the past, does a race begin to move towards the fulfilment of its powers with the certainty of a man who knows where he wishes to arrive, and how to find his way thither.

5. *Psychological Aspects of the Third Stage.*

Psychologically, the difference between this stage and the preceding is entirely a matter of improved articulation and wider comprehension. It is not that new faculties are introduced, but that old faculties receive a fresh development. The old question, whether animals reason, is a question which people will go on putting for ever until they arrive at a definition of reason which will satisfy everybody. How far an animal or a man must be held to understand the grounds of his action before we can say that he acts rationally, is in one sense a question of terms; in another, a question of degree. We might parry the question whether animals reason by asking whether man reasons, and there would not be wanting plausible grounds for answering the latter question with a negative. What man has ever fully taken into account all the premises of any practical or theoretical conclusion to which he commits himself? Philosophy is aware that common action rests upon assumptions of which it is wholly unconscious, and she is also aware that she herself can only analyse out and justify those assumptions in an incomplete manner. A chicken avoids a caterpillar because he dislikes the taste. We perhaps refuse to allow that the chicken reasons because he does not know what it is that makes the caterpillar taste bad. After the chicken follows the chemist, who finds that the caterpillar secretes a certain acid. We clap our hands and applaud him as a reasoner who has explained everything. But will the chemist explain why a given acid should have an acrid taste, or show how the experience of unpleasantness should modify subsequent action ? A horse learns to lift a latch. We do not think he reasons. He merely has found out how it is done, and does it. A man explains to a child the action of the latch, and shows how by pressing it at one point you lift it out of a catch at another. He, we say, reasons because he analyses the process and how it is done. But a physicist might point out that the man knows nothing whatever about it unless he sees that the principle of the lever is involved in a simple form, and a metaphysician might add that the physicist cannot be said to understand the principle of the lever unless he is prepared to decide whether it is a principle which holds true of reality, and if so, on what epistemological grounds.

If we allow reason to the human species in general, and yet restrict it to that species, it must be by identifying the term reason arbitrarily with a certain grade in the development of analysis. It would be true to say that abstract or explicitly general reasoning emerges in the level of intelligence under consideration, but we have seen that abstractness is only one side of generality, and that the generality of human as opposed to animal reasoning is once more primarily a matter of explicitness. At bottom the function of mind in this as in the lower stages is to organise life by the correlation of experiences. As in every stage of mental growth what is new is that the work of the mind becomes on the one hand more explicit or articulate, on the other, more comprehensive in scope. That these two movements, if not at bottom identical, are closely interwoven, is seen in the relations of analysis to comparison. We clear up our experiences by bringing them into relation, and being so cleared up, the thought that emerges is the more truly universal in its application. It is this double movement, then, which forms the world of ideas by tracing experience to the underlying affinities on which both universal and individual conceptions rest. In these affinities we arrive at the basis of the more primitive inferences of the practical intelligence, and in this sense we might be tempted to say that human Reason gets at the ground upon which animal intelligence works without knowing it. But it will be better to avoid using the term Reason to characterise any one stage in distinction from others. The particular organisation of experience which we are now describing rests on the detached idea or the concept as its unit, and, if it is to have a name, may be best qualified as the stage of Conception, the Conceptual Judgment and Conceptual Reasoning.

What is true of the Reason is true also of Self consciousness. A dog or ape looks after "itself." It has a self, *i.e.*, a pervading identity and permanent character, is aware at least of its present needs and seeks to satisfy them. What we miss is evidence that the self is present to it as a persistent identity in such a way, for example, as to shape the choice of immediate ends by considerations of lifelong welfare. The self of which the animal is conscious is a very small fragment as compared with the self of which the man is aware. The light of consciousness reaches but a short way before and after in the animal, and since there is nothing to show that his conception of himself acts otherwise than his conception of his present end, there is no point in attributing to him knowledge of self. A man, on the other hand, who, for example, rejects a desired end on the ground that it is unworthy of him, shows that his consciousness of self is a permanent regulative force distinct from the desires or plans of action which he forms from day to day.

On the same ground, Will in a special sense may be said to emerge along with Conceptual Reasoning. We have wedded Desire to Concrete Experience and the Practical Judgment on the ground that the Practical Judgment knows its concrete end, and that where the end is known,

the impulse towards it is rightly characterised as Desire.
Facts also compel us to admit a conflict of desires in that
stage.  What then is there in Will beyond the victory of
one desire over another ?  The true answer to this question, which is of considerable interest in view of the
above discussions, seems to be given by those thinkers
who identify the will with the total or resultant
influence of character as a whole, while desire rests upon
some single and separate impulse.  The will is not to be
regarded as an additional impulse, or as a force existing
outside impulses and operating upon them.  It is rather
the system or synthesis of impulses, the broad practical
bent and tendency of one's nature.  Now here as elsewhere the development as we pass from a lower to a
higher stage consists primarily in a growing explicitness.
It is quite possible that even in animal life, when there is
a conflict of desires, that one tends to prevail which is
most intimately bound up with the animal's whole mode
of life.  And at least among the domestic animals, we see
symptoms of shame and remorse when under the stress of
momentary excitement such an impulse is violated—and
remorse is precisely the tingling with which the permanent
character, the real self, comes to life again.  The new
development is merely that those broad tendencies of the
character which before operated, if at all, obscurely and
unconsciously, have now a definite conception to guide
them.  The nature of the self, its character, its duties, the
wider life of which it is a part, now become conceptions,
ideals, or principles which appeal to the personality as
a whole, just as particular satisfactions appeal to special
impulses.  Just as the special impulse when it formulates
its end into an idea becomes Desire, so what we have called
the broad impulses of the personality when their end is
defined by conception constitute Will.  The will, with its
broad, permanent ends, presents itself as overriding and
independent of impulse, and out of this appearance the
fiction of the motiveless Will has very naturally grown
up.  We are aware of the Will often not as desire, but
as constraint overcoming Desire, and when Will and
Desire coalesce there is still something added to desire

which we express as Resolve or Determination. The reason is that even in human experience, the basis of the Will is too wide and too deep to be brought within the scope and limits of a single act of consciousness. The Will is more than we can feel at any one moment, for it is the whole self, or ourself acting as a whole. This action of the self as a whole is called out and directed by the broad ends of life, and things seen to be bound up therewith. It therefore belongs to the grade of mental development under discussion.

6. The development of moral impulses into the moral will determines in principle the advance in the content of morality—the objects on which the moral will insists— in the human as compared with the animal world. One side of this advance we have already found to be implied in the growth of the conception of Personality (pp. 339–341). On this side the change is a development rather than a revolution. Most of the higher animals have rudiments of a family life for which they labour and not infrequently sacrifice themselves. Many of them are also capable of a wider social life based on mutual help and friendliness. More than this can hardly be said universally of all races of men, and within all races numerous individual exceptions would have to be made of those who are far from being capable of as much. Yet the moral change is no less profound than the intellectual, of which it is indeed one expression. We attribute sympathy and attachment to the higher animals. That is to say, we credit them with desire to relieve the distress or satisfy the wants of another, to feed the young, to defend a com-panion, to gratify a master. Take them at their highest, and these are still desires addressed to immediate ends. It is true that in many, probably in most cases, they actually serve the permanent good of the object of affection. But if the feeding, warming, and protection of the nestling all actually subserve its permanent health and growth, this is merely a very familiar illustration of those co-ordinations of instinct by which desires are brought into general harmony with needs. We have no more right to credit the mother bird with a conception of the future career of her nestling,

than to suppose that she originally accepted the attentions of her mate with a view to maintaining the numbers of the species. In this grade, it is only so far as action is instinctive that its ends are broad and permanent. So far as it is intelligent and based on experience, its aims are near and concrete. Obviously, this limitation of view must apply to social action in this grade.

Now the characteristic of human intelligence as we have defined it is that it widens out so as to grasp the permanent in experience, and comprehend life in some sort as a whole. Thus widened, the same impulses that we saw before in the narrow concrete sphere develop into the manifold relations of personality. Sympathy, for example, becomes a regard not merely for the immediate needs, but for the career, the character, the mental development of another. The hen that clucks to her chick, and the mother that plans out a child's education with a view to physical health, growth of character, and the profession that must be taken up twenty years hence, are both moved by the parental impulse, but there is a difference in comprehensiveness of aim. Conversely, in the same way, we can conceive an animal—a sentinel deer, for example —performing the service immediately necessary for its herd. We can hardly conceive it as having the good of the herd as a permanent object of action. Animals may have selfish impulses, that is, desires for their own gratification as opposed to that of another. Man alone is swayed by self-interest ; that is, an intelligent subordination of desire to his permanent welfare as he conceives it. And just as his own permanent welfare becomes an end to him, so in proportion to his moral qualities does the permanent welfare of other people. It is in this way that the social qualities of animals are transformed in becoming human.

7. Morality is not ordinarily conceived as consisting in the devotion to certain broad and comprehensive purposes so much as in conforming to certain rules. Without inquiring here how far this conception is adequate, we may point out that the mass of rules, traditions, customs, laws, moral judgments, religious conceptions, which make up the

accepted code of conduct in any society, naturally subserve the broad end of the maintenance of that social system on which they are dependent. They are the *media axiomata* by which conduct is brought into relation to the broad requirements of the welfare, or, at lowest, the maintenance of society. Ordinary unreflecting morality is therefore conduct adjusted to the maintenance of the existing social type. It stands at a lower grade than the conduct deliberately regulated by some general principle, but in several respects at a higher grade than the highest development of the " Practical Judgment." For to begin with, though a rule may not be referred back to the principle which underlies and justifies it, it is still a rule, still general; that is to say, it is as such independent of impulse, and dependent on a general conception recognised not only by the agent, but by onlookers. In other words, it is a standard of conduct. Thus it becomes relatively independent of the caprice of the individual and the whim of the moment. The social sanction is there to guide the errant individual, and the moral sanction—the man's permanent conception of himself—to check the errant whim. To illustrate by a single point : the difference is that between an act of kindness based on an impulse of sympathy or affection, and an act of justice, based on an acknowledged duty or right. It is proverbially easier to be generous or kind than to be just ; and the reason is, that while kindness springs from an impulse which its object, from whatever cause, happens to have excited, justice is required, whether the impulse is there or not. Such a requirement can only be fulfilled where there is the recognition of a universal law applying under specified conditions to all individuals, and under all circumstances, without reference to the feelings or desires of the agent. Thus with the apprehension of general rules, social relations cease to rest merely upon instinct and impulse, and pass instead into a system of acknowledged rights and duties.

Two corollaries follow from the standardising of conduct. One is the possibility of adapting conduct to a highly complex social structure. Of this something has already been said. The other is, that while social behaviour becomes more stable, it is also more capable of development. Social changes are on the average far more rapid than those changes in the physical constitution of a species upon which instinct ultimately rests. Change of behaviour through modification of instinct must proceed with the same geological slowness which marks all the stages of physical evolution. Through submission to the social standard, conduct may be made to accommodate itself to the changing requirements of social life, without lagging more than two or three generations behind the requirements themselves.

Thus by the standardising of morality a force grows up outside of instinct to regulate conduct. In the end, this force no doubt owes its origin to hereditary tendencies, but it is a heredity modified, on the one hand, by tradition : on the other, by the rational apprehension of what is required, one may say of its own ultimate meaning. What is recognised as right in accordance with this standard may in many cases be very far removed from the inborn impulses of the individual. Under its guidance, the social impulses develop into a recognition of what is due to others, placed above momentary caprice or personal desire. Such a standard admits of development into a code, adaptable to the thousand details of a complex social structure ; while finally, as the needs of social life change, the standard is capable of organic modification along with them, in accordance with the reasoned appreciation of necessity.

In this place, I am only concerned to contrast animal behaviour with human morality taken in the rough and as a whole. How morality as a contribution to the organisation of life develops within the human race to the stage thus roughly indicated, would have to be the subject of a separate inquiry. To the same inquiry would belong the consideration of the steps by which it further advances to something higher. What the nature of this higher stage is, will be briefly indicated in a later chapter.

8. *The position of instinct.*

It needs no argument to show that intelligence, when developed to the point now reached, must very largely replace instinct as the guide of conduct. Indeed, the tendency of ordinary thought is to exaggerate this effect, and to contrast the reason which governs man with the instinct that rules animals. But man is no more regulated by pure reason than animals by pure instinct. As has been indicated above in Chapter VI.,[1] the basis of human conduct is hereditary character : the hereditary tendency to feel, to think, to act in a determinate manner. Properly considered, the impulse to reason is itself a hereditary propensity ; and the methods by which we reason, the " laws of thought," are, in the first place, inherited methods of reaction to the appropriate object. They are indeed improved and refined under the guidance of experience and reflection, but in this respect their history is quite parallel to that of the humbler instincts of animal life.

But now if hereditary character, mental and moral, be the ultimate basis of human conduct, can we say in general terms how far it is remodelled by the rational use of experience ? What is principally important for our purpose is to compare the remodelling as effected in this stage with the corresponding process in the next lower grade of intelligence. In that grade, we found, first of all, that the instinctive use of means to an end might be remodelled, as when in the course of training a dog works out a way of meeting the special tricks of different kinds of game. We found, secondly, that out of random actions, or out of mere observation, methods could be built up which have no specific basis in instinct at all. We found, thirdly, that even the ends of action might be in some respects modified by the nature of the individual objects to which by instinct an animal's interests are attached, as when the dog is said to take his character from his master. In all these three cases, instinct on the one hand, and the direct experience of the individual on the other, come into immediate contact ; and a certain modification, whether in the choice of ends or of means, results. What is peculiar to human intelligence—apart from the developed influence of rational control in the individual—is the rise

[1] Cf. especially pp. 99—106.

of tradition as a third force impinging upon the other two. The innate propensities of each individual human being are in contact throughout his life with the body of beliefs, moral judgments, social institutions, rules of art or craft that make up the tradition of the society into which he is born. These enter into his character, interpenetrate his hereditary impulses, not only encouraging and restraining, but with more subtle power, prescribing to each impulse the sphere within which it is to move, and the object on which it may exercise itself. And the character so formed is all the while in interaction with the results of experience in the narrower sense of that which the individual finds out for himself, as opposed to that of which he is told. Tradition, in the broad sense in which it is here taken, rests of course principally on language, and language, as we have seen, is both the parent and the child of the Universal. Hence it is that though there is a rudimentary form of tradition among the higher orders of animals, it cannot there fill the place which we here attribute to it. The rudiments of instruction which an ape, a cat, or a bird can furnish to its young, are limited to a few acts of restraint and encouragement, supplementing, or, rather, anticipating the lessons which individual experience would teach. In human society, on the other hand, tradition goes to the root-principles of action, both as shaping the ends recognised as desirable, and as furnishing rules of method of which but few could be found out in the course of individual experience, and those only by exceptionally gifted or exceptionally fortunate persons. In a word, tradition as based on the Universal brings the experience of the race to bear on individual conduct in a new sense. If we are right in holding that instinct is due to heredity, while heredity works through natural selection, then, as we have already seen, there is a sense in which instinct itself utilises the experience of the race to guide the individual. What is performed at that stage by the constant elimination of the majority of individuals born, and by the stereotyping of the structure of those which survive, is executed at this higher stage by the organisa- tion of the experience of those who have lived, and rests upon the plasticity of those who learn by it.  In short, at this stage, we have organised racial experience largely taking the place of that hereditary structure which represents the result of an infinity of conflicting and chaotic experiences in past generations.  In fine, in the highest animal species, instinct lays the ground plan of conduct, within which details may be remodelled by individual experience.  In the human species, the ground plan is itself reconstituted by the organised experience of the race.

9. To bring together the main heads of our account, we have suggested that human intelligence develops out of a lower form by growth in those features of Comprehension on the one hand, and Articulateness on the other, by which the higher stage of animal intelligence was marked out from the lower.  (a) Mind, it is suggested, differs from mind in the degree in which these powers are developed, in the area of experience which it can comprehend, and in the articulateness with which it can comprehend it.  But here, as elsewhere, there come points in growth where change of degree becomes change of kind.  The constitution of a physical body is understood to be determined by the energy of movement on the part of its constituent molecules.  Increase the vibration of the constituent molecules, and a solid body gets warmer to the touch, and expands in volume.  Increase it still further, and other physical characteristics are changed.  The body perhaps becomes soft and pliable.  Presently there comes a point at which the solid body becomes liquid, the energy of movement having overcome the forces which cause each swinging molecule to return constantly to the same point.  Increase it yet again, and the liquid becomes a vapour, the energy of movement having altogether overcome that of cohesion.  Thus do successive increments of quantity, as they pass certain critical phases, produce changes of quality.  In the instance just taken, the change of quality is, as I understand, due to the disturbance of the relation between the force that is increasing and the force that remains constant.  In the mental world, the change may be explained in this way : that

as the scope and clearness of mind increase, certain points are successively reached at which quite new achievements become possible. Those achievements, once possible, carry with them a whole train of consequences. And thus the species that has just succeeded in turning the corner finds itself in a different world from that which has just failed.

To understand then the rise of the specifically human intelligence, we have to suppose a mind capable of holding together more elements of experience than the highest animal can cope with, and of noting each several element more clearly. Where separate experiences are thus held together, they have an effect which we have already noted in the animal world upon the movements of attention. Common qualities and differences rise into notice. In proportion as the elements of each experience become conspicuous, they react upon association, bringing to mind other experiences, partially but not wholly identical. Through their influence in turn the points of identity and of difference are thrown into relief. In other words, acts of comparison and analysis aid one another, extending the scope of judgment, and adding to its precision.

The first critical phase in this development, marking the transition to human intelligence, is that in which the common element obtains a firm enough hold over attention to be responded to with a name of its own. How this stage arose in the race we cannot tell, but it arises in the individual as a rule between the tenth and fourteenth month, by a process which seems to be at least in part instinctive. At any rate, the instruction given by mother or nurse has the instinctive babblement of the baby to work upon, and as soon as a word is acquired, the child seems to feel an instinctive satisfaction in its use. But this stage, as we have seen, is only the rudiment of the Universal, and the mere fact that a word is used after this fashion no more proves intelligence than any other simple and uniform reaction to stimulus. The importance of the word lies in the part which it plays as mechanism in the further stages. For just as the content first suggests the word, so the word being learnt suggests the content ; and therefore the combination of words the combination of contents.

Now, it is not the mere disentangling of common characters that is essential to the higher stage, but, as we have seen, the power of recombining. We are at the edge of the plane of general reasoning as soon as the mind can make for itself, without the aid of perception, an intelligible synthesis of common qualities. It may then be said to have a practical command of that attributive relation upon which the general concept is based. This synthesis the child no doubt learns to make largely from others. If, as is here assumed, the evolution hypothesis is correct, the human race must have learnt it step by step alongside with the development of language.

(b) Given the power of operating with common qualities as units, all that we have called the world of ideas becomes possible. Henceforward the experience of each individual dwells alongside with a body of thought distinct from but related to it. For this body of thought is in large part a heritage from others, and in turn helps to regulate the direct experience of the individual. This perpetual cross reference between acquired ideas and direct experience is the fundamental feature of human thought, of the existence of which in the animal world there is not the slightest trace.

(c) The contrast in explicitness and comprehension between this stage and the preceding sufficiently appears from the nature of the Universal itself. We saw that logically the procedure of the lower stage was an argument from particulars to particulars. Such an argument implies the universal truth ; i.e., it is the common character of the two cases that operate within the mind to produce the inference, while if the mind reflects upon its own process, it is compelled to recognise that the process is only valid if the universal truth holds. In the present stage the Universal, we have seen, is recognised ; i.e., the implication of the lower form of inference is now made explicit. And what is true universally, is recognised as being true necessarily. Logical sequence not merely directs the operations of mind, but is recognised by the mind, and not merely by the reflecting mind of the logician, but by every one who has learnt the use of " therefore " and " because." We have already compared the two lower stages of intelligence to a syllogistic process in varying degree of explicitness. In the first stage we saw that what corresponds to the major premiss is a certain formed disposition, what corresponds to the minor, a stimulus, what corresponds to the conclusion, a response. The premisses in this case are antecedent conditions from which the response follows, but there is no evidence that either of them is grasped in relation to the response or its results. In the second stage we held that the starting point is a complex of related percepts—as of action and consequence—an "observed particular," and the result a judgment equivalent to the combination of minor premiss and conclusion, the major being still represented only by the mental habit which predisposes towards the combination. In the third stage the major premiss itself becomes explicit and the syllogism complete. We have the universal judgment, the particular, and their combination in the conclusion. I do not mean that ordinary reasonings are cast in syllogistic form, but that each of the three (or including antecedent experience four) phases which are formulated in syllogism is now a distinct mental content, a distinct judgment. All along there were general qualities and universal relations contained in the world of experience. All along these guided the mind whether in action or in the formation of judgments. Now they not merely guide the mind, but are apprehended by the mind, and they become in their turn units or terms which can enter into higher combinations as the order of experience and the laws of thought may determine. So far, then, the apprehension of the Universal appears as a turning round of the mind upon its previous operations ; a bringing into clear consciousness of what it was doing before.

(d) But the Universal has another aspect. It sums up in itself the results of a set of experiences when compared and analysed ; and it refers to a whole class of facts, of experiences actual or potential. Thus to reason in Universals is to bring classes of facts into relation with one another. Experiences already correlated by the affinities which have led us to class them together become for us now a unit which may be correlated with any other units similarly constituted ; and this correlation may reach any degree of complexity. The characteristic of this stage, in short, is the correlation of experiences in groups or masses by the elements of permanence and universality pervading them. The Universal is not the only form in which experiences are grouped. The great Collective and Individual concepts on which much of human thought is based are arrived at on similar principles, and in great measure have similar functions. They rest on pervading identities traced by the comparison and analysis of diverse experiences, and their reference covers indefinitely great masses of experience, future and potential, as well as past or present. Of such a kind are the substances of ordinary thought, the personality of self and of others, the society to which the individual belongs, to say nothing of the wider and deeper concepts belonging to the higher stages of human intelligence. A very little reflection shows that conceptions of this kind are no less important than true universals in the correlation of experience by human thought.

(e) It is in particular in virtue of the co-ordination of a certain set of experiences under the conception of self, that man is credited with self consciousness. In the determination of conduct by comprehensive ends or broad principles answering to the permanent character of the self as against the cravings of the moment he manifests Will as opposed to Desire.

(f) But with the conception of Will we pass at once into the ethical side of the development. The same co-ordination which builds up the conception of self, builds up the conception of other personalities, and the sympathetic impulse of the animal world develops into a rational regard for the wealth and welfare of others. A similar development builds up the human society, with its system of rights and duties in which each individual finds his place. In such a system, again by a parallel development, the social and selfish impulses of the animal are elaborated into rules of conduct resting on the relatively permanent character of human beings and their societies, and recognised as superior to momentary impulse and even to the individual will. In other words, conduct is standardised.

(*g*) It is an essential feature of the change described that the part formerly played by instinct, as the basis upon which individual experience has to work, is now largely taken over by tradition. Instinct does not disappear, but on the one hand, the individual becomes capable of grasping and even criticising the ends to which it urges him, and on the other, he is born into a society with rules and principles of art and of life which in part combat, in part fuse with and modify, the hereditary impulses of common human nature. In the highest plane of animal intelligence we found that the scheme of life was still determined by instinct, though it might be modified by individual experience. In the present stage, the outlines of the scheme itself are as much determined by the organised experience of the race represented in " tradition," as by its unorganised experience, represented by the forces of heredity. In short, the organised experience of the race now enters into the principles and bases of conduct, fusing with instinct or displacing it.

To conclude. In the present stage the affinities—be they elements of common character or of continuous individual identity—which link diverse perceptual experiences, are analysed out and correlated in their turn. This correlation, in which the concept is the distinctive psychological feature,

(*a*) makes explicit the connections on which correlation in the previous stages depends, and

(*β*) makes a comprehensive reference through the medium of common character to masses of related experience. Thought in this stage may therefore be typified in the completed syllogism with explicit major premiss as contrasted with the truncated syllogisms of the previous stages.

In scope, it effects a correlation of the elements of permanence and universality in experience racial and individual. It organises given facts under connecting principles and practical purposes under comprehensive ends and general rules, the results of the first group being subordinated to those of the second partly as contributing to their formation, partly as guiding the choice of means to the ends which they prescribe.

Under its ethical aspects, this correlation appears as a direction of conduct by Will guided by general conceptions of the welfare of self, others, or the community, as well as by the code of rules in accordance with which the life of any given society is organised.

As a result, not only does individual experience (as in the previous stage) modify the general plan of behaviour resting on instinct, but the recorded experience of the race is brought to bear on its hereditary tendencies, engendering an explicit conception of the main ends desirable in the life to be lived by man.

# CHAPTER XVI

## SYSTEMATIC THOUGHT [1]

1. THE central feature of the stage of intelligence described in the two preceding chapters is that comprehensive reference to the permanent conditions of experience which we know as the concept. We might regard the ideal action of this stage as directed by generalisations which embody vast masses of previous experience towards an end which will comprehend vast masses of future experience. And it is not merely the individual but the race whose experience is thus organised. Through this organisation, not merely the particular actions but the general setting or framework of life comes to rest quite as much upon tradition as upon instinct. A mass of social customs, political obligations, religious beliefs, environ a child from the first, and are often in marked conflict with his inherited impulses. Instinct as modified by social tradition is now the ground-work of life, while apart from simple reflexes, there is very little in the detailed adjustment of means to ends in daily life in which acquired knowledge does not take the principal part.

But no words are needed to show how incomplete even at this stage is the organisation of life. Man is man, but not yet master of his fate. All that he has done by centuries of progress is to reclaim a little garden plot out of the vast wilderness of unknown and unmanageable

---

[1] The substance of this chapter has been more fully dealt with in the writer's *Development and Purpose*. I have thought it better not to attempt to incorporate fresh matter, and have therefore left it with trifling corrections as originally printed.

forces of nature, among which the forces of his own
nature are not the least terrible and by far the most
incalculable.  Nor if he could bend all nature to his
bidding would he yet understand fully to what end to use
his power.  The world of human ends is not yet an ordered
community owning the sway of a single comprehensive
principle.  It is a scene of bitter and perpetual strife,
where rival philosophies and fratricidal religions contend,
the crowd of ignobler passions often joining in the fight.
The reason that is within us forces us to hold that whatever is right and good cannot be destructive of other
things right and good, but rather must co-operate with
them to the same ultimate end.  But human ethics as we
know them provide no such harmony.  Half the energies
of the best men are taken up in combating others no less
well intentioned than themselves.  It is no doubt right
provisionally that both should fight for their principles,
just as in war men on both sides, fighting for their own
country, are as individuals justified.  So far the comprehensiveness of the modern spirit can bring in a certain
ethical harmony.  But it is a harmony which deepens the
tragedy that it ennobles, and ennobles it only by pointing
to a still loftier harmony resting on the common nature
that underlies all differences and the greater far off end of
human kind which all actual effort but dimly apprehends.

Reason, as the impulse to harmonise and unify, keeps
constantly before us the ideal of a principle which should
explain the world, and a purpose which should rationalise
human effort.  Man has not reached his goal, but he has
made some progress since the days when he chipped the
flint spear heads of the river-drifts.  This progress is
most apparent on the side of knowledge, and we will
consider that first.

2. In what has been said hitherto of the organisation of
human experience, we have had in view thought as it
exists among men in general, not thought as specially
developed in art, religion, science, or philosophy.  We
have in short been dealing with " common-sense " knowledge and common-sense ways of thinking.  We may
now briefly contrast the characteristics of common sense

with those of that higher organisation of experience which constitutes science.

We have seen that in the third stage generalisations are made explicit, and becoming explicit, they may be further correlated with one another as well as with fresh perceptions. As this correlation proceeds, loosely organised masses of thought arise. We know that common sense abhors trains of reasoning and abjures close analysis. Nevertheless in our common knowledge ideas already exist in combinations. Tacit combinations they may be, but they are real, as we find from the numbers that rush to the defence when any cherished thought is assailed. The ideas connected with our daily life, our homes, belongings, occupations, politics, form combinations of this kind. We do not reduce them to system, but we might do so if there were an adequate motive to set us to work. But though there are combinations at this stage, they are loose and ill organised, as is sufficiently shown by the contradictions which arise when the generalities of common sense are taken literally as universal truths. Common sense, indeed, tolerates a good deal of contradiction. It does not distinguish very carefully between " never " and " hardly ever," and tacit saving clauses are part of its stock in trade. For the rest, common sense admits that it does not know everything, and is always ready to live and learn.

Suppose, however, that instead of tolerating contradictions we seek to resolve or explain them. The explanation will have to be found in the drawing of fresh distinctions based upon a more thorough analysis. With this analysis, we are already on the way towards turning our rough generalisations into relatively exact universals. With exact universals to work with, our loose inferences turn into rigid proofs, and we find that we have passed from common sense to science.

*Character of Science.*

The best single term for describing the general character of Science as opposed to common sense is System. Science works the data of experience into a whole of interconnected facts. It may be objected that there is interconnection of facts in all reasoning, and that the distinction is therefore a mere matter of degree. But even in the Third Stage systematisation is an underlying principle, not the explicit object of mental effort. Common sense carries interconnection as far as is necessary for the purpose in hand. But a new step is taken when the purpose in hand is that of making interconnection complete, and this is the step taken when we begin to investigate a subject for the sake of understanding it through and through. In science system becomes the explicit purpose.

Science is systematic in the first place because it seeks to be complete. It takes a certain subject matter and examines it not from the point of view of some practical or imaginative interest, but for the sake of understanding its essential nature as exhibited in all its developments. Thus the beginning of science is the marking off, often by a crude distinction which is afterwards revised, of a department of experience for its field of operations. Next, since the business of science is thorough understanding, it must discover as well as it can the real connections of things. This involves going beneath the generalities of common sense, with their "practical certainty," to the most definite and precise conceptions attainable. For this purpose both terms and their relationships must be accurately defined, and hence the saying—a one-sided saying—that science is measurement. Hence also the part played by definition, the true place of which is neither at the beginning nor at the end of science, but all along its march—the definitions being modified as knowledge of the subject advances. To form some idea of the relation between accuracy and systematic interconnection, we might compare common sense to the implements of a handicraft, and science to a modern machine. The parts of the locomotive or the printing machine must be adjusted with the minutest accuracy to fit into a scheme of rigid wheels and levers. The craftsman's tool may deviate from the normal, and the craftsman himself will correct the deviations. He gets to know his implement and accommodates himself to its individuality. The slightest deviation stops the perfect but rigid system of the machine. In the same way, common sense makes use of its rough generalities without disaster, but for elaboration and system there must be accuracy in each part, to the last millionth of an inch.

It must be added that science goes more deeply than common sense into the fact of connection itself. It does not merely go beneath the practical efficiency of good working rules to the strictly defined and conditioned universal on which the rules rest. It goes beyond the universal itself, seeking its why and wherefore by breaking it up into elements and discovering further affinities. In so doing, it tries to trace its way up to the central point, what Aristotle called the essence of the subject, and works from the centre outwards, drawing the radial lines so as to preserve affinities and follow the lines of vital distinction. The preparatory work of such a system is that of classification, the final work, that of Explanation. As the highest of the "systematic forms," Explanation exhibits the fact explained not merely as dependent on another fact, but as necessarily occupying its assigned place in a system of connected facts. Whether it resolves compound laws into their elements, traces derivative truths to their origin, exhibits the character as a part as dependent on its place in a structure, or deals with an event or process as some special phase in the genesis of an organic growth, the tendency of science seems always to be to a systematisation of thought which shall not be merely a connection of some one element with some other, but rather the reference of all elements to a whole into the plan of which they fit.

3. The beginner in science has been sometimes re-presented [1] as turning to a new method because of his disgust with the contradictions to which he was brought by following the unreflective, unanalysed workings of common sense. However this may be, there must speedily arise in science a tacit recognition of the divergence between thought and truth, or between "truth" as it appears to man, and Reality. At a certain stage of

---

[1] *E.g.* by Plato, Rep. VII.

reflection, the mind begins to recognise that its opinions are in a sense of its own making. The natural man does not question that he is in daily and hourly contact with reality ; he makes no question about the validity of the conclusions which he draws from this seeming reality by steps which appear no less self evident. Common sense may be convinced of error as of illusion, but while it revises its results, it neither calls its own methods into question nor doubts its senses. It is satisfied to be right in its own world. It does not ask about the limits of that world, nor inquire whether its experience is the same thing as reality. Yet the human mind, like the human body, is the outcome of a long and highly specialised evolution. It is a very elaborate structure, with determinate functions of its own, and its every act and thought, every inference, perception, and feeling depends as much upon this structure as upon the outer world which acts upon it, and stimulates it to reaction. We thus contribute to the making of our own experience—that experience which at first we all take as though it had a sort of absolute value wholly independent of ourselves. The full realisation and discussion of this difficulty is the central problem of philosophy, but it is important to recognise that it makes itself felt in one way and another even in the special sciences. The world of science is not the same as the world of common sense. The material universe as conceived by molecular physics is not the universe as known to sight and touch, only rather more completely known. The conceptions of Life, of Personality, of Society are not merely deepened and widened in scientific treatment, but in great measure they have to be taken to pieces and thought out anew. In many sciences, we get, by the use of instruments, into a new world of perceptions, and are thus forced to realise incidentally the relativity of our own sense-experience. In all science we constantly find that the conceptions which have grown up uncritically, and which we began by using confidently as moulds into which reality must fit, are spontaneous products of our limited experience, which a wider experience would transform out of all recognition.

B B

But with this scepticism about fundamental conceptions, we are thrown back on first principles. We shall need a criterion of certainty, that is to say, a Logic. We shall need an examination into the relation between the world of our thought, and the world of ultimate reality, *i.e.*, a Metaphysic. And in these inquiries there is wrapped up another which is, strictly speaking, a special science, but yet is concerned with those mental processes which are at work in building up science itself, *i.e.*, Psychology. Clearly, if we want to evaluate the human factor in human thought, we must understand the laws of growth by which our ways of thinking have arisen. Historically, therefore, Psychology has arisen in close connection with Logic and Metaphysics. This is not the place to argue the precise delimitation of the spheres of Logic, Metaphysics, and Psychology. What I have to do is to call attention to the work which these three branches of investigation have shared between themselves. This work has a double aspect. On the one hand, it is essentially an analysis of the work of mind, and to many people this would seem to be the differentiating mark between philosophy and science. Thus, if we wish to contrast the highest stage of mental development with all those that have gone before, we might say that while in all the other stages the mind is at work correlating its experiences, in this stage for the first time it turns to analysing the principle and method of correlation itself, the laws that govern it in its system-making. On the other hand it is only by evaluating this unknown quantity that we get a determinate relation between thought in any sphere, and reality. That is to say, this analysis is the primary condition of a completed synthesis. If the partial systems of science can be conceivably built up into a unified science revealing the true nature of things, this analysis must be the keystone of the arch.

4. This unification of experience is the ideal to which philosophy points. For in the search for first principles, philosophy finds itself brought up against something that looks very like an insoluble contradiction. We cannot go outside experience in order to judge experience. We may

push a science back to its first principles, but may still ask on what those first principles rest. We may distinguish true ways of thinking from false, and yet be reminded that the true ways are only ways of thinking. Are we then landed ultimately in pure assumption as our starting point ? Or may we recognise that the search for a peg outside the world of thought to which thought may be hung, is the result of an illusion, by which we transfer to thought as a whole methods justly applicable only to a part ? If this is so, the ultimate justification of thought and experience is to be found within the world of thought and experience itself. As I have argued at length elsewhere, it is to be found in point of fact in its character as a coherent system, a whole in which the diverse parts support and necessitate one another. The goal of philosophy is therefore a system which should embrace all experience.

There have been two views of the function of philosophy which at first sight are difficult to reconcile. One is, that philosophy is the unification of the sciences ; the other, stated broadly, is that it is the analysis of the presuppositions of thought. In the view here taken, these two conceptions coincide, for it is in the possibility of harmonising the results of thought that the test of thought is ultimately to be found, and such a unification is not possible without taking exact account of the way in which thought goes to work in building up its conceptions. The correlation of the sciences on the basis of an analysis of experience seems then to be the fuller statement of the work of philosophy. It is by such a correlation, if at all, that we get back from the world of thought which has arisen uncritically out of human experience and human evolution to the Reality which we still hope to be attainable. We find the need of such a correlation obscurely felt in the special sciences when in trouble about their elementary conceptions, explicitly recognised in modern metaphysics, but not yet satisfied by any philosophic system. The ideal unity of the philosopher, however far beyond the reach of human attainment, may serve as a " regulative concept," indicating the direction in which the advance of thought moves and the principles by which it is guided. The prime feature which distinguishes this movement from the work of common sense is the emergence of the idea of systematic interconnection from its position as an underlying principle into the forefront of the struggle as the avowed object of effort. The exactness of science and its disengagement from practical interests are corollaries of this principle. But secondly, the idea of system necessitates in the way described a criticism of method, and thirdly, the result of this criticism is a remodelling of the whole conception of experience and the truth that can be built upon experience, in such a way as to evaluate the work of mind, and determine the relation of thought to reality. Explicit systematisation, criticism of thought processes, and the consequent "return to reality," are thus the three factors determining the philosophic movement of thought. In other words, here, as in the other advances of thought that we have traced, the methods of lower phases are made explicit, and as a consequence the character of the systematisation is remodelled. Ordinary human thought makes explicit the universal that underlies animal experience. Philosophy makes explicit the principles of correlation that underlie the use of the universal. And thus, while the bodies of common-sense knowledge are fragmentary and rough-hewn, the ideal philosophic system is an accurate piecing together of experience into a single coherent whole. Thus philosophy grows out of common sense, and completes its work. But it completes it only by taking it to pieces and putting it together again. It is ordinary thought not merely extended, but in a measure transformed.

Philosophy then, in its narrower sense as the analysis of mind, may be said to deal with the conditions under which the general truths and inferences of common sense arose. Meanwhile the sciences deal with what is in a sense the same problem in a different form. For, as we have seen, they trace the rough rules of common sense to the true universals that underlie them, and out of these universals they make their system. Finally, philosophy in the wider sense is the effort towards the ideal unification of these processes, the system of adequately defined truths in which contradictions are resolved, and errors and half truths alike explained. Putting these points together, we may formulate the work of systematic thought in general as the effort to discover the conditions under which the general truths of common sense arise, and by the correlation of these deeper truths to complete the systematisation of experience.

5. *Self-conscious development.*

The ideal unity of thought is, as has been indicated, rather a "regulative concept" than an attainable goal. But there is a point in the movement which it guides which may also be very remote, but whether remote or near, seems to indicate the natural terminus of the whole development which we have been following. We can conceive as not indefinitely remote a stage of knowledge in which the human species should come to understand its own development, its history, conditions, and possibilities, and on the basis of such an understanding should direct its own future, just as an individual who thoroughly understands himself and the conditions of his life may mark out his career for himself. Such a development must be intellectual on the one side and ethical on the other. Intellectually, the whole progress of the sciences and philosophy may be regarded as so many steps towards it, the lower sciences as giving man control of nature, the higher as yielding the requisite knowledge of human life, physical, mental, and social. Moreover, as Comte and others have shown, the lower or more abstract sciences lead up to the higher or more concrete,—Mathematics to physics, physics and chemistry to biology, biology to the mental and social sciences. If we imagine the higher sciences as complete as they are at present rudimentary, we should have in them a general theoretical account of the conditions of human development, physical and moral. Thus prolonging in imagination the line of mental development traced in the foregoing pages, we are led to the conception of a scheme embracing the whole problem of human life and destiny on earth. We start with a consciousness limited to the reaction of the moment, and knowing nothing of the past which determines its action, nor of the future which its action will affect.  Step by step, as we advance, more of the past and the future come within the scope of intelligence, and we end at a point where all that has made the race what it is is brought into the account and made to prove what it has in it to be.  At this stage the mind of man is first fully self-conscious in the strict sense—conscious of its own nature, of the conditions under which it lives and works, of the future to which it may aspire.

6.  But " self-consciousness " of this kind is not attained by scientific theory alone.  It rests on a spiritual truth, and must be applied by a moral force.  Now moral force is not a method of intellectual development, and spiritual truth cannot be grasped by the intellect unaided.  A race devoid of moral feeling could not appreciate its own unity, which is essentially a moral truth.  Along with the intellectual development of which we have spoken must therefore go a certain evolution of ethical conceptions which we must attempt briefly to characterise.

The moral conceptions of men rest in the end on the moral impulses of human nature.  This does not always hold of the individual, for the conceptions which a man accepts intellectually and follows more or less involuntarily are in great part worked out for him by society, and imposed upon him first by his spiritual pastors and masters, and then by the requirements of social life.  Thus in ordinary life we are painfully conscious at times of the divorce between moral theory and practice.  Nevertheless, if we take human society as a whole, the Aristotelian position holds true, that the conception of virtue rests on the practice thereof.[1]  That is to say, the whole system of moral tradition governing the life of a society is evolved from the practical impulses and feelings at work in the past and in the present.  It is from these as they operate on each other, and are reacted upon in turn by the physical conditions of life, that the social system with its complex rights and duties and the moral traditions in which these

---

[1] *Nic. Eth.* VII. 8, 4.  οὔτε δὴ ἐκεῖ (ἐν τοῖς μαθηματικοῖς) ὁ λόγος διδασκαλικὸς τῶν ἀρχῶν, οὔτε ἐνταῦθα, ἀλλ' ἀρετὴ ἢ φυσικὴ ἢ ἐθιστὴ τοῦ ὀρθοδοξεῖν περὶ τὴν ἀρχήν.

are formulated evolve. There is indeed one other regulative condition, namely, the stage of intellectual development reached. This has an important influence in more than one shape, as we shall presently see, but it is not the basis of the matter.

From a very early if not the earliest stages of development onwards, the maintenance of the species rests on two conditions, conditions often so closely related as to be almost identical, but at times thrown into sharp contrast and antagonism. The first of these is what we may call the principle of self-maintenance, "the will to live." We have observed this principle at work in the processes to which we do not attribute consciousness at all, in the form of that tendency to self-maintenance which we attribute to organisms as such. It persists in the various impulses tending not merely to the maintenance of life, but to the maintenance of the individual in his own character, the fulfilment of his impulses or desires, the realisation of his individuality. But this principle is from an early stage limited and controlled or modified in its action by another. In all but the lowest stages, the life of a species depends not only on the efforts of each individual to maintain himself, but on a certain unique relation between different individuals composing the species. At least as soon as distinction of sex appears, the individuals of a species begin to have need of one another. They are not complete each in himself, but need a complement, which they find in another individual possessing the same fundamental specific character developed with certain differences. The most obvious and most permanent need of this kind is that of sex, but in the highest orders this relationship takes a thousand different shapes. The young needs the parent, and so also does the parental instinct cry out for young ones to satisfy it. The gregarious instinct runs far down into the lower animal world, and in human life every man must needs have some other human being by him, if only to annoy him. Even rivalry and hatred rest on some sort of consciousness of a common nature subjected to difference, and of mutual help and love we need not speak.

One need not waste words in showing that this relation to other individuals must profoundly modify the workings of "self-assertion," either by directly thwarting it, as when love enjoins self-sacrifice, or perhaps by entering into and modifying it, as when a man makes the pursuit of revenge the object of a lifetime. The genesis of morality may be said to consist in the development and interaction of these two principles.

In the stage of pure instinct, the influence of the elementary relationships appears chiefly in the sexual and parental impulse. We cannot regard these as unselfish, any more than we can regard the impulse to eat and drink as selfish. Both terms imply a conception of ends, which is alien to pure instinct. The conception of a primitive egoism on which sociability is somehow overlaid is without foundation either in biology or in psychology. Indeed, it has been said with more truth of Nature—

> " So careful of the type she seems,
> So careless of the single life."

For the impulses of sex and provision for young, if not unselfish, at least do not tend to self-maintenance. In some instances, as the act of procreation in the fly, and courtship in the case of the male spider, they are dangerous, and even fatal, while if we allowed the solitary wasps any sort of understanding of the purpose of their actions, we should have to admire the self-devotion of their unremitting toil to build and provision an abiding place for the grub which they never see. We do not impute such reflection, and we therefore reckon the actions mentioned as neither selfish nor unselfish. What is clear is that in following out these instincts the animal is acting as a part of a whole, as a member of a species. He is stimulated by his affinity to another individual, and his actions are of service to individuals that come after him. It does not seem that the " social principle," so to call it, makes any marked advance in the first stage of intelligence. We have seen that the attention shown to the young is of a rudimentary character, and that social life is little more than a manifestation of the gregarious instinct. It is indeed diffi-

cult to see how the experiences operating within the
limitations of this first stage could teach anything with
regard to the effect of conduct on others. So far, it is
only when the consequences of action make themselves
apparent in the feelings of the agent that they influence
subsequent conduct, and under that limitation it is hard to
think that the effect of action upon others can be in any
way apprehended. It is in the stage of concrete experience, where we get on the one hand purposive action, and
on the other recognition of and definite feelings towards
individuals, that action first becomes interesting from the
point of view of the ethical inquirer. In this stage life is
still dominated by the struggle for existence, but the animal
builds up for himself a little ring fence within which the
impulses making for co-operation are allowed full play.
Family life has a definite development in this stage.
Mating is often relatively permanent—conspicuously
among many species of birds—and the care for the young
is carried to a high pitch. In many cases herds and flocks
are found which live in the main in a state of internal
peace, and in which mutual helpfulness and sometimes a
simple division of labour are found. In these little communities we have already seen that many of the fundamental
social and self-regarding impulses appear. There is every
sign of sympathy and attachment, and equally of pride,
jealousy, anger, and hatred—qualities also implying a
relation to others as individuals, though a relation of
antagonism. Upon the whole, the higher animals appear
to act on the Mosaic precept, " Thou shalt love thy friend
and hate thine enemy." The greater part of the world is
either an enemy or a prey, and accordingly the animal
must live principally by taking care of himself and being
ready to fight. Hence self assertion is the dominant note
of his character if he is strong, self protection if he is weak,
and he must have the qualities known as " self-regarding,"
which belong thereto. But there is a little bit of the
world which is a friend, and in relation to this little bit he
develops a different side of his character, and becomes a
social animal. Thus in this stage the " social principle,"
that is, the fundamental identity of the species appearing

in different forms according to age, sex, and individuality, becomes the foundation, first, of certain distinctive relations which we might almost call "personal," with the appropriate emotions of love, hate, sympathy, attachment, jealousy. Secondly, it is the foundation of little social structures, families, flocks, herds, resting on a certain community of interest, admitting of a simple division of labour, and possessing some permanence. To maintain these little societies there must be a considerable measure of mutual understanding and assistance. That is to say, among the concrete or practical ends which we recognise at this level of development, the satisfaction of mate or young or even comrade may figure along with the satisfaction of self. We may say broadly that in this stage, on the basis of Sympathy, actions are adapted to concrete social ends. It must further be recollected that such action rests neither on blind impulse nor on any general conception, but is directed to the particular practical end preferred at the moment—that is, it is based upon desire. Human morality rests on the same fundamental conditions at a higher stage of development. Our common human nature is the ultimate basis of moral conceptions. Upon the emotional need we have of each other rest the affections, and with them the relation of family and friends. On the same creed extended and reinforced by common understandings and common interests which enjoin mutual help and mutual self-restraint rests society. In short, upon the basis of a common nature is reared a common interest and understanding. But this common interest is not at first explicitly recognised. It is rather a principle embedded in the structure of society, and fostering its life and growth. What comes before consciousness in the earlier stages is rather the mass of rules and customs prescribing those dealings of individuals with one another on which the existing social structure rests. These rules and customs evolve later into written laws on the one hand, and moral judgments supplementing and correcting established laws on the other. Human society is from the first differentiated from any animal society that we know of by the fact that the individual actions on which it rests are not left either to fixed instincts and habits on the one

hand, or to the desires of the moment on the other, but
are embodied in general rules forming a permanent standard
which society itself will enforce.   In this formulation of
the general rules of action prescribed by the conditions of
life, and particularly of social life, we find the foundation
of human moral systems.

It follows that effective moral theory is broadly relative
to the practical exigencies of the existing social structure.
Now the existing social structure rests on a very partial
application of that principle of a common human nature to
which it owes its existence.   In primitive life, societies are
small, and often, particularly among the more vigorous
stocks, mutually hostile.   The common interest which
unites the men of group A makes them collectively hostile
to group B.   Nor is this all.   The relations within any single
group are by no means dominated by the social principle
to the exclusion of any other.   The actual structure of
any society is a kind of compromise between the claims of
self assertion and the recognition of what is due from man
to man.   The pure social principle would demand the
suppression of every instinct of antagonism and personal
aggrandisement.   Effectively recognised morality has
never demanded anything of the kind.   It recognises
self-assertion, rivalry, competition, and antagonism, within
their limits, and seeks so to adjust them that they shall
not be destructive of the social order.   The social principle is, as it were, Society's collective instinct of self-pre-
servation, and it reduces the other instincts to order as
best it may, but its original aim is not to conquer but to
compromise with them.   It is at a later stage, when
the social principle has become more explicitly realised,
that there arises a moral theory going beyond actual
morality.   Hence also comes about a divorce between the
moral ideal, or religion and philosophy on the one hand,
and the effective morality which is the generalised
expression of customary conduct and the recognised
requirements of social life, on the other.   We are told,
for example, to love our enemies, but the primitive man,
and we are all primitive men when it comes to the point,
loves his friends and hates his enemies, and his conceptions

of right and wrong rest on the hate as much as on the love. The average man learns in church to love his neighbour as himself, but he keeps the lesson for Sundays and holy-days, *i.e.*, days on which he has nothing to do. It does not enter into his practical consciousness of right and wrong. When he sets about to best his neighbour, he has no sense of wrongdoing as he has when he steals or lies. We are not to think of the conception of doing to others as we would be done by as a principle which appeals to the average man in the light of a duty against which he habitually transgresses with a certain sense of remorse. On the contrary, it does not for the most part appeal to him as standing in any relation to practice at all. It is just a pretty formula which he likes to hear repeated, as long as the preacher does not use it to draw uncomfortable conclusions bearing on practical life. Under the veneer of Christian ethics, the average man has a code of his own. It is a mistake in the opposite direction to suppose with the cynic that the natural man recognises no purely moral obligation. On the contrary, he is constantly surprising the attentive observer by showing a regard for some kind of code in quite unexpected ways. But it is a code of his own—a code, one may conjecture, differing more or less from class to class and from nation to nation, and based in each case on the realised relations of a man's life, on the nature and exigencies of the particular part which it falls to him to play, the special form which the struggle for existence takes for him. Life remains for the average man a game which he plays against others, and he has the character and the sentiments appropriate to a player. His morality consists essentially in recognising the rules of the game. If you condemn the game altogether, in the name of something higher than war and competition, he simply does not understand you, or he classes you with those ministers of religion who preach upon the blessings of peace one day, and the next lead with voices raised to highest sanctimonious pitch the popular howl for war. The average man not only plays his game against others, but in his heart approves of and

respects them when they play it well against him.   Still,
he expects them to keep to certain rules.   If they hit, it
must be above the belt, and if they cheat, it must be
all in accordance with the regular tricks of the trade.
The average man has, as we say, his code.

. . . "What passes as the moral consciousness of mankind is
no more purely and unreservedly moral than mankind itself.   It
is a highly complex product of very various sentiments, many of
them beautiful, most of them respectable, but some of them
irrational and ugly.   To make sure of this, it is only necessary
to take the average moral sentiment of workaday life, consider not
the phrases which it employs, but the application which it makes
of them, and compare it with any well-known example of the
genuine ethical spirit, say the Sermon on the Mount, which
comes almost as near as is humanly possible to unalloyed ethical
truth.   The difference resolves itself into this, that whereas the
Sermon on the Mount is an expression of pure love, the average
moral sentiment is an expression of regard for others tempered by
rivalry and fear.   It is a compromise between the primitive
struggle for existence and the sense of an identical nature and
purpose.   Hence, to illustrate by a single point, its regard for
success as such, and its contempt and dislike of failure ; its feeble
criticism of successful violence and its self-righteous zeal in
devising fresh degradation for those who are already disgraced.
There can be little doubt that the average moral man thoroughly
enjoys the punishment of an offender and feels his own righteous-
ness enhanced thereby.   Objection to cruelty seems to be a
comparatively modern feeling, still in its infancy and limited to
a small percentage of people.   An unauthorised shot at a rabbit
is still a far more serious offence than beating a child with a
poker, and *pecca fortiter* remains a tolerably safe motto.   In the
same spirit, when the average man talks of honour he is not really
thinking of a moral quality, but of something which makes a man
respected and feared by others, which puts him beyond the reach
of insult or injury.   It is only in this sense that a duel can be
called an affair of honour, and it is in just the same sense that a
nation's honour is thought to be more seriously menaced by a
frank admission that it has done a wrong, than by the most un-
scrupulous use of force against the people that it has injured.   In
short, force, self-assertion, and all that contributes to the market
value of man or woman, are natural objects of admiration for the
consciousness which is immersed in the struggle for existence,
and they remain constantly at strife with the ideas of love, self-

surrender, and mutual service which arise with the dawning consciousness of a common human nature."[1]

7. Ordinary unreflecting morality is in line both with lower and higher developments in its ultimate basis. The common character and interests of the species, its unity for certain purposes, go to determine the instincts, and later, the sympathies and antipathies of animals; in human thought they become, within certain limits to be insisted on presently, explicitly realised. Our social morality rests on our knowledge that others are made of like clay to ourselves. But what the average man knows of others is that while for some purposes or in some relations he may rely on their help, for other purposes he must also be prepared to maintain himself against them. Now within a society, as order develops, the average man comes to conform himself well enough to the customs, laws, and understandings which establish a certain compromise between his self-assertion and his regard for his neighbour. He recognises, to use our former expression, the rules of the game. But outside the organised society, all men are primitively enemies, and here, at least, it is astonishing how primitive we still are. The result of social morality in its lower stages is to organise men into competing groups. Nowhere, as we all know, is the paradox of the moral consciousness more conspicuous than in the contrast between the relations upon which it insists within a well ordered society, and those which it tolerates or encourages towards the foreigner. Dr. Wallace gives an idyllic account of the Dyaks of Borneo, who appear to be the most charming and orderly of people—only they have an unfortunate habit of head-hunting. The heads, of course, are only taken from the inhabitants of other villages. Here, surely, is the human moral consciousness in a nut shell. All the great work of social reorganisation that constitutes the progress of 100 years has gone to make the states of Europe more determined adversaries in a more deadly struggle.

For the natural man, rights and obligations effectively

---

[1] From the writer's "Ethical Basis of Collectivism," *International Journal of Ethics*, Jan. 1898, pp. 151, 152.

extend only to the Group to which he belongs.  In any society but the most primitive tribe, which is too small and too feebly organised to admit of much differentiation, the differences and antagonisms that keep different tribes apart are reproduced, if somewhat more faintly, in the relations of groups, classes, or castes within the tribe.  All the world over, a man has one morality which he keeps for his peers, and another for those " beneath " him.  It is instructive to note how the moral distinction survives the disappearance of the political forms or legal barriers in which it is originally expressed.  It is in the most democratic communities that we are apt to find the shades of social inequality most nicely marked off.  The average man cannot genuinely feel that an inferior class deserves or even really desires the kind of treatment which he expects for himself, and recognises as due from him to others of his own order.  " Libbaty's a kinder thing that don't agree with niggers " is a maxim which, *mutatis mutandis*, governs social morality all the world over.

If we trace the moral paradox to its root, we shall find that it grows out of an inadequate conception of that common human nature upon which morality rests.  The duties that we recognise towards others, the rights of our own to which we expect them to pay regard, are founded on the common human nature which makes possible the broad reciprocity, the give and take of social life.  To this principle civilised morality invariably does lip-service, but it is so imperfectly realised, and its obligations are so faintly felt, that it is only applied where other motives come to its support.  These motives fall roughly into two main classes.  There are, first, those of affection and sympathy on which rest family life, and, in a less degree, the intercourse of friends, and the relations of a man to those whom he recognises heartily as his "neighbours."  There is, secondly, the community of interests, not necessarily mere self-interest, but the sense of an end common to a certain group, be it a class, an organisation, a party, or a nation.  We have already seen how this community of interest underlies the formation of social groups, and develops along with them, being at once the cause and effect of their life and growth.

8. The social structure at any given place and time, and the moral system appertaining to it, is a partial organisation of many conflicting forces. The self-assertion of individuals, the collective selfishness of families and other minor groups are not subdued, but come to a kind of compromise with the necessities of social union, and the fighting spirit is permanently maintained by the hostile or at best unsocial and unorganised relations of society as a whole to other societies. But from an early period the sense of a common human nature makes itself felt above the limitations of the ordinary workaday morality. There is, for example, a certain chivalrousness towards enemies apparent even at the level of barbarism, and the impulses of sympathy and tenderness occasionally well up over all barriers of class or race or creed. A moral revolution is introduced as soon as the conception of common humanity becomes recognised as the fundamental moral truth which is to be thanked for such advances in social organisation as have been already made. With the explicit recognition of this principle begins the organisation of life on quite a different scale and with altogether higher ends.

The first and most striking effect of the humanitarian principle is its levelling tendency. In the ancient world, the Stoic doctrine of the fatherhood of God, and the consequent brotherhood of man, was instrumental in breaking down the barriers raised by differences of race, nationality, and even caste against the universal application of moral truth. The older morality of Greece and Rome was civic. It was concerned with the reciprocal obligations and rights of free men in a city state, and but faintly concerned itself with duties to slaves or foreigners.[1] The Stoic doctrine was better suited to be the ethical creed of the great denationalised Roman Empire. In proclaiming the moral equality of the slave with his master, Stoicism overleapt class boun-

---

[1] Nevertheless the utter cynicism of Athens in the fifth century B.C. shocked the Greek world, just as France at the beginning of the nineteenth century, England at the end of it, and, above all, Germany in 1914, have shocked the modern world. The Melian dialogue followed by the dramatic retribution of the Sicilian catastrophe is Thucydides' testimony to this feeling of his contemporaries. But Plato's conclusions (Rep. 469-571) show how narrow was the conception of humanitarian duties in the fourth century.

daries as well as race boundaries, and made quite clear for
the first time in Western Civilisation that a man is to be
judged, not by his birth or fortune, but by what he is worth
as a man.[1] The absorption of humanitarianism in supernatural religion has at once popularised and corrupted it.
Between the great world-religions of Buddha, Christ, or
Mohammed, and the more ancient tribal or national religions,
there is a broad difference, roughly parallel to the difference
between humanitarian and nationalist ethics. The world-
religion at least seeks to include all men in its scope. If
all men could be persuaded to believe the same thing, this
would be well enough, but as in matters of theology this
ideal is never realised, the effect of religious teaching is
ordinarily to draw a very vital distinction between those
who are of the household of faith and those who dwell
without. Hence the revived humanitarianism of modern
times has often had to protest against the ethics of religion,
and for a time found itself allied with science in combating the Church. There were however sufficiently strong
humanitarian elements in the Christian creed to assert
themselves against the degradation of religion, and the
modern humanitarian movement from the Evangelical
revival of the Eighteenth century down to the Christian
Socialism of our own day, has been as much furthered by
the established religion on certain sides as it has been
hampered and obstructed by it on others. It is but just to
add that in the modern world the humanitarian spirit has
also had to fight the crudities of an incomplete and over
confident science. The humanitarianism which, whether as
a force interpenetrating older creeds or as itself a religion, is
familiar to the modern world, is principally associated with
the series of political and social changes to which it gives
unity of meaning and purpose. Many of these changes
have a negative or destructive aspect. Such, for instance, are
the abolition of slavery, the destruction of class privilege,
the establishment of equality of opportunity. But the
humanitarian principle is not negative but inclusive, and

---

[1] A single passage in Aristotle (*Eth. Nic.* VIII. 11, 7) may be said
to admit this truth by implication, but rather by way of exception to a
rule than as a fundamental axiom of life.

aims at destruction only so far as is necessary to the removal of barriers by which its operation is limited. It is as much concerned for the extension of corporate responsibility as for the free self-development of the individual ; but the social order which it seeks is that of a higher organisation in which differences are not obliterated, but preserved. Similarly it holds the unity of the human race for a principle which transcends all differences and rivalries of nations, whence its persistent opposition to warfare ; but it has no less often been the champion of nationality because it recognises that the problem is to make divergent types contribute to a vast harmony, not to reduce them to the dead uniformity of a bureaucratic machine-world. Hence politically its problem is on the one hand to create a state which, without derogation to present freedom, shall be a true community with no outcast or disinherited class ; on the other, to make each state part of one greater community in which without loss of national vitality there would be an overruling sense of the common human heritage. I speak only of its efforts, and do not here attempt to measure its success.

9. But there is another aspect of the humanitarian spirit of which it will be well for our purposes to form some conception, however imperfect. Its doctrine, as we have put it, is that a man is to be judged by his worth as a man. Properly speaking, it would carry this conception a step further, and insist that moral and social values themselves are to be measured and estimated in accordance with the requirements and possibilities of human nature. The importance of this position is that current doctrines of right and wrong and the current estimate of comparative values may diverge very greatly from what is best suited to the normal development of the human species. For this divergence there are several reasons. In the first place, we have seen that the moral standards of a people are evolved in correspondence with the practical needs of that people. They must accord with the social structure assumed under pressure of that necessity. Clearly such necessities may be of a temporary character, and they may be such as to stunt or distort the social growth. Now the influence of

tradition tends to maintain moral rules after the need for
them has passed away.    Morality is like a plant growing
in a confined space, which cannot at once resume its natural
form as soon as the confining barriers are removed.    This
obstacle to free development is much aggravated by the
tendency of moral conceptions to crystallise into precepts
arrogating to themselves a supernatural sanction, and
accordingly an absolute fixity.    This assumption, which
doubtless strengthens moral authority as long as the
supernatural basis is firmly believed in, and the ideal
preached is thoroughly in harmony with the desires and
better tendencies of the time, tends to undermine the hold
of morality altogether as soon as the possibility of a wider
and completer life is opened out.    Religion is a progressive
force when it seizes on a new moral truth and presents
it convincingly to the popular imagination.    It becomes
retrogressive when in presence of a still higher truth it
obstinately maintains the absolute validity and fixity of
the old.

Against the tendency to bring conceptions of right and
wrong to the bar of tradition or of supernatural truth, it has
to be said that both tradition and religion have rather to
be brought before the bar of human nature.    It is out of
the needs of common human nature that morality is originally built up.    Could we arrive at a complete conception
of human nature and its possibilities, we should possess
final moral truth.    The humanitarian spirit has at least
reached the point of conceiving human nature as an
organism with a natural growth of its own.    The growth
of the individual is limited in morality as in actual fact
by the corresponding growth of others.    There is as it
were a moral struggle for existence, no less than a physical,
and the character arrives at maturity at the expense of
some loss.    Like the individual, the species has also a
possible and natural growth, made up necessarily of the
growth of its members, but differing in this, that it can
go on from generation to generation.    The full meaning
of the humanitarian principle is to conceive of this growth
as a whole as the end and aim of all human effort, and to
judge existing conceptions of right and wrong thereby.

Human development may be instructively compared and contrasted with simple organic growth.   If we consider a seed, we know that it contains within it certain possibilities of development.   In the proper soil and under assignable conditions its growth will follow a normal course, and it will come to the perfect flower.   What is true of the seed is true of the human being at birth.   For each there is normal development, a possibility of full and perfect realisation, resting on certain conditions and laws of growth.   There is however this difference, that the flower may become perfect at the expense of its neighbours, while for the man, this method of attaining perfection destroys it.   The perfection of the human soul is a function of the perfection of others.   Thus from individual development we are driven on to social development, and from that, to the development of the whole race.   For the race to be perfect, the individuals must be perfect, and an essential part of their perfection must lie in their mutual relations.   This again is a peculiarity of the human world. The general idea of a racial development is of course applicable to the plant as well as to the man.   Just as the botanist studies the growth of the individual rose, its normal course, its perfection, the conditions of health and disease, so he investigates the evolution of the species or the variety, shows how a generic type exhibits the promise and potency of a specific form, and discovers the conditions under which that form evolves.   So does the sociologist with the human species : he treats it as something that has evolved, and is evolving, and he seeks to discover what further developments it holds in germ.   In this way the study of growth, human evolution, is to the humanitarian spirit what botany is to the gardener, who would not only bring the flowers that he has to the summit of their perfection, but would seek to derive from them new and more beautiful varieties.

This scanty sketch will serve its purpose if it suggests that the ethics of the civilised world is a field of thought in which two principles, or more strictly, two phases of development, are confusedly intermingled.   On the one hand is the morality of the natural man, a morality that has grown up in correlation with the facts of individual and social life, and this morality tends to be the effective rule of conduct.    On the other hand is a higher morality, based on a conception, more or less perfect, of what life means.    This morality appeals too strongly to the conscience or reason of mankind to be overtly rejected when fairly presented, but it is not as yet strong enough to overcome established practice when the two conflict.    Hence those " conventional lies," by which a faulty civilisation seeks to make the best of both worlds.    Hence also the pitiable state of the recognised religious bodies, most of which admit large fragments, more or less distorted, of true ethical teaching which as parts of the established order they dare not apply.

It will readily be seen that " natural morality " corresponds to the Third Stage of intellectual development. It has already been characterised in describing that stage. At that level experience is organised into conceptions, and similarly conduct is formulated in general rules, but as there is no penetrating analysis of the conceptions, so there is no striving after the underlying purpose that might justify but might also remodel the rules.    This analysis, which involves moral as well as intellectual insight, is the foundation of a higher moral teaching, which has historically become current in a fragmentary manner and in very diverse forms.    The central idea which gives unity to these differences is that humanity is the object of man, *i.e.*, that the business of the human race is to work out all that it has in it to be.    In this conception the social structure and even the current morality are treated as servants rather than masters of human life.    And if we follow out this doctrine into all that it implies, we are led to think of an ethical system which will be guided by the conception of the human race as a whole, bound together by the ties of a common nature, and capable under ascertainable conditions of a future for which all earlier evolution is preparatory.

10. Such a principle might serve as a basis for that comprehensive harmony of conduct which we should expect to find at the highest stage of development.    In

this respect again it contrasts with the fragmentary and more or less inconsistent rules which satisfy unscientific thought.   But it is worth adding that a transition from the lower or fragmentary to the higher or systematic ethics may be seen at the  point at which without any scientific analysis, some general conception arises, comprehending and subordinating to itself all minor rules of conduct.   Such a conception may be social or religious ; the end that it proposes may be the welfare of society, or it may be obedience to the will of God.   In either case, though with very different results, such a conception endows life for the first time with real unity of purpose, and under its guidance a man's every action comes to be devoted to a single end.   Such an end, however, rarely includes within it the whole of human nature.   Those who consecrate their lives to a single cause tend, as we are often tragically made aware, to limit themselves in proportion to their success in concentration.   There are very few men who can be as ardent in their patriotism as Mazzini, and yet at the same time conceive of their country as the servant rather than the mistress of humanity.   The ordinary patriotism is, if made the highest end of life, a narrow, exclusive, and in the long run a self-destructive idea.   Conversely the greatest modern statesmen in our own country have been noted for qualifying the insular by the " European " view. Nor need we waste words in describing how religion often tends to narrow as well as to elevate.   A man's God is a crystallisation of certain elements of his own nature.   It is therefore a limited being, narrower than the man himself.   To find the true God is to understand the Spirit which moves and works in all things and strives towards realisation, and it is only this God whose service is the perfect freedom which consists in following the plan which is at once natural and divine.

The ideal of moral philosophy is also to bring the conduct of life under the unity of a single comprehensive purpose.   But this unity, it is suggested, is formed by a deliberate synthesis of the divergent but not necessarily conflicting possibilities of human development.   Nothing,

if the method is true to itself, can be left out that is permanently necessary or desirable in the formation of human
character.  Hence the ethical religion claims the privilege
of concentrating, like other religions, all life and all its
powers on a single aim, but it concentrates without narrow-
ing.  Its ideal is to bring to their highest pitch all the
faculties of man so far as they are capable of harmonious
development.  Its enemy is everything that conflicts with
such harmony, and of this it finds much in the established
order, and even in the recognised moral and religious
teaching of the best ordered societies.  It has therefore
constantly to go back from the recognised ideal to its own
deeper ideal.  Its work is constantly to revise social relations and moral values in accordance with the realities of
human nature and social life.  In this formula we arrive
by another road at the point reached when discussing the
goal of scientific thought.  We saw then that the development of science and philosophy pointed to the ideal of a
completed system in which the results of race experience
should be so far co-ordinated as to make possible a just
understanding of the true lines of race-development.  We
saw that this ideal postulated a certain development of
the ethical consciousness, since it is for this consciousness
that the race becomes a unity, while even to apprehend,
and, much more, to translate it into a practical correlation
of conduct and ideal, an ethical principle was needed as the
underlying motive.  We have now sketched the course of
ethical development so far as to show that it leads us to
the same result, that the highest ethical consciousness
postulates an understanding of the possibilities of race
development, and consists in the effort to remodel social,
moral, and religious life in accordance therewith.  As in
theoretical, so in practical science, the higher development
consists in a double process.  Like philosophy, it is a completion of the co-ordination of conduct which we find in all
moral ideas by the formation of a single comprehensive
system.  Like philosophy, it proceeds by tracing existing
conceptions back to underlying principles, finding in such
principles a keystone of the arch.
    The parallel between ethical development and the general

growth of system and co-ordination of which it is a part, may indeed be carried through all the four intellectual stages which we have distinguished. In the first stage we have impulse not explicitly related to its end. Accordingly we have no evidence of purposive action for the good of another. In the second stage we have concrete, practical ends. Corresponding with this, we have sympathy and attachment binding one individual to others, and correlating his action with their immediate needs. In the third stage, action rests on general conceptions, and is adapted to comprehensive ends. Ethically it is guided by moral rules, and may be subordinated to an end as comprehensive as the permanent welfare of a great community. In the fourth stage general conceptions being traced back to their principles are formed into a comprehensive system in which any particular thought or action must find its definite place in relation to all the rest. Ethically this general conception is the realisation of the full promise of human nature in the effort towards which it is conceived that human effort might find a unity which should not be a limitation.

## SUMMARY.

The last stage of development that we have traced consists, like the earlier ones, in a double advance in explicitness and comprehension. Once again, there is no breach of continuity, but a series of changes amounting as they are summed up to a difference of quality. Going below the reasoning of the previous stage and its conditions in reality, thought now interconnects the universal Truths which constitute these conditions and forms of them a system, the aim of which is to render experience intelligible as a whole. From first to last the mind works by correlating experiences. In the highest development of the present stage, the principles and methods of correlation themselves become objects of consciousness, and form a distinguishable element in the system which they build up. We have compared the earlier stages to distinct phases in the apprehension of a logical syllogism. The lowest stage

we compared to a syllogism in which the conclusion alone
was explicit, the premisses being represented by psychological
forces which, without being grasped as such, produced
their result. The second stage we took as equivalent to
the inference from minor to conclusion, where a major
premiss was still unrecognised. In the third stage, the
major was brought into the conscious process, and we had
major, minor, and conclusion explicitly recognised as a
coherent whole. It remains that in this last stage the
theory of syllogism, the character of the Universal and the
Particular, the assumptions involved in reasoning, in a
word, the whole thought-process operating as a psychological force in the lower stages, should be analysed out,
and become, like its data and its products, an object of
examination and criticism. The highest operation of
thought, as we know it, is to be conscious of its own principles. And this applies, of course, to the moral and
practical as well as to the theoretical functions of thought.
We demand at this stage a similar analysis of the basis of
the moral judgment : of religious conceptions : of the
social structure. In the lower stages of human development these conceptions grow like natural products.
Though their life is in the thought and action of intelligent individuals, yet the action of man on man, of thought
on thought, of the social structure on the individual, of
the individual on his environment, is so subtle and so
complex that though each step in the progress of any
great change may be the conscious act of a rational agent,
the change as a whole proceeds unconsciously and without
plan. Gradually to weld the vast mass of interrelated
cause and effect that constitutes history into an intelligible
whole will be the latest result—for it is a result not yet
achieved—of the highest science. In point of explicitness,
then, the work of the highest human philosophy is to
analyse and bring into its system the principles upon which
that system rests.

These principles form the keystone of the arch, which
for the first time embraces the whole of human purpose
within its span. In the previous stages we have seen how
the organisation of experience began modestly, with the

readjustment of instinctive processes, and developed to the point where in human life it uses the recorded experience of the past to form a basis of conduct, and a setting for the life and purposes of the individual. But up to this point, though experiences are grouped together, the results are not systematically co-ordinated *inter se*, nor has life one purpose, plan, or rule, but rather many that contend with one another. It remains for the highest stage to reduce the whole of human experience to a single system, and to make the future of humanity the all-embracing purpose of action. Remote as this ideal organisation of life may be, it is suggested that the trend of theoretical science is towards the discovery of the conditions of human development, while the trend of the ethical spirit is towards making that development the supreme object of action. In the union of these movements, human thought would seem to come as near as possible to the limiting conception of the correlation of all experience with all action. At any rate, knowledge of the underlying conditions of development would become the basis of a system of conduct designed to promote development. The life of the species would become self-conscious, and its growth self-determined. It remains only to note that the force of instinct or heredity would not disappear, but it would no longer be a force operating outside the system of knowledge. On the contrary, it would enter into the system and be duly allowed for among the fundamental conditions affecting the possibilities of growth.

# CHAPTER XVII

SUMMARY OF THE STAGES OF CORRELATION

1. THE broad fact dealt with in the preceding chapters is the adaptation of human and animal action to the requirements of life and growth. Such adaptation we have found to involve a certain correlation, to put it in the most general terms possible, between the experiences and actions of the individual and of the race. In the character of the correlation found at different stages there is an immense difference, and as is the nature of the correlation, such is the adequacy, subtleness, and comprehensiveness of the adaptation, and such also the "requirements of existence" which the organism seeks to meet. At one end of the scale we have a method of correlation based on the principle of heredity, and working out in the course of many generations and through the extinction of a majority of individuals, a structure fitted to respond with something approaching the regularity of a machine, to those promptings of the environment or of the inward mechanism which concern the safety of the individual and the perpetuation of the species. Adaptation at this stage, though often a model of precision in its working, is seen nevertheless in its narrowest and most primitive shape. For each act is merely a response to a stimulus or set of stimuli which under normal circumstances gives the required result, but, where the environment deviates from the normal, there is little or no power of making the necessary readjustments. Lastly, the requirements of existence which action is adapted to secure are the requirements of a

bare existence, or, to put it more fully, of the maintenance
of the specific type. Action is not adapted to the improvement of the type, nor even to making the life of the
individual or of other individuals better or fuller or more
comfortable.

From this stage of correlation we passed to those in
which the behaviour of the organism is less and less rigidly
defined by heredity, while the part played by experience
becomes greater. Adaptation becomes at the same time
more many-sided and directed to remoter and more
comprehensive aims, including conceptions of welfare
which involve something more than the bare existence of
the species. As the development proceeds, the experience
of the race is once more brought into play in a new form,
as acting not merely through inheritance, but through
tradition and history, and finally as the basis of scientific
inductions. In a parallel fashion, the conception of the
ends of conduct widens until it grasps the welfare of the
race as a whole as its object. At this point Development, at first blind and mechanical, advancing through
stress of conflict and competition, becomes directed and
purposeful—an organic growth, and yet the growth of
an organism that knows its own destiny, and by knowing
achieves it.

This process is, as we conceive, the fundamental fact of
Orthogenic Evolution. We have now to summarise the
main features of the successive stages as they have appeared
in the preceding chapters.

*I. Correlation by Heredity.*

There is, as we have seen, an indirect correlation of
experience, reaction, and welfare, before intelligence, that
is, the capacity of the individual to learn from experience,
comes into play. Response to stimulus is in this stage the
outcome of an inherited structure, and if a certain variation
of structure gives a more suitable response, that is, one
better adapted to preserve the organism or its offspring,
such a structure would tend to be " selected." That is to
say, individuals possessing it would have an advantage in
the struggle for existence. In this way inborn tendencies
to a given method of response may be correlated with the

past experiences of the race. The points to be summarily noted here as to this method of adaptation are :—

1. Such correlation is not achieved within the experience of any individual, but only through a succession of individuals, resting upon the destruction of most of them.

2. The "welfare" subserved by the adaptation is simply the survival of the race under the existing conditions of its environment.

3. Adaptation is limited by stimulus ; that is to say, if the normal stimulus fails or is greatly modified, the power of carrying out the "ends" which the adaptation subserves is small, and often altogether absent.

4. The growth of adaptation (*i.e.*, the evolution of a Reflex or any structurally determined response) is limited by the condition that each stage of change must be directly more beneficial than that which it supersedes (*i.e.*, without regard to the question whether a further development on similar lines would be still more beneficial or not).

It follows that (as compared with correlation effected within the experience of the individual) the rate of change is indefinitely slow, and there is no necessary tendency to a higher type, but merely to one which will under existing circumstances maintain itself more efficiently.

*II. Correlation by Coexistent Conditions.*

We could not carry our study of behaviour far in any direction without coming on a factor clearly distinct from the operation of a hereditary mechanism, and indeed in appearance from any mechanism whatever. The distinction was that mechanical process is unaffected by its consequences. The new factor, which we called generically conation, is conditioned by its relation to the results arising from it. We found traces of this factor in very low stages of the animal world, and it is probably co-extensive with animal if not with all life. It expresses itself in action in the uniqueness and originality with

which diverse elements affecting the organism are so
correlated as to secure suitable results. Such correlation
among ourselves involves the condition of consciousness.
Consciousness is known to each of us only by introspection, only therefore within himself. But we do not
hesitate to impute it to other human beings and to
attribute to them modifications of consciousness similar
to those which we each know in ourselves on the ground
of similarity of behaviour. We found that among
animals processes exist which proceed from causes and
perform functions closely corresponding to those which
among ourselves involve consciousness in various forms,
and we decided to characterise such processes in terms of
consciousness, without implying thereby that if we had
a sense which could directly acquaint us with what
passes within the animal we should find it exactly like
the conscious state that we know in ourselves. We also
speak freely of conscious processes as causes of behaviour
without postulating a theory of the relation between the
conscious and the physical. Every conscious process
may, for anything that has here been said, have a physical
side or concomitant, and it may be only through its
physical side that it operates on physical processes. But
even so the physical state involving consciousness is
distinct from all others in its causes and effects, and it is
the nature of this distinction which we have been pointing
out. When we speak of any form of consciousness as a
link in causation, then we refer to the operation of that
process, be it physical or psychophysical, in which, among
ourselves, that form of consciousness is an integral
factor.[1]

The function of conative consciousness in general is
to effect fresh correlations within the life of the individual,
correlations which could not be achieved by hereditary

---

[1] That the psychical element is a true cause, *i.e.*, that psychical energy
exists, is, however, my belief. I have worked out the reasons in my own
fashion in *Development and Purpose*, Part II. Ch. IV. The impossibility
of a mechanical view of mind and the weakness of the presumptions on
which it rests is ably shown by Dr. McDougall in his *Mind and Body*,
however much the Animistic theory in the form which he proposes may be
subject to criticism.

mechanism. In its earliest forms this appears in the
relation established between the act and the present conditions of the organism. The crudest instance is the
maintenance of action, with repeated reversals and variations under the influence of some persistent stimulus.
This behaviour tends at last to bring relief, and may be
regarded as determined, in an indefinite or negative
fashion, by its tendency, since it is the discomfort of the
present that excites action and maintains it at high
tension while the failure to give relief causes its reversal
and modification. In the sensori-motor action we found
a more definite direction given to effort. Various circumstances and movements are uniquely correlated in the act
of attention and (if we exclude ideas) we must regard
the sense of approximation to the result as the factor maintaining the appropriate action and inhibiting deviations.

The result thus indirectly determining action (as the
point to which the conation tends) is the performance of
some function in the life of the organism. In our consciousness it is that which at the moment satisfies. Where
one object is attained, others come into view, and in
certain cases a train of objects may be formed leading up
to some total result. Such a line of behaviour may be
laid down by the hereditary structure of the organism,
and the enduring interest which governs it is called an
Instinct. In Instinct then successive conations are correlated so as to secure some ultimate result, *i.e.*, to subserve
some organic function, but this correlation, so far as it is
purely instinctive, is not effected by consciousness. The
instinct at any given stage arouses interest in the object
appropriate at that stage and conative consciousness is
limited to the achievement of that object. In so far as
remoter aims come into view and intermediate stages
losing their independent interest are treated merely as
means, a higher factor of correlation comes into play and
we pass from the sphere of pure Instinct into the stage
in which Instinct is merged with Intelligence.

So far, then, consciousness as such effects a correlation
of present conditions. Acting under correlations determined by heredity, it serves to make these more plastic

and efficient in adapting themselves to variety and overcoming obstacles.    We have now to examine the extension
of its scope to Past and Future.

*III. Correlation based on Individual Experience.*

Of this process, which we have considered the special
work of Intelligence, we have distinguished four great
stages.

*Stage I. Inarticulate Correlation.*

While inherited behaviour, whether instinctive or
reflex, consists of the response to stimulus of a preformed
structure, we find in this stage a modification of such
response by experience of its effects.    This process may
be regarded as the germ of all subsequent correlation.
In this first stage, the correlation is to be understood as
follows :—

The feeling consequent upon instinctive or random
reaction to a stimulus modifies the reaction to similar
stimuli in a manner determined by the nature of the
feeling.    Simple instances are those of the spider refusing
after a few trials a fly which had been dipped in turpentine,
or of the fish which learns to come for food on the
approach of human beings.

To the observer it is clear that the basis of the
modification is a certain relation of stimulus, reaction, and
feeling.    But for the intelligence at this stage, these
elements and their relations are not explicit.    They have
no distinct function each for itself, but act as a whole so as
to effect the particular modification described.    We have
described this as a *Correlation of Empirical Results*, or
negatively, as *Inarticulate Correlation*.    As a thought
process we have compared it to a syllogism in which the
mind is explicitly aware of the practical conclusion alone,
the premisses being presented by a certain combination of
psychological forces from which the conclusion follows.

The distinctive conscious function involved is an
impulse-feeling attached to a sensory excitement in consequence of previous experience.

The scope of the experience co-ordinated is the *relation
between reaction upon stimulus and the immediately attendant feeling.*    The scope of the adjustment effected is pre-

cisely the same—that is, *adaptation of reaction so as to produce the most suitable feeling.*

Correlation of this type prunes and perfects hereditary tendencies and forms useful habits out of random acts. The general biological effect is to render instinct more plastic.

Ethically considered, action in this stage is *Impulsive*, and so far as determined by experience, must be regarded as limited to adjustments based on and relative to the feeling of the individual alone.

*Stage II. Concrete Experience and the Practical Judgment.*

It is clear that in the first stage the scope of intelligence is at a minimum, being confined to the felt character of the excitement of the moment. This character must[1] contain a motor impulse more or less definite, but is not in any way differentiated into distinct elements. Hence discrimination is also at its lowest point. The first advance in both these respects brings us to the second stage. Psychologically, the new departure which has taken place in this stage is that the related term which in the previous stage merely influences action, is now brought explicitly into consciousness. In other words, the perceptual relation, the concrete whole in which distinct terms are united, now appears to be the basis of action, or even to enter, along with other experiences, into higher combinations. Thus in the previous stage, where an excitation A led to a consequence B, it acquired thereby a motor character $\beta$. But in proportion as $\beta$ becomes accurately defined and individualised in each new case, it comes to be equivalent to what is in human consciousness a motor idea of B in a definite relation to A. The content thus arrived at is a whole constituted by related elements.

The judgment in which distinct elements are held in relation must rest upon a perception, and thus the foundation of the change we are describing must lie in the growing distinctness and comprehensiveness of perception whereby related objects can be apprehended distinctly and yet together. Such apprehension again becomes possible as

[1] At least in the lower stages. The development of sensation into Perception does not depend exclusively on motor impulses.

the perception proper becomes disengaged from the motor impulse, so extending its scope and becoming a perceptual judgment.[1]   Such a perceptual complex when freely reproducible, becomes the basis of the recognition of individual objects, persons, and places, and of the succession of events.   Action is now no longer tied to a specific motor stimulus, but is based on a relation whereby means and end are connected.

We have called this the stage of Concrete Experience and of the Practical Judgment.   The correlation which it effects is a degree more complex than that of the preceding stage.   Its terms are themselves complexes of related elements.   In the percept-complex which forms the starting point, experiences which are distinct are already combined to form a whole.   The adjustment of means to ends is again, as we have understood it, a distinct act of correlation, and the one relation is based on the other. We may express this increased complexity by describing this stage as the correlation of interrelated elements or Articulate Complexes, the one complex being perceptual, the other practical.   Both are essentially concrete, that is to say, we deal in this stage not with the relation as such, but with two or more related objects of experience.   From this it follows that while the " particular " relations are " conscious " or " explicit," the "universal " that connects them operates unconsciously.   In a given case a consequence is anticipated on the basis of a parallel experience, but there is no consciousness of the implied generalisation, nor even an analysis revealing the point of identity as against the individual differences between the two cases. The inferential process involved is thus parallel to the argument from particulars to particulars, or, if we regard the application of experience alone, to an argument from minor premiss to conclusion.   In this argument the major premiss is not an explicit object of consciousness, but is

---

[1] In sensori-motor action we already have a certain correlation of distinct elements.   But this correlation is purely subservient to the motor response.   We have no evidence of the apprehension of the complex as a distinct state until we find it "reproduced" in an idea.   We may therefore speak of perception in relation to sensori-motor activity but not of the perceptual judgment.

represented by the psychological effect of past experience, which makes the mind draw its inference.

The increased scope of correlation in this stage is most clearly seen in the fact that in reaching it we pass from the sphere of motor reaction and attendant feelings to that of perception and the anticipation of events. The organism can now be said to "know" outer objects (as having distinct qualities, for example) to recognise persons and other animals and to anticipate their behaviour. Its instincts as bearing relation to other individuals, etc., are thus subject to modification in accordance with experience, while it is also possible for it to learn modes of action to which there is no instinctive tendency at all, and that not merely by the fortunate effect of random successes. On the other hand, the animal's action appears to be limited to what may be called its concrete environment and immediate practical ends.

On the ethical aspect, the important points to note are, first, that action being prompted by an idea of its end, we may say that in this stage Impulse is replaced by Desire, and since desires may conflict, the germs of deliberation and even of self-control appear. Secondly, with the knowledge of individuals and their behaviour comes the possibility of emotional states in relation to them. For our purposes the most significant of these states are Sympathy and Affection, whereby the experiences of another become an object of desire along with one's own. The sympathetic desires and feelings are in the first place the conscious rendering of the instincts tending to the maintenance of the species, but observation shows that they may be transferred under the workings of experience to other beings (*e.g.*, men) to whom they do not attach instinctively.

To sum up.

The work of intelligence in this stage, may be described as a *Correlation of articulate complexes in the perceptual order*.

The distinctive conscious functions involved are the perceptual judgment in which distinct elements are held in relation, and the practical idea based upon it which relates to the future. In the correlation which these functions effect the universal relation is the implicitly operative force. Comparing it in this respect with the previous stage, we see that the concrete relation which was there merely an element in the " process " has here passed over with the content. The underlying identity remains outside. The process of correlation is thus comparable to a Syllogism in which minor premiss and conclusion are avowed, while the major premiss is suppressed.

In scope, the experiences co-ordinated are those of the *concrete objects and events in their relation*, with which the mind comes in contact through perception. The scope of purpose is the *adoption of means to practical ends*.

In sphere this co-ordination is limited to *ends determined in general character by instinct*. In general biological effect, its tendency is to throw instinct back to the outlines or plan of action, and to replace it in detail by individual experience and mutual help and even tradition.

Under its Ethical Aspect its distinguishing feature is the determination of behaviour by *Desire* having for its object the experience of others as well as of the Agent.

*Stage III. Conceptual Thinking and Will.*

In the last stage, the connection between the perceived relation and the action based on it remained unanalysed. It rests on an element of identical quality and implies a generalisation which are not in that stage made explicit. The steps by which this bond of connection is analysed out as a distinct content of thought lead us to the third stage.

The starting point, logically, of this process is the act of analysis which renders distinct the common element in different instances. This analysis, which represents a higher development of articulateness in perception, is conditioned by comparisons which throw the common point into relief by exhibiting it in varying contexts. Such comparisons are rendered possible by the increased scope of experience, and are in turn facilitated by the analytical tendency which they cultivate. Thus through increase in the scope and clearness of intelligence a new kind of correlation grows up, resting on the common characters which run through experience, and their specific differences.

We have called such correlation cross-relation, because it runs across the order of direct perceptual or practical activity in which the relations of the previous stages have been found. Of the working out of this correlation, language, both as cause and effect, is the central feature.

This cross connection then appears as the backbone of the third stage. The terms which it connects are not merely related percepts. They are qualities as such, relations as such, elements of continuous identity as such. We have called them collectively elements of affinity between different portions of the world of percepts. These affinities are now explicitly recognised and correlated with one another, thus forming generalisations in which the connection between experience and action always operative is for the first time clearly expressed, and felt in consciousness as connection, as inference. On the other hand, the methods by which the generalisation is drawn from and applied to experience still remain uncriticised. The work of correlation becomes at length comparable to a complete syllogism in which both premisses are made explicit. Yet there is at work a thought-process which, with all the assumptions involved in reasoning on the basis of experience, is not yet taken into account.

In scope, the correlation that is now made possible is immeasurably widened. In the conceptions of this stage, thought first finds itself possessed of contents set free from the line of practical interests, and also—through the possibility of freely breaking up and inter-connecting detached concepts—from the perceptual order. In this way a " world of ideas " is formed, going beyond as well as behind experience, and the conceptions which form this world—whether logically universal, or like the Self and the State, Individual—are equally schemes of reference to great masses of experience, past or future. Thus the permanent elements in experience are grasped, and in experience we must now once more include the experience of the race as handed on by tradition. Similarly, action is subordinated to purposes of comprehensive and abiding interest and to rules of universal applicability.

Conduct is adjusted to meet the requirements of self or others as Persons, of Society as an abiding structure, or Morality as a system of universal rules. In fine, the correlation is now between the permanent and universal in experience on the one hand, and broad purposes of life or general standards of conduct on the other.

Though the part played by experience and thought operating on experience is so greatly increased, it must not be supposed that the instinctive basis of action has disappeared. On the contrary, experience and the use made of it are determined in the first place by the inherited structure. The same fundamental conditions are at the root of the ideals of life, and largely even of the theories of reality which emerge in this stage. Yet at all points, in a manner which we do not in this work seek to determine in detail, instinct is now infused with experience, if in experience we include tradition. The nature of man's ends can now no more be called purely instinctive than the means whereby he learns to achieve them.

From the ethical point of view, we note, first, the emergence of Will as something more than a balancing of Desires—more, because it expresses the personality as a whole which now for the first time has a comprehensive end or scheme of life to guide it. As desire is transformed into will, so sympathy is transformed into regard for the personality of others, and the social impulses of the previous stage pass into an ordered conception of social life and its duties, with a felt obligation of its own that is independent of passing impulse. Conduct is standardised, and becomes explicit morality.

To sum up: the work of intelligence in this stage is the correlation of the elements of affinity pervading and connecting masses of diverse experience.

The distinctive conscious function involved is the conception wherein such an element being distinguished from any given experience becomes a medium of reference to bodies of experience. Correlation through this function is comparable with the completed syllogism with explicit Major Premiss, and comparing it with the preceding stage, we see that the pervading identity which was there the central feature of the inexplicit "process," has now passed over into the recognised "content," leaving outside those general methods and assumptions of thought by which the universal and all other products of intelligence are built up.

The scope of intelligence in this stage extends to the permanent and substantial in the world of experience and to the causal relations underlying its variations. It includes the permanent interests of the individual or of society among its ends, and regulates behaviour in accordance with general rules.

Intelligence thus extends its sphere of influence to the *permanent conditions under which life is maintained,* and of the great ends that make it desirable. In this it partly replaces and partly remodels hereditary tendencies. Yet by these tendencies it is itself unconsciously guided, and for this reason its grasp of the conditions remains partial and uncertain.

Under its Ethical Aspect, this is the stage of *Will guided by general conceptions* of the permanent welfare of self, others, or the community, as well as by the code of rules in accordance with which the life of any given society is organised.

*Stage IV.   Rational System.*

The interconnection of experience with experience, which is the essence of what we mean by system, has been seen at work in all the preceding stages, and in the third stage the work of systematisation has gone so far as to group experiences and purposes into more or less organised bodies. Nevertheless it is a familiar characteristic of "common sense" knowledge that it is unsystematic. This is as much as to say that its systematisation is inexplicit and incomplete. We may consider that the fourth stage begins when system, *i.e.,* the formation of a coherent, self supporting, exact and exhaustive body of knowledge upon a subject—begins to be made an explicit object of mental effort. The stage would be complete when such a system should embrace the conditions and possibilities of human evolution.

From an early stage of its development, the effort

to systematise induces two consequences. The first is a criticism of the principles upon which thought has hitherto dealt with experience, the second a criticism of experience itself, or perhaps rather of the result constructed by thought operating in and upon experience. In this move-ment, the work of analysis, of rendering thought articulate, reaches its final stage, at which it attacks the principles, methods, and processes of thought itself. We compared the inferences of the last stage to a syllogism in which both premisses and conclusion were completely explicit ; but in this stage there is yet another point that is explicit, *i.e.*, the assumptions involved in syllogising, in building up and applying universal conceptions.

Ideally, intelligence at this stage also reaches its highest development in point of scope, for its ultimate goal is nothing less than the complete synthesis of reality as a whole. This goal we have treated as merely a " regulative concept." Reality is infinite, but the conditions affect-ing human life and its development are finite, and there is no reason why they should not come within the scope of science. The knowledge of the conditions of human life and the possibilities of the human race would there-fore constitute the scope of intelligence, if we conceive the scientific stage to have arrived at maturity. The result would be a system including not all reality, but all that affects practical life.

The application of such a system would be a deliberate organisation of life, in which the development of the race is itself the supreme object. And of such an organisation the highest ethical consciousness supplies the necessary basis. If we imagine the tendencies which we see in germ to have reached maturity, we should have brought the de-velopment of mind to a point at which the slow and uncer-tain growth emerging through conflict and competition with forms that are often stronger though less worthy, would be replaced by an orderly development moving steadily towards an ascertained goal, and master of the conditions, internal and external, of its advance. Thus the scope of correlation at this stage is inclusive of all matters affecting action. The whole experience of the race is used to guide the whole future of the race.   From race-experience—in that widest sense in which moral, spiritual, and imaginative experience are comprehended—is derived that understanding of man's own nature, the meaning of his life on earth, by which action is so shaped as to bring about the consummation in which the human spirit " comes to itself," and in so doing enters on its kingdom. We express this by saying that the conditions and character of human development are made the basis of conduct directed to the perfection of that development.

At this point the hereditary factor undergoes its final transformation.   For under one aspect the special work of this stage consists not in eliminating but in evaluating that factor.   The methods upon which correlation rests remained unconscious and implicit in the third stage. They are of course methods resting on a hereditary structure modified by such gradual and unnoticed operations of experience as are no more conscious or deliberate in their workings than the growth of physical structure itself.   While science and philosophy have to criticise methods of inference, they have also to take account of the limitations of sense-experience—limitations of course depending on the inherited structure of the sense organs.   But perhaps most important of all is the evaluation of the hereditary factor in the moral consciousness.   We have seen that in the previous stage the moral impulses gave rise to definitely formulated rules and standards of action.   They also fuse with the conceptions coming from other sources to make the religions of the world.   But though they give rise to explicit conceptions, they themselves are far from being clearly analysed.   Nowhere is the contrast between clearness of result and obscurity of process more marked or of more serious importance than in the sphere of practical conduct. What is contributed by instinct, what by tradition, how much rests on conscious or unconscious adaptation to economic or political circumstances, how far theories of the supernatural have elevated, debased, or in any way modified ethical conceptions, are questions of which ethical theory has hardly yet touched the fringe.   The problem

on solving which the possibility of " self-conscious development" depends is to find the value of all these unknown quantities, and by evaluating them, to determine how
much of moral truth is contained in recognised morality.
This is, in other words, to determine what is meant by
the best and highest development of the human soul, and
what conduct is essential thereto.

Summing up : The work of intelligence in this stage
may be described as the *Correlation of the governing conditions of the life of mind, that is, of the methods and aims of
correlation itself—a correlation of correlations.*

Its distinctive psychological unit is the *apprehension of
the principles and processes underlying thought*—the process of thinking made conscious. This is the process
implicit in all the preceding stages, and in bringing it into
consciousness so that the whole of the " thought process"
now passes into the content, the reasoning of this stage is
as a syllogism in which the assumptions involved in
syllogising should be taken into account.

In scope, the work of Intelligence is to *correlate the
permanent underlying conditions of racial development with
its ideal goal.*

Its sphere is thus *coextensive with life,* and includes
the due appreciation of the conditions imposed on development by heredity.

Under its Ethical Aspect, we may call this the stage of
the *rational Will* in which social standards are subordinated
to and unified in the real conditions of human welfare and
development.

At this fourth stage of development, the wheel has come
full circle. We start from a condition in which ancestral
" experience" acting indirectly through heredity and the
elimination of the less adapted fits responses to stimuli into
an order suited to maintain the racial type in the environment in which it finds itself. Passing out of this condition,
we enter on a process in which life is more and more
dominated by intelligence.

In the lowest stage of this process, a dimly felt mass of
experience gradually remodels reaction to stimulus. In the
second stage, the perceptual world becomes clear and con-

crete, and its relations are used intelligently in the service
of desire.   In the third stage the mind dissects out the
threads of common quality that bind the moving show of
perception, and by their aid grasps the permanent inexperi-
ence, and subordinates action to large and general purposes.
Finally, in the fourth stage, it works down to the principle
whereby these great fragments of knowledge and of purpose
are pieced together into a rational system, comprehending
in a synthesis of thought and action the summed experience and purpose of the race.    The first stage is a correlation of massive results, the second of articulate complexes
in  the  perceptual  order,  the  third  of  transperceptual
affinities, and the fourth of the processes of correlation.
In the first we have consciousness of the present, in the
second conscious reference to past and future, in the third
the self-consciousness of the individual, and in the fourth
that of the race.    Impulse and feeling, perceptual judgment  and  desire,  conceptual  inference  and  will,  critical
reason and ethical spirituality mark the successive steps.
In each stage, as the sphere of experience grows, that of
heredity is transformed.    In the first stage it is rendered
plastic  and  general  instead  of  being  relatively  particular  and  rigid.    In  the  second,  it  begins  to  fuse
with experience as the basis of action.    In  the  third,
it tends to disappear as a separate force,  being  partly
formulated into rules of life, partly fused with tradition,
and  partly  overlaid  thereby.    Meanwhile,  Experience
in  the  form  of  recorded  history  is  extending  over  the
ancestral line through which heredity acts, and thus in the
fourth  stage  we  come  to  the  point  in  which  the  whole
field at first covered by unconscious physical forces is
now overrun by experience and thought.    Race experience,
race maintenance, and race-future are still the determining
factors, but all now fall within the scope of the Reason, and
purposes equally with methods are transformed accordingly.
It  is  not  the  maintenance  of  the  type,  but  its  perfection,
which  is  sought :  not  mere  adaptation  to  circumstances,
but the domination of the rational spirit in the world.

NOTE.—It should be superfluous to say that the above division of intellectual growth into stages is of a hypothetical character, and is not

regarded by the writer as, at best, anything more than a first approxima-tion to the truth. Such as it is, the scheme has a twofold origin : (1) in an analysis of developed experience ; (2) in the observation of less developed experience. The fourfold method of correlation differing stage by stage (a) in respect of the factors explicitly taken into account, and (b) therewith in extent of the sphere comprehended, appears to the writer to be realised in human consciousness as we run the gamut from philo-sophical reflection down to the quasi-mechanical response of habit. Whether these stages into which developed human reason can be analysed correspond to stages by which it *grew* is of course another question—a question only to be answered by a much wider knowledge of animal psychology and of the distinct processes of human development than we at present possess. If we accept evolution, analogy suggests that human intelligence is a specific and higher development of a more general form of intelligence. Hence, if we cut away the higher development, we should come to something roughly common to man and the higher animals. If we cut further, we should come to something common to man and a wider class of animals, and so forth. But there is a caution to be borne in mind. No two species will come to a quite identical de-velopment. No part of the physical structure of man, I suppose, is precisely equivalent to the homologous part in another mammal, still less in another vertebrate of a different class. It is the same with the mental structure. We must not expect to find any animals whose intelligence falls readily into any classification based on the analysis of human ex-perience. We can only expect to find homologous developments. That being understood, it may be said that the method of the preceding chapters, so far as they relate to animals, has been to analyse out the phases of intellectual development as distinguishable in human experience, and to discover what homologous structures are to be found in the animal world. In accordance with these homologies animals are ranked in the classification.

# CHAPTER XVIII

## ORGANISATION, CONFLICT, AND EVOLUTION

1. WE assumed in Chapter I. that Orthogenic Evolution must be identical with the evolution of Mind. This evolution we have now traced, and found to consist in a gradually developing organisation of life. This intelligent organisation, however, is but the natural development and expansion of a process which in its lower stages is purely biological. The growth of intelligence and of social life rests on a high development of physical organisation. To grasp the process of Orthogenic Evolution as a whole we must therefore extend our view. Speaking generally, it is an advance towards a higher organisation, a development of the organic principle in life. But what is a "higher" organisation? Can any definition be found which will not bring us back to the conception of Mind or to some human judgment of value?

Some light on this question may be gained by considering what we mean by organic unity. By an organic whole, is understood one which (*a*) has a certain general character or individuality, while (*b*) it consists of distinguishable parts each with a certain character of its own, but (*c*) such that they cannot exist unmodified apart from the whole, while the character of the whole is similarly dependent upon them. By a mechanical whole, the negation of this interdependence is intended. It may indeed be doubted whether a purely mechanical whole exists as a reality *in rerum natura*. Thus, a heap of cannon balls, which has sometimes served as an instance, may be said to have a certain character of its own which in some degree affects the individual balls —by pressure, for example, which imperceptibly alters their figure, and presumably their molecular structure. The definitions then must be taken as laying down two *limiting conceptions* to which actual things approximate more or less closely, and which are used in ordinary thought. Thus, *e.g.*, by the mechanical view of society is meant the theory which treats human beings as being constant quantities, whether in or out of their social relations. The organic view of society recognises an interdependence whereby the individual is modified by the very social relations which he himself helps to build up. Without going deeper into the nature of the organic principle, these simple considerations may lead us to distinguish two main lines of organic development. There is, first, degree of organic unity. A whole is more organic in proportion as the interdependence of parts is more complete, and one line of advancing organisation will consist in perfecting this unity. Then there is, secondly, scope of organisation. Very simple elements may be very completely organised. Much more numerous, diverse, or complex elements may be less completely organised. In the first case, there is a perfect organism of low or narrow scope. In the second, an imperfect organism of a higher or wider scope. Scope of organisation is proportioned to the diversity of elements which go to build up its unity. A Rhizopod is not so completely a unity as man is, but even if it were, it would be a lower organism. It is a unity including much less of differentiation. From this distinction, it will readily appear that there are two methods by which organic unity may develop. One is by the gradual obliteration of the distinctive characters of the parts, wherein all that is opposed to unity and organisation is worn away. The other is by the working out of a type of organisation in which there is room for more of difference and of what was before contradiction. It is clear that it is only the latter form of development by which organisation can grow in perfection and in scope simultaneously. Taking the two tests of Unity and Scope together, we may regard them as conjoint tests of " higher " organisation, and we may define orthogenic evolution as the process by which such organisation is attained.

2. Now the organisation of the life of a species as a whole depends on three more elementary forms of correlation. These are :—

(1). The correlation of the constituent parts of the individual—perfection of structure and function.

(2). The correlation of the several acts and experiences of the individual.

(3). The correlation of the acts and lives of different individuals.

With the two latter we have dealt. It remains to show in a summary way how their development is associated with an advance in physical organisation from the lowest organisms to man. The Protista are classed as the lowest organisms on account of their " simplicity," *i.e.*, the narrow scope of their organisation, confined as it is to a single cell. Among the lowest Metazoa, the unity of the distinct cells that constitute the living being is so loose that it is often difficult to say whether a certain aggregation of cells should be regarded as one individual or many.

"When from sundry points on the body of a common polype, there bud out young polypes which, after acquiring mouths and tentacles and closing up the communications between their stomachs and the stomach of the parent, finally separate from the parent ; we may with propriety regard them as distinct individuals. But when in the allied compound, Hydrozoa, we find that these young polypes continue permanently connected with the parent ; and when by this continuous budding-out there is presently produced a tree-like aggregation, having a common alimentary canal into which the digestive cavity of each polype opens ; it is no longer so clear that these little sacs, furnished with mouths and tentacles, are severally to be regarded as distinct individuals. We cannot deny a certain individuality to the polypedom." [1]

Long after organisation is sufficiently developed to leave no doubt as to the unity of the organism, the separate

[1] Herbert Spencer, *Principles of Biology*, Vol. I. p. 246. Cf. Verworn, pp. 63, 64.

parts still retain powers which show that their mutual dependence is still far from complete. The most remarkable
of these powers is that of Regeneration, which, as is well-
known, diminishes roughly in proportion as organisation
advances. For example, among Worms, it is common to
find Regeneration not only of the tail, but even of the
head.[1] No Vertebrate could imitate this feat of growing
its head anew, but the lower Vertebrates retain a considerable though diminished power of regenerating lost
limbs and other organs. Thus, the larval Salamander
regenerates the lens of the eye from the posterior layer of
the iris.[2] The Salamander can also regenerate an am-
putated limb, if the bone is cut across, but not if it is
exarticulated. These powers however are by no means
common to all the lower Vertebrates—the frog's limb, for
example, would merely heal without growing again—and
are, I imagine, wholly lost in the higher class of birds
and mammals, where the power of regeneration is confined
to that fresh growth of the adjacent tissues which we are
familiar with in the healing over of a wound, or in the
mending of a bone.

As the loss of regenerative power points to a growing
centralisation of the vital functions, so also does the
gradual loss of independence on the part of the lower
nerve-centres point to the growing centralisation of the
nervous system. In passing from the higher to the lower
vertebrates, the relative independence of the spinal reflexes is well marked ; but it is as nothing to the powers of
separate nerve centres among the higher Invertebrates.
Thus, the loss of the hind quarters does not prevent a
bumble bee from continuing its meal, nor an ant from
persisting in a battle.[3] Wasmann mentions cases of an ant
or wasp fighting with its own severed limbs.[4] On the
other hand, according to Forel,[5] the severed head of an ant
still distinguishes a friend from an enemy. On the same
authority we learn that crickets deprived of the cerebral
ganglia can be stimulated by touch to oviposition. At

---

[1] See e.g. Wilson, op. cit., p. 325.        [2] Wilson, p. 329.
[3] Wasmann, Instinct und Intelligenz, p. 93.        [4] Ibid.
[5] Aperçu de Psychologie comparée, Année psychologique, 1895, p. 25.

this stage it is clear that the unity of the nervous system is not the unity with which we are familiar in man, or in animals which approach man in the general plan of their structure. In truth, unity of nervous organisation is less necessary and perhaps less possible where behaviour consists mainly of a series of instinctive reactions. Reflexes and instincts may be efficiently carried out, each by its own appropriate mechanism, and their mutual dependence may be slight. But in proportion as the organism comes to rely upon its own experience for guidance, it becomes more and more necessary that different actions and different experiences should be brought to bear upon one another ; and for this purpose different parts of the nervous system must be more intimately correlated. Thus completeness of physical unification serves as a condition of that still higher organisation of life which is the work of intelligence.

In the same way, social life has its ultimate basis in a refinement of physical organisation whereby the play of separate individual lives becomes interwoven. This is first seen at a low stage of the animal world in the distinction of sex whereby each individual becomes an incomplete organism, needing union with another to fulfil its vital functions, and endowed accordingly with means of finding and uniting with the other. It is seen, secondly, in the physical relation of mother and young both before and after birth—a relation which, as has been shown, steadily grows in importance as we ascend the orthogenic scale. In both cases physical bonds unite otherwise distinct individuals [1] to form temporarily or permanently a higher organisation. As intelligence in general starts from the organised unity of the individual, so the social intelligence —the organising principle which makes a unity of separate individual lives—starts with a physical organisation which does the same work in little.

Thus from first to last the essence of orthogenic evolution is a progress in Organisation. Such a progress

---

[1] In the case of the embryo indeed we get a doubt as to the distinctness of individuality quite parallel to that which we have noted in regard to the component parts of the lowest Metazoa.

takes two forms. There is a development in organic unity or "organicity," as parts and wholes come to be more and more completely interdependent. And there is increase of scope, as the life or purpose of the organisation becomes more and more comprehensive. The lower phases of this movement are worked out by biological forces. The higher are the work of mind.

But is this antithesis final and complete ? We oppose the operation of Mind to that of biological forces so far as these are mechanical and, like natural selection, act blindly without regard to results. But in everything living we have seen traces of a principle which is not mechanical, which in its most definite shape we identify with conation. If conation is co-extensive with life, then there is at least the germ of Mind in all life, and this is what differentiates it from the inanimate. When we oppose Mind to biological forces, then we mean those forces taken in abstraction from the element of Mind, without which it would seem nothing actually lives. What part then is played in building up organic unity by Mind in the lower forms of conation on the one side and by mechanism on the other ? This is a question which Biology does not as yet enable us to answer with definiteness or certainty. In every individual we find a mechanism co-ordinating parts in subservience to the life of the whole. In every individual also we find conation supplementing this mechanism and perfecting it. The relationship is not that of two wholly independent factors. For (a) conation itself depends upon pre-existent structure and stimulus,— hunger, for instance, or the sex impulse arising from a physical condition in response to a physical stimulus and issuing in a pre-formed process which, in the lower stages, the conation only modifies in minor detail. (b) The conation that has done its work affects structure and leaves a modified mechanism behind it, so that the process which has been conscious and conative sinks to the purely mechanical. This latter relation suggested one of the earliest evolutionary theories of instinct, viz., that it arose from the inheritance of habits themselves originally due to intelligence. No one would now maintain this view. But we must observe : (*a*) the only ascertained cause of determinate modification in the individual is conation. (*b*) Conation modifies the individual structure. (*c*) The cause of germinal variation remains wholly unknown except in so far as it is due to the combination of different gametes, and this leaves the variations of the individual gamete unexplained. (*a*) The denial that modification due to conation may affect the germ plasm has been erected into a dogma on account of the difficulty of understanding it, experimental evidence leaving the question open. The early origin of the germ cells within the body is not decisive because we do not know all the ways in which distinct cells affect one another. It is just possible that modifications impressed from without (*e.g.* mutilations) should not affect the germ cells while conations arising from within do in some way work upon them. It is clear that any considerable change of the parent organism must affect the environment of the germ cells, and therefore call forth from them new efforts to maintain themselves within the body tissues, and it is conceivable that such effort should involve a modification of structure congruous with and comparable to the change in the tissue which surrounds them. We must not therefore exclude the possibility that conation is at work through the generations building up the organic structure, and if that is the case the whole of organised life would be referable ultimately to the working of Mind, the " mechanical " factors being merely conditions prescribing the limits of its operations. Such an explanation, which would unify the whole evolutionary process, must, however, be left for the present as a mere possibility.[1]

[1] Apart from this possibility it must be maintained that later research on heredity has made any evolutionary theory of Instinct far more difficult than before. According to the later lights we are to rule out the small variations, the "fluctuations" about the parental mean that occur in every individual. We are to rely on certain definite mutations of appreciable magnitude occurring once for all and founding each time a new and relatively fixed type. In relation to instinct this theory postulates a succession of divine chances. What first causes a spider to spin a web on this view? The addition to or the omission from the fertilised ovum of a physical element. How any physical element destined to produce web spinning comes into existence plumply before any web has been spun is a question which admits of no answer unless we appeal to special creation.

3. We saw in Chapter III. that all organic life rests on adaptation. The means of maintaining life differ from species to species, and improvement of organisation—the method of Orthogenic Evolution, is one means among the rest. It may be shown that this method is not only (as we have assumed) a higher, but also a more efficient method than any other. If we look on the life of a species, its structure and normal functions, as something adapted, I will not say to perfecting, but merely to maintaining itself, it is clear that the efficiency of the adaptation may be measured broadly by the proportion of individuals that it is able to preserve through their normal life span. If the normal life span is difficult to measure, we may take instead the less severe test of maturity, and measure the efficiency of organisation by the number of individuals which it is capable of maturing to the point at which they in turn can propagate the species compared with the number of those that perish by the way.

Of this proportion we can judge in a rough and ready way by the birth-rate of any given species. For unless the numbers of the species are to increase or decrease in geometrical proportion, the adults must year by year be replaced by, on the average, an equal number of the new generation, neither more nor less. For this purpose, the less efficient the species, the greater the number of young that will be required. Accordingly, unless in any species we have evidence for a steady growth or diminution of numbers, we may fairly take the birth-rate as a rough test of efficiency of organisation. The better the species is adapted to maintain itself, the lower will be the birth-rate, and conversely.[1]

The theory supposes a physical change occurring for physical reasons, and carrying with it a change of behaviour which happens to suit the organism—a pure chance which must be repeated every time a new instinct or new variety of instinct arises. The element of continuity which was the essence of the older evolutionary theory has disappeared and we are left with a succession of leaps, which if they only landed us in varieties of form might be credible, but when they end in complexities of behaviour accurately adjusted to need pass the limit of belief in casual coincidence.

[1] The birth rate for this purpose means the average number of young

Bearing this in mind, we find much significance in the enormous differences in fertility that are to be found in different divisions of the organic world. This fertility seems to be at its highest where individual organisation is lowest, that is to say, among Protozoa. It is at its lowest in the human race.[1] It is calculated that a single Paramœcium would, if unchecked, produce two hundred and sixty-eight billions of descendants in one month, while another Infusorian is credited with a possible progeny of a hundred and seventy billions in four days.[2] The birth and death roll of many parasites is small in comparison with these figures, but it has been computed that 60,000,000 eggs are contained in the body of a single Nematode,[3] while, to pass to insects, Huxley calculated that the helpless Aphis, the prey of countless insects, is so prolific that in ten generations the produce of one individual would contain more substance than 500,000,000 men.[4] Speaking generally, it appears that Invertebrates are more prolific than Vertebrates, excepting fish,[5] while among Vertebrates we find on the whole a regular descent from Fish, through Amphibia and Reptiles to Birds and Mammals. This is brought out in the following figures which I take from Mr. Sutherland's valuable work.[6]

Number of young produced per annum by each female.

| | |
|---|---:|
| Fish | 646,000 |
| Amphibia (average of 20 species) | 441 |
| Reptiles (average of 39 species) | 17 |
| Birds (average of 2000 species) | 5 |
| Mammals (average of 82 species) | 3·2 |
| Higher orders of Mammals | 1·3 |
| Ape and Man | $\frac{1}{2}$ |

In interpreting these figures, we must bear in mind that we are not always comparing like with like. In the case

per adult, not per annum. A comparatively slow breeding animal may in this sense have a high birth rate if it is long lived. (See Weismann, *Essays in Heredity*, " On the Duration of Life.")

[1] The Elephant is perhaps less fertile than man, but the Elephant is dying out, while the human race is increasing in numbers.

[2] Ray Lankester, *Comparative Longevity*, p. 74.

[3] *Cambridge Natural History*, Vol. II. p. 162.

[4] *Op. cit.* Vol. VI. p. 589.    [5] Ray Lankester, *loc. cit.*

[6] *Op. cit.* p. 41.

of fish, we are for the most part reckoning unfertilised ova, vast quantities of which in fact miss fertilisation. In the higher classes we are reckoning either fertilised eggs or living young. But when all deductions are made, enough seems to remain to justify the general truth of Mr. Herbert Spencer's view that fertility and high individual development in the main tend to vary inversely.

. . . "Individuation and Genesis are necessarily antagonistic. Grouping under the word Individuation all processes by which individual life is completed and maintained ; and enlarging the meaning of the word Genesis so as to include all processes aiding the formation and perfecting of new individuals ; we see that the two are fundamentally opposed. Assuming other things to remain the same—assuming that environing conditions as to climate, food, enemies, &c., continue constant ; then, inevitably, every higher degree of individual evolution is followed by a lower degree of race-multiplication, and *vice versa.* Progress in bulk, complexity, or activity, involves retrogress in fertility ; and progress in fertility involves retrogress in bulk, complexity, or activity.

This statement needs a slight qualification. For reasons to be hereafter assigned, the relation described is never completely maintained ; and in the small departure from it, we shall find a remarkable self-acting tendency to further the supremacy of the most-developed types. Here, however, this hint must suffice." [1] . . .

There are doubtless many great deviations from the general tendency. One species may be more preyed upon than another of no higher organisation. If so it must either be more fertile in order to maintain its numbers, or its numbers must fall till they reach a point compatible with greater security. Again, there are countless devices for protection which do not imply an advance, and may even involve retrogression in general development. Such, I imagine, are the hard outer shell of the tortoise, the disagreeable taste of certain insects, and the " protective mimicry " of others. The point is that with all the fluctuations due to these causes we find upon the whole a gradual diminution in fertility as we pass from the lowest organisation to the highest.

[1] *Op. cit* Vol. II. p 429

4. So far of organisation generally. There is further evidence, general and special, for the efficiency of the two higher developments of organisation—Intelligence and the Social Life. The efficiency of Intelligence is best measured by contrasting it with that of Instinct—the next highest stage of organisation reached in the organic world. After what has been said, a single reflection will make clear the superiority of Intelligence. Under natural selection Instinct is made and kept perfect only by the ruthless elimination of the majority of individuals. Any diminution in the severity of the struggle will tend to diminish the perfection of the instruments by which it is waged. The species under such circumstances, far from dominating nature, is still struggling for existence, and only its most capable members survive. The condition of their survival is not organised co-operation, but internecine struggle with one another and with the rest of the world. If from the maintenance of Instinct we go back to its growth, we find its inefficiency as compared with that of intelligence in the slowness and indirectness of adaptation to novel circumstances, and in the consequent waste of individual life during the process. Whatever advance there is proceeds at a rate which we may call geological. It requires in all probability generations to perfect itself, and once perfected it sticks. Compared with such sluggishness, the social changes which appear to us slow enough are as the express train to the stage wagon. Between the England of Alfred's time and the England of to-day how many changes of specific value would an accurate sociological classification have to admit ? The reason of the difference is very simple. Whatever its end, intelligence sees it in advance, and goes towards it as straight as circumstances permit. Natural selection, or whatever other biological force is responsible for instinct, does not see its goal at all, but merely favours the breed which most nearly approaches it, and by the preponderance of success in that direction, the species is at length transformed as a whole into a new type. Thus the replacement of instinct by intelligence as the guide of life means a complete revolution in the rate of change. There may be

progress—Orthogenic Evolution—under natural selection, but if so, it must be fortuitous, indirect, and incomparably slow.  It is only under the guidance of intelligence that progress can become the normal condition.

Unfortunately it is only in its most developed form that intelligence takes rank as a serious factor in the evolution of higher species.  In its beginnings, indeed throughout the animal world, intelligence is but one among many qualities through which a species maintains itself, achieving the ends prescribed by its structure.  At this stage, intelligence develops under the influence of natural selection, and therefore at " geological " speed.  Probably the same thing holds of primitive man.  It is only as the mind, in the course of this advance, widens its scope and begins to form general conceptions of social welfare, of religion, of the principles of a science or a handicraft, that the movement begins to go forward steadily.  We do not indeed find a steady general advance of civilisation, for the human mind has not yet grasped the conditions of civilisation as a whole, but here and there, as some new conception arises, we find results worked out with unexampled rapidity, and out of many such movements arises a social evolution.  If in the animal world we find intelligence active mainly in adapting means to ends from day to day, in the human world we find in it also the underlying cause of great changes of type.  Here again it replaces the purely biological forces.

One aspect of organisation remains to be considered— the correlation of the lives and actions of different individuals.  Here again there is evidence that wastage diminishes as correlation improves.  In the animal world this correlation depends mainly on two factors.  One is an organic change whereby the young remains to a later and later stage within the body of the mother.  The other is a psychical change whereby the parent comes to maintain and care for the young with more and more persistence and efficiency.  The first change brings about an enormous decrease in the number of young requisite for the maintenance of the species.  Indeed, the viviparous fish is a far more economical breeder than the nest-builders.[1] Summing up on the fertility of fish, Mr. Sutherland says:—

" Of species that exhibit no sort of parental care, the average of forty-nine give 1,040,000 eggs to a female each year ; while among those which make nests or any apology for nests the number is only about 10,000. Among those which have any protective tricks, such as carrying the eggs in pouches or attached to the body, or in the mouth, the average number is under 1,000 ; while among those whose care takes the form of a uterine or quasi-uterine gestation which brings the young into the world alive, an average of fifty-six eggs is quite sufficient." [2]

Now, the mere postponement of birth is of course a purely physical development. Still, it is an important step in the organisation of life and in curtailment of the struggle for existence. The higher development of correlation between separate lives begins with parental care in the ordinary sense. Its efficacy is best seen in the higher Classes. For example, Mr. Sutherland[3] divides Birds into three grades, his account of which[4] may be summed up in tabular form :—

| Lowest grade. | Middle grade. | Highest grade. |
|---|---|---|
| The young are capable. | Young dependent but can run at birth. | Young callow. |
| There is no nest. | Loose nest. | High skill in nest building or in finding substitutes. |
| Average number of eggs 12·5 per annum. | Average 7·66. | Average 4·5. |

Here it will be seen that with the development of intelligence and of parental care, though the young are more callow, fewer of them are needed to maintain the numbers of the species.

With more complication of detail, Mr. Sutherland shows that the same law holds among Mammals. Thus from the lowest organisms up to the highest, culminating

---

[1] We must except the most efficient nest-builders, such as the stickleback, who hatches from 20 to 90 eggs only at a time (Sutherland, p. 36.)

[2] *Op. cit.* Vol. I. p. 40.      [3] *Op. cit.* p. 58.

[4] *Op. cit.* pp. 54–71.

in Man, we find, with many fluctuations due to other causes, a steady tendency to decrease of fertility, implying a diminution of waste, and a better organisation of life.[1]

5. Now, the further the birth-rate falls, the smaller is the field in which natural selection can be exercised. And yet the higher types are well maintained, and within the highest type the forward movement is most rapid of all.

[1] How far does this process continue in human species? Is it the case that as civilisation advances, the waste of life is less? The question is of the greatest interest, but cannot be answered by considering fertility alone.

If we compare one nation or one grade of civilisation with another, the birth-rates alone will not be sufficient, since in many cases population is notoriously increasing, while in others, and particularly in the lower races, it is diminishing, and even dying out. Moreover, as to the birth-rate itself, no trustworthy figures exist for non-European peoples. Another method of investigation would be to find in any given nation the proportion of children who actually survive to a marriageable age. But here again, anything like accurate information would be limited to civilised nations.

Looking, however, to the actual facts, scanty as they are, we observe first, that among European countries, the most backward are those in which infantile mortality is highest. According to Mulhall (*Dictionary of Statistics*, p. 178) the number of children out of 1,000 who complete the fifth year of life is :—

In Russia . . . . . . . . . . . . 425
„ Spain . . . . . . . . . . . . 571
„ Austria . . . . . . . . . . 614

as against :—

In France . . . . . . . . . . . . 751
„ Denmark . . . . . . . . . 755
„ Belgium . . . . . . . . . . 756
„ England . . . . . . . . . . 762
„ Scotland . . . . . . . . . . 780
„ Sweden . . . . . . . . . . 783
„ Ireland . . . . . . . . . . 837
„ Norway . . . . . . . . . . 838

It agrees with this that the birth-rate per marriage is also highest in Russia, where it is 5·7 as against 4·2 in England and 3·0 in France.

In France, with the birth-rate per family mentioned, population is practically stationary, the increase having been ·08 per 1,000 in the five years 1891-5. (Newsholme's *Vital Statistics*, p. 15.)

This affords us a rough measure of the wastage of life in a modern civilised country, which corresponds fairly well with the figures for between four and five thousand Danish families given in Professor Karl Pearson's *Chances of Death*. (Essay on *Reproductive Selection*, p. 98.) In these figures, the average gross fertility of families in the professional, commercial, and artisan class is given, compared with the net

The truth is that organisation as a method of maintaining the species is set from the first in antithesis to Natural Selection. Natural Selection rests on destruction. It maintains the type only by sacrificing the majority of

fertility arrived at by taking the number of survivors, first after 15, then after 25 years of married life.

GROSS AND NET FERTILITY (DANISH FIGURES).

| | | No. of cases. | Duration of marriages (15-24 years). | No. of cases. | Duration (25 years and over). |
|---|---|---|---|---|---|
| Professional class | Gross | 944 | 4·24 | 898 | 4·80 |
| | Net | — | 3·25 (·77) | — | 3·38 (·70) |
| Commercial . . . | Gross | 2,009 | 4·32 | 1,622 | 4·91 |
| | Net | — | 2·91 (·67) | — | 3·13 (·64) |
| Artisan . . . . . | Gross | 2,934 | 4·79 | 1,457 | 5·26 |
| | Net | — | 3·12 (·65) | — | 3·17 (·60) |

The broad result for our purposes is to show that the proportion of children surviving to the age at which they might in turn marry and have children varies from 60 per cent. upwards. We shall therefore not be far wrong if we take three children, or a fraction over, to a marriage, as the number required to maintain the level of population in a modern civilised country of the first rank. We seem, further, to be pretty safe in assuming that a higher rate is required in a country of distinctly lower civilisation, such as Russia. Passing to non-European countries, we find a wild confusion of assertions as to the birth-rate. It has been suggested on the basis of such statements as are to be found collected in Ploss's *Das Weib*, that the non-European birth-rate tends to be rather lower than the European, averaging perhaps four to the family, or a fraction below. But here three remarks suggest themselves. The first is, that the tendency of casual observations of this kind is almost undoubtedly to underestimate. A missionary in a savage tribe finds three children with the father and mother, and takes that as the number of the family, ignoring the grown-up, the dead, and the unborn. Mr. Sutherland indeed says roundly that "wherever travellers have taken pains to discover, not the number of children actually alive, but the number that had been born to a savage woman, the result comes out about seven to ten for each." The second point is, that even if we took the low figures given as fair samples, and assumed the birth-rate of non-European nations to be below that of Europeans, still it does not follow that the wastage of life is so low. To settle this point, we should have to know further, whether in less civilised countries increase of population is found to go along with the lower birth-rate. And that brings us to the third point, *i.e.*, the well-known fact that many savage tribes, where the birth-rate is known to be low, are actually becoming extinct.

So far then, the slender and unsatisfactory evidence available would seem to show that the diminution of wastage, which is one of the most

individuals. Organisation, especially in the form of Intelligence, sets itself rather to maintain the individuals, and in so doing improves the type. The rational organisation of life, from the dawn of parental care upwards, tends to suspend the struggle upon which natural selection rests, and there is here, for the believer in progress through natural selection, an insoluble contradiction. The solution

prominent facts of biological evolution, from the lowest organisms to man, has been continued, though at a slower rate, within the limits of human evolution.

An indirect confirmation of this view is the greater variety of civilised as compared with uncivilised man. The many-sidedness of civilisation as compared with barbarism, and of higher civilisation as compared with lower, is one of the central features of historical development. According to Professor Karl Pearson, this increased variability extends even to physical structure (*Mathematical Contributions to the Theory of Evolution*, Proc. Royal Society, Vol. LXI. No. 375), and he rightly points out that this increase of variability implies a diminished pressure on the part of natural selection. But there is a further point to be considered. We are comparing the capacity of different societies to maintain their members. But the difficulty of so doing increases, within limits and under conditions that need not be specified here, in proportion to the density of population. It is here that we find the greatest differences between civilised and lower races. The greater part of the savage and barbarian world is thinly peopled, and no great aggregations of population are to be found below the level of the great European and Asiatic civilisations. Elsewhere it appears that density of population is confined to small specially favoured areas, such as the Gilbert Islands and certain spots in the Black Belt of Africa. For great masses of population we must go to the civilised lands of China, Japan, India, or Western Europe. In the case of the first three the growth of population is dependent as much on natural advantages as on the social order, though in the third case the maintenance of the Pax Britannica has been responsible for an enormous growth during the past century. There remains the case of Western Europe, which we assume to be the home of the highest civilisation of all. Here the average density is indeed below that of China, but it implies a still higher grade in the mastery of the conditions of life. Density and increase of population become at this stage independent of natural advantages, or more accurately, men adapt to their use and profit conditions which at a lower stage they would find unfavourable or impossible to cope with. Hence of course the far spreading range of the white man and his dominance in climates not his own. Thus in uncivilised countries population is generally sparse, in civilised countries of the second rank it becomes dense under favourable conditions, while in the higher civilisation it becomes relatively independent of the bounties of nature. There can then be little doubt that the power to maintain the life of its members by which we have measured the "efficiency" of a species increases in a very marked degree as we pass from the lowest to the highest phases of human development.

I have not thought it necessary to complicate this note by the insertion of more recent figures which would only emphasise the general argument. In England in particular the fall in the infantile death rate in response to deliberate and organised effort has been marked since 1900.

is to find progress not in the laws of inheritance—except in so far as these may be used by intelligence for its own purpose—but rather in the organisation of life culminating in the deliberate self-development of a race under the guidance of reason. Organised life rests not on internecine rivalry, but on mutual interdependence.

This organisation is at first physical or biological. It is extended by intelligence, the essential function of which is to correlate experience and action. The development of intelligence consists in widening the scope of this function, as well as in perfecting its execution. There is an organisation of individual experience, an organisation of social life. Of this organisation in both these forms we have roughly sketched the growth. Life is indeed in a sense organised without intelligence, but only in a rudimentary way. Without intelligence, the race is not master of its fate. It is so built as to behave itself appropriately within a certain groove. Outside of that groove it is lost. Its instincts may prompt a measure of co-operation, but this, again, will be within limits mechanically defined. It is never at this stage master of its surroundings, for the very perfection of its hereditary adjustments rests on a constant elimination of the great majority of its component members. Its rate of progress at the best is such as can be attained by a gradual elimination of the less efficient individuals. In all these respects the growth of mind works a gradual revolution, reorganising life on the basis of knowledge, realising the unity of the race, and deliberately working out its capacities for development.

6. But not only is the organisation of life made more efficient by intelligence, but its very purpose is gradually revolutionised. To complete our account, we must trace the steps of this revolution. The first change introduced by the intelligent use of experience lies in the substitution of pleasures and pains for life and death as the "sanctions" of conduct. It is a necessary consequence of this truth that we should hold with Mr. Herbert Spencer that the pleasurable and the life-giving, the painful and the death-dealing tend to coincide. So much would be determined

by natural selection. We must only bear in mind, first, that it is the life of the race which natural selection has metaphorically in view. There is to the biologist no paradox in the pleasurableness of self-sacrificing effort on behalf of children, descendants, or even the species as a whole. Secondly, as life becomes more complex, we must remember that what is pleasurable from one point of view may be overwhelmingly painful from another. This understood, we may say that in the first stage of intelligence pleasure and pain are substituted as "masters" of conduct for life and death. The first result is that readjustments which natural selection might take an epoch to effect, are carried through by the direct method within a single lifetime, and perhaps ultimately through a single experience. The readjustment, besides being swifter, is obviously less wasteful of life; and lastly, it favours an improvement of type. This it does in two ways. From the first, it makes possible a pliability of nerve-structure which, while incompatible with detailed instinct, forms a basis for more various and therefore broader development. If width of scope is one test of development, we see here the beginnings of an upward movement. Secondly, since pleasure and pain instead of life and death are now the determining factors, we see a possibility that modes of action may be built up not concerned with the mere maintenance of the species, but with anything that may yield pleasure to its members. The primitive pleasures and pains will doubtless be connected with race maintenance (as the pleasures of eating, drinking, and sex), and as we have seen both feelings must throughout development be limited in the main by natural selection. This however is a limiting condition only. Pleasures must not be preponderantly unhealthy. It does not follow that pleasures may not arise that have no bearing one way or other on the life of the species. And if experience lights on unexpected sources of pleasure, it will certainly attend to them, and work them for what they are worth. Further, since we find pleasure in the full development of faculty, it is a possible and indeed a probable case that among the pleasures on which experience lights should be some connected not with the maintenance of the race at its then level, but with the further expansion of its powers. Such an expansion may be of little use to it as a means of survival for the present, but it means progress hereafter. Something like this would seem to be the history of those mathematical and æsthetic " faculties " which have been a stumbling block to natural selection.

7. Even among the higher animals the exercise of faculty seems to be intrinsically pleasant, to be desired upon its own account and independently of its value in maintaining life. When we pass to the human level of development, it is not merely pleasure, but a deeper and more comprehensive end which plays a similar part. As is Pleasure to Desire, so is Happiness to Will. Will is not Desire, nor merely a resultant of desires, but an expression of the whole personality. Desire is the impulse towards a particular end in which a partial and temporary satisfaction is found ; Will, the impulse to a broader end, in which the whole being of the agent is concerned. Pleasure is the satisfaction of Desire : Happiness the satisfaction of Will, the attainment by a man of what he feels to be his true being's end and aim. Now, the conception of Happiness will vary, not only according to individual temperament and circumstances, but also according to the current ideas of life and society. For in all but the most degraded, and perhaps even in them, the conception of personal worth and of the part that a man is expected to play in life enters as an ingredient, perhaps as the determining ingredient, into the conception of his own happiness. And besides his function in this life, there is the conception of another life, or of his duty to God, which profoundly influences the notion of happiness formed by great numbers of men. Finally, the happiness of others, which in a greater or less degree a man identifies with his own, is determined in the concrete form which it takes by a similar multiplicity of influences. I am not here concerned to go into these influences in detail, or to analyse the actual conception of Happiness that prevails at different times or under different conditions. I call attention to two points only. One is, that as it actually develops,

Happiness as an end is something very different from life as an end. There have been important sects which have even held the suppression of life, or of important elements in life, essential to man's temporal or eternal happiness. And apart from abnormalities of this kind, one may say generally that to live well is not the same thing as to live. Happiness does not mean necessarily increased quantity of life, but a special quality.

The second point is what we may call the relativity of Happiness. The conceptions of value are, as we have hinted, largely a matter of social tradition ; largely, again, dependent on religious belief. Thus, apart from philosophic analysis and reflection, they are to be numbered among those determining conceptions of life which grow up in a spontaneous semi-unconscious way with the life of society. And taking the world over from China to Peru, they may differ within very wide limits. No doubt here, as lower in the scale, natural selection operating in the background keeps a certain check on the growth of ideas. If the conception of well-being comes to conflict too violently with the real conditions of life, the society which it dominates will obviously tend to succumb. The ideal of celibacy, for example, can only weed out the community or the class which faithfully puts it in practice. But generally speaking natural selection drives humanity with a sufficiently loose rein. Man is by so much the most dominant of animals, that he can afford himself a good deal of latitude, and yet preserve himself from destruction.

8. This latitude is indeed a necessary condition of the highest development. Natural selection can preserve and augment nothing that is not immediately useful. If the pigment-fleck which is the first rudimentary germ of the eye is preserved and developed, it must be because it is useful as a pigment-fleck. The plea that it will later develop into a magnificent sense-organ of the highest possible utility could not avail it in the court of natural selection unless it could prove services actually rendered by itself. So is it with all the faculties ; and most of all with the higher faculties of man. The philosopher, as Plato's contemporaries complained, occupies himself

with things superfluous.  He is wont to walk into the well while gazing at the stars ; and he may be thankful with Plato himself if he is able to get under the shelter of a wall, and philosophise there unmolested by the storms that beat outside.  Originality is the greatest disadvantage to its possessor in the intellectual market.  The same point is more obviously true on the moral side.  Every one of the Christian virtues is obviously a disadvantage to its possessor in the struggle for existence, more particularly in a Christian community.  The greatest offence a man can commit against society is to be in any respect better than society.  For such the criminal law has always reserved its worst tortures.  But these germs of higher qualities, so dangerous to their possessors, are destined in their fuller development to carry human life to a higher level.  What was a short time ago a struggling ideal, is now placidly accepted as normal.  The world wonders how it could ever have got on without it.  The martyr of the past generation is duly canonised, while the gridiron is being cheerfully heated for the prophet of a still higher creed.

Natural selection no doubt plays a beneficent part in human life in curing the worst aberrations of the moral or social standard.  And this is not all.  The higher principle, if it is given time to develop far enough and deepen its hold, is also stronger than any lower principle, and fairly beats it in the struggle for existence.  Mr. Sutherland has shown at great length how first the parental and then the social principle are positively fortified and confirmed by the struggle for existence.  The most careful parents will bring the largest proportion of their family to maturity, while the children of the careless and the callous are allowed to die.  Similarly at a higher remove the best ordered State is at an advantage over its competitors. But here at once we trench upon the limits of this method of progress.  The good order necessary to a successful war may, as we well know, be secured at the cost of individual liberty, and of much besides.  Hence an iron despotism may overthrow a state containing within it the elements of a higher order, which, if it came to maturity, would be

not only better but also stronger than its conqueror.   And
this is but one instance of a rule pervading all relations of
life.   If the man of genius is endowed with unusually
strong will, or is placed in exceptionally favourable circumstances, he not merely escapes disaster, but imposes
his genius on the world, and is recognised as one of its
great men.   The inventor is not always ruined, and if
not ruined, he makes a fortune.   The loving temperament is not always crushed, and if not crushed, it is the
foundation of the most enduring happiness.   But it remains that in the ordinary course of the world, the virtues
and excellences belonging to the highest type are a disadvantage to the individual in the naked struggle for existence.   They need the shelter of a social order in which
the reign of force is suspended or mitigated, and in that
shelter they reach a maturity in which they are found to
be after all the strongest as well as the most beautiful
growth.

9. The suspension of the struggle for existence makes
possible a many-sided development.   In some directions
this development is all good, in others it is a mixed good,
in yet others it may lead to evils which the unmitigated
struggle would never allow to come into existence.   But
upon the whole, this many-sidedness means that human
life becomes fuller, and that the infinitely varied capacities
of human beings find more and more room for satisfaction.
And this again is as much as to say that life reaches a higher
stage of organisation.   For the highest organism is that
which, while maintaining its unity, allows the fullest development of individuality in its parts.   The controlling
factor needed to replace the rude efficacy of the struggle,
is the intelligent apprehension of the organisation possible
for human life, and the subjection of current standards of
value to that principle.   At this point the conditions of
existence cease to act as a check on intelligence from outside.   They are absorbed into its system as part of the
knowledge which it uses for its own ends.   The philosophic science of the highest stage brings us back to the
conditions of existence as the source of laws for conduct
from which we started in the sphere of instinct, but the

conditions and the existence are transformed. The conditions are used by the mind as its instruments, and the existence which it contemplates is not that which it knows, but the higher life which it sees to be possible. In a certain sort we have treated mental development throughout as a process in which an implicit purpose gradually comes into view. But we must bear in mind that in proportion as it comes into view, it is changed in character. The implicit purpose of the lower type is to maintain itself, to satisfy the wants and impulses belonging to that type. But the very fact that impulse comes to understand itself as desire implies that the type is changed to something better, and the same holds at each higher stage. If a man understood the real mental and moral forces that underlie his cherished ambitions, his ambitions would thereby be changed. We must therefore understand the organisation of life as changing not only in method but in plan, as it passes from the control of heredity and the struggle for existence to that of Reason and purpose. At its lowest it is an organisation of behaviour directed to the maintenance of the type. It passes to organisation directed to the attainment of purposes varying in scope and character, and ultimately becomes an organisation for the comprehensive purpose of bringing life itself to the perfection of its development.

# CHAPTER XIX

## SELF-CONSCIOUS DEVELOPMENT

Our object in the present work has been to ascertain the character and function of Mind as the organising principle in Evolution. In the absence of intelligence and in its lowest stages, Life is, as we expressed it, relatively "unorganised." The successive actions of an individual are not properly correlated.) As between different individuals there is conflict rather than co-operation. In the process by which species are formed there is an even more complete lack of plan. The fact that biological evolution rests on a struggle for existence is itself enough to show a want of that organic unity in which the good of one part is necessarily the good of the rest. Were a species to become a unity, and its development organic, the fundamental condition would be that each individual should find the furthering, the development, of his own nature in that which furthers and develops others. Evolution by natural selection is thus the direct negation of an organic growth. It is in no way parallel to the regular unfolding of a germ. It is an irregular backwards and forwards movement in which now an individual of one type prevails, now an example of another, and little by little, the battle swings over to the one side. This is not development. It is more like a slow process of sifting, in which, by a long series of stages, and with many pauses, grains of one kind tend to come together in one heap. In such a process, clearly the accidental as well as the more permanent character of the environment must play a notable part.

Accordingly evolution biologically considered exhibits no comprehensive plan or pervading tendency. It produces, not necessarily a higher type, but one that deals more effectually with its particular environment. It may be said perhaps to tend towards variation, but the variation is not necessarily towards anything higher or better.

(1. The development of Mind in animals and Man means in our view the gradual introduction of a higher principle of organisation into this relatively chaotic state. The first function of mind is to organise individual experience, and from this it proceeds through the organisation of social life till finally it reaches the conception of the development of the entire race as its starting point and its goal. This conception brings into organic relationship elements formerly at strife. It is true that on the ethical side in asserting a common human nature as supreme over all differences it is in a manner recognising a unity that was there before, but in recognising this unity it transforms it. The fundamental kinship of men is a fact before it is admitted, but it is only when it is admitted that it becomes a bond of union. Thus the unorganised struggle of biological evolution gives place to an organic principle. At the same time its purposeless movement gives way to an articulate plan. As soon as the past and present evolution of man are understood as the opening stages of a much nobler growth, as soon as that further growth becomes sufficiently understood to operate upon standards of morality and conceptions of social effort, evolution becomes conscious and full of purpose. Now, if not before, it has a goal, or, if we prefer it, a standard of perfect development to which it moves forward with that orderly unrolling of powers which we find in organic growth. When, further, the previous course of mental evolution is conceived as a process by which the intellectual and moral unity necessary for this growth were prepared, we carve out of the whole of evolution one great process of " orthogenic evolution " of which the tendency and direction are one from first to last—the

evolution of Mind as the dominating principle in this
world.  If still further extending our view we take
into account on the one hand the organic growth on which
intelligence rests, on the other hand the generic function of
Mind in the world, we may describe the whole process as
the development of organisation and trace its beginning
to the first germ of life.  Whether this unity of tendency
can be properly regarded as the expression of a purpose is
not so clear.  What is clear is that in the earlier stages no
such purpose is realised by any of the individuals concerned in the evolutionary process.[1]  There are elements,
fragments of the purpose, realised in the lower stages, and
these gradually come together into that wider purpose
which makes of subsequent evolution an organic development.

2. But are we right in calling it an organic development ?  Should we not rather, if we wish to understand
what human progress as designed by man would be,
compare it to a purpose executed by human fore-thought ?
There is certainly one point which should be noticed. An
organic growth in the ordinary sense follows a strictly
determinate course.  Not only its beginning and end, but
each intervening stage follows in rigid sequence, each
depending on and arising out of that which went before.
Certainly there may be deviations of a kind, but these
proceed by equally uniform laws from abnormalities of the
environment.  Now, if the development of humanity
were fixed in this way, there would be no need of intelligence.  The function of intelligence is to adjust
variable relations, but if the development of the human
species were, like the physical development of each in-

[1] Since certain biological processes have somehow engendered that
bodily organisation which is capable of mental life, those particular
processes must be deemed a part of orthogenic evolution.  But this is not
to say that there is any plan in the conditions determining survival as such.
On the contrary the sort of organism that is a fit vehicle for mind is only
one among many that are fitted to survive, all of which are in fact fostered
by the biological conditions with the impartiality of complete indifference.
If we assume the efficacy of conation in determining structure we may (as
shown above, p. 419) impute the entire work of organisation to the action
of Mind, but even so it would not in the lower stage be a mind conscious
of its supreme purpose, but dimly conscious, fragmentary in effort, and
not in the full sense purposive at all.

dividual, based on a determinate interaction of structure and environment, it may be questioned whether human intelligence could do anything to affect it. But human development is not fixed in this sense. Its proper aim, and, we may say, its general course, are fixed by the germinal possibilities of human nature, but wherever intelligence can act, the limitations of ordinary organic growth may be overstepped. An organic growth must, as we have tried to show, always hold on its course, an unfolding now of this structure, next of that, being the due order never departed from. Intelligence, on the other hand, may execute any sort of curve to get to its ultimate end. It cannot, indeed, break any law of nature, but within the limits of the laws of nature, it can alter the course by which it reaches its goal at its pleasure. Since in the intelligence which we presuppose in our "self-conscious evolution," we have all the mastery of the forces of nature, organic and inorganic, that the sciences give, with the knowledge of man and his social life added thereto, we should surely have not less but more of this intelligent disposition of events than in the contrivance of any ordinary human scheme.

But if we conceive future evolution as essentially a human purpose, we must be on our guard against an opposite fallacy. From such a conception we should be apt to infer in it something mechanical and also something arbitrary. Man imposes his purposes as it were on things without regard to their wants and requirements. Bars and rivets and wheels of steel or brass do not spontaneously come together to make a steam-engine, nor in a steam-engine have they ever that organic relation which subsists between cells of the animal body. They are simply brought into shape by an agent acting upon them, an agent which they do not set in motion. Human evolution, on the contrary, is the work of man—the product of the being who evolves. Man does not stand outside his own growth and plan it. He becomes aware of its possibilities as he grows, and, if we are right, there comes a stage when conception of the perfected growth seizes upon him, and makes him intelligently work towards it. There is here on the one hand no distinction between the worker and his material. It is the material which does the work. On the other hand, the "material" is not "indifferent" to its destiny. It is out of human nature as it is that the conception of the ultimate purpose and destinies of man is evolved, and human nature being what it is, this purpose must appeal to it in the end with compelling force.

If then self-conscious evolution is like the working out of a human purpose in allowing unlimited license of method, it resembles an organic growth in that its moving principle is within. It resembles an organic growth in that the broad possibilities of development are already determined in the germ, but differs from it in that the actual growth is determined by the conception of the end itself and may be modified as that conception requires. It is therefore an organic growth and something more ; it is a purpose and something more. This we have tried to express by calling it a self-conscious evolution. It should be added that there is one point in which both human purposes and organic growths agree. Both are definitely making by different methods for an ascertained goal. In this they differ from the process of biological evolution, which arrives at a goal without making for it. One may perhaps convey some conception of the difference by an image. Three persons start for a certain place. One does not know the way, but is directed to follow a certain road. Keeping to this road, he arrives safely and speedily unless there should be any unforeseen obstacle, such as a broken bridge, in which case, as he knows no other paths, he is blocked. This is the case of "organic growth." Another, Intelligence, knows where the point is and finds his way there, going by a detour if the direct road is impassable. The third wanders at random, but as everywhere there are hedges and walls preventing him from getting far out of the way, and as hedges grow up behind him to prevent his return, he gradually arrives by eliminating all possibilities of going anywhere else. This is the evolutionary process. We might vary the image by substituting three companies for three individuals. Of the first company, three or four out of ten would arrive, and

that speedily, but the remainder would be unable to swim
the stream where the bridge was broken.   Of the second
class, all would arrive, and, on the average, still more
speedily, since, taking obstacles into account, they know the
best way.   Of the third, the different members would start
together and gradually disperse, and, having a tendency to
keep apart, one out of the number would in time happen on
one of the paths leading to the right spot.

3. Self-conscious evolution, then, differs from previous
evolution in having a purpose towards which it steadily
makes its way.   This difference not only affects the
method by which it advances, but also the rate at which
it moves.   I referred at the outset to the growing rapidity
of social changes as orthogenic evolution advances.   The
whole life span of the human species, even if we take the
highest estimates of its antiquity, is a very small fraction
of the millions of years occupied by organic evolution.
But it is not too much to say that the extension during
that time in the scope of Mind and its power to control
natural forces and direct its own life is as great, and in
some respects greater than all that was effected in the
vastly longer period preceding the appearance of man.
But this is not all.   If we accept a high antiquity—of
anything over 100,000 years—for the human race, the
result follows, that the greater part, eight- or nine-tenths
at least, of that period belongs to the lowest stage of
culture—the stage in which men had not learnt to grind
and polish their stone tools and weapons.   The first
rudiments of civilisation in the great river valleys arose
from 6,000 to 8,000 years ago, but this again was a
civilisation judged by modern standards of an extremely
stationary type.   It is only with the rise of Greek civilisation that anything like a forward movement began, and
civilisation since that day has had not only to maintain
and improve itself, but to absorb and control the vast
masses of barbarism which have constantly threatened to
submerge it.   To this day the outlying mass of savagery
and semi-civilisation still threatens us, not with the open
conquest which has haunted perverted imaginations, but
with the far subtler danger of internal corruption.   Civilised

man as we have seen too often in recent years, has a painful
tendency to adapt his manners and his standard to those
of the lower races whom he conquers.   The master takes
his character from the slave.

Nevertheless, the facts briefly adverted to, which might
be   drawn   out   effectively   in   great   detail,   illustrate
sufficiently   the   self-accelerating   tendency   of   mental
growth.   Of the total growth of mind in scope and power
during the existence of the human race, at least one half
must be assigned to the comparatively short period from
the beginnings of Greek history to the present day.   But
it must be remembered that the greater part of this period
still lies outside the scope of "self-conscious evolution."   It
is only in modern times, as I hope to show in detail on
another   occasion,   that   the   threads   begin   to   be   drawn
together to weave the larger purpose.   Up to this point
civilisation still moves in large measure through conflict,
though the social systems, the principles, the purposes that
conflict   are   wider,   and   give   more   scope   for   internal
development.   As civilised societies become more highly
organised and their ideas more comprehensive, the onward
movement in each becomes more sure and its orbit more
vast.   And yet, to this day, how great a proportion of
the energies of the best and ablest men is spent in
combating one another.   If we can imagine all this
energy harmonised by the conception of a great pervading
purpose, we can form some conception of the increased
efficiency with which "self-conscious evolution" would
bring its forces to bear.

4. The conclusion to which we have been led is that
among the manifold conflicting movements of evolution,
there is one tendency of which the significance is not
obscure.   In orthogenic evolution we find a constant
development of Mind in scope, and accordingly in power.
Slow at first, the development gathers speed with growth,
and finally settles into the steady movement of a germ
unfolding under the direction of an intelligent knowledge
of its powers and of its life conditions.   The goal of the
movement, as far as we can foresee at present, is the mastery
by the human mind of the conditions, internal as well as

external, of its life and growth. The primitive intelligence is useful to the organism as a more elastic method of adjusting itself to its environment. As the mental powers develop, the tables are turned, and the mind adjusts its environment to its own needs.*) " Mihi res non me rebus subjungere conor " is the motto that it takes for its own. With the mastery of external nature, applied science has made us all familiar. But the last enemy that man shall overcome is himself. The internal conditions of life, the physiological basis of mental activity, the sociological laws that operate for the most part unconsciously, are parts of the " environment " which the self-conscious intelligence has to master, and it is on this mastery that the *regnum hominis* will rest.

The development in its highest stage is beyond doubt purposive. The purpose is conceived in the human mind itself. Are we now to throw the purpose back, and to conceive the whole course of orthogenic evolution as determined thereby? We can conceive such a purpose in one of two forms. We may place it within the evolutionary process, attributing it to the beings taking part therein, or we may place it outside the process in a hypothetical Being who contrives the whole movement, and shapes it towards the end defined. In the former alternative, we are forced to characterise the purpose as an unconscious purpose, and this threatens to be a contradiction in terms. At most, we can say that there are in the earlier stages elements of purpose and understanding which are gradually blended and fused into coherence. The latter alternative would bring us to the conception of an unconditioned creation of the world-order, which can never be accepted by the intelligence without stifling the moral sense. Is there any third possibility?

5. I have argued elsewhere [1] that a close examination of the postulates of knowledge leads us to conceive Reality as a single comprehensive system in which all things and all processes have their place in accordance

---

[1] In the *Theory of Knowledge* (1896). I leave the following section as it was originally written, but may be allowed to refer to a fuller and in some respects a modified exposition of the argument in *Development and Purpose* (1913).

with a single pervading scheme. This scheme cannot be something foreign to the elements which compose it, for there is nothing outside it to impose it upon them. It is the expression of their nature as a whole, and upon it they in turn depend for their existence. If we would figure such a relationship in terms of a familiar experience, we may think of a living organism in which the life process rests on the working of every part, and in turn makes that working possible. The life cannot be more than the parts make possible, yet the parts are not conditions that limit it as from without, but are its constituent elements, and apart from the whole have no existence.

So, far, however, there is nothing to show that either development or purpose are necessary parts of such a scheme. We might still say that what the whole order and framework of the universe is now, is determined by what it was yesterday, and so on to infinity. But over and above the postulate of thought, there is an ideal of thought which we cannot regard as valueless for truth, though it may be both unrealised and unprovable. The methods of thought are valid, and give us reality. If, tracing them onwards in their natural direction, we find them pointing to a certain end as the goal of completed thought, we cannot easily avoid the belief that such a goal is in fact attainable. Now the goal of thought is a system intelligible in itself and without passing outside it. Whether such a system must be finite or not is a different question. If we could attain to it, the conceptions of finite and infinite would probably be changed from what they are for us now. But whether the system were to shed light on a finite or infinite reality, the principle which is to make all things intelligible must lie wholly within it if it is to be complete.

Now, it is easy to show that in such a system the ultimate grounds of interconnection can neither be purely mechanical nor purely teleological. Reality is or includes a time process. Now, if we take any time process, and consider its beginning, we are dealing with a partial fact, and for every partial fact, thought demands an explanation

which will connect it with Reality as a whole.   For the
cause of the origin of a process, then, we may look in two
directions, to its results or to its antecedents.   If we look
to the latter, we are clearly going outside the process.
But if the process is one in which the whole nature of our
ultimate system is to be expressed, we cannot go outside
it without denying the claim of our system to be complete.
We are therefore thrown forward towards the results of
this system.   But neither can the purpose achieved by the
process stand alone, for the necessity of the process must
also be made plain.   If an unconditional purpose were the
secret of the universe, there could be no explanation of
the means, the process, and the effort through which the
purpose is realised.

6. From the conception of purpose, then, we are again
thrown back on origins, just as these throw us forward to
their purpose.   We have, in short, to conceive a single
principle not realised in full at any one phase, but pervading the whole world-process.   In this principle, the possible
and the actual in a sense come together, for what it is to
be is an integral condition that goes to make the world
what it is.   We cannot take any phase of Reality as an
absolute starting-point and regard it as determining everything that follows upon it mechanically, or everything that
precedes it teleologically.   If we conceive any process as
making up the life of an intelligible world-whole, we must
conceive its origin and issue as dependent on and implying
one another.   That is, we must conceive it as determined
organically.   And the word is the more appropriate
because, just as we saw at first that the relations of a
comprehensive plan to its elements could be figured in the
penetration of all the organic elements by the life of the
whole, so now when we treat the plan as the plan of a
process, we find its nearest analogy in the struggle of life
within its physical conditions to realise its full nature.
The life that, determined on one side by its constituent
elements, is equally determined from the first by its own
possibility and promise, displays a history in which end
and origin, broad principles and detailed conditions, form
a systematic whole.

If this ideal of thought may be taken as adumbrating the ultimate nature of Reality, nature is neither wholly blind, nor wholly the creature of intelligent purpose. Origin and purpose are mutually dependent parts of one scheme. What was in the beginning was in order that what shall be might be realised. But what shall be, and the way in which it shall come about, are equally the creations of that which was at first. If we seek to realise in some concrete fashion what this means, we shall think once more of the germ of a soul in a living organism. The soul would not exist in germ, but that there is laid up in store for it a futurity which repays the travail of development. Neither could it exist but for the physical conditions in which it is immersed. Its development is a war with these conditions which maintain and yet limit it and its triumph is the submission of the conditions to its perfected nature. In this image we have a brief account of the whole process of the evolution of Mind as traced in these chapters, and therewith the process of evolution upon this earth appears as the working out in concrete shape and on this relatively narrow stage of the vaster process which we dimly conceive as constituting the essential life of the world.

# APPENDIX

## THE ELBERFELD HORSES

ALL preconceived opinions as to the limitation of animal intelligence have been called in question of late years by the experiments of Herr von Osten and Herr Krall with their learned horses. It is impossible for anyone who has not himself seen the horses to make any contribution to the subject that is worthy of attention. I had hoped to have an opportunity of forming an independent opinion upon their performances before revising this work, but events intervened, and I have been compelled to rely on the evidence of others. It may be well, however, to set forth briefly the admitted facts, to indicate the conclusions, or rather the alternative conclusions, to which these point, and to show what bearing they will have on the view of animal psychology arrived at in the preceding chapters. The broad facts are well known, but it will be convenient to summarise them very briefly.

Herr von Osten had a horse called Clever Hans, which was able apparently to solve arithmetical questions by rapping out the appropriate numbers with his hoof, and to communicate with his master by an alphabetical code, in which a number of raps corresponded to letters. The performances of Hans attracted attention in Germany, and were investigated by a commission of psychologists, who came to the conclusion that he was guided by involuntary signals telling him when to begin rapping and when to stop, and that no further intelligence was involved in the operations of the horse. After Herr von Osten's death, however, the matter was taken up by a believer, Herr Krall, who has trained a number of other horses on similar lines. The alleged arithmetical performances of these horses include the four primary rules, a knowledge of fractions, use of brackets, the extraction of roots to the 4th and 5th root, complex sums involving multiplication of roots, and the solution of simple equations. They have further a spelling code, whereby they can communicate with their master; they can read words, describe a picture, ask for bread or a carrot—which is one of their favourite rewards—have at times made spontaneous utterances in their code, and carry on conversations. An illustration of the latter may be given from Herr Krall's book : [1]

"I wrote on the board : 'What is sugar ?' Muhamed, the horse, answers ' Sweet.' 'But that is no proposition. What must you say as well ?' 'Z. ist.' 'What can you say further of sugar ?' 'Sugar is white.' 'What besides ? Consider again.' 'Z. schmkt gud.'

"The next day I say to Muhamed : ' You said yesterday sugar is sweet and white and tastes good. Now consider again whether you can say something more about sugar,' and I put a bit of sugar before him. Muhamed answers : 'Z. ht 4 ek,' i.e., sugar has 4 corners. While noting down this, he says, quite of himself, 'Iohn.' Johann asks : 'What am I to do ?' The answer is : 'Mgbn' (i.e., möhre geben—carrots)."

Feats of this kind are attested by a large number of witnesses, many of whom are men of scientific eminence, and while some have remained unconvinced, others are sure of the genuineness of the performance, and nearly all believe the problem is worthy of serious investigation. The marvel is not diminished by the account Herr Krall gives of the method of education :

The horses Muhamed and Zarif were originally taught to count by raising the foot once or twice, as the case might be, while the number 1 or 2 was placed before them conspicuously and the name of the figure uttered clearly. On the first day the numbers 1 and 2 alone were employed. On the next day 3 was added and 0, which was to be expressed by the horse by a turn of the head from left to right. Each horse had an hour and a half to two hours' training per diem. After a few days we are told the horses had learnt they must paw with the foot in answer to the command " Count," and on the fifth day the figures 1, 2, and 3 were put up in a row, the horses were allowed to touch them, and take a bit of bread placed on each number. After about a week Herr Krall began to write the numbers on a blackboard and to use a counting machine to assist in addition. On the 13th day Muhamed began to give the numbers from 1 to 4 correctly, and practice in addition, with the aid of the counting board, was begun. A piece of the actual record of the lesson may be subjoined, it being understood that the horse has before him, along with the written figure on the blackboard, the counting board, on which the appropriate row of dots is placed under each number.

[1] *Denkende Tiere*, p. 157.

"Count 4." Muhamed answers rightly 4.

The 5 is then displayed on the counting board, written on the blackboard, and named several times.

"Count 5."          Answer 5
"Count 3."              „    3
"Count 2."              „    2
"Count 4."              „    4
"Count 5."              „    5
"Count 3."              „    3

Then, as above, the 6 is produced.

"Count 6."    Muhamed answers 6.

Now begins the first instruction in a sum, accompanied with pointing to the dots on the counting board :

$$1 + 3$$
$$. + . . .$$

"When I add 1 + 3, how many do I get ?"          Answer 4

"    „    „    1 + 4,    „    „    „              „    5
"Now I add    1 + 5,    „    does that make ?"    „    6
"    „    „    1 + 6, tell me how many does
                              that make ?"    „    7

After Muhamed has pawed 7 times, the 7 is named.

"6 less 1 is how many ?  Here I have 6 (pointing to the counting board, saying 1, 2, 3, 4, 5, 6). If I take away 1 (this is done, the outer point being pushed under the 1 and then covered) how many remains over ?"    Answer 5.

And so it goes on, by the end of the lesson Muhamed being able to add $2 + 1 + 8$ and to multiply 2 by 3 and 3 by 3. The marvellous rapidity of this progress is only to be surpassed by the speed with which Muhamed acquired the conception of a square root. This lesson may also, with advantage, be transcribed.

He is apparently already familiar with the notion of a power. $2^2$ is written up and he is asked how much does that make ?

                              Answer 4
"Once again ? "              „    4
"$2^3$ That makes ? "          „    8

$\sqrt[2]{4} = 2$ is then written up, and Herr Krall says : "See, that is called a root. $\sqrt{\ }$ is the sign of a root. $\sqrt{\ }$ or $\sqrt[2]{\ }$ is called the second root or square root. What comes from it, 2, gives, when raised to the second power, the number which is placed under the root sign, so 2 gives 4, as you have already said, and the second root out of 4 gives 2."

After this luminous explanation $\sqrt{16}$ is written up. But Muhamed has not yet grasped the matter completely.

"How much does the second root from 16 give?" Muhamed answers 82 and then 6. We are not surprised to learn that the above explanation is repeated in an altered form, and then $\sqrt{16}=4$ is written up. It is pointed out to the horse that the second root of 16 is 4. "Then $4^2$ is how much?" Muhamed: 16. $4^2 = -$ is then written up. "You see you have there the number which is placed under the sign of the root, now deal with it." Apparently there is no result, but $\sqrt{25} = -$ is written up in the same way. "I point to the open space behind the sign of equality: Here must be the number which, multiplied by itself, gives 25. So?" Muhamed answers 5.

"You have done that well. Once again." Muhamed: 5. After this, with one or two errors, Muhamed gives $\sqrt{49}$ as 7, but fails to extract the root of 36, so that the conclusion is that he has not yet conceived the matter rightly. On the evening of the same day, however, the answer 4 followed at once when he was asked for the root of 16, and the understanding of Muhamed adapted itself to this kind of sum in a short time, so that he could soon do the sum $\sqrt{81}+\sqrt{49}=16$, or $\sqrt{81}-\sqrt{25}=4$.

Thus, if we are to believe that Muhamed's answers are given by genuine process of thought, we must suppose that in a single lesson, by dint of sheer explanation, he advances from the power to count 4 to that of adding 3 numbers and understanding multiplication; while again, in a single lesson, he was able to grasp the meaning of a root and the general notion of an inverted operation. Apart altogether from the miraculous results achieved by the horse, the method of instruction would suggest a totally different conclusion. It convinces us that, in these lessons at any rate, whatever might be the case afterwards, the horse must in reality have been responding to voluntary or involuntary signs indicating which foot he is to use,[1] when he is to begin to paw, and when he is to stop.

Such are the broad facts, which might be indefinitely multiplied, and how are they to be explained? The obvious hypothesis is that the horse responds to a sign, voluntary or involuntary, on the part of his master or of the groom, or, if someone else is conducting the experiment, of the experimenter himself. As to this it must be remarked first of all that the theory of conscious fraud is not suggested as against Herr Krall, even by his bitterest opponents. All observers appear to have come away convinced of Herr Krall's honesty, and the most that can be said by his critics is that he is a fanatic, who may have the failings of fanaticism but who undoubt-

---

[1] The horses give units first, reckoning them with their right foot. They then give the tens with their left foot, then the hundreds with the right, and so on. Confusions as to the foot account for some of the errors in their computations, *e.g.*, we easily get 45 instead of 54 by this method.

edly believes in his own case.    There are of course others about the horses, grooms and attendants, to whom less attention has been paid, but it is to be remarked that experiments have been made in the absence of Herr Krall, and also in the absence of any groom, so that apparently the horse is in contact with no one but the experimenter himself.    Under such circumstances complicated sums have been solved ; for example, Monsieur G. Bohn reports that in the absence of Krall and the groom he has seen the following performance :

$$\sqrt[4]{2825761} - \sqrt[4]{531441} = 14$$

Close attention has been given to the behaviour of Krall and the groom and nothing in the nature of a sign has been detected.    To this, however, there is one exception.    In order to eliminate the possibility of visual signs, Krall acquired a blind horse called Berto.    Herr Wigge, witnessing a performance with Berto, observed that the groom twitched the bridle at the point when the horse had stamped the right number.    He had the two reins in his hand and jerked the right or left for the units or the tens.[1] Herr Krall's reply to this accusation is that what Herr Wigge was witnessing was not a demonstration of a performance but of the method of teaching a beginner.    But this reply is not wholly satisfactory.    Dr. von Máday[2] points out that no mention is made of the use of the bridle in any of Krall's accounts of training ; that the incident related by Wigge occurred after Berto had had six weeks' training, whereas Krall maintains that Berto could count up to nine in a fortnight.    However, Haenel, one of Krall's most vigorous supporters, six weeks later than Wigge, mentions the substitution of a pull for the actual guidance of the feet, and says that he was witness of the important moment at which the hand could be left off.    At the lowest, this indicates serious lacunæ in Krall's account of the training of the horses.    It confirms the suspicion, based above on internal evidence, that the horses do not, at least at the outset, really count when Krall supposed them to be doing so, but were responding to a signal, which he did in fact use.    But if this throws an element of doubt on the method of training, it does not enable us to account for the actual results.

To the theory that the horses give their replies in answer to involuntary signs, there are four replies.    The first is that, with the one exception noted, the signs are incapable of detection.    This has already been considered.    The second depends on what we may call the loophole experiments.    The third on experiments in the absence of Krall and the groom ; and the fourth on experiments in which the answer is wholly unknown even to the experimenter himself (Unwissentliche Versuche).

[1] *Tierseele*, Heft I. p. 59.        [2] *Gibt es denkende Tiere*, pp. 241-2.

Loophole experiments have been described by Claparéde, who is, on the whole, our best and most impartial witness. Krall, in Claparéde's presence, wrote a problem on the board and retired along with Claparéde from the stable. The horse was left alone and his proceedings watched through a loophole from outside. The first sum so given was $\sqrt{614656}$, and the answer, given in some seconds, was 28, which is right. The next was $\sqrt[4]{4879681}$, for which Muhamed, after 30 seconds, gave 117 and then 144. The right solution, which is 47, Muhamed did not find. For the next fourth root, where the right answer was 56, he gave the following attempts :—43, 73, 267, 34, 74, and 84, and then, being set another sum, he rapped out 56, which would have been right in the previous case. The results of this experiment are curious and I think instructive. The only sum which the horse does right is the first. It looks as though this answer might have been somehow conveyed to the horse, or that possibly he had the figure or the appropriate rappings for the figure 28 in his memory previously. We shall find some corroboration for this suggestion in other answers given by the horse. After the first one he fails, but in the same curious way he seems to have the right answer to sum No. 3 in his mind, for it comes out, though on the wrong occasion. It is clear that Claparéde's record, taken alone, is unsatisfactory for the defenders of Muhamed, and with regard to the loophole experiments in general Dr. Máday points out [1] that, so far as our descriptions go, the use of audible signs is not altogether excluded. In several cases the door is partly open, for instance, and Krall habitually talks to the horse from outside. In 21 out of the 22 recorded cases Krall himself wrote up the problem. Four of these cases were so-called Kuvert Versuche, that is to say, the sum set was put inside an envelope, which Krall opened immediately before writing it up on the board, and in these four the proportion of false answers to the right was large. One was not solved at all, but here again, as in Claparéde's case, the answer was given when the next sum was set. But in these experiments again an awkward incident occurred. The horse gave 33 as a cube root where the answer should have been 23. Krall called out "False," and told the groom to give the horse a stroke of the whip, whereupon, after another error, the horse gave 23. This occurred, says Dr. Buttell Reepen, notwithstanding that he had not told Krall the right solution. Krall's explanation is that, in many cases, he knew a false answer from the manner of pawing, but it must be admitted that the incident throws considerable doubt upon the value of experiments in which Krall is supposed to be ignorant of the answer to be given.

[1] *Op. cit.* p. 297.

(2) That Dr. Haenel writes as an enthusiast.

(3) That it may not be so easy as he takes it to be to secure complete ignorance of the figures placed on the board. In one instance, as a fact, he mentions the half glance, and it must be borne in mind that the horse, on the face of the record, itself frequently makes a number of uncertain efforts before he gets to the right one, a process which still suggests that he is in some way waiting for a sign. It is at least reasonable to suspend judgment until further experiments of the type of this record by Dr. Haenel have been made under careful observation, by two or more experimentalists in co-operation.

Let us now for a moment discuss the apparent results, seeking to dismiss all preconceived opinions as to the capacity or incapacity of horses. Let us suppose that we have merely the results before us, without knowing whether they were produced by a civilised man, a savage, a little boy, or an animal, and that we were therefore free to enquire what sort of intelligence, if any, they presuppose. We should, to begin with, find in them some strong reasons against the supposition that they rest upon a genuine understanding of arithmetical operations. This reason is to be found in the nature of the mistakes made by the horses, and of the method by which they approach solution. Quite easy problems are missed by these advanced students ; for instance, Zarif gives $4^2 = 15$, and corrects it to 24.[1] Now, any horse as familiar with squares as Zarif was supposed to be by this time ought to know that a square number cannot be odd. The talented Muhamed, at quite a late date, fails, in the presence of Dr. Sarasin, to add $4 + 6$, and also to multiply $6 \times 6$. This in the same *séance* wherein he succeeds in finding $\sqrt[4]{2313441}$. Berto can divide 21 by 3, and gives 7, but immediately afterwards he supposes that $5 + 6 = 41$, and corrects to 14.

These are not casual mistakes. They are written all over the record, and though they are imputed to obstinacy or wilfulness on the part of the horse, it must be pointed out that they are often punished with a hearty smack. It is indeed doubtful whether years of practice make the horses really more competent in dealing with the simple than with very difficult questions. On this point there is some conflict of evidence. Dr. Plate put together a number of lists of successes and failures, classified in accordance with the difficulty of the problem. The gist of these is given in the appended table. Column I. includes additions and subtractions involving not more than two figures, enumeration, reading the date of the month, and so on. Column II., additions and subtractions of more than two figures, division and multiplication, or in Berto's case, counting of figures written on the back. Also spelling,

[1] Claparéde, *Archives de Psychologie*, XII p. 273.

It may be remarked here that experiments in the extraction of roots, of which Herr Krall is particularly fond, are in reality very unsuitable as tests of arithmetical power. Roots can be very rapidly guessed by anyone who has once got the trick, and fifth roots, which sound the hardest, are in reality the easiest of all because the terminal digit is always the same, and unless we run into three figures, only one of them remains to be guessed. On the whole, the loophole experiments add very little to our knowledge. We pass to cases in which Krall is altogether absent. Doctors Sarasin and Brunies give an account[1] of experiments made when Krall was away, the groom coming in only when the horse declined to answer, except in the case of blind Berto, who is apparently unmanageable without him. Experiments with Zarif failed completely. The pony Hänschen read 23 correctly after certain failures, failed to add 2 and 3, asked to count 63 gave successively 53, 33, 63 ; for $4 \times 5$ gave 45 and then 54. Having thus disgraced himself he was energetically smacked and set the sum of $25 \times 5$, which, after two failures, he gave correctly : 125. There followed a series of trials with Muhamed, which included some failures in very simple operations, *e.g.*, $4 + 6$ and $6 \times 6$. But Muhamed extracted $\sqrt{225}$ correctly after one failure, $\sqrt{5625}$ correctly after two failures, and $\sqrt[4]{2313441}$ correctly after four failures. He then tapped the name of Albert the groom, thus : A l p b a i d. Asked which letter is wrong he says the sixth, which should be r. R is, in fact, given by thirteen taps and i by thirty-one, so that Muhamed's error is excusable. Shown a book and asked what it is, he taps b u, and then after accidental interruption, g.

There followed some experiments with Berto, but as the groom was present in these they need not be regarded.

Monsieur Bohn's successes with Muhamed in the absence of Krall have already been referred to. It may be added that when he proposed to the horse an addition, he got a result which he thought was mistaken until he saw that he was himself responsible for the error, having made the vertical sign of the plus so faint that Muhamed had taken it for a minus and carried out a subtraction, which was worked correctly.

Monsieur Claparéde's results under similar conditions were hardly so favourable. On his first visit Krall wrote up the following sum on the blackboard and then left the room :—

$$(\sqrt{1296} - \sqrt{81}) \times (\sqrt{144} - \sqrt{49}).$$

Muhamed, says Monsieur Claparéde, threw a glance at the board and instantly replied 115, which is wrong. Krall then called to

[1] *Tierseele*, Heft I. p. 184.

him from outside to begin again, and he gave 25, and then 125, which is still wrong. After this Muhamed persisted in knocking numbers of his own and made an undecipherable word. He then returned to the sums and gave a correct answer to the one written above, namely, 135, without any preliminary mistake, and later on he solved a fourth root when Krall had left the stable after writing up the problem. Monsieur Claparéde then being left alone with Muhamed, gave him some simple additions, but the answers were wrong and not clear.

In a second visit Monsieur Claparéde obtained some rather better results when he knew the answers to his own questions. Hänschen failed in several cases, but succeeded in getting $24 + 12 = 36$ at the third shot. Muhamed failed the first day, and Zarif altogether, but on the second day Muhamed gave some right answers in the absence of the assistants. These results, if not as clear as might be wished, show that it is at least possible to obtain a correct answer from the horses when neither Krall nor any of the attendants is there, at least, so far as the experimenter is aware, but I do not notice that any attention has been given to the question of the possibility of a dishonest person operating in some manner from outside the stable.

But the matter is of less critical importance than might appear, because if the solution of the whole matter is communication with the horse by a sign, which cannot be detected and which may be involuntary, it is quite as possible that the experimenter himself may give this sign without knowing it, and that is the suggestion which has to be met by the upholders of the intellectualist interpretation of these performances. The decisive test would then lie in the power of the horse to answer a question when the right solution was unknown to the experimenter himself. The importance of this test was seen by Monsieur Claparéde, who, in the experiments which he made when alone with the horses, attempted by the use of cards to set them problems unknown to himself. His results are as follows :—

Hänschen's answers were wrong, but in one case gave the number 42 for 45.

Muhamed failed on that day with numbers known to Claparéde, and therefore was not tested with the unknown. On the next day, after Muhamed had given some right replies as mentioned above, in cases where Monsieur Claparéde knew the answer, the test of the unknown was applied. In all cases Muhamed's answer was wrong. There followed an addition, in which Monsieur Claparéde knew the figures, $22 + 15$, given correctly as 37, but after this no results were given by the horse. Monsieur Claparéde considers the result of this investigation to be negative. It fails to disprove the horses' powers, but it does not show a clear issue. The

horse makes numerous mistakes when Claparéde knows the answer, and we cannot therefore say decisively that his failure when Monsieur Claparéde does not know the answer is due to the absence of an unconscious sign. Other cases are, first, that of Monsieur Bohn, mentioned above, in which the horse subtracted instead of adding. This feat convinced Monsieur Bohn. He had the wrong solution in his mind, and therefore certainly could not have signalled the right one. On the other hand, it must be said it is permissible to doubt Monsieur Bohn's interpretation. After all, he wrote a plus, not a minus, and the suggestion that the horse read the plus as a minus is merely his own hypothesis Muhamed might simply have made another of his frequer mistakes.

We come finally to Dr. Haenel's record. Herr Krall absent. Dr. Haenel sent the groom out of the stall, quite vinced himself that nobody remained behind the door of the which had to be kept open for the sake of the light. H took a packet of cards, with the numbers 1 to 9 on them, plus on the board, and put two cards one on each side of it seeing what they were. Muhamed, after several respo were not clear, gave decisively 15. Dr. Haenel then the numbers and found they were 7 and 8. Muham the same way with 3 and 2, and with $8 + 2 +$ followed a case in which Dr. Haenel had a half g numbers as he put them up, and summed them to 1 however, gave 16, which proved to be right. additions were correctly given, two of them afte failure, and he then substituted the multiplying and put up two figures. Muhamed gave 27, an $9 \times 3$. For the two next figures Muhamed repeated it, but the numbers were $7 \times 6$. I ment Muhamed gave $9 \times 2$ correctly as 18 for a repetition gave 12, 2, 29, and then 1 Muhamed gave 65 and then 48. There f problems, which were not solved, and unfortunately, are not given us, and the sé the extraction of $\sqrt[4]{7890481}$ given corr for a repetition of this, Muhamed wave succession 4, 55, 33, 23, and 54. Th by Herr Krall to Dr. Haenel on the pr was unknown to Dr. Haenel.

This record is without doubt the series, and if we could suppose D able precautions, would compel involuntary signs once for all. F

(1) That the door was open.

explaining pictures, and squaring one or two figures. Column III. includes roots and cubing or raising to the fourth power. The results are as follows :—

|  | Correct without preliminary failure. | | | Complete failure. | | |
|---|---|---|---|---|---|---|
|  | I | II | III | I | II | III |
| Muhamed ...... | 44·8 | 41·2 | 10·0 | 13·8 | 32·4 | 20 |
| Zarif ............ | 77·3 | 53·8 | — | 13·6 | 26·9 | — |
| Hänschen ...... | 44·4 | 31·0 | — | 18·7 | 26·2 | — |
| Berto ............ | 47·7 | 31·1 | — | 10·8 | 19·7 | — |
| Total......... | 51·5 | 36·8 | — | 12·7 | 25·0 | — |

This table was made when Muhamed and Zarif had had over four years' instruction, Hänschen one year, and Berto six months. Dr. Máday notes that Muhamed still errs in nearly one out of two of the simplest problems, and although he is the most accomplished performer of the party, Hänschen and Berto equal him in the simplest cases. Still these figures certainly show a reduction of successes in proportion to difficulty, but particularly in the case of Muhamed this reduction is by no means what one would expect from a genuine intelligence which was undergoing a genuine education. We should expect more like 90 or 95% of successes in very simple sums at such a stage. Modjelewski's figures, however, are much more damaging to the intellectualist view. He was present along with Monsieur Claparéde and enumerated all the cases witnessed by him, distinguishing the more complex, in which he included all calculations and the reading of verbal numbers, from the remainder. His results showed that in the first *séance* the horses gave right answers in 11% of all cases but in 13% of the more complex. This is the very opposite of what we might expect from an intelligent schoolboy.

The answers, as we have seen, are often senseless, wholly wide of the mark, even numbers given as the root or square of odds, and so on. But beyond this, right answers seem to be arrived at by a process of groping; for example, for $\sqrt{117649}$ Muhamed gives successively 4, 13, 346, 347, and 343. Apparently he gets by successive stages to three figures, and at the third shot he has got two digits right. At the fourth shot he has got 7 as a terminal digit, which is a possible square root for a number ending in 9. That being wrong, 3 is the only alternative, and is correctly given. It certainly looks here as if some mind was groping for the right answer, but hardly that any mind was calculating. So again $\sqrt[4]{2313441} = 37$, 16, 19, 49, and 39 (r). The first shot

is nearly right and 7 is a possible fourth root for a number ending
in 1, but it must have been a mere shot, whoever is responsible for
it, for it is followed by 16, which is hopeless, and then by 19,
where the terminal is, for the first time, right. Shots are then
made at the first figure, which is got at the third try. Compare
the very next sum :

$$7 + 8 + 3 + 11 + 5 = 25, 33, 34.$$

Here we have an operation which seems rather more consequent.
The approximations are successive. The first figure is probably
influenced by the terminal 5. The second shot brings us very
nearly right.

One of the most suggestive cases is recorded by Monsieur
Claparéde (*Archives*, XII., p. 289), $\sqrt{99225} = 315$. For this
Muhamed gives the following answers : 134, 155, 113, 135, 153,
235, 134, 175, 325, 215. Monsieur Claparéde rightly notes that
the digits group themselves about 315. Two digits are right
in every shot, and in several cases all three digits. Anyone
applying our test, knowing only that someone had given these
solutions without knowing who it was, would say that that
someone had got a notion of the digits constituting the number,
but no notion whatever of the operation by which the number is
obtained.

With these results we may associate the tendency to answer
wrong questions, which we have already noted. If, without
knowing it was a horse, we learnt that the answer 56 was given
to one sum when it belonged to a previous one for which the
answers propounded had been hopelessly wrong, we should infer
that the person who did that sum had somehow got the number
56 implanted in his mind and that it came out on the wrong
occasion. The previous sum might have set in motion the
train of association destined to call it forth, but it had worked too
slowly and come up at a moment when quite another figure was
required. On the whole, on these considerations we seem warranted in drawing at least one negative conclusion. The horses
do not work sums of any complexity as arithmeticians. They
arrive at their results by some other method. Whatever that
may be, this method involves a great deal of guessing and groping,
and the same appears to be true of the words attributed to the
horses. Dr. zur Strassen gives as his opinion [1] that the horses
produce senseless words at first, and that then when their
rappings give some sense, which their modes of spelling render
easy, they seem suddenly to know what they mean to say ; indeed,
the formation of words is no test, for the operation of signs is

[1] *Tierseele*, Heft III. p. 265.

It may be remarked here that experiments in the extraction of roots, of which Herr Krall is particularly fond, are in reality very unsuitable as tests of arithmetical power.   Roots can be very rapidly guessed by anyone who has once got the trick, and fifth roots, which sound the hardest, are in reality the easiest of all because the terminal digit is always the same, and unless we run into three figures, only one of them remains to be guessed.   On the whole, the loophole experiments add very little to our knowledge.   We pass to cases in which Krall is altogether absent.   Doctors Sarasin and Brunies give an account[1] of experiments made when Krall was away, the groom coming in only when the horse declined to answer, except in the case of blind Berto, who is apparently unmanageable without him.   Experiments with Zarif failed completely.   The pony Hänschen read 23 correctly after certain failures, failed to add 2 and 3, asked to count 63 gave successively 53, 33, 63; for 4 × 5 gave 45 and then 54.   Having thus disgraced himself he was energetically smacked and set the sum of 25 × 5, which, after two failures, he gave correctly : 125. There followed  a  series  of  trials  with  Muhamed,  which included some failures in very simple operations, e.g., 4 + 6 and 6 × 6.   But Muhamed extracted $\sqrt{225}$ correctly after one failure, $\sqrt{5625}$ correctly after two failures, and $\sqrt[4]{2313441}$ correctly after four failures.   He then tapped the name of Albert the groom, thus :  A l p b a i d.   Asked which letter is wrong he says the sixth, which should be r.   R is, in fact, given by thirteen taps and i by thirty-one, so that Muhamed's error is excusable.   Shown a book and asked what it is, he taps b u, and then after accidental interruption, g.

There followed some experiments with Berto, but as the groom was present in these they need not be regarded.

Monsieur Bohn's successes with Muhamed in the absence of Krall have already been referred to.   It may be added that when he proposed to the horse an addition, he got a result which he thought was mistaken until he saw that he was himself responsible for the error, having made the vertical sign of the plus so faint that Muhamed had taken it for a minus and carried out a subtraction, which was worked correctly.

Monsieur Claparéde's results under similar conditions were hardly so favourable.   On his first visit Krall wrote up the following sum on the blackboard and then left the room :—

$$(\sqrt{1296} - \sqrt{81}) \times (\sqrt{144} - \sqrt{49}).$$

Muhamed, says Monsieur Claparéde, threw a glance at the board and instantly replied 115, which is wrong.   Krall then called to

[1] *Tierseele*, Heft I. p. 184.

him from outside to begin again, and he gave 25, and then 125, which is still wrong. After this Muhamed persisted in knocking numbers of his own and made an undecipherable word. He then returned to the sums and gave a correct answer to the one written above, namely, 135, without any preliminary mistake, and later on he solved a fourth root when Krall had left the stable after writing up the problem. Monsieur Claparéde then being left alone with Muhamed, gave him some simple additions, but the answers were wrong and not clear.

In a second visit Monsieur Claparéde obtained some rather better results when he knew the answers to his own questions. Hänschen failed in several cases, but succeeded in getting $24 + 12 = 36$ at the third shot. Muhamed failed the first day, and Zarif altogether, but on the second day Muhamed gave some right answers in the absence of the assistants. These results, if not as clear as might be wished, show that it is at least possible to obtain a correct answer from the horses when neither Krall nor any of the attendants is there, at least, so far as the experimenter is aware, but I do not notice that any attention has been given to the question of the possibility of a dishonest person operating in some manner from outside the stable.

But the matter is of less critical importance than might appear, because if the solution of the whole matter is communication with the horse by a sign, which cannot be detected and which may be involuntary, it is quite as possible that the experimenter himself may give this sign without knowing it, and that is the suggestion which has to be met by the upholders of the intellectualist interpretation of these performances. The decisive test would then lie in the power of the horse to answer a question when the right solution was unknown to the experimenter himself. The importance of this test was seen by Monsieur Claparéde, who, in the experiments which he made when alone with the horses, attempted by the use of cards to set them problems unknown to himself. His results are as follows :—

Hänschen's answers were wrong, but in one case gave the number 42 for 45.

Muhamed failed on that day with numbers known to Claparéde, and therefore was not tested with the unknown. On the next day, after Muhamed had given some right replies as mentioned above, in cases where Monsieur Claparéde knew the answer, the test of the unknown was applied. In all cases Muhamed's answer was wrong. There followed an addition, in which Monsieur Claparéde knew the figures, $22 + 15$, given correctly as 37, but after this no results were given by the horse. Monsieur Claparéde considers the result of this investigation to be negative. It fails to disprove the horses' powers, but it does not show a clear issue. The horse makes numerous mistakes when Claparéde knows the answer, and we cannot therefore say decisively that his failure when Monsieur Claparéde does not know the answer is due to the absence of an unconscious sign. Other cases are, first, that of Monsieur Bohn, mentioned above, in which the horse subtracted instead of adding. This feat convinced Monsieur Bohn. He had the wrong solution in his mind, and therefore certainly could not have signalled the right one. On the other hand, it must be said it is permissible to doubt Monsieur Bohn's interpretation. After all, he wrote a plus, not a minus, and the suggestion that the horse read the plus as a minus is merely his own hypothesis. Muhamed might simply have made another of his frequent mistakes.

We come finally to Dr. Haenel's record. Herr Krall was absent. Dr. Haenel sent the groom out of the stall, quite convinced himself that nobody remained behind the door of the stall, which had to be kept open for the sake of the light. He then took a packet of cards, with the numbers 1 to 9 on them, wrote a plus on the board, and put two cards one on each side of it without seeing what they were. Muhamed, after several responses that were not clear, gave decisively 15. Dr. Haenel then looked at the numbers and found they were 7 and 8. Muhamed dealt in the same way with 3 and 2, and with $8 + 2 + 3$. There followed a case in which Dr. Haenel had a half glance at the numbers as he put them up, and summed them to 13. Muhamed, however, gave 16, which proved to be right. Three other additions were correctly given, two of them after a preliminary failure, and he then substituted the multiplying sign for the plus and put up two figures. Muhamed gave 27, and the figures were $9 \times 3$. For the two next figures Muhamed again gave 27 and repeated it, but the numbers were $7 \times 6$. In the next experiment Muhamed gave $9 \times 2$ correctly as 18, but on being asked for a repetition gave 12, 2, 29, and then 18 again. For $8 \times 6$ Muhamed gave 65 and then 48. There followed seven similar problems, which were not solved, and the details of which, unfortunately, are not given us, and the *séance* was wound up with the extraction of $\sqrt[4]{7890481}$ given correctly as 53. Being asked for a repetition of this, Muhamed wavered considerably, giving in succession 4, 55, 33, 23, and 54. This number had been given by Herr Krall to Dr. Haenel on the previous night. The solution was unknown to Dr. Haenel.

This record is without doubt the most remarkable in the whole series, and if we could suppose Dr. Haenel to have taken all suitable precautions, would compel us to dismiss the theory of involuntary signs once for all. But it must be remarked :—

(1) That the door was open.

(2) That Dr. Haenel writes as an enthusiast.

(3) That it may not be so easy as he takes it to be to secure complete ignorance of the figures placed on the board. In one instance, as a fact, he mentions the half glance, and it must be borne in mind that the horse, on the face of the record, itself frequently makes a number of uncertain efforts before he gets to the right one, a process which still suggests that he is in some way waiting for a sign. It is at least reasonable to suspend judgment until further experiments of the type of this record by Dr. Haenel have been made under careful observation, by two or more experimentalists in co-operation.

Let us now for a moment discuss the apparent results, seeking to dismiss all preconceived opinions as to the capacity or incapacity of horses. Let us suppose that we have merely the results before us, without knowing whether they were produced by a civilised man, a savage, a little boy, or an animal, and that we were therefore free to enquire what sort of intelligence, if any, they presuppose. We should, to begin with, find in them some strong reasons against the supposition that they rest upon a genuine understanding of arithmetical operations. This reason is to be found in the nature of the mistakes made by the horses, and of the method by which they approach solution. Quite easy problems are missed by these advanced students ; for instance, Zarif gives $4^2 = 15$, and corrects it to 24.[1] Now, any horse as familiar with squares as Zarif was supposed to be by this time ought to know that a square number cannot be odd. The talented Muhamed, at quite a late date, fails, in the presence of Dr. Sarasin, to add $4 + 6$, and also to multiply $6 \times 6$. This in the same *séance* wherein he succeeds in finding $\sqrt[4]{2313441}$. Berto can divide 21 by 3, and gives 7, but immediately afterwards he supposes that $5 + 6 = 41$, and corrects it to 14.

These are not casual mistakes. They are written all over the record, and though they are imputed to obstinacy or wilfulness on the part of the horse, it must be pointed out that they are often punished with a hearty smack. It is indeed doubtful whether years of practice make the horses really more competent in dealing with very simple than with very difficult questions. On this point there is some conflict of evidence. Dr. Plate put together a number of results of successes and failures, classified in accordance with the difficulty of the problem. The gist of these is given in the appended table. Column I. includes additions and subtractions involving not more than two figures, enumeration, reading the date of the month, and so on. Column II., additions and subtractions of more than two figures, division and multiplication, or in Berto's case the counting of figures written on the back. Also spelling,.

[1] Claparéde, *Archives de Psychologie*, XII p. 273.

explaining pictures, and squaring one or two figures. Column III. includes roots and cubing or raising to the fourth power. The results are as follows :—

|  | Correct without preliminary failure. | | | Complete failure. | | |
|---|---|---|---|---|---|---|
|  | I | II | III | I | II | III |
| Muhamed | 44·8 | 41·2 | 10·0 | 13·8 | 32·4 | 20 |
| Zarif | 77·3 | 53·8 | — | 13·6 | 26·9 | — |
| Hänschen | 44·4 | 31·0 | — | 18·7 | 26·2 | — |
| Berto | 47·7 | 31·1 | — | 10·8 | 19·7 | — |
| Total | 51·5 | 36·8 | — | 12·7 | 25·0 | — |

This table was made when Muhamed and Zarif had had over four years' instruction, Hänschen one year, and Berto six months. Dr. Máday notes that Muhamed still errs in nearly one out of two of the simplest problems, and although he is the most accomplished performer of the party, Hänschen and Berto equal him in the simplest cases. Still these figures certainly show a reduction of successes in proportion to difficulty, but particularly in the case of Muhamed this reduction is by no means what one would expect from a genuine intelligence which was undergoing a genuine education. We should expect more like 90 or 95% of successes in very simple sums at such a stage. Modjelewski's figures, however, are much more damaging to the intellectualist view. He was present along with Monsieur Claparéde and enumerated all the cases witnessed by him, distinguishing the more complex, in which he included all calculations and the reading of verbal numbers, from the remainder. His results showed that in the first *séance* the horses gave right answers in 11% of all cases but in 13% of the more complex. This is the very opposite of what we might expect from an intelligent schoolboy.

The answers, as we have seen, are often senseless, wholly wide of the mark, even numbers given as the root or square of odds, and so on. But beyond this, right answers seem to be arrived at by a process of groping; for example, for $\sqrt{117649}$ Muhamed gives successively 4, 13, 346, 347, and 343. Apparently he gets by successive stages to three figures, and at the third shot he has got two digits right. At the fourth shot he has got 7 as a terminal digit, which is a possible square root for a number ending in 9. That being wrong, 3 is the only alternative, and is correctly given. It certainly looks here as if some mind was groping for the right answer, but hardly that any mind was calculating. So again $\sqrt[4]{2313441} = 37, 16, 19, 49,$ and 39 (r). The first shot is nearly right and 7 is a possible fourth root for a number ending in 1, but it must have been a mere shot, whoever is responsible for it, for it is followed by 16, which is hopeless, and then by 19, where the terminal is, for the first time, right. Shots are then made at the first figure, which is got at the third try. Compare the very next sum :

$$7 + 8 + 3 + 11 + 5 = 25, 33, 34.$$

Here we have an operation which seems rather more consequent. The approximations are successive. The first figure is probably influenced by the terminal 5. The second shot brings us very nearly right.

One of the most suggestive cases is recorded by Monsieur Claparéde (*Archives*, XII., p. 289), $\sqrt{99225} = 315$. For this Muhamed gives the following answers : 134, 155, 113, 135, 153, 235, 134, 175, 325, 215. Monsieur Claparéde rightly notes that the digits group themselves about 315. Two digits are right in every shot, and in several cases all three digits. Anyone applying our test, knowing only that someone had given these solutions without knowing who it was, would say that that someone had got a notion of the digits constituting the number, but no notion whatever of the operation by which the number is obtained.

With these results we may associate the tendency to answer wrong questions, which we have already noted. If, without knowing it was a horse, we learnt that the answer 56 was given to one sum when it belonged to a previous one for which the answers propounded had been hopelessly wrong, we should infer that the person who did that sum had somehow got the number 56 implanted in his mind and that it came out on the wrong occasion. The previous sum might have set in motion the train of association destined to call it forth, but it had worked too slowly and come up at a moment when quite another figure was required. On the whole, on these considerations we seem warranted in drawing at least one negative conclusion. The horses do not work sums of any complexity as arithmeticians. They arrive at their results by some other method. Whatever that may be, this method involves a great deal of guessing and groping, and the same appears to be true of the words attributed to the horses. Dr. zur Strassen gives as his opinion [1] that the horses produce senseless words at first, and that then when their rappings give some sense, which their modes of spelling render easy, they seem suddenly to know what they mean to say ; indeed, the formation of words is no test, for the operation of signs is

[1] *Tierseele*, Heft III. p. 265.

in this case quite impossible to exclude. Monsieur Claparéde, cool observer as he in general is, was greatly impressed at the outset of his experiments with Zarif by the fact that the horse spontaneously rapped out in his code S c h l p r r d. Allowing for the resemblance in German of Sch to C and for the absence of vowels in the horse's notation, this is equivalent to the name Claparéde. Commenting on it, Krall at first said that Zarif had never heard the name, but afterwards corrected himself and said that Claparéde's coming had been mentioned before the horse that morning. The legitimate inference is not that the horse wanted to show that he knew Claparéde's name, but that when his spontaneous rappings began Herr Krall tended involuntarily to check them successively at the point at which they made an intelligible letter, and as the shaping of these letters into a name proceeded, the process would become more certain.

In fact, whatever may be said against the horses as arithmeticians may be said with greater force against them as grammarians. It is on their handling of arithmetical problems that they must stand or fall, and on this point we may conclude negatively that, at any rate, they do not do arithmetic after the manner of the arithmeticians. But if the horses have not all the powers claimed for them, are we to conclude that they have none at all beyond a preternatural gift of responding to signs which no human observer can detect ? In advancing this theory we are in some danger of falling as deep into the bog of the miraculous on the one side as the opposite party do upon the other. It is quite useless to bring in telepathy to our aid, for telepathy would not explain the cases in which the experimenter himself does not know the problem. We have seen that genuine cases of success under these conditions are very few, and our principal witness, Dr. Haenel, is not wholly satisfactory, for he is apparently an enthusiast, and in his enthusiasm omits some details which we should very much wish to have. Let us, however, for the moment take his evidence, assuming its soundness, and consider what powers it implies. It will be seen that the experiments with Muhamed fall into three divisions. The first consist in simple additions and very simple multiplications, which were for the most part solved accurately. The second consist of a series of problems described as similar, in which the horse failed and which, most unfortunately, he does not specify. The third consists of the extraction of the fourth root. Now this last problem was handed to Dr. Haenel by Krall himself, and it is not an unfair inference that it is one in which the horse might be expected to succeed. If that is so, it was because the horse had memorised it, and we have seen evidence of memorising, partial or complete, in some of the errors already referred to. At any rate, without either calculation or memorising, on the actual face of the evidence, we cannot explain Muhamed's success in this case. Let us assume for the moment that it was memorising—what does that mean? It means that Muhamed could associate a double series of taps, 3 with the right, 5 with the left foot, with a complex symbol; and if memorising is a serious part of the explanation of the horse's achievements, it means that he was capable of forming many such associations. This is a very wonderful capacity to attribute to a horse, but less remote from what we already know of animal intelligence than *bonâ fide* arithmetical calculation. In mitigation of the difficulty the frequency of mistakes must be borne in mind, and the tendency of all the horses to prefer certain numbers to others. I think that this must be admitted as a bare possibility.

We then come to the simple sums which Muhamed did. Most of these are additions. It is barely possible that Muhamed can so far be said to read the figures, 1, 2, 3, etc., as to respond to them with the appropriate number of taps. This again is what no one would readily believe of a horse, but it is less difficult to believe than to credit him with some of the powers claimed by Herr Krall. Now if Muhamed can in this sense read 6, 7, and 3, it is possible that when 6 + 7 + 3 is put on the board, he should tap out 16 in all, not adding them in the strict sense of the term, but tapping them in succession. The test here is a simple one. If there were true addition Muhamed would render the 16 by 6 taps with the right and 1 with the left foot; if the figures were read off, he would give all 16 taps with one foot. Most unfortunately, Dr. Haenel does not tell us which he did, but all the additions which he mentions amount to small sums, which might have been tapped with one foot without great fatigue.

Lastly, there remain four simple multiplications, two of which were given wrong in the first instance and which again might conceivably be memorised. In a word, if we keep to the cases in which, if the report is accurate, any possibility of a signal is excluded, we find that they postulate a definite memorising, both of simple and complex signs, that is to say, the association with such signs of the number of taps. But it must be admitted that this alone is a forced explanation, and that it would be natural on the ground of these experiments alone to attribute to the horse at least the capacity for simple addition and possibly of very simple multiplication. The alternative is to reject Dr. Haenel's evidence *in toto*.

There, for the moment, the matter must rest until further evidence is available. The question will hardly be solved until some more general evidence of intelligence is available than these highly specialist methods provided; for example, when we find that the horse wholly fails to understand a statement that Monsieur

Claparéde has a carrot for him and that he is to come and get it, we find it exceedingly difficult to believe that he can himself make up sentences about carrots and communicate them in a code to his master.[1] But we may do well to consider the bearings of the whole question upon the general theory of animal intelligence, which may be very briefly stated. Should the whole or even a small portion of Herr Krall's claim be substantiated, it would rather show the immense effect of training on drawing out the potentialities of the mind than alter our view as to the normal level of animal intelligence. Ordinary horses do not perform any such feats as those of Muhamed and Zarif. They are incapable of communicating with their masters in any such fashion. If they were, their whole position in the world's economy would be different and men would not be upon their backs. If anything like Herr Krall's view is true, we must infer that powers like those of fixing a concept like a number independent of anything seen, heard, or felt, and operating with it in some determinate fashion, are capable of being elicited by training in a mind, which normally makes no use of any such faculty. That is to say, the transition from the level of intelligence characteristic of the normal animal of the higher type to that characteristic of the human being is capable of being made, not by the evolution of a new type of brain but within the limits of modifiability of a single brain through the stimulating powers of the teacher. This would corroborate our view of the essential difference between the animal and human intelligence as a difference due to the development of the means of inter-communication, though it would attribute to this factor far more preponderating influence than we have ventured to assign to it, far more even than, with all Herr Krall's evidence before us, we can think is really probable.

## NOTE

The case of Rolf, the Mannheim terrier, may be more cursorily treated. The truth is that, as Dr. Máday says, the story of Rolf reads almost like a skit upon performances of the Elberfeld horses. Rolf learnt his arithmetic while listening to the children's lessons and helps them with their sums when in any difficulty. He gives orthodox answers to Jesuits and keeps a private theology of a more up to date kind for his friends. Almost everything he has done he has done in the presence and with the knowledge of his mistress, and the evidence for unseen experiments is slight and unsatisfactory. It consists, as far as I know, first of Mackenzie's statement that he showed the dog certain cards which he described. "I am sure," says Mackenzie, "that absolutely no one saw the design except the dog." No details are given, and it is obviously exceedingly difficult to be sure of such a point when there are many people in the room. Secondly, we have the observations of Doctors Gruber and Wilser. Dr. Gruber gave certain cards to Rolf, which he thought he concealed from everybody else. In

---

[1] *Archives de Psychologie*, XII. p. 278.

these experiments Rolf's mistress was present. On the same day apparently Dr. Gruber and Dr. Wilser interviewed Rolf in the absence of his mistress and also tried unseen experiments. The dog, however, paid no attention but gaped impolitely, and after many remonstrances brought out the following sentence, "wholly unexpected and astonishing to all present" :—"Very many pictures seen and said what they are with Ziegler (who had been with him two days before). It is enough. Will not say any more what it is. . . . . All men give me the hump." We may sympathise perhaps, but we shall not agree with Dr. Wilser that in this remark obviously nobody could have helped him. He then went on to describe a picture correctly as a fat pig, but this picture—here said to have been shown in the absence of his mistress—corresponds precisely with one of the unseen experiments described by Dr. Gruber. Finally, after returning to his mistress, Rolf gave some beautiful proofs of his capacity.

It follows that, in fact, experiments in the absence of his mistress, the answer to which was unknown to the experimenters, failed. Instead of performing them the dog produced this ridiculous sentence which substituted astonishment and laughter for enquiry. Monsieur Claparéde ("Claparéde et Des Bancels," *Archives de Psychologie*, XIII. p. 377), who attempted unseen experiments, found, as a careful observer would, considerable difficulty in satisfying himself as to the conditions, but finally succeeded in so satisfying himself in two cases, in one of which the dog gave a correct description of a picture, in the other a vague one. As to this success, Monsieur Claparéde says judiciously : "We affirm that Mdme. Moekel did not look at the pictures, and we believe that it would have been very difficult to see them even involuntarily." But affirmation is not a proof, and this proof would be necessary to secure the experiment all its value. Monsieur Claparéde wished to continue the experiments the next day. Rolf, in the meantime, had been taken ill. He concludes that his observations did not suffice to establish the facts proposed to be verified. "Without doubt the experiments that we report seem to attest in the dog the possibility of a spontaneous speech, and would demonstrate its real existence if they had been executed in conditions which could defy criticism. But we cannot offer them as entirely satisfactory in this respect. We are obliged to insist, on the other hand, that Rolf, sympathetic as he is, does not, under ordinary circumstances, as far as we have the means of judging, pass the level of a dog reputed to be intelligent, and that under the tests to which he is constrained he often shows signs of marked *ennui*." This is but a cold criticism to follow the enthusiastic article of Professor Mackenzie (*Archives de Psychologie*, XIII. p. 379). The authors add that they had wished to show Rolf a card saying, "There is some sugar for you behind the drawing-room door." This test, which it may be agreed would have been a most decisive one, was prevented by Rolf's indisposition.

# INDEX

463

THE END

PRINTED IN GREAT BRITAIN BY
RICHARD CLAY AND SONS, LIMITED,
BRUNSWICK STREET, STAMFORD STREET, S.E.,
AND BUNGAY, SUFFOLK.

# CLASSICS IN PSYCHOLOGY

AN ARNO PRESS COLLECTION

Angell, James Rowland. **Psychology: On Introductory Study of the Structure and Function of Human Consciousness.** 4th edition. 1908

Bain, Alexander. **Mental Science.** 1868

Baldwin, James Mark. **Social and Ethical Interpretations in Mental Development.** 2nd edition. 1899

Bechterev, Vladimir Michailovitch. **General Principles of Human Reflexology.** [1932]

Binet, Alfred and Th[éodore] Simon. **The Development of Intelligence in Children.** 1916

Bogardus, Emory S. **Fundamentals of Social Psychology.** 1924

Buytendijk, F. J. J. **The Mind of the Dog.** 1936

Ebbinghaus, Hermann. **Psychology: An Elementary Text-Book.** 1908

Goddard, Henry Herbert. **The Kallikak Family.** 1931

Hobhouse, L[eonard] T. **Mind in Evolution.** 1915

Holt, Edwin B. **The Concept of Consciousness.** 1914

Külpe, Oswald. **Outlines of Psychology.** 1895

Ladd-Franklin, Christine. **Colour and Colour Theories.** 1929

**Lectures Delivered at the 20th Anniversary Celebration of Clark University.** (Reprinted from *The American Journal of Psychology*, Vol. 21, Nos. 2 and 3). 1910

Lipps, Theodor. **Psychological Studies.** 2nd edition. 1926

Loeb, Jacques. **Comparative Physiology of the Brain and Comparative Psychology.** 1900

Lotze, Hermann. **Outlines of Psychology.** [1885]

McDougall, William. **The Group Mind.** 2nd edition. 1920

Meier, Norman C., editor. **Studies in the Psychology of Art: Volume III.** 1939

Morgan, C. Lloyd. **Habit and Instinct.** 1896

Münsterberg, Hugo. **Psychology and Industrial Efficiency.** 1913

Murchison, Carl, editor. **Psychologies of 1930.** 1930

Piéron, Henri. **Thought and the Brain.** 1927

Pillsbury, W[alter] B[owers]. **Attention.** 1908

[Poffenberger, A. T., editor]. **James McKeen Cattell: Man of Science.** 1947

Preyer, W[illiam] **The Mind of the Child: Parts I and II.** 1890/1889

**The Psychology of Skill: Three Studies.** 1973

Reymert, Martin L., editor. **Feelings and Emotions:** The Wittenberg Symposium. 1928

Ribot, Th[éodule Armand]. **Essay on the Creative Imagination.** 1906

Roback, A[braham] A[aron]. **The Psychology of Character.** 1927

**I. M. Sechenov:** Biographical Sketch and Essays. (Reprinted from *Selected Works* by I. Sechenov). 1935

Sherrington, Charles. **The Integrative Action of the Nervous System.** 2nd edition. 1947

Spearman, C[harles]. **The Nature of 'Intelligence' and the Principles of Cognition.** 1923

Thorndike, Edward L. **Education:** A First Book. 1912

Thorndike, Edward L., E. O. Bregman, M. V. Cobb, et al. **The Measurement of Intelligence.** [1927]

Titchener, Edward Bradford. **Lectures on the Elementary Psychology of Feeling and Attention.** 1908

Titchener, Edward Bradford. **Lectures on the Experimental Psychology of the Thought-Processes.** 1909

Washburn, Margaret Floy. **Movement and Mental Imagery.** 1916

Whipple, Guy Montrose. **Manual of Mental and Physical Tests:** Parts I and II. 2nd edition. 1914/1915

Woodworth, Robert Sessions. **Dynamic Psychology.** 1918

Wundt, Wilhelm. **An Introduction to Psychology.** 1912

Yerkes, Robert M. **The Dancing Mouse** and **The Mind of a Gorilla.** 1907/1926